THE TEACHING MINISTRY OF THE CHURCH

INTEGRATING BIBLICAL TRUTH WITH CONTEMPORARY APPLICATION

DARYL ELDRIDGE

BROADMAN
& HOLMAN
PUBLISHERS

Nashville, Tennessee

4210-87
0-8054-1087-2

Dewey Decimal Classification: 268
Subject Heading: Christian Education \ Religious Education
Library of Congress Card Catalog Number:94-34202

Unless otherwise noted all Scripture quotations are from the Holy Bible, New International Version, copyright © 1973, 1978, 1984 by International Bible Society; New American Standard Bible. © The Lockman Foundation, 1960, 1962, 1963, 1968, 1971, 1972,1973, 1975, 1977. Used by permission; and the King James Version.

Page Designer: Trina Hollister Fulton

Library of Congress Cataloging-in-Publication Data
The teaching ministry of the church: integrating biblical truth and contemporary application / Daryl Eldridge, editor.
    p. cm.
Includes bibliographical references.
    ISBN 0-8054-1087-2 : $24.99
    1. Christian education—Philosophy.   2. Christian education—Teacher Training. I. Eldridge, Daryl, 1951-
    BV1464.T42   1995
    207—dc20   94-34202
                                           CIP

10 11   05 04 03

CONTRIBUTORS

---

1. Daryl Eldridge, Associate Professor, Foundations of Education, Southwestern Baptist Theological Seminary

2. Norma S. Hedin, Associate Professor, Foundations of Education, Southwestern Baptist Theological Seminary

3. Terrell M. Peace, Assistant Professor in Foundations of Education, Southwestern Baptist Theological Seminary

4. William A. "Budd" Smith, Professor in Foundations of Education, Southwestern Baptist Theological Seminary

5. Jack Terry, Jr., Dean of the School of Religious Education and Professor of Foundations of Education, Southwestern Baptist Theological Seminary

6. Rick Yount, Associate Professor of Education, Southwestern Baptist Theological Seminary

CONTENTS

PREFACE

James Smart writes, "The voice of the Scriptures is falling silent in the preaching and teaching of the church and in the consciousness of Christian people, a silence that is perceptible even among those who are most insistent upon their devotion to the Scriptures."[1] Richard Osmer raises the same concern: "What is missing from mainline Protestantism today is a vital teaching office by which the foundations of Bible and Christian doctrine are taught to members of most congregations. In the absence of such a teaching office, individuals are left to sort out their own understanding of God and the moral life or turn to groups offering absolutes to fill the void they are experiencing."[2]

We might easily dismiss these comments. After all, we are evangelicals. We are *Am Hassifer*, people of The Book. But do the facts bear that out? The following statistics are from one of the fastest-growing evangelical churches in America. It ranks in the top one percent of its denomination in size and number of baptisms. The figures are given per thousand members and do not represent the actual number of members.

- 650 are enrolled in Bible study (The denomination's average is 55 percent).

- 300 persons will attend Bible study (The denominational average is 25 percent).

1. James D. Smart, *The Strange Silence of the Bible in the Church* (Philadelphia: Westminster Press, 1970), 15–16.
2. Richard Robert Osmer, *A Teachable Spirit: Recovering the Teaching Office in the Church* (Louisville: Westminster/John Knox Press, 1990), x.

- 60 people will have studied their lesson, 30 of those will be teachers.

- 125 persons (12.5 percent) will be involved in an educational study group which explores Christian ethics, church polity, discipleship, Christian theology, and Christian history.

- 10 persons will be involved in a one-on-one discipleship relationship.

- 43 persons will be baptized (in other words, it took 22 members to baptize one person).

- 1 family out of 100 will have a family Bible study.

Recent research shows that two out of every ten born-again Christians do not read the Bible in a typical week. Among those who attend worship services regularly, thirty-five percent do not read the Bible. Only twenty percent of evangelicals read the Bible every day.[3] What is more distressing is that six out of ten Christians believe that "God helps those who help themselves," is a Scripture verse.[4]

In studying Protestant congregations, Search Institute discovered that in general, Christians in the United States do not have mature faith. According to the criteria used in the study, only thirty-two percent of adults have a mature faith, and sixty-four percent of youth have an undeveloped faith. They concluded that for most people in our churches, faith is dormant and inactive.[5]

Do these statistics mean that Christian education is ineffective? That Sunday School needs to be abolished? On the contrary, in evaluating congregational effectiveness, researchers discovered that Christian education is the most important vehicle within congregational life for helping people grow in their faith. Christian education, when done well, has more potential for promoting spiritual growth than any other area of congregational life.[6]

Unfortunately, there are Christian leaders and those preparing for ministry that feel Christian education is simply "cutting and pasting." I've heard some people joke that the Christian education degree is shorter now because there are electric staplers and pencil sharpeners. Christian education is more than ordering literature and making sure there is plenty of construction paper. The spiritual growth and vitality of a church is dependent upon an effective teaching ministry. As Smart writes: "The Church must teach, just as it must preach, or it will not be the Church. . . . Teaching belongs to the essence of the Church and a church that neglects this function of teaching has lost something that is indispensable to its nature as a church."[7]

Unfortunately, Christian educators are expected to raise the numbers in their programs by using Madison Avenue techniques. Church leaders employ short-term

3. George Barna, *What Americans Believe* (Ventura, Calif.: Regal Books, 1991), 289–90.
4. Ibid., 301.
5. Eugene Roehlkepartain, *The Teaching Church* (Nashville: Abingdon, 1993), 19.
6. Ibid.
7. James D. Smart, *The Teaching Ministry of the Church* (Philadelphia: Westminster Press, 1974), 11.

strategies that result in beefing up the numbers in our educational programs while neglecting quality Bible teaching. Simply providing Bible studies and small group educational experiences with teachers that are inadequately prepared and ignorant of Scripture will not suffice. God is worthy of our best efforts in teaching his Word. The Bible demands our best study. The people of God deserve equipped, skilled artisans of teaching. We cannot permit mediocrity in the teaching ministry. There is too much at stake. "The restoration of a church that can teach with authority . . . may be the pressing issue before mainline churches today. . . . The American mainline Protestant churches are at a crossroads. Which path they take may very well rest on whether they can restore the teaching ministry of the church to its rightful place of importance."[8]

The purpose of this book is to elevate Christian education among Christian leaders by reexamining the biblical purpose and nature of the teaching ministry. In part 1, we discuss how the teaching ministry of the church is founded on the very character of God. He is the ultimate teacher, as Job declared, "Who is a teacher like him?" (Job 36:22). From the beginning of time, God has been teaching his creation who he is. In other words, God teaches to reveal himself to us. The purpose of revelation is not intellectual enlightenment, but the establishment of a personal relationship with him.

The revelation of God achieves its consummation in Jesus Christ. While Jesus was often a healer and performer of miracles, he was always a teacher. In fact, over forty-eight times in the Gospels Jesus is referred to as teacher. In none of the Gospels is Jesus called preacher. The fact that Jesus was called Rabbi indicates the respect the people had for his teaching. Jesus was the Master Teacher. Not only did Jesus come teaching, he commanded us to teach. In his Great Commission Jesus said: "All authority in heaven and on earth has been given to me. Therefore go and make disciples of all nations, baptizing them in the name of the Father and of the Son and of the Holy Spirit, and *teaching them* (italics mine) to obey everything I have commanded you" (Matt. 28:18–20).

Christ commands us to teach, but he provides the Holy Spirit as his grace agent, teaching us the things of the Spirit. The teaching ministry of the church is dependent upon the empowering of the Holy Spirit.

Parts 2 and 3 take a practical look at equipping teachers in preparing and planning effective Bible studies. The book concludes with a discussion of how Christian leaders can develop a cadre of well-trained effective teachers who can help others mature in their faith.

The writers of this work owe a great debt to those who have gone before us. LeRoy Ford and Leon Marsh served on the faculty of Southwestern Baptist Theological Seminary in the Department of Foundations of Education until their respective retirements. They are our mentors in the teaching ministry. LeRoy Ford is a won-

8. Osmer, 5.

derful craftsman in the art of teaching and lesson planning. Leon Marsh showed us how to love students, and continues to encourage us to spend more time with them, for they are the reason we teach.

We are grateful to the many students who have enriched our lives. Through their questions and stimulating discussions, they have challenged us to be our best, both in the classroom and in our church ministries. These gifted students, the "rabbis of the twenty-first century," will provide the leadership necessary for our churches to restore the teaching ministry to its rightful place of importance.

Leon Marsh once told us: "Some people wait too long to write and some don't wait long enough." When you read this work, our prayer is that we are in God's perfect timing.

Part One:
Biblical Foundations for the Teaching Ministry

1. God as Teacher

2. Jesus, the Master Teacher

3. The Role of the Holy Spirit in Teaching

4. The Bible as Curriculum

5. The Disciple: Called to Learn

6. The Church's Role in Teaching

7. The Family's Role in Teaching

8. The Pastor as Teacher

9. The Goal of Christian Teaching

CHAPTER 1

GOD AS TEACHER

—JACK D. TERRY, JR.

God is exalted in his power. Who is a teacher like him? (Job 36:22).

Every religion has valued education for its members. Even cultures which preceded the Hebrews, including the Chinese, Egyptians, Assyrians, Babylonians, Greeks, and Phoenicians, had systems for instructing religious converts. Wherever an active belief exists, there follows the necessity to educate converts in the precepts of the faith and to provide religious instruction for the young. Instruction in faith, an imperative for the pagan convert, was likewise important in the Judeo-Christian tradition for understanding and growing in the belief of a true and living God.[1]

The Hebrews surpassed all others in their emphasis on tribal and family origins. In contrast to the nations around them, the Israelites preserved a clear picture of their simple beginnings in the midst of complex migrations that brought them into contact with many diverse religions and peoples of the ancient world. Even though the Israelites mingled freely with different nations and observed contradictory and unusual religious practices, the constancy of their religious heritage and the worship of a single Deity (Jehovah) gave them a national identity. This central focus, and the educational system that accompanied it, set the Israelites apart from the rest of the world.

From the beginning of creation when "God created man in his own image" (Gen. 1:27), Jehovah purposed that one day the whole human race would acknowledge him as God. Paul writes: "From one man he made every nation of men, that they

---

1. Jack D. Terry, Jr., "History of the Doctrine of Education" in *Disciple's Study Bible* (Nashville: Holman Bible Publishers, 1988), 1728.

should inhabit the whole earth; and he determined the times set for them and the exact places where they should live. God did this so that men would seek him and perhaps reach out for him and find him, though he is not far from each one of us. For in him we live and move and have our being" (Acts 17:26–28).

However, man failed in all that God sought for him to do by direct command, conscience, and government. Self-willed man disobeyed God, chose to direct his own destiny, and devised all kinds of wickedness and ungodliness. It became necessary for God to destroy the majority of this rebellious race, but he saved a remnant. One individual in this remnant received God's revelations and passed them on to his physical and spiritual descendants.

It was through Abraham and the nation that descended from him that God brought this revelation to pass, "and all peoples on earth will be blessed through you" (Gen. 12:3). Through the people that sprang from Abraham it was God's intention to make himself and his ways known to all nations and in the fullness of time to bring forth the Redeemed of all mankind.[2] It was likewise God's intention that his chosen people would carry on a process of education as the means of achieving this plan.

GOD AS TEACHER THROUGH THE PATRIARCHS

Abraham, a descendant of Shem, was from Chaldea. The Babylonians, from whom Abraham came, had an exceptionally advanced civilization. The greatest king of the Old Babylonian dynasty wrote the famous Code of Hammurabi.[3] From this stock, three centuries later, Abraham emerged as the one chosen of God to bring mankind to the Redeemer.

Abraham was a man of culture and superior intelligence. "He was a person of great sagacity, both for understanding all things and persuading his hearers, and not mistaken in his opinions."[4] Abraham came to the conclusion that the gods worshiped by the Chaldeans were under the control of God, the Creator of the universe. He also determined that this Creator God should be the only one worshiped. That he continued to pay high homage to God after entering Canaan is affirmed in Genesis 18:19: "For I have chosen him, so that he will direct his children and his household after him to keep the way of the Lord by doing what is right and just, so that the Lord will bring about for Abraham what he has promised him."

Education in Abraham's time was natural and informal, accomplished through example. The wandering nomads had no established schools, but they modeled their beliefs in daily activities. What Abraham, Isaac, and Jacob did in relationship

---

2. C. B. Eavey, *History of Christian Education* (Chicago: Moody Press, 1966), 44.
3. Ibid, 45.
4. William Whiston, trans. *The Complete Works of Flavius Josephus*, translated from the original Greek (Philadelphia: David McKay), 49.

to God, in like manner their children learned and did the same in their relationship to God. Everything they learned came from the great lives of their distinguished fathers.

The effectiveness of Abraham's teaching is evident in Isaac, who was completely obedient to the will of God even in the face of death. He responded to God's request for an acceptable offering as his great father taught him. Abraham's example inspired emulation in Isaac's total obedience to Almighty God.

Isaac and Jacob continued to be obedient to the teachings of Abraham and transmitted them to their children. In the end each of them received a confirmation from God of the covenant delivered to Abraham. Surely this covenant would not have continued with Isaac and Jacob had they been untrue to the teachings of God. In the pilgrimage of Jacob's family to Egypt, continued obedience to the preserved teachings of God carried them through the centuries of their sojourn. In the final analysis, God heard and answered their cry for deliverance from bondage in Egypt, vindicating the beliefs and instruction they received from the patriarchs.[5]

GOD AS TEACHER IN THE PENTATEUCH

During the seventh generation of Abraham's descendants, God delivered his people from Egypt through an Israelite named Moses. Supernaturally preserved by God while an infant (Exod. 2:2–9), Moses was reared in the instruction of both the Hebrews and the Egyptians. Acts 7:22 declares: "Moses was educated in all the wisdom of the Egyptians and was powerful in speech and action."

Much of Egyptian education during the period of Moses was contextually related to the deity worshiped at the time. Egyptian religion was dominated by the priesthood of the god Amun at Thebes. Amun's synthetic figure gradually absorbed the major deities, becoming far more important than any other Egyptian god. However, in 1365 B.C. the young Amenophis IV broke completely with the cult of Amun and replaced it with a solar monotheism centered on a deity named Aten. Aten had many qualities resembling those of Jehovah, the God of Israel. Both emphasized teaching, and their worshipers held each in a position of unequalled superiority. Aten was, like Jehovah, considered the creator of everything. Worship of Aten was an extremely prominent feature in the Egyptian education of Moses.[6]

In such a religious and educative climate the young man Moses was schooled. Taught at the knee of his biological mother in the things of God and by his adopted mother in the finest schools of Egypt, Moses grew in his faith in God while acquiring the vast knowledge of the Egyptians. When the time came for Moses to make a choice between the pleasures of Egypt and the people of God, it became apparent

---

5. Ibid., 47.

6. W. F. Albright, *The Biblical Period from Abraham to Ezra* (New York: Harper & Row, Publishers, 1963), 15–16.

that the instruction given by the members of his Hebrew family was the most lasting and enduring. From them he learned the promises of Abraham, kept alive through faith by the Israelites.

Moses, chosen by God to deliver his people from the yoke of bondage in Egypt, was called the greatest of schoolmasters. Given the privilege of doing signs and wonders by the hand of God, he taught the Israelites and the Egyptians the omnipotence of God and his judgment on those who opposed him.

As a demonstration of that omnipotence, God instituted the Passover (Exod. 12), an event that would become an important means of education for all Jews in every generation. God taught the children of Israel a great lesson about his mighty power through the experience of the Passover. He commanded the people and all succeeding generations to celebrate this memorable day. "This is a day you are to commemorate; for the generations to come you shall celebrate it as a festival to the Lord—a lasting ordinance" (Exod. 12:14).

God gave the people of Israel many instructions to accompany the commandment to celebrate this seven-day religious holiday. These included eating bread without yeast, removing yeast from their houses, holding a sacred assembly, refraining from work, and preparing enough food for everyone to eat. These requirements are educational reminders of the omnipotence of God. As they are carried out in each succeeding generation, the people recall the great power of Jehovah God. The feast is twofold in nature, pointing back to deliverance from Egyptian bondage and pointing forward to deliverance from the bondage of sin through Christ Jesus our Lord. The whole feast is educational and the master teacher is God.

When God's people were delivered from Egypt by the hand of God through mighty signs and wonders, they were in a position to receive further instruction in the way God wanted them to live. They needed explicit regulations to guide them as they moved toward their final destination, Canaan, the Promised Land. At Mount Sinai God gave the Law (the Ten Commandments), which became the pedagogue of his kingdom. These Ten Commandments would teach the impossibility of pleasing God through acts of obedience. "So the law was put in charge to lead us to Christ that we might be justified by faith" (Gal. 3:24). Therefore, the main purpose of the Law was instructional.

The Law has three specific parts: the commandments, setting forth the holy will of God (Exod. 20:1–26); the judgments, or the rules governing social life (Exod. 21:1–24:11); and the ordinances, or the rules for worship (Exod. 24:12–31:18).[7] The central core of Jewish education was the Law given at Sinai. It regulated every feature of life: how to operate in the home, how to dress, what to eat, how to work, personal conduct, the possession of property, political involvement, civil life, and especially religious life. The Law regulated education, and if it had been completely followed it would have led Israel to a successful inhabitance of the land of promise.

---

7. Eavey, 49.

Even with their failures, the people of Israel have remained a distinct people because of their adherence to the instructions of the Torah.

EDUCATION THROUGH THE LAW

To the Hebrew, God was explicitly revealed not only in history, but also in the Law. The Law gave the Hebrews the profound confidence that they could, through his covenant relationship, teach their young to likewise put their confidence in God. The commandments reminded the young not to forget the works of God and to follow his teachings. The education of the young was the primary concern of Jewish parents. Josephus wrote: "Our principal care of all is this, to educate our children well; and we think it to be the most necessary business of our whole life to observe the laws that have been given to us, and to keep those rules of piety that have been delivered down to us. Our legislator [Moses] carefully joined two methods of instruction together; for he neither left the practical exercises to go without verbal instruction, nor did he permit the hearing of the law to proceed without the exercises for practice."[8]

The family was the primary educational institution of the Law and the entire Jewish faith. Both the father and the mother were to teach the child, "Listen, my son, to your father's instruction and do not forsake your mother's teaching" (Prov. 1:8). Edersheim quotes Philo as saying, "The Jews from their swaddling clothes, even before being taught either the sacred laws or the unwritten customs, trained by their parents, teachers and instructors to recognize God as Father and as the Maker of the world and that having been taught the knowledge (of the laws) from earliest youth, they bore in their souls the image of the commandments."[9] Josephus is quoted as saying, "from their earliest consciousness they had learned the laws, so as to have them, as it were, engraved upon the soul."[10]

One passage etched deeply in the Hebrew consciousness was Deuteronomy 6:4–9, called the Shema. Apparently, this passage set the agenda for the home and the nation. The instruction of the Shema spoke not only to the nature of God but also to the important place of education in the life of the Jew. "Hear, O Israel: The Lord our God, the Lord is one. Love the Lord your God with all your heart and with all your soul and with all your strength. These commandments that I give you today are to be upon your hearts. Impress them on your children. Talk about them when you sit at home and when you walk along the road, when you lie down and when you get up. Tie them as symbols on your hands and bind them on your foreheads. Write them on the door frames of your houses and on your gates" (Deut. 6:4–9).

---

8. Cited in Nathan Drazin, *History of Jewish Education from 515 B.C.E. to 200 C.E.* (Baltimore: Johns Hopkins Press, 1940), 11.
9. Alfred Edersheim, *In the Days of Christ: Sketches of Jewish Social Life* (Boston: Bradley and Woodruff, 1876), 111.
10. Ibid., 112.

Education has always been a passion with the Hebrews. The curriculum of the Hebrew faith was always the Scripture. First, the study of the Torah. Later the Prophets and the Writings. Added to this curriculum was the Mishna, the oral tradition handed down from family to family and generation to generation, eventually ending up as the Talmud. Much later in the synagogues during the postexilic period, the Apocrypha and the Pseudepigrapha were added to the curriculum of the Hebrew child.

Recitation, story-telling, symbolism, question and answer, parables, and other learning activities were used in the lessons to build a cultural consciousness of an omnipotent God. Monotheism was the major theme of study, transmitted through daily and weekly rituals, life events, and religious feasts and festivals.

EDUCATION THROUGH TABERNACLE WORSHIP

The most complete and reliable source of information regarding the tabernacle and its educational significance for the Israelites is the Bible, especially Exodus 25–40. The Tabernacle, with its design and worship implements, encouraged the Israelites to meet with God and to worship him. The entire family participated in the worship activities at the tabernacle. The four kinds of offerings, all of which involved the shedding of blood (the burnt offering, the peace offering, the sin offering, and the guilt or trespass offering), allowed worshipers of all ages to become part of God's redemptive process. Participation in the offerings is carefully explained in Leviticus 1–6. The father was the prime source of instruction for tabernacle worship and he was responsible for preparing the family to participate in the various worship exercises. He was to detail the meaning of the physical structure, the drapes and coverings, the altar and laver, and the furnishings of the Holy Place and the Holy of Holies. Because of the instruction provided by the father, the family was better prepared to enjoy and understand tabernacle worship.

EDUCATION THROUGH CELEBRATIVE ACTIVITIES

Not only were the people of God to have the words of Jehovah God firmly in their hearts, but they were to bind them upon their hands, place them upon the frontals of their heads, and put them on the doors and gates of their homes (Deut. 6:4–9). Every activity was to be an educational reminder of the providence of God in the life of the person. Prayer, a vital part of life in the home, was said each morning and evening and before every meal. Many other household rituals were instructional and performed on a regular basis.

- Putting on the phylacteries (the leather box placed on the forehead as a reminder to place God's words between the frontals of your eyes), with the leather strap going down the left arm to the fist and forming the letter Shin, was a reminder of the Lord's name, Shadiah.

- Lighting the Sabbath lamp each week on Friday evening after sundown and then partaking of a Sabbath meal.

- During the eight-day celebration of the Passover, regular bread was replaced with unleavened bread.

- Families made pilgrimages to Jerusalem for the three feasts commanded in Deuteronomy: Passover, Pentecost, and Tabernacles.

All of these home worship activities reminded the family of the importance of the Eternal God in their daily lives.

The Hebrew word *hanak*, "to educate or to train," comes from the root word meaning "to dedicate or to consecrate."[11] "Train a child in the way he should go, and when he is old he will not turn from it" (Prov. 22:6). The education of a Hebrew child was considered an act of consecration. The word *hanak* also means "to rub the palate or gums." The Word of God was conveyed to the young child using the imagery of delicious food. When a child began to study the Torah, honey and sweet cakes were used as an incentive. Perhaps this is why the psalmist refers to the Law as sweeter than honey: "How sweet are your words to my taste, sweeter than honey to my mouth" (Ps. 119:103). Ezekiel, when told to eat the scroll, said "So I ate it, and it tasted as sweet as honey in my mouth" (Ezek. 3:3).

The Sabbath, feasts, festivals, and one fast commanded in Leviticus 23 also afforded opportunities for the education of the children through participation in the celebrations. "The Lord said to Moses, 'Speak to the Israelites and say to them: These are my appointed feasts, the appointed feasts of the Lord, which you are to proclaim as sacred assemblies'" (Lev. 23:1). These holy days were means by which the Ultimate Teacher instructed his people. Through their observance, God taught the Israelites who he was and what he wanted them to be.

1. The Sabbath was of divine institution and is so declared in passages where ceasing to create was called "resting" (Gen. 2:3; Exod. 20:11 and 31:7). According to the Mosaic law the Sabbath was observed by the cessation from labor and by a holy assembly. Girls participated in the celebration by assisting in lighting the Sabbath lamp and preparing the Sabbath meal. Conversation at the table was to remind the children of God's sanctification of the day.

2. The Passover is the most important of three great annual festivals of Israel. The Hebrew word *pesah* means "to leap over, to show mercy," or "to spare." The Passover was instituted in memory of Israel's preservation from the last plague visited upon Egypt, and the subsequent deliverance from bondage (Exod. 12:1–28). The blood of an unblemished lamb was brushed on the door frames of Hebrew homes. Those homes covered by

11. Werner C. Graendorf, *Introduction to Biblical Christian Education* (Chicago: Moody Press, 1981), 27.

the blood were passed over when the death angel came to kill the first-born son in every household in Egypt.

All Hebrew males were required to attend the three annual feasts if they lived within a twenty-five mile radius of Jerusalem. If they lived outside that radius they could choose to attend one of the three. Most chose to attend Passover because of its significance to the Jewish people. "The deliverance of Israel from Egypt was accompanied by their adoption as the nation of Jehovah. For this a divine consecration was necessary that their outward severance from Egypt might be accompanied with an inward severance from everything of an Egyptian or heathen nature. This consecration was imparted by the Passover, a festival which was to lay the foundation of Israel's birth into a new life of grace and fellowship with God and to perpetuate it in time to come."[12]

In present Judaism, the Passover is celebrated by the use of a *Seder* and the *Haggadah*. Seder, which means "order," refers to the special meal and ceremony of the first night of Pesach (Passover). The Haggadah, a book that dates back almost two thousand years and contains parts of the old songs the Jews recited when the second Temple still stood in Jerusalem, helps tell the story of Passover. Children are an integral part of the celebration. They ask four questions to which the father responds with explanations appropriate to their age and development. The children also search for the *afikomon* (a broken piece of matzah that is wrapped in white linen and hidden beneath a cushion before the meal begins). The afikomon is closely guarded by the father because one of the children will attempt to steal it from him. Should the child succeed, the father must offer a gift before the child returns it. The four questions are among the oldest parts of the Haggadah. For a long time the Haggadah was part of the book of common prayer. Not until late in the Middle Ages did it become a separate book.[13]

Passover is an eight-day celebration that includes the Feasts of Unleavened Bread and First Fruits in the seven days immediately following the day of Passover. As originally commanded, a special sacrifice was offered every day after the regular morning sacrifice. Everyone ate only unleavened bread, and no work was allowed during the entire seven days. Grain (generally an omer of barley from the sheltered Ashes valley across the Kedron) was waved before the Lord on the Day of First Fruits, the day after the Sabbath following Passover. Children were encouraged to accompany their father in the preparation and waving of the grain presented to the Lord.

3.   The Feast of Pentecost is called *Shovuos* in Hebrew, which means "weeks." This is the festival which ended the weeks of the grain harvest. It is the second of the three great annual festivals, the others being Passover and

---

12.   Merrill F. Unger, *Unger's Bible Dictionary* (Chicago: Moody Press, 1965), 353.
13.   Hayyim Schauss, *The Jewish Festivals* (New York: Schocken Books, 1973), 84.

Tabernacles. The festival was called the Feast of Weeks because it celebrated seven completed weeks, culminating fifty days after Passover. It is also called the Feast of Harvest because it concluded the harvest of the later grain. Part of the ritual was offering the Lord two loaves of bread made from fine flour. Detailed instructions for making and baking these loaves were given in later times. Each loaf had little horns at each corner, like the horns of the altar. These were the only leavened Temple offerings, showing that they stood for ordinary, everyday bread. The sight of these loaves was bound to awaken many questions and again afforded priests and parents an opportunity to teach.[14]

Significant to the celebrants was the connection of Pentecost with the giving of the Decalogue. Exodus 19 indicates that the Law was delivered to Israel on the fiftieth day after the Exodus. A connection between that event and this festival may be hinted at in the reference to the observance of the law in Deuteronomy 16:12.[15] Schauss agrees with Unger as he writes: "It appears that as far back as the days of the second Temple, Shovuos was a twofold festival. It was the festival of the wheat harvest, when a sacrifice was offered from the new wheat crop; it was also considered the observance of the pact entered into between God and mankind. . . . The holiday first gained importance when it became the festival of the giving of the Torah, of God revealing Himself on Mount Sinai."[16]

According to the injunction of Leviticus 23:15–16, the Jews regularly count every evening of the fifty days from the second day of Passover until Pentecost and recite a prayer over it. Perhaps, as is true with Passover, the festival expresses the fact of a nation chosen and separated from other nations. Pentecost is the solemn termination of the period of consecration preceding it.

4. The Feast of Trumpets, or Rosh Hashana, falls on the seventh month (Tisri) and is also called the Feast of the New Moon. This feast differs from the ordinary celebrations of the new moon because of the symbolic meaning of the seventh or sabbatical month. This feast also marks the beginning of the civil year. Because of the multitude of offerings associated with this feast day, the beginning of this month is distinguished above all other months of the year.

The educational significance of this day of rest and celebration is different in instruction and atmosphere from other Jewish festivals. Because this New Year feast day is closely connected with Yom Kippur, the attitude of the feast is solemn and subdued. Unlike the days of exalted joyfulness characterizing the other feasts, the Day of Trumpets and the subsequent days

---

14. William Barclay, *Educational Ideals in the Ancient World* (Grand Rapids: Baker Book House, 1974), 21.
15. Unger, 356.
16. Schauss, 89.

leading toward Yom Kippur are called the "Days of Awe." These are profoundly serious days, marked by a consciousness of the heavy moral responsibility we all bear.[17]

The fact that Tisri was the great month for sowing might easily have suggested the thought of commemorating on this day the finished work of creation. Because of this rabbinical thought, the Feast of Trumpets came to be regarded as the anniversary of the creation of the world.[18]

5. The Feast of Trumpets is dynamically attached to the Sabbatic Year and to Jubilee. The observance of the Sabbatic Year began on the first day of every seventh year. During the Sabbatic Year the soil, vineyards, and olive groves had complete rest from cultivation. This period provided the opportunity for physical rest and spiritual renewal. Through its observance the Israelites were to learn two things. First, the earth was created by God for man, though man's energies were not to be solely invested in the cultivation of the fruit of the earth for profit, since man was created to worship and glorify God. Second, cessation from work allowed the Israelites to enjoy the fruits of the earth that God had given them and would ever give them if they kept his covenant. It was a reminder of their dependence upon God for their sustenance.

6. In a similar manner, the Year of Jubilee, also called the Year of Liberty, began on the first day of the fiftieth year. At Jubilee all property, fields, and houses situated in villages or unwalled towns that the owner had been obliged to sell through poverty and had not been able to redeem was to revert without payment to its original owner or lawful heirs. The lesson taught in the Year of Jubilee is that Yahweh is a God of freedom and grace, the Redeemer who releases the captive, delivers the poor, and spiritually revives the weary.

7. The Day of Atonement, or Yom Kippur, was celebrated on the tenth day of Tisri. The day was a high Sabbath on which no work was done. The Mosaic law prescribed only one public occasion of strict fasting and it was once a year on the Day of Atonement. All the people were to afflict their souls (fast from the evening of the ninth to the evening of the tenth) under the penalty of being cut off from Israel. The link connecting the Day of Atonement with the death of Aaron's sons (Lev. 10:1–5) was intended to point to the importance and holiness attached to the entrance into the innermost sanctuary of God (Lev. 16:1–2).

The Day of Atonement was pregnant with opportunities for teaching and instruction. On the morning of the Day of Atonement the high priest bathed and put on the holy garments—the coat, undergarments, girdle,

---

17. Ibid., 112.
18. Unger, 350.

and headdress of white cloth, signifying that he was entirely cleansed from the defilement of sin and dressed in holiness.

The centerpoint of this feast was the expiation offered by the high priest after the morning sacrifice. The high priest first sacrificed a bull for himself and his house and then entered the Holy of Holies with a censer to cover the mercy seat with a cloud of incense, a symbol of prayer. After returning to the altar of sacrifice to take some blood from the bull, he reentered the Holy of Holies and sprinkled the blood on the mercy seat seven times.[19]

He then presented two goats before the Lord at the door of the tabernacle and selected the goat that would be the scapegoat by casting lots upon them. One goat was killed as a sin offering, sprinkling its blood before the mercy seat in the same manner as he had done with the bull's blood. The priest entered the Holy of Holies at least four times to make atonement for the sins of the people. The priest then laid his hands upon the second goat (the scapegoat) and confessed over it all of the sins of the people. The goat was then led into the wilderness by the hand of a Levite and let loose. As soon as the high priest was informed that the scapegoat had reached the wilderness, he read lessons from the Torah and offered prayer. After this the high priest returned to the Holy of Holies, bathed himself again, and put on his usual royal blue robes with gold trim. Then he offered two rams as burnt offerings (marked dedication to his service), one for himself and one for the people.

All of the rituals and ceremonies of the Day of Atonement raised questions that gave the priests numerous opportunities to explain their significance. This high holy day had so many physical and symbolic activities attached to its observance that lessons were taught through conversations and discussions in the home and in the places of worship. It was a most instructive day in the life of the Jewish individual.

8. Feast of Tabernacles, or Sukkot, is the seventh and last of the celebrations commanded by God in Leviticus 23. It is the Jewish autumn festival. The feast is connected with Succoth, the first halting place on the Israelites' march out of Egypt (Exod. 12:37). The word *Sukkah* means booth or temporary dwelling. For the duration of the feast, all the people live in temporary dwellings or huts, in remembrance of the last booths their ancestors lodged in prior to entering the desert.

    This celebration is the most joyous of all the feasts and commemorates the labor of the ingathering of the field and the fruit of the earth. The act of building and dwelling in booths was to be a joy to the people of Israel. The booths instructed the people by reminding them of the fatherly care and protection of Jehovah while they journeyed from Egypt to the promised land of Canaan. As the families lived outdoors during the festival of Sukkot,

19.   Schauss, 135–39.

many opportunities for conversation and discussion arose from the various activities that took place during the feast.

Jerusalem opened its gates wide to welcome countless thousands of Jews three times a year. However, at Pesach and Sukkot the pilgrims flocked to the city from all parts of Palestine and from every foreign land known to harbor a Jewish community. Although Pesach (Passover) brought a greater number of pilgrims to Jerusalem, it was far more interesting and joyous to make the pilgrimage at Sukkot. The celebration during Sukkot involved parades and ceremonies, thus providing opportunities for the children to be instructed. Since the festival was so joyous and invited revelry, the celebrant felt more free at Sukkot than at other feasts.

The daily parades wound their way from the Mount of the Temple to the Spring of Siloam. A large golden pitcher of water was drawn to pour on the altar. During other parades the people gathered long willow branches that were placed alongside the altar with their points inward. The priest held the pitcher above the altar and poured out the water libation on the altar. The trumpet blew and the priests with the long willow branches stood in choir formation and sang the Psalms of Praise. Each day the water libation at the altar instructed the people in the generosity of God as the provider of the necessity of life, water.

Each evening of the feast in the great Court of the Women four tall golden menorahs were lit. They were fifty yards high with four branches that terminated into huge cups in which oil was poured. Ladders were placed against each menorah so four young priests could continue to put oil into the cups to keep the wicks burning. The wicks were made from the worn-out garments of the priests. The light of these menorahs attained such a high intensity that all of Jerusalem was lit by them. The people were reminded of the Shekinah glory of God as his presence in days past had filled the tabernacle and especially the Temple (1 Kings 8 and 9). As the lights flared, the sound of flutes was heard. The fine men of Jerusalem gathered in the court with torches in their hands dancing and waving the torches, throwing them in the air and catching them again. Late into the night the dance went on. Early toward morning, with the priest retired, the congregation chanted psalm after psalm. The festival went on before the great congregation gathered in Jerusalem.[20]

It can easily be seen that the Jewish feasts and festivals were unparalleled opportunities for instruction in history and in the generosity of God. Before there was ever a school to teach him, a son would learn from his father the history of his country, the holy righteousness of God, and the bounty of God in the world of nature. In the Jewish home the father was bound to

---

20.   Ibid., 180–89.

accept the duty of the religious education of his son. It was a holy and reverent responsibility.

GOD AS TEACHER IN THE MONARCHY

In the early days of the monarchy of Israel there was hardly time for the establishment of formal schools. The first king of Israel was a warrior who led his nation in victorious military encounters. Depending on the prophets for any educational nurturing, the early monarchs thought little of education and more of political expansion. Education was still primarily in the hands of the father, who was responsible for explaining the educational significance of the feasts, sacrifices, and later the Temple worship.

> Jewish law laid it down that a father must explain the great festivals to his son. When a son asked the meaning of "the testimonies, the statutes and the judgments" his father must be ready with an explanation (Exod. 13:8; Deut. 4:9; 6:20). Now, what is not sufficiently realised is that these great festivals had not only a historical significance; they had also an agricultural significance. They did not only commemorate events in history; they also marked out the cycle of the agricultural year; and it may well be true that their agricultural significance was more primitive than the historical significance which was attached to them. Their historical significance was as follows. The Passover commemorated the deliverance of the Jewish people from slavery and bondage in Egypt; Pentecost commemorated the giving of the Law on Mount Sinai; The Festival of Tabernacles with its living in booths made from branches, commemorated the journey through the wilderness to the promised land.[21]

Though a military genius who surely spent most of his time and effort in that dimension of monarchical activity, Israel's second king was a sensitive scholar at heart. As musician and lyricist, King David is unexcelled in Old Testament literature.[22] David was not given permission by God to construct the Temple, but because he loved Jehovah he was very concerned about the type of worship that would take place in the Temple when it was eventually built. Toward the end of his reign a completed system of levitical services was organized with thirty-eight thousand Levites given various job responsibilities. In addition, singers, minstrels, Temple servants and door keepers were trained to prepare for service in the Temple that his son would build.[23]

Education in the monarchy cannot be totally understood until the vast instructional capability of King Solomon is taken into consideration. The educational value of the book of Proverbs alone will never be surpassed for its elevation and distribution of wisdom. Education began to take on a more personal dimension in the writings of Solomon and the wise men.

---

21. Barclay, 19–20.
22. Kenneth O. Gangel and Warren S. Benson, *Christian Education: Its History and Philosophy* (Chicago: Moody Press, 1983), 26.
23. Ibid., 26–27.

WISE MEN AS INSTRUCTORS

There were a number of God-fearing wise men who, like Solomon, composed proverbs, answered "hard sayings," and gathered these sayings into an orderly arrangement of written teachings that were current among the people. Proverbs 1:2–6 explains the goal of the teaching of the men wise in the ways of Jehovah.

These words indicate that the purpose of the wise men of Israel was to teach wisdom that was not simply intellectual but involved the whole man, wisdom which had its origin in the fear of God, a wisdom that was God-given, not the product of the thinking of man apart from God. Along with wisdom, spiritual education was to be given, that is, instruction in wise, just, and fair dealing. Wise men stressed the harm and evil of impurity, falsehood, pride, dishonoring parents, unjust practices, cruelty, intemperance, and irreverence. They highly exalted such virtues as truth, honesty, fairness, patience, courage, humility, and godliness. The instruction they gave was individual and personal. While adults were certainly not neglected, the wise men gave special instruction to the young as those who, if they would but take heed to their ways when they could learn readily, would be able to live soberly, righteously and godly when they came to maturity.[24]

PROPHETS AS INSTRUCTORS

The instructional prominence of the prophets developed during the divided monarchy. Although this process began with Samuel, when the nation fell into military and economic turmoil, the prophets became the center of education and remained so until the destruction of the Temple and the city of Jerusalem.

When civil agencies failed to function in Israel and Judah, God raised up the prophets to fill the educational gap.

> Probably no nation has ever produced a group of religious and moral teachers comparable with the prophets of ancient Israel. Through their spoken public addresses and writings they became creators of national religious and social ideals, critics and inspirers of public policies, denunciators of social wrongs, preachers of individual and social righteousness, and the source and channel of an ever loftier conception of God and of the mission of Israel. In fulfilling each of these capacities they were acting as public teachers. In every national crisis they were at hand to denounce, to encourage, to comfort and always to instruct. They were the public conscience of Israel, the soul of its religion, the creators of its public opinion, its most conspicuous, its most revered, its most convincing teachers.[25]

The prophets were divinely called by God. It was no mere profession that prompted them to begin instruction. These men spoke to the people for God while the priest spoke to God for the people. As the priests began to adulterate the

---

24.   Eavey, 57.
25.   Fletcher H. Swift, *Education in Ancient Israel from Earliest Times to 70 A.D.* (Chicago: The Open Court Publishing Company, 1919), 38.

spiritual dimension of Temple worship, the place of education began to shift. Rather than the people coming to a central location such as a tabernacle or temple, the prophets took God's message wherever they could find people who would listen. Their messages were highly ethical as well as dynamically theological. Because of the lack of justice, mercy, and generosity of God's people toward one another, the messages of the prophets were dominated by the themes of mercy and justice. This was an attempt to call their nation back to God and the provisions of his covenant. The prophets knew the people were on a downward collision course with the judgment of God, and they tried to educate the Israelites about the appropriate response to God's commandments. Of great importance in this era was the development of the schools of the prophets. These were mainly associated with the ministries of Elijah and Elisha. It appears from biblical writings that these schools were informal bands of disciples not unlike those who lived and learned with Jesus during his three years of earthly ministry. But in spite of the prophets' efforts, the die was cast and dark clouds of destruction were on the horizon.

Because the present generation seemed to be lost in greediness and gain, the prophets taught about the future and "the great day of the Lord" at which time God would reveal himself. This glorious future, they taught, would be realized through the Messiah. There is no doubt that Isaiah 53 is a representation of a new level in the nation's understanding of the coming Messiah. Gangel and Benson write: "Educational processes among the prophets were geared to deepen religious insight, increase its favor, and develop a better and more intimate knowledge of Jehovah, which would ultimately consummate in a personal righteousness. Unfortunately, most of their efforts were unsuccessful, and God's judgment had to fall when His people would not heed the message of His teachers."[26]

INSTRUCTION DURING THE EXILE

Many of the people of the southern kingdom of Judah remained in Judah during the captivity in Babylon. Numerous innovative forms of worship evolved during the years after the destruction of the Temple in 586 B.C. The center for Jewish worship, the Temple, was no longer a place for worship and study. It became necessary for each Jewish community to establish a place for meeting. The impetus for these meeting places appears to have come from Jeremiah who urged the captives to pray for the city of their captivity.[27] As the captives gathered to pray, they also began to have fellowship with one another and to study together. The community meeting place became the synagogue.[28]

During the fifth century B.C. the synagogue became the central place of instruction in Hebrew theology. The Torah reigned supreme again, although Aramaic in-

---

26. Gangel and Benson, 28.
27. A. Sanders, "Dispersion," in *Interpreters Dictionary of the Bible* (Nashville: Abingdon Press, 1962), 1:855.
28. Clarence H. Benson, *A Popular History of Christian Education* (Chicago: Moody Press, 1943), 24–25.

stead of Hebrew had become the spoken language of the people. Because of the necessity of reading theological books in Hebrew, that language became a major subject of instruction for anyone who desired to serve in an official religious capacity. The synagogue became the first formal educational institution the Hebrews developed. The Torah emerged in written form in the Talmud and high qualifications were required for all teaching.[29]

CONCLUSION

God chose the people of Israel and set them apart to carry out the plan he had established for all mankind. Through the people of Israel, God taught all of us the total insufficiency of man and the abundant sufficiency of God through grace. God educated Israel for separation. From the day he commanded Abraham to leave his country to the time when the nation went into captivity, God was training the Israelites to be a separate people devoted to him alone.

God also sought to prepare the people of Israel to carry his truth to all other nations. Even though they were perverse in their attitudes toward God and their self-righteous pride made them ineffective to deliver God's purpose to other nations, God still used their contrary course in history to bring Christ into the world.

The Law, which occupied the centerpoint of Jewish national life and education, was God's means of revealing human sinfulness and insufficiency. Through the Law God taught all humankind its need for a Redeemer. The Law brings the sinner into the depths of despair in the realization that he is dead, and thereby leads him to lay hold on life in Christ.

May God be as patient in his education of us, his children in Christ, as he was with the "dull of ear and slow of heart" Israelites from Abraham to the Exile.

FOR FURTHER STUDY

1. What is the relationship between God's role in teaching and revelation?

2. Compare the content of instruction and the teaching methodology of the period of the Patriarchs with the period of the Pentateuch.

3. Explain the instructional aims of each of the following celebrations of Israel:

    a. Sabbath

    b. Passover

    c. Unleavened Bread and Feast of First Fruits

    d. Pentecost

---

29. Gangel and Benson, 30.

  e. Trumpets or New Moon

  f. Day of Atonement

  g. Feast of Tabernacles

4. God used the feasts and festivals to teach his people. How can we employ religious holidays to communicate faith to our children?

5. The tabernacle served as an educational vehicle for transmitting the Hebrew faith. Write an essay on "Worship as Education." Include a discussion of how today's worship services could be strengthened as a teaching medium.

6. How did God use daily traditions and rituals to teach his people?

SUGGESTED READING

Albright, W. F. *The Biblical Period from Abraham to Ezra*. New York: Harper & Row Publishers, 1963.

Barclay, William. *Educational Ideals in the Ancient World*. Grand Rapids: Baker Book House, 1974.

Bloch, Abraham P. *The Biblical and Historical Background of the Jewish Holy Days*. New York: KTVA Publishing House, 1978.

Cardozo, Arlene Rossen. *Jewish Family Celebrations: The Sabbath, Festivals, and Ceremonies*. New York: St. Martin's Press, 1982.

Eavey, C. B. *History of Christian Education*. Chicago: Moody Press, 1966.

Gangel, Kenneth O., and Warren S. Benson. *Christian Education: Its History and Philosophy*. Chicago: Moody Press, 1983.

Graendorf, Werner C. *Introduction to Biblical Christian Education*. Chicago: Moody Press, 1981.

Pazmiño, Robert W. *Foundational Issues in Christian Education: An Introduction in Evangelical Perspective*. Grand Rapids: Baker Book House, 1988.

Reed, James E., and Ronnie Prevost. *A History of Christian Education*. Nashville: Broadman & Holman, 1993.

Schauss, Hayyim. *The Jewish Festivals*. New York: Schocken Books, 1973.

CHAPTER 2

JESUS, THE MASTER TEACHER

—RICK YOUNT

When Jesus landed [on the shore] and saw a large crowd, he had compassion on them, because they were like sheep without a shepherd. So he began teaching them many things (Mark 6:34–35).

The crowds were amazed at his teaching, because he taught as one who had authority, and not as their teachers of the law (Matt. 7:28–9).

We discovered in the last chapter that God revealed himself as Teacher. It is no surprise, then, that Jesus, though he healed and preached and met physical needs, was known as Rabonni, Master, Teacher. Jesus clearly connected himself to the Father when he states, "I and the Father are one" (John 10:30). He further connected himself to the Father as *teacher*: "For I did not speak of my own accord, but the Father who sent me commanded me what to say and how to say it. So whatever I say is just what the Father has told me to say" (John 12:49–50). And again, "Don't you believe that I am in the Father, and that the Father is in me? The words I say to you are not just my own. Rather, it is the Father, living in me, who is doing his work" (John 14:10).

Nicodemus acknowledged that Jesus was "a teacher . . . come from God" (John 3:2). Jesus came teaching what he had learned from his Father. And what was the result? Sherwood Eddy, in his book *Maker of Men*, writes:

He was allowed less than three years in which to do His work; little more than a year in His public ministry, and a year in retirement training His pathetic remnant. He was cut off in His young manhood, a little past the age of thirty. Socrates taught for forty years. Plato for fifty. Aristotle had lived long and filled libraries with his learning. Buddha and Confucius had fulfilled their three score and ten. He was among a crushed people, under an oppressive legalism, zealously opposed and

21

hated by scribes and Pharisees, betrayed by Jews and crucified by Gentiles. He left no book, no tract, or written page behind Him. He bequeathed no system, no philosophy, no theology, no legislation. He raised no armies, held no office, sought no influence, turned His back forever on might, magic, and cheap miracle.

Yet He transformed the bigoted Jew and universalized his religion; He showed the philosophizing Greek the highest truth; He won the proud Roman to plant the cross on his standard instead of the eagle; He stretched out His hand to the great continents and transformed them—to Asia, to savage Europe, to darkest Africa, to America.[1]

Therefore, if we are to have a Christ-centered focus in our teaching ministry, we should focus our attention on Jesus as Master Teacher. What kind of students did he have? What characteristics did he display? What methods did he use? What principles did he espouse?

In exploring these questions we face a danger. A botanist destroys a delicate flower as he analyzes it; a zoologist destroys a living organism as he dissects it. We must approach our study of Jesus as Teacher with a proper sense of awe and reverence. He is our Lord and Master and not a case study to be played with for the sake of academic exercise. And so we honor him as Lord and Teacher even as we look to him as a model of how we should teach.

THE STUDENTS OF JESUS

A friend of mine, a fellow minister of education, invited me to join him for a cup of coffee at a local cafe. He was as depressed as any minister I'd ever known. As he poured out his heart, he returned again and again to the same lament: "If I only had some committed people to work with!" or "If I had some members with the leadership skills to direct our programs!" Seminary had taught him about programs for children and youth and adults; singles and seniors; outreach and inreach; organization and enlistment; church council, weekly workers' meetings, and appreciation banquets. But where do you find the people to make these programs come to life? Where do lay leaders come from? Seminary had exposed him to a wide variety of Christian ministry ideals. He now found himself in the ordeal of local church ministry, and he was sinking fast.

His experience is not unique. I suppose every minister has had feelings like these from time to time. Even seminary professors fall prey to the idea that our teaching could be so much more effective "if only" our students were more creative or motivated or something. It is a fantasy of the imagination. We are not called to some abstract ideal. We are called "to prepare God's people for works of service" (Eph. 4:12). We take them as they are and lead them to become all they can be. That is our calling. And that is exactly what Jesus did with his disciples.

---

1.   Sherwood Eddy, *Maker of Men* (New York: Harper & Bros., 1941).

We tend to think of the disciples—especially Peter, James, and John—as great men of faith. This they became. But they were not "great men of faith" when Jesus chose them. Though they were chosen carefully and prayerfully (Mark 6:12–16), they were very human. Let's look at some of the basic characteristics of the twelve men Jesus chose as his closest students.

THE DISCIPLES WERE IMPERFECT

Scripture provides us ample evidence that the twelve were rough in character and demeanor. James and John, the sons of Zebedee, were short-tempered—so much so that they were nicknamed the "sons of Thunder" (Mark 3:17). It was James and John who wanted to call fire down from heaven to destroy a Samaritan town because they did not welcome Jesus. Jesus rebuked them for their outburst and went on to another village (Luke 9:54–55).

Simon, son of John, was impetuous and unstable. Though Jesus gave him the name Peter (Petros, "the rock"), Peter gave little evidence of stability. Jesus told the disciples about his impending death in Jerusalem, but Peter protested. When the guards came for Jesus in Gethsemane, Peter drew a sword and cut off Malchus's ear. Though Peter had bragged that he would die for Jesus (John 13:37), he denied being a disciple to a servant girl, to one of the men standing by the courtyard fire, and to one of the high priest's relatives (John 18:17, 25–27). Peter was impetuous and unstable, even after three years of living with the Master.

Thomas was a realist. He wanted cold hard facts. He had been absent the first time Jesus had appeared to the disciples (John 20:24). When told that they saw Jesus, Thomas exclaimed, "Unless I see the nail marks in his hands and put my finger where the nails were, and put my hand into his side, I will not believe it" (John 20:25). Where had he been the last three years? He had witnessed many miracles at the hands of Jesus. He had lived and worked with these men. Why was he so stubborn? But he was honest. When the facts presented themselves, he did not hesitate to act on them. A week later Jesus stood among them and invited Thomas to test his wounds. Thomas's reaction was immediate and absolute: "My Lord and my God!" (John 20:28).

Then there were the political power brokers, Judas Iscariot and Simon the zealot. These two saw in Jesus a chance to overthrow Roman oppression. They sought to use him in their political struggle. Judas was a thief. He pilfered money from the disciples' common purse, which he was responsible to keep (John 12:4–6).

The disciples were far from perfect.

THE DISCIPLES WERE SLOW TO LEARN.

Jesus chose the Twelve during his first year of ministry.[2] For nearly three years they followed and observed Jesus; they ate with him; they witnessed his numerous miracles. But they were so slow to learn.

---

2. Alexander Balmain Bruce, *The Training of the Twelve* (4th ed., New York: A. C. Armstrong & Sons, 1894; reprint, New Canaan, Conn.: Keats Publishing, 1979), 12. See also Alfred Edersheim, *The Life and Times of Jesus the Messiah*, vol. 1 (London: Longmans, Green and Co., 1890; reprint, Grand Rapids: Eerdmans, 1969), 348.

He talked to them of his impending death and resurrection (Matt. 16:29), and yet they were shocked when he actually died, and surprised by his resurrection. Look:

> [The angels said to the women,] He is not here; he has risen! Remember how he told you, while he was still with you in Galilee: "The Son of Man must be delivered into the hands of sinful men, be crucified and on the third day be raised again." Then they remembered his words. When they came back from the tomb, they told all these things to the Eleven and to all the others. It was Mary Magdalene, Joanna, Mary the mother of James, and the others with them who told this to the apostles. But they did not believe the women, because their words seemed to them like nonsense (Luke 24:6–11).

Even when he appeared to them after his resurrection, some of them doubted! (Matt. 28:17). They were slow to learn.

THE DISCIPLES WERE SELF-CENTERED

Judas and Simon the Zealot had accepted Jesus' call to further their own political purposes. But the self-centeredness of the disciples went far deeper. As Jesus and the Twelve made their way to Jerusalem, Jesus focused his thoughts on the cross. Peter, however, was thinking about all the sacrifices they had made—and what had it gained them? "We have left everything to follow you! What then will there be for us?" (Matt. 19:27).

At another time, Jesus told the disciples they were going to the other side of the Sea of Galilee (Mark 4:35). As they were making their way across the lake, a violent storm arose and nearly swamped the boat. What was their reaction? "Teacher, don't you care if we drown?" (Mark 4:38). Jesus' response clearly revealed their self-centeredness: "Why are you so afraid? Do you still have no faith?" (Mark 4:40). He had told them they were going over to the other side and drowning in a storm had not been part of his plan.

Still another example of their self-centeredness is revealed at the arrest of Jesus. We've already noted Peter's false bravado: "I will lay down my life for you" (John 13:37). And again, "Even if all fall away on account of you, I never will" (Matt. 26:33). Then Jesus told Peter he would disown him three times before morning (v. 34). "Even if I have to die with you, I will never disown you. And all the other disciples said the same" (v. 35). But when the reality of Jesus' arrest arrived, "all the disciples deserted him and fled" (v. 56), and by morning, Peter had denied even knowing Jesus three times (vv. 69–75).

THE DISCIPLES WERE UNEDUCATED AND UNPROFESSIONAL.

The center of higher learning in Jesus' day was Jerusalem, and many of the inhabitants of Judea were well educated in the Law. Galilee was a different matter. Galilee provided rich soil for farming, an abundance of hard workers for a vast array of trades and businesses, and a bountiful lake for fishing. Its beauty may have led some to meditation and prayer, but it certainly did not evoke the morbid fanaticism of the faithful in Jerusalem. So, while Galilee was home to generous spirits, warm hearts, simple manners, and earnest piety, it was looked down upon by the rabbinic leaders in the south.[3] Edersheim reports the following as a common saying: "If a person wishes to be rich, let him go north; if he wants to be wise, let him come south."[4]

Jesus began and built his ministry in Galilee (Luke 23:5), and chose men of the north to be his disciples. They were not learned men, but, being sick of the righteousness then in vogue, they hungered for real righteousness. They demonstrated the rudiments of faith and devotion. They displayed a willingness to grow and to learn. Jesus saw great potential in these men.[5] That's why he could call unstable Simon "Petros, the rock," because he saw the "rock" that Simon would ultimately become.

THE DISCIPLES WERE APPRENTICES, NOT MERE LEARNERS

The differences between north and south can also be seen in two words used for "learner." Coleman makes the distinction between *mathetas* (apprentice) and *talmid* (scholar).[6] A. B. Bruce underscores the idea of *mathetas* when he writes that Jesus "desired not only to have disciples, but to have about him men whom he might train to make disciples of others." And again, "The careful, painstaking education of the disciples secured that the Teacher's influence on the world should be permanent; that His kingdom should be founded on the rock of deep and indestructible convictions in the minds of a few, not on the shifting sands of superficial evanescent impressions on the minds of the many."[7]

The disciples were not trained, but they were trainable. They had not been taught, but they were teachable. Nothing more in learners should a teacher desire, and nothing more does a teacher need!

In summary, the disciples were rough hewn, imperfect, self-centered, and untrained when Jesus chose them. In short, they were normal people, with all the problems and potential of people today. Yet from among these Twelve came leaders who turned the entire known world upside down for the Lord. How can we teach so that our people can become *mathetas* and, in time, leaders and teachers of others? What can we glean from Jesus' words and actions that will help us develop our skills in the teaching ministry of the church? It is to the Teacher that we now turn our attention.

---

3. Edersheim, vol. 1, 224–5.
4. Ibid., 223.
5. Bruce, 5–8.
6. Lucien Coleman, *Why the Church Must Teach* (Nashville: Broadman Press, 1984), 23.
7. Bruce, 13.

THE CHARACTERISTICS OF JESUS AS TEACHER

In both the Ten Commandments and the Sermon on the Mount, "Who we are in the Lord" comes before "What we do for the Lord." The best teaching flows not merely out of our mouths, but from our hearts. So before we look at the methods of Jesus, we need to learn something of the person of Jesus.

JESUS WAS WHAT HE TAUGHT

I once explained to my students that Jesus was a model of what he taught, but what some understood by that missed my intention. Jesus did not "model his teaching" like a fashion model parading the latest fad. His lifestyle was not a put-on conceived to strengthen the words he spoke. Jesus simply lived what he taught. What he taught flowed out of who he was. One day after Jesus was finished praying, one of the disciples asked Jesus to teach him and the others to pray (Luke 11:1–2). Educators call this kind of event a "teachable moment." Creating a climate of teachable moments, particularly in a formal class setting, is difficult. Jesus wasted no time responding to the request of the disciple.

From Jesus' life flowed teaching. His words and actions reinforced each other with an authority that amazed his hearers. "What we are" speaks more loudly than "what we say." Faith learning is more "caught from" than "taught by" a teacher. Some thirty years after Jesus had ascended to heaven, Peter wrote to pastors: "Be shepherds of God's flock that is under your care . . . not lording it over those entrusted to you, but being examples to the flock" (1 Pet. 5:2–3). Jesus was the example to Peter and to the Twelve and to all who would follow him. If we are to pattern our teaching after Jesus, we too must strive to be examples.

JESUS WAS COMFORTABLE WITH PEOPLE OF ALL KINDS

Teachers must be able to establish rapport with learners if they are to be effective. Rapport building is a social skill which requires some degree of sensitivity to those you teach. The Scriptures reflect Jesus' amazing ability to be "at home" with a wide range of people—whether they were poor or wealthy; Jew, Gentile, or Roman; male or female. Let's look at just a few examples.

- Jesus spoke earnestly and confidently with Nicodemus, a devout Jewish leader and showed no anxiety as he taught a member of the ruling Sanhedrin (John 3).

- He invited himself to the home of Zacchaeus, a tax collector, for dinner, and demonstrated no discomfort being in the company of wealth (Luke 19). He chose another tax collector, Matthew, as one of his disciples (Matt. 9:9–12).

- He conversed openly with a Samaritan woman who had come to draw water from a well and appeared to be unconcerned that, in the custom of his day, a respectable man did not talk with women in public, nor a respectable Jew to Samaritan "half-breeds." But Jesus broke social customs to draw this Samaritan woman to faith in himself. And through her, he reached into her village (John 4:28–30).

- Jesus healed the demon-possessed daughter of a heathen woman after he taught her who he was (Matt. 15:22–28).[8]

- The disciples rebuked parents for bringing their little children to Jesus, but the Lord welcomed them: "Let the little children come to me, and do not hinder them, for the kingdom of heaven belongs to such as these" (Matt. 19:14).

Besides these instances, Jesus surrounded himself with people of all kinds. He healed all sorts of diseases in crowds and drove out demons from the possessed (Mark 1:34). He healed the deaf (Mark 7:32ff) and the blind (John 9:1ff), the lame (Matt. 21:14) and the leprous (Matt. 8:3). During his arrest he even healed the ear of Malchus, one of the high priest's servants (Luke 22:51; John 18:10).

We naturally tend to stay with "our own kind." We like people like us. Discomfort mounts as we deal with people much richer or poorer than ourselves. It isn't easy to deal with people of a different race, language, or age bracket. To do so requires an extra degree of energy and commitment. But the teacher who can build bridges to all people will be the most effective.

JESUS WAS COMPASSIONATE TOWARD HIS LEARNERS

Jesus protected the disciples from harm (John 17:12). He gave the disciples instructions before he sent them out (Matt. 10). Whether he used a strong rebuke (Matt. 16:23; Luke 24:25) or a gentle explanation (Matt. 16:21; Luke 24:27), his focus was on the disciples' welfare: ". . . the Son of Man did not come to be served, but to serve, and to give his life as a ransom for many" (Matt. 20:28).

Jesus cared more for his learners than for lessons. One day Jesus was teaching about fasting (Matt. 9:14–17) when Jairus, the ruler of the local synagogue, appeared and asked him to attend to his sick daughter. Which was more important to

---

8. The Canaanite woman entreats Jesus, "Lord, Son of David, have mercy on me!" Jesus' behavior appears rude: "Jesus did not answer a word" (Matt. 15:23). When she continued, "Lord, help me!" (v. 25), his language sounds strangely harsh: "It is not right to take the children's bread and toss it to their dogs" (Matt. 15:26). Edersheim explains that the woman's approach to Jesus was "not as the Messiah of Israel but an Israelitish Messiah . . . this was exactly the error of the Jews which Jesus had encountered and combated, alike when he resisted the attempt to make him King, in his reply to the Jerusalem Scribes, and in his Discourses at Capernaum. To have granted her the help she so entreated, would have been, as it were, to reverse the whole of his teaching, and to make His works of healing merely works of power. . . . And so He first taught her, in such manner as she could understand—that which she needed to know, before she could approach Him in such a manner—the relation of the heathen to the Jewish world [dogs, children] and of both to the Messiah, and then He gave her what she asked" (vol. 2, 39).

Jesus, finishing his lesson on fasting or helping Jairus' daughter? "Jesus got up and went with him" (v. 19).

JESUS HAD A STRONG SELF-CONCEPT

Our society has gone overboard with the idea of self-esteem and positive self-concept. A recent research study showed that American high schoolers are significantly more confident in their math and science skills than are their Japanese counterparts. The only problem is that the Japanese high schoolers are significantly more capable in math and science than American students.[9] For twenty years we have worshiped "feel good" at the expense of "think well" and "do well," resulting in more self-esteem problems than ever. Still, a healthy self-concept is important. For Christians, knowing to whom we belong is an essential part of learning who we are. And knowing who we are in the Lord gives us the confidence we need to teach others. Let's look briefly at the evidence that Jesus had a healthy self-concept.

Jesus was a man on a mission. This gave him power. He did what he did because he was sent by the Father (John 5:23). His work was what the Father had given him to do (John 5:19–36). His work was a result of the Father working through him (John 14:10). Jesus' self-concept was not based on the "me first" philosophy of our day. It was based on a "Father first" philosophy. He sought his Father's will and did it, not turning to the left or right. He was a man on a mission—and knowing what he came to do gave him power to teach with authority.

Each of us has spiritual gifts that we are to use in Kingdom service. We have a unique yoke—his yoke—a mission to perform. When we find that mission and accept it, we find rest and refreshment in the Lord and learn from him (Matt. 11:28–30). In short, we find our "self" as God created us to be. This discovery of "self" is far better than trying to make something of ourselves for the Lord! Find the Lord's place for you and give yourself to it.

Jesus was a man of dynamic humility. Nowhere in the Gospels do we find Jesus demanding worship from the disciples. We cannot find a hint that Jesus fretted about a lack of recognition, or grumbled that those he healed weren't more grateful, or that the religious leaders didn't give him the respect he deserved. Though he did not demand worship or honor, he did on at least one occasion acknowledge it when it was given. But look how he used it: "You call me 'Teacher' and 'Lord,' and rightly so, for that is what I am. Now that I, your Lord and Teacher, have washed your feet, you also should wash one another's feet. I have set you an example that you should do as I have done for you. I tell you the truth, no servant is greater than his master, nor is a messenger greater than the one who sent him. Now that you know these things, you will be blessed if you do them" (John 13:13–17).

---

9. Jerry Adler, et al, "Hey, I'm Terrific: The Curse of Self-Esteem," *Newsweek*, 17 February 1992, 46–51.

Jesus came as the "Suffering Servant" (Isa. 53; Matt. 16:21). Yet his humility was not passive. He never played the victim, apologetically kicking the dirt because people—his own people—rejected him. His was a dynamic humility, an energetic submission. Even when he stood before Pilate, the one man who, humanly speaking, could rescue him from the cross, we see our Lord submissive and powerful: "You would have no power over me if it were not given to you from above" (John 19:11).

Jesus did not put himself down, except to exalt the Father (Luke 18:19). He never belittled his ministry. He never grinned with embarrassment when people praised him. He displayed the dignity of authority.

He did not reject worship when it was offered him. When the rich young ruler fell on his knees before him, Jesus did not exhibit embarrassment. Rather, he simply dealt with the man's desire (eternal life) and his need (to be rid of his wealth) in order to follow Jesus (Mark 10:17–22). When Thomas saw Jesus after the resurrection and exclaimed, "My Lord and my God!" Jesus gave no indication that Thomas's adoration was out of line (John 20:28–29).

Jesus did not degrade himself or his ministry. Neither did he flaunt himself or his powers. His dynamic humility was not the self-effacing "I'm sorry I didn't do better" kind of passive, put-down humility nor was it the arrogant self-promoting "Why can't you be as good as me?" kind of dynamic. Jesus' dynamic humility was a vigorous meekness, a vital submissiveness, an aggressive lowliness.

Jesus' calmness under attack shows his strong self-concept. Jesus healed two demon-possessed men[10] by casting the demons into a nearby herd of pigs. Those tending the pigs ran into town and told what had happened. The whole town went out to confront Jesus over their loss "because they were overcome with fear" (Luke 8:37). They feared Jesus' power and were angry over their loss. There is no more volatile mix of human emotions than fear and anger. They pleaded with Jesus to leave (Matt. 8:34).

How did Jesus react? Apparently without a word of defense or explanation he "stepped into a boat, crossed over and came to his own town" (Matt. 9:1).

If I were in that situation I would want to defend myself and my actions. I would want to explain to the villagers that I was the Son of God, and I had just restored two men to their right minds by casting out a legion of demons. I would want them to understand that what I had done had been for the best.

Jesus' patience with his disciples showed his strong self-concept. Insecure teachers easily lose patience with students because they see a negative reflection on their own teaching ability when students fail to learn. Secure teachers simply back up and try again until their learners master the subject. As we have seen, the disciples had many

---

10.   Mark and Luke record that Jesus healed one demon-possessed man (Mark 5:1, Luke 8:26). Edersheim explains this by saying, "From these tombs the demonized, who is specially singled out by Mark and Luke, as well as his less prominent companion, came forth to meet Jesus" (vol. 1, 607). See Matt. 8:28.

weaknesses. Yet Jesus never gave up on them. "None has been lost except the one doomed to destruction so that Scripture would be fulfilled" (John 17:12).

He demonstrated patience when they lacked faith during the storm: "Why are you so afraid? Do you still have no faith?" (Mark 4:40). He demonstrated patience when they were unable to heal the demon-possessed boy: [Why could you not heal him?] "Because you have so little faith" (Matt. 17:20). He demonstrated patience when they fell asleep in the Garden: "Could you men not keep watch with me for one hour?" (Matt. 26:40). He never gave up on his disciples because they were a part of his mission: "I pray for . . . those you have given me, for they are yours" (John 17:9).

Jesus identified with the Father through prayer. At the beginning of the chapter, the dependence of Jesus on the Father for his work and teaching was underscored. The connection between them was prayer. We find several specific references to Jesus' prayer life. He went out "very early in the morning, while it was still dark . . . to a solitary place, where he prayed" (Mark 1:35). On another occasion, Jesus "spent the night praying to God" (Luke 6:12). Luke tells us that Jesus often prayed in lonely places (Luke 5:16). The disciples recognized that prayer strengthened Jesus, and they asked him to teach them how to pray (Luke 11:1). Later, Jesus reinforced the importance of prayer through the use of a parable that taught them they "should always pray and never give up" (Luke 18:1). Further, Jesus underscored the importance of asking the Father (Matt. 7:11; 18:19; Luke 11:13; John 14:13; 15:16; 16:23, 26).

Prayer—connection with the heavenly Father—was an essential part of Jesus' self-concept. And if Jesus, the Second Person of the Trinity (Matt. 28:19) in whom the fullness of the Godhead dwelt bodily (Col. 2:9), needed time alone in prayer, how much more do we?

However, we have grown up in a society saturated with existential thinking. "I am who I make myself. The only true reality is the reality I choose for myself. I am important because I am me. Good is what is good to me. Beauty is what I choose it to be. I am my own god. I choose my own universe. I make my own rules." Such philosophy leaves no room for submission, obedience, sacrifice, or surrender to the Lord. Nor does it allow for the absolutes of God or his Word, which says, "See to it that no one takes you captive through hollow and deceptive philosophy, which depends on human tradition and the basic principles of this world rather than on Christ" (Col. 2:8).

Prayer is the connection. The Word is the means. The Spirit is the power. Jesus is our Lord and Example. All combine to remake us after his image. And as you make this holy journey, you will find you have no problem with your self-concept, because Jesus declares that he came so you "may have life, and have it to the full" (John 10:10).

JESUS KNEW HIS LEARNERS

One of the reasons Jesus' teaching was so special is that it focused on the real life needs of those whom he taught. Jesus knew his learners, and he used that knowledge to focus his teaching for maximum effectiveness in each situation.

Jesus' knowledge was both divine and human. Being divine, he could read the hearts and minds of the people around him. When the Pharisees claimed Jesus' miracles were done by Beelzebub, the prince of demons[11] (Matt. 12:24), Matthew tells us "Jesus knew their thoughts" (v. 25). When many people believed in him because of the miracles, John writes, "Jesus would not entrust himself to them, for he knew all men. He did not need man's testimony about man, for he knew what was in a man" (John 2:24–25). Later, when many of his followers began to desert him, John tells us, "Jesus had known from the beginning which of them did not believe and who would betray him" (John 6:64).

Mark gives us the clearest picture of Jesus' ability to discern the thoughts of others. One day four men brought their paralytic friend to Jesus to be healed. They could not get inside the house, so they made an opening in the roof and let him down on his mat. "When Jesus saw their faith, he said to the paralytic, 'Son, your sins are forgiven.' Now some teachers of the law were sitting there, thinking to themselves, 'Why does this fellow talk like that? He's blaspheming! Who can forgive sins but God alone?' Immediately Jesus knew in his spirit that this was what they were thinking in their hearts, and he said to them, 'Why are you thinking these things?'" (Mark 2:5–8).

Even though Jesus had the power to read thoughts and hearts, he greatly depended on his human knowledge of people. Much of what he knew about people he learned the same way you and I do—through observation, conversation, or by asking questions. "What do you think, Simon?" (Matt. 17:25). To the Pharisees, "What do you think about the Christ? Whose Son is he?" (Matt. 22:42). To Pilate, "Is that your own idea, or did others talk to you about me?" (John 18:34).

Whether Jesus used divine or human knowledge, he used that knowledge in order to teach. He knew the Samaritan woman's need for water and, on a deeper level, a satisfying marriage, and deeper still, salvation. So he taught her about himself with water and husbands. Jesus understood the heathen woman's ignorance of the true Messiah, and so he taught her about himself with children and dogs before granting her request. Nicodemus was a teacher of Israel (John 3:10); yet he did not understand the meaning of what he taught until Jesus instructed him. Jesus knew his learners and he used that knowledge to mold and focus his teaching.

---

11.   Edersheim renders the name "Beelzebul" rather than "Beelzebub" which is a reference to Baal-zebub, the "fly-god of 2 Kings 1:2." He translates "Beel" (Master) and "zibbul" (sacrificing to idols), so "Beelzebul" means the "lord or chief of idolatrous sacrificing," vol. 1, 648.

JESUS WAS A MASTER OF THE OLD TESTAMENT

While the Scribes and Pharisees had embellished the Old Testament with their own corollaries and exceptions, Jesus displayed a fluent mastery of Scripture. For example, the Pharisees hated Jesus because he healed on the Sabbath (Matt. 12:9–14). They justified their hatred and indignation by reckoning Jesus' healing as "work," which was forbidden on the Sabbath (Exod. 20:8–11). Jesus pointed out their hypocrisy and interpreted the Law in light of the whole Old Testament: "If any of you has a sheep and it falls into a pit on the Sabbath, will you not take hold of it and lift it out? How much more valuable is a man than a sheep! Therefore it is lawful to do good on the Sabbath" (Matt. 12:11–12).

For the Pharisees, principles were more important than people—the Pharisees derived their power from holding principles over people. Jesus explained it this way: "[The Pharisees] tie up heavy loads and put them on men's shoulders, but they themselves are not willing to lift a finger to move them" (Matt. 23:4). For Jesus, people were more important than arbitrary principles. The Jewish leaders had twisted the Old Testament to their own purposes of power and control. The "Sabbath rule" was one example of this. They would rather a man or woman go unhealed rather than violate their interpretation of Sabbath rest.

> Indignant because Jesus had healed on the Sabbath, the synagogue ruler said to the people, "There are six days for work. So come and be healed on those days, not on the Sabbath." The Lord answered him, "You hypocrites! Doesn't each of you on the Sabbath untie his ox or donkey from the stall and lead it out to give it water? Then should not this woman, a daughter of Abraham, whom Satan has kept bound for eighteen long years, be set free on the Sabbath day from what bound her?" When he said this, all his opponents were humiliated, but the people were delighted with all the wonderful things he was doing (Luke 13:14–17).

So, which was primary in the Old Testament, principle or people, rules or relationship? Jesus spoke plainly when he said, "the Sabbath was made for man, not man for the Sabbath" (Mark 2:27). Even the Old Testament accuses the Pharisees: "Will the LORD be pleased with thousands of rams, with ten thousand rivers of oil? Shall I offer my firstborn for my transgression, the fruit of my body for the sin of my soul? He has showed you, O man, what is good. And what does the LORD require of you? To act justly and to love mercy and to walk humbly with your God" (Micah 6:7–8).

When the Pharisees threw the adulterous woman at Jesus' feet, their intent was to uphold the Law and trap Jesus (John 8:5–6). The Law was clear. There was no shade of gray: "must be put to death" (Lev. 20:10). They cared nothing for the woman. Their intent was to destroy this one who questioned their authority and power. Principle and power, not people.

In contrast to the Pharisees, Jesus cared for the woman and led her away from her sin. He displayed the loving-kindness of Jehovah God of Israel. His challenge, "If any one of you is without sin, let him be the first to throw a stone at her" (John 8:7), refocused their attention on themselves and their own need. The oldest, and evidently the wisest, were the first to understand Jesus' meaning. They dropped their stones and left, followed by the younger men.

Jesus acted as he did because he was Master of the heart of the Old Testament. In a fanatically religious nation, religion was the means to power. The scribes and Pharisees were trapped, as it were, by their own egotistical need for power. The Word of God was merely another tool to be used to maintain control. But for Jesus, the Old Testament was God's Word, the revelation of his Father. The entire Law and all of the prophets could be summarized in two brief statements of relationship: "Love the Lord your God . . . and love your neighbor as yourself" (Matt. 22:37–40). These were not New Testament teachings. Jesus was quoting the Old Testament: "Love the LORD your God with all your heart and with all your soul and with all your strength" (Deut. 6:5). "Do not seek revenge or bear a grudge against one of your people, but love your neighbor as yourself. I am the LORD" (Lev. 19:18).

Jesus had analyzed the teachings of the Old Testament and he synthesized the central thrust of the Father's perfect loving-kindness. But he went beyond knowledge of the Scripture and understanding. He expanded the Old Testament in his "you have heard it said . . . but I say unto you" teachings (Matt. 5:21, 27, 33, 38, 43).

Have you noticed the balance in Jesus' teaching? He was Master of the Scripture, and yet he focused that mastery on teaching people where they were. People were his focus. Scripture was his means. As he applied Old Testament Scripture to real problems in his students, he provided solutions uniquely suited to each one. The Eternal Word meeting today's personal need: the result was changed lives.[12]

JESUS' METHODS OF TEACHING

Now that we have an idea of who Jesus was, let us explore the way he taught. What methods did he use? What were his primary emphases in teaching? We will look at ten such areas.

JESUS ESTABLISHED RELATIONSHIP WITH HIS LEARNERS

Teaching from mouth to ear is very different from teaching heart-to-heart. If "getting the lesson across" is the main goal, there is little need for relationship between teacher and student. But if transforming students toward Christlikeness is the goal, a warm positive relationship is essential.

Jesus "appointed twelve to be with him" (Mark 3:14). Bruce indicates that their selection passed through three stages. In the first stage, the Twelve were simply believers in him as the Christ and occasionally accompanied him at their convenience.

---

12.   The Eternal Word and the needs of people are the two foundation stones in the Disciplers' Model. Chapter 1 of *The Disciplers' Handbook* discusses the practical problems in teaching associated with imbalance.

The second stage involved leaving their secular occupations and traveling with him. The third stage began when they were chosen by the Lord and formed into a select band, to be trained for the great work of apostles.[13]

The apostles lived together and ate together. They witnessed the miracles of Jesus together. They suffered rejection together. All the while, Jesus loved them, taught them, protected them.

Like coals in a fire, their mutual support and service strengthened them. Pull a coal from the fire, and it soon cools down. Peter's denials. Thomas's doubt. Scattering at Jesus' arrest. Despite obstacles, Jesus fanned the individual sparks of the Twelve into a family of fire, and within that context, he taught them.

JESUS STIMULATED AND MAINTAINED INTEREST

Jesus stimulated interest with dramatic illustrations and exaggeration. His illustrations included an unmerciful servant (Matt. 18:23ff), equal wages for unequal work (Matt. 20:1ff), murdering tenants (Matt. 21:33ff), undeserving wedding guests (Matt. 22:1ff), unprepared virgins (Matt. 25:1ff), wise and foolish investors (Matt. 25:14ff), wise and foolish builders (Luke 6:46ff), a good Samaritan (Luke 10:30ff), a rich fool (Luke 12:16ff), a lost sheep and coin and son (Luke 15:3ff), a shrewd manager (Luke 16:1ff), a rich man in hell (Luke 16:19ff), and the condemned Pharisee and forgiven tax collector (Luke 18:9ff). Such stories seized the hearts of Jesus' listeners because they came directly out of their own frustrations and disappointments.

Jesus also used exaggeration in his teaching. If your hand or foot causes you to sin, "cut it off" (Mark 9:43, 45). If your eye causes you to sin, then "pluck it out" (Mark 9:47). The only way to be Jesus' disciple is to "hate [your] father and mother, [your] wife and children, [your] brothers and sisters—yes, even [your] own life" (Luke 14:6). Illustrations and exaggerations helped to stimulate interest.

Jesus also maintained the interest of his listeners. He asked questions. He focused his teaching from the perspective of his students. He used parables with the masses, but waited until he was alone with his disciples to explain them (Matt. 13:10–18; Mark 5:33–34). Those who truly hungered for righteousness would follow, learn, and grow. Those who were merely curious would fall by the wayside.

JESUS TAUGHT BY EXAMPLE

We have established that Jesus was what he taught, focusing on his Person. Here the focus is on his method. Jesus inspired his disciples to imitate him. Pray as I prayed. Love as I loved you. Serve as I served. Take up your cross as I took up mine. Care for the sheep as I cared for the sheep. Finish your course as I finished mine.

---

13.   Bruce, 11–12.

The best teachers are living case studies of their subject matter. Thirty years after Jesus returned to the Father, Peter wrote to young pastors "Be shepherds of God's flock that is under your care, serving as overseers . . . not lording it over those entrusted to you, but being examples to the flock" (1 Pet. 5:2–3). Bible study, whether it be in church or at a college or seminary, should mold us into better examples of the Truth, not merely living libraries of it.

JESUS TAUGHT PEOPLE, NOT LESSONS

Not once in Scripture do we find Jesus sitting down to teach and saying, "Our lesson for today is Leviticus, Scroll 3." His teaching flowed out of the needs of the people he taught. It flowed out of problem situations they presented. It flowed out of the real crises of life.

This is not to say that an organized curriculum is unnecessary. Curriculum writers provide enormous assistance to teachers in our churches. Well-designed materials target a wide range of issues relevant to growing in the Lord. But the emphasis in our classes must be the people in the chairs, not the lines in the lesson. God's Word is Truth. But it becomes truth-that-matters-to-me as it intersects me where I live.

Jesus understood the balance of Scripture and needs. Many teachers in our churches, both volunteer and ministerial, do not understand this balance. The overriding goal in many classes is to "Cover the Lesson." In the name of "covering the lesson," questions are ignored, comments curtailed, personal experiences restricted. The teacher who says, "Mildred, I wish we could spend some time dealing with your question, but I have four more verses to cover," may finish the lesson, but he hasn't taught Mildred. Plan for interruptions and questions. Encourage discussion and openness. Teach people, not lessons.

JESUS EMPHASIZED CHARACTER MORE THAN CONTENT

The Pharisees knew their content. They memorized the five books of Moses. They mastered the myriad details of proper prayer, almsgiving, and fasting. Their religion was a superficial, technical, and external show of rote actions and memorized rules, a tedious rule book that led them to become "sanctimonious faultfinders."[14]

Jesus described the ethics of the kingdom as a "stream of life, having charity for its fountainhead; a morality of the heart."[15] Character focuses on the heart: mind, emotions, and conduct. The mind focus is "How do you comprehend this?" The emotional focus is "How do you value this?" The conduct focus is "What will you do with this?" These questions form a trilogy of character-building teaching.[16]

For learners to grow in their character, they must have freedom to think and decide for themselves. Jesus understood this. His disciples freely chose to follow him.

---

14. Bruce, 27.
15. Bruce, 43.
16. See Chapter 9 for an in-depth discussion of this trilogy.

The rich young ruler freely chose not to. Judas chose to betray Jesus. Thomas chose to doubt. Peter chose to deny the Lord. The disciples chose to run away when Jesus was arrested.

The Pharisees hated this freedom, for their concern was to control. The following incidents reveal the inability of the Pharisees to accept the freedom Jesus taught.

> Then some Pharisees and teachers of the law came to Jesus from Jerusalem and asked, "Why do your disciples break the tradition of the elders? They don't wash their hands before they eat!" Jesus replied, "And why do you break the command of God for the sake of your tradition? For God said, 'Honor your father and mother' and 'Anyone who curses his father or mother must be put to death.' But you say that if a man says to his father or mother, 'Whatever help you might otherwise have received from me is a gift devoted to God,' he is not to 'honor his father' with it. Thus you nullify the word of God for the sake of your tradition. You hypocrites! Isaiah was right when he prophesied about you: 'These people honor me with their lips, but their hearts are far from me. They worship me in vain; their teachings are but rules taught by men.'"

> Jesus called the crowd to him and said, "Listen and understand. What goes into a man's mouth does not make him 'unclean,' but what comes out of his mouth, that is what makes him 'unclean'" (Matt. 15:1–11).

> At another time, Jesus went through the grainfields on the Sabbath. His disciples were hungry and began to pick some heads of grain and eat them. When the Pharisees saw this, they said to him, "Look! Your disciples are doing what is unlawful on the Sabbath."

> He answered, "Haven't you read what David did when he and his companions were hungry? He entered the house of God, and he and his companions ate the consecrated bread—which was not lawful for them to do, but only for the priests. Or haven't you read in the Law that on the Sabbath the priests in the temple desecrate the day and yet are innocent? I tell you that one greater than the temple is here. If you had known what these words mean, 'I desire mercy, not sacrifice,' you would not have condemned the innocent. For the Son of Man is Lord of the Sabbath" (Matt. 12:1–8).

The disciples did not follow the Pharisees' rules, and the Pharisees hated Jesus for it. But Jesus was more interested in the disciples' "Kingdom character," which Bruce describes like this: "humble, retiring, devoted in singleness of heart to God . . . contentment, cheerfulness, and freedom from secular cares for its fruits; and finally, as reserved in its bearing towards the profane, yet averse to severity in judging, yea, to judging at all, leaving men to be judged by God."[17]

For all their religious content, the Pharisees were whitewashed tombs "which look beautiful on the outside but on the inside are full of dead men's bones and everything unclean" (Matt. 23:27).

---

17.   Bruce, 43.

JESUS FOCUSED ON EVER SMALLER GROUPS

"Large crowds from Galilee, the Decapolis, Jerusalem, Judea and the region across the Jordan followed [Jesus]" (Matt. 4:25). Throughout his ministry, Jesus taught the crowds (Matt. 5:1; 8:1; 9:36; 11:7; 12:46; 13:2; 13:34; 14:13; 15:30; 19:2; 20:29; 21:8; 23:1).

From the crowds Jesus chose two specific groups of workers. He first chose the Twelve (Matt 10:1ff) to be trained as apostles to carry on the work after he left. Later "the Lord appointed seventy-two others and sent them two by two ahead of him to every town and place where he was about to go" (Luke 10:1). The Twelve were chosen to be with him; the Seventy-two to go before him. Both groups were given power to drive out demons, but only the Twelve were given power to heal diseases (cf. Matt. 10:1 and Luke 10:1, 17).

From the Twelve, Jesus chose three for special attention: Peter, James, and John. These three men experienced things with Jesus that the other nine did not.

- They witnessed the transfiguration of Jesus (Matt. 17) while the nine remained at the bottom of the mountain.

- They accompanied Jesus into the home of Jairus when Jesus raised his daughter from the dead (Mark 5:37) while the nine remained outside (Luke 8:51).

- When Jesus and the disciples went to Gethsemane, the nine stayed back while the three moved forward with Jesus into the Garden (Mark 14:32–33).

According to Paul, Peter, James, and John became pillars in the early church as a result of their advanced training and personal attention (Gal. 2:9).

Of the three, Jesus paid the greatest attention to Simon. He gave Simon the new name of Peter [*Petros*, rock] (John 1:42). He healed Peter's mother-in-law (Matt. 8:14–15). He allowed Peter to try something miraculous and fail (Matt. 14:28–33). Lastly, Jesus even recommissioned Peter after he denied him (John 21:15ff). Peter served his Lord faithfully until his death.

Howard Hendricks recently said he was finished with building great churches. He wanted to give the rest of his life to building great people. "Even if you build a church of 3,200 people, if none of them develops, 3,200 times 0 still equals 0. But 1 times 1 equals 1, and that is 100% better. The question you must ask is "Whose life are you impacting?"[18] This approach to ministry is certainly in line with that of Jesus, who poured himself into ever-smaller groups.

---

18.   Student report on conference notes, Howard Hendricks, February 10, 1992. Dr. Hendricks is Professor of Christian Education at Dallas Theological Seminary in Dallas, Texas.

JESUS RECOGNIZED THE WORTH OF HIS LEARNERS

Local church ministry is people-intensive. We can plan programs, but without people to lead and staff the programs and reach others to participate in them, our planning is in vain. In the hustle bustle of church ministry, it is easy to focus more on "getting the job done" than on those who are doing the job. In this kind of corporate atmosphere, learners are no more than the means by which we do ministry. It is a utilitarian view of people: "You are valuable so long as you can produce. Fail to meet organizational standards and we'll replace you with someone more dedicated to the company." The bottom line to all this is that, in many churches, the people of God are being abused in the name of reaching strangers.

The disciples were not merely the means of Jesus' ministry. They were the end of it. Jesus did not use (i.e., abuse) his disciples to reach the crowds. In fact, Jesus pulled away from the crowds in order to teach the disciples. They were not tools in the hands of a clever public relations man, but rather beloved children. Jesus poured his own heart into them, and after he left they carried on his work.

Many in our churches are hungry for ministers who care about them for who they are, and not merely for what they can do for the minister's own career. Before being challenged to reach "ten more next Sunday," they would like to know that we've noticed them, that we care for them, that we love them. Discipleship and evangelism go hand in hand (Matt. 28:19–20). Our flock is worthy of compassion and we are called to lead with compassion (1 Pet. 5:2).

JESUS EMPHASIZED QUALITY OF EFFORT OVER QUANTITY OF LEARNERS

The "quality vs. quantity" debate has long raged in Baptist circles. Those who emphasize "quality Bible study" in Sunday school may create classes that are self-sufficient, satisfied, and indifferent toward outsiders. Those who emphasize "quantity" through outreach efforts may create classes that are shallow and spiritually stagnant, and whose members are indifferent to each other. The Great Commission calls for both reaching (evangelism) and teaching (discipleship). Jesus' preference between the two is clear and Bruce describes it well: "The careful, painstaking education of the disciples secured that the Teacher's influence on the world should be permanent; that His kingdom should be founded on the rock of deep and indestructible convictions in the minds of a few, not on the shifting sands of superficial evanescent impressions on the minds of the many."[19]

A common question among ministers is "Howmanyjahave?" When we start a new Sunday school class, "Howmanyjahave?" When an early worship service is begun, "Howmanyjahave?" A new course in discipleship training begins, "Howmanyjahave?" Someone hears that a recent revival produced many baptisms, "Howmanyjahave?" It is pervasive, almost second nature, to ask that question. Ev-

19.   Bruce, 13.

ery measure of spiritual vitality seems to be tied to how many people attended, not what happened in those people because they attended. Jesus did not brag or exaggerate about the crowds of people who gathered around him to be healed or fed or taught. Attendance levels was not his concern; people were. Okay, I know that numbers are people. But when I am overly concerned about "ten more next Sunday," I don't really care about who those ten are—so long as I have ten. This is different from looking for Sally, Tom, Jane, and Stan. Put it in a business sense. My goal is to sell ten thousand hamburgers this month. Do I care whether a particular customer gets a bad hamburger? If I reason that I can still sell ten thousand with or without him, then my focus is quantity. If I reason that I want to make every customer satisfied with my food and service, then my focus is quality. Ask McDonald's—or for that matter, Ford and Honda—and they'll tell you the one who focuses on quality not only increases sales now, but increases sales for a long time.

Later, Jesus did not change his message when the crowds began to leave him. As he focused on life surrender and "yokes" and "crosses," people began to drift away. The rich young ruler walked away from Jesus, unwilling to pay the cost of discipleship. But Jesus did not change his style or his message. He did not evaluate the quality of what he was doing by the quantity of people following him. He knew he was in the Father's will, and he was faithful.

One other story illustrates this quantity/quality issue. There were money boxes in the Temple where the faithful deposited their tithes and offerings. The coins were deposited in metal cones, made in the shape of a trumpet. When a person dropped several coins into the opening, they clinked and clanked as they fell through the cone. This was called "sounding the trumpets." The Pharisees loved to deposit a bag of coins into the box, so that people within hearing distance would know they had made a large offering. Then one day . . . "Jesus sat down opposite the place where the offerings were put and watched the crowd putting their money into the temple treasury. Many rich people threw in large amounts. But a poor widow came and put in two very small copper coins, worth only a fraction of a penny. Calling his disciples to him, Jesus said, 'I tell you the truth, this poor widow has put more into the treasury than all the others. They all gave out of their wealth; but she, out of her poverty, put in everything—all she had to live on'" (Mark 12:41–44).

It was the quality of the gift, not its quantity, that caught Jesus' eye.

JESUS EMPHASIZED ACTION MORE THAN KNOWLEDGE

Jesus defined the terms "wise" and "foolish" not on the basis of what one knows, but on the basis of what one does with his words (Matt. 7:24, 26). When your students leave your class, have you helped them practice what they've learned from God's Word? They have heard the words, but do they practice them? If not, then Jesus says we have sent them out as fools. When your congregation leaves the sanctuary after worship, they have heard the words, but do they practice them? If so, then Jesus says we have sent them out as wise.

Encouraging students to practice what they learn in the study of God's Word is worthy of serious attention. This can be achieved through assignments done during the week; case studies in class; personal experiences related to the subject; and mission projects. Putting the Word into practice is essential in developing biblical wisdom in our learners.

JESUS FOCUSED ON STRUCTURE MORE THAN DETAIL

As a Master of the Old Testament, Jesus taught its key themes. Jesus majored on truth, the Pharisees on trivia. Jesus majored on love, the Pharisees on legalism. Jesus majored on justice, the Pharisees on judgment.

When you teach, say, the story of the Good Samaritan, are you more interested in covering every verse in the story or helping your learners become good samaritans? Do you curtail questions from learners in order to complete your lecture? When there are five major truths in a given lesson, are you more inclined to cover all five equally or would you rather choose the one that relates best to your class needs and focus on it?

The central truth of Scripture is summed up in Jesus' own statement, "I have come that [you] may have life, and have it to the full" (John 10:10). The pinnacle of our teaching ministry is lifting high the Lord Jesus and letting him draw all our learners to himself. There is no greater reward in teaching than to see a life transformed by the love and power of the Lord. May God grant you many such rewards as you offer your teaching ministry to him.

It is easy to get lost in the details of a particular study and miss the central truth God is conveying. My son is an active Bible driller at our church. He has just passed the associational drill competition with flying colors and is headed to the state competition. He knows his memory work! We were practicing his verses the other day. After he perfectly quoted an Old Testament verse, I asked him what it meant. "We don't have to know what the verses mean, Dad. We're just supposed to memorize them!" Great on details; weak on structure. So I explained the meaning of the verse. Take care not to lose your learners in a mass of detail, even if the detail is God's Word.

JESUS STRESSED LONG-TERM RATHER THAN IMMEDIATE RESULTS

We have already noted that Jesus consciously chose to pour his life into a select band of believers, who could then carry on his mission after he left. He did this even though he could have drawn a crowd anywhere he went with his dramatic teaching and miraculous works. Jesus made this choice because the in-depth training of the Twelve formed the foundation for the early church, which then carried his gospel around the world.

In one sense, Jesus' training of the Twelve was preparation for ministry. His words and explanations and parables formed the raw material out of which the disciples learned to be apostles. But even at the end of Jesus' ministry, as he prepared to return to the Father, the disciples were ill-suited to take on the power of the Sanhedrin and the power of Rome. They had been trained but they lacked the power to carry out their mission. However, Jesus promised them that they would "receive power when the Holy Spirit comes on you; and you will be my witnesses in Jerusalem, and in all Judea and Samaria, and to the ends of the earth" (Acts 1:8).

And so, on the Day of Pentecost, the Holy Spirit filled the believers and empowered them to do all that Jesus had commanded them. They had been prepared. Now they were transformed. The day of Pentecost forever divided history into two eras: the first, in which the Holy Spirit was imparted to God's chosen for specific purposes and short periods; and second, in which the Holy Spirit takes up permanent residence (Eph. 1:13) in the life of the believer in Jesus (1 Cor. 12:3).

Jesus knew that he had to return to the Father so that he could return, by the Spirit, to dwell in the hearts of all believers everywhere: "But I tell you the truth: It is for your good that I am going away. Unless I go away, the Counselor will not come to you; but if I go, I will send him to you" (John 16:7). But the work of the Counselor, the Holy Spirit, is to glorify Jesus, not himself (John 16:14). He does not speak on his own, but speaks only what he hears—presumably from Jesus (John 16:13). And in his earlier teaching on the Holy Spirit, Jesus intimated that he himself would be coming to them (John 14:16, 18). Both Peter and Paul used the terms "Holy Spirit" and "spirit of Christ" interchangeably—so when Christians say that Jesus is in our hearts, we reflect this dual meaning.

The point of this is that the teaching of Jesus provided the raw material for the transformation that took place at Pentecost by the Holy Spirit. The Spirit called to remembrance all that Jesus had taught the disciples, and used that teaching to grow them into the leaders of the early church.

Paul writes to the Corinthians, "I planted the seed, Apollos watered it, but God made it grow. So neither he who plants nor he who waters is anything, but only God, who makes things grow (1 Cor. 3:6–7). We may teach or preach our hearts out, week after week, and see little spiritual fruit resulting from our efforts. Then one Sunday, for no apparent reason, the Lord moves in the hearts of several of the members and a spiritual breakthrough occurs. There is an insidious temptation to do whatever works in order to make the church grow. This is fleshly, worldly thinking. Ends seem to justify the means. We do not make the church—God does.

Does this mean we simply wait for God to do whatever he is going to do? No. Paul continues, "The man who plants and the man who waters have one purpose, and each will be rewarded according to his own labor" (1 Cor. 3:8). There is a work to be done. And what is that work? Praying and teaching the Word: that is our labor. And God grows his church by his Spirit—in his time and in his way.

Lord, give us the heart and mind to labor in accomplishing our essential tasks of praying and teaching, so that we might provide "spiritual nourishment so that the saints might take up the work of ministry."

FOR FURTHER STUDY

1. How do you react when you work hard to do a good job, but no one congratulates you on your efforts? When you serve faithfully in a difficult position and few seem to notice? When you've done your best to be fair, honest, and open in a church issue and several people accuse you of petty self-interest?

2. How do you react when someone you've helped says, "Thank you"? When someone in your church praises you to your face? When someone praises you in a public gathering?

3. What gives you real satisfaction: Having a big crowd in your class or seeing one come to the Savior?

SUGGESTED READING

Baxter, Margaret. *Jesus Christ: His Life and His Church*. Philadelphia: Westminster Press. 1987.

Bruce, Alexander Balmain. *The Training of the Twelve*, 4th ed. New York: A. C. Armstrong & Sons, 1894; reprint, New Canaan, Conn.: Keats Publishing, 1970.

Coleman, Lucien. *Why the Church Must Teach*. Nashville: Broadman, 1984.

Edersheim, Alfred. *The Life and Times of Jesus the Messiah*, vol. 1. London: Longmans, Green and Co., 1890; reprint, Grand Rapids: Eerdmans, 1969.

Horne, Herman Harrell. *Jesus the Master Teacher*. New York: Association Press, 1942.

Hull, Bill. *Jesus Christ Disciple Maker*. Colorado Springs: Navpress, 1984.

Manson, T. W. *The Teaching of Jesus*. Cambridge: Cambridge University Press. 1963.

Price, J. M. *Jesus the Teacher*. Nashville: Convention Press, 1946; revised, 1981.

CHAPTER 3

THE ROLE OF THE HOLY SPIRIT IN TEACHING

—DARYL ELDRIDGE

> Mr. Bailey was late again for our boys' mission education class. He gave his typical apology for not having prepared a lesson. "But," he said, "on the way to church the Holy Spirit spoke to me and told me what to say." I was curious. I knew God spoke to Saul on the road to Damascus. I'd been told that God sometimes spoke in a loud voice. Did God speak to Mr. Bailey in that same way? Did his sons in the back seat hear God, too?
>
> There wasn't anything spectacular about the lesson. In fact, it was similar to last week's lesson. It was one of his favorites, the eleventh commandment. Maybe you've heard it: "Women shall not wear pants in church." As a nine-year-old boy, I didn't mean to be disrespectful to God, but it seemed to me he could have given Mr. Bailey a better lesson.

The Holy Spirit is often credited with the thoughts or "lessons" we teach. Comments like, "God spoke to me," or "The Holy Spirit revealed this truth to me," may be expressions of an encounter with the living God or they may be attempts to pass the responsibility for lack of preparation to the divine. Lawrence Richards says there are two ways to distort the role of the Holy Spirit. "The first is to discount it, and to see Christian growth as simply a natural process. The second is to make it a magical thing, demanding that God work against all natural processes and intervene in spectacular ways."[1] Just what part does the Holy Spirit play in our preparation? What role does he play in the teaching/learning process? Can we understand the teaching role of the Holy Spirit or is it an unexplainable mystical experience?

---

1. Lawrence O. Richards, *A Theology of Christian Education* (Grand Rapids: Zondervan, 1975), 323.

There is no denying that the Holy Spirit is the most important person in the teaching/learning process. Teachers need divine guidance. Learners need help in understanding and applying biblical truth. Teaching is a spiritual task, involving spiritual truths to meet spiritual needs. This requires spiritual power.[2] This power comes from the Holy Spirit. There are many names for the person of the Holy Spirit, but there are several that especially emphasize his role as teacher. These include the Spirit of Truth, Counselor, Spirit of Wisdom and Revelation, the Spirit of Knowledge and the Fear of the Lord, and the Spirit of Counsel and Might. Let's look at each of these.

THE HOLY SPIRIT AS TEACHER

THE SPIRIT OF TRUTH

"But when he, the Spirit of truth, comes, he will guide you into all truth" (John 16:13). The very character of God is truth. There is no error in him. There is no better illustration of the phrase, "Like father, like son," than the resemblance of the Heavenly Father and his Son. Our Lord not only knew the truth, he was truth. Jesus stated, "I am the way, the truth, and the life" (John 14:6). Our Savior's character is contrasted to that of Satan. Referring to the devil Christ stated, "When he lies, he speaks his native language, for he is a liar and the father of lies" (John 8:44). Since God is truth, he is trustworthy and reliable. We can always count on him to tell the truth.

As the agent of God, the Holy Spirit does not misrepresent the truth. The Spirit of truth keeps believers from doctrinal error. Jesus said, "You will know the truth and the truth will set you free" (John 8:32). Truth liberates. Lies incarcerate. Those under the influence or teaching of the world cannot receive the teaching of the Spirit, for he does not reside in them (John 14:17). God does not want us to wander from the truth. A believer can have full confidence that the Spirit of truth is at work to keep us from wrong thinking and wrong living.

Christ prayed that his disciples would be rendered pure, cleansed from sin (John 17:17). We are consecrated, set apart for a holy purpose (See 1 Thess. 5:23; 1 Cor. 6:11). Sanctification is the process of becoming more like Christ and less like the world. We become like Christ through his truth. Truth is a representation of how things really are, and it is the Holy Spirit that helps us to see things as they really are. He helps us see God as pure and see our sin as it really is. Things are not the way the world sees them. When you are with a person you are influenced by him. When you are worldly, you see things as the world sees them. When you are taught by the Spirit, you see things from his perspective. His interests become our interests. It is only as the Holy Spirit teaches us that we come to know him and know the truth (John 14:17).

---

2. Roy Zuck, "The Role of the Holy Spirit in Christian Education," chap. in *The Christian Educator's Handbook on Teaching* (Wheaton, Ill.: Victor Books, 1988), 32.

COUNSELOR

"But the Counselor, the Holy Spirit, whom the Father will send in my name, will teach you all things and will remind you of everything I have said to you" (John 14:26). The Greek word *parakletos* is translated "comforter," "counselor," or "advocate." It literally means "one called to another's side." The idea is that the Holy Spirit is right at one's side to take another person's part. The translation of *parakletos* to "advocate" or "counselor" does not give the full force of the Greek rendering. In modern usage, these terms have a legal connotation—one going to the judge on our behalf. While the Holy Spirit plays this role, the term "parakletos" is more personal. He is close by, right at our side, ready to stand by us and take our part when help is needed.[3] The Holy Spirit did not comfort the grieving disciples by long distance. He was right by their side, erasing their loneliness, and he is right by our side, ready to help us when we need him.

Moses wanted to be excused from God's call to deliver his people from Egypt because he lacked eloquence of speech. How many prospective teachers have felt this same inadequacy? However, God promised Moses that he would teach him what to say and how to say it (Exod. 3:10–13).

The Spirit of God instructs his disciples for the tasks they are called to perform. He teaches us those things we were once not prepared to receive nor could understand. He brings into remembrance the life and teaching of Christ. The Holy Spirit made use of the disciples' memories to comfort and encourage them. The role of the Spirit is to teach disciples the meaning of those things that the Lord has spoken (John 15:26).

Today's teachers have this same helper at their disposal. We have one who stands right beside us, teaching us and encouraging us. In reality, without this helper we could teach nothing (John 15:5).

SPIRIT OF WISDOM AND REVELATION

"I keep asking that the God of our Lord Jesus Christ, the glorious Father, may give you the Spirit of wisdom and revelation, so that you may know him better" (Eph. 1:17). The Holy Spirit helps us understand the Lord, his character and nature. The Holy Spirit is the author of wisdom and the revealer of all truth. The Holy Spirit reveals Christ to us. Revelation in this passage is not a reference to future things. God wants to reveal, or disclose himself to us. The things of God are a mystery that cannot be understood without the work of the Holy Spirit. Our understanding of God is dependent upon him revealing himself to us (1 Cor. 1:18–25). He wants us to know him intimately and completely.

---

3. R. A. Torrey, *The Person and Work of the Holy Spirit*, revised ed. (Grand Rapids: Zondervan, 1974), 58.

SPIRIT OF KNOWLEDGE AND THE FEAR OF THE LORD

"The Spirit of the Lord will rest on him—the Spirit of wisdom and of under-standing, the Spirit of counsel and of power, the Spirit of knowledge and of the fear of the Lord" (Is. 11:2–3). God wants our hearts and our heads to be right. Christians need to be right thinkers about God. Sin has marred our understanding of God and his purposes. The Holy Spirit helps us understand and apply the truths of God to our own circumstances. The more we know about God, the more we understand how much more there is to know. There is an unfathomed depth of knowledge of God. "The fear of the Lord is the beginning of knowledge" (Prov. 1:7). To know God is to respect (fear) him. As our relationship with him grows we understand the greatness of our God.

SPIRIT OF COUNSEL AND MIGHT

The Scriptures are full of examples where the Spirit provided might and counsel to God's children (Is. 2:2) . The Holy Spirit gives us the power to accomplish what he has called us to do. We are competent because of his power (2 Cor. 3:4–6). Jesus told his disciples they would receive power when the Holy Spirit came upon them (Acts 1:8). The power referred to here is help or aid in witnessing about the resur-rected Christ.

The Spirit also provides guidance to believers. "You guide me with your counsel" (Ps. 73:24). Because the Spirit is our "standbyer," he is right there to direct our lives and our ministry. The Spirit guided Philip to witness to the Ethiopian eunuch (Acts 8:29). The Spirit kept Paul and his friends from going into Asia and directed them into Europe (Acts 16:6–7).

The names for the Holy Spirit discussed above do not describe discreet func-tions. However, by examining each of these terms we obtain a fuller picture of the Holy Spirit's role in the teaching ministry. The Holy Spirit is reliable in teaching believers truth, for he is the Spirit of truth. He is our helper in understanding the revelation of God. It is the Holy Spirit that makes us wise to the ways of God and teaches us the knowledge of God. The Holy Spirit also guides believers and disclos-es God's will. It is through the power of the Holy Spirit that teachers are effective. Indeed, without the Holy Spirit, it would be impossible for us to know God.

THE HOLY SPIRIT IN THE TEACHING PROCESS

HIS WORK THROUGH GOD'S WORD

While the natural man may intellectually understand the facts and information contained in Scripture, it is only through the Holy Spirit that man can receive spir-itual truth (1 Cor. 2:12, 14). This enlightenment by the Holy Spirit is referred to as the ministry of illumination. "Apart from the Holy Spirit, the Bible will utterly fail to penetrate and transform the human heart. With the Spirit of God comes illumination—true understanding of what has been written. Every believer has the one who inspired the writers of Scripture residing in him. Without his illuminating ministry to us, the truth of Scripture could not penetrate our hearts and minds."[4]

Christians are fortunate to have the author of the greatest book in the world to take up residence in us. The Bible's author is at our immediate disposal to help us interpret and understand Scripture. This, however, does not negate the need for preparation or the help of others. Some sincere but misguided persons misinterpret 1 John 2:27: "As for you, the anointing you received from him remains in you, and you do not need anyone to teach you. But as his anointing teaches you about all things and as that anointing is real, not counterfeit—just as it has taught you, remain in him."

An example of this misunderstanding is one elderly Sunday school teacher who told his young minister that he didn't need to come to weekly teachers' meetings. In his own words, "God is my only teacher." This, of course, is contrary to other passages of Scripture. The Bible stresses the importance of teachers in the church. Jesus commanded us to go and teach all nations (Matt. 28:19–20). The early ministry of the apostles was a ministry of teaching. In Acts 5:42 it is recorded that the apostles "never stopped teaching." Paul stayed a year-and-a-half in Corinth "teaching them the word of God" (Acts 18:11). In Rome, Paul "taught about the Lord Jesus Christ" (28:31). Paul admonishes Timothy, "And the things you have heard me say in the presence of many witnesses entrust to reliable men who will also be qualified to teach others" (2 Tim. 2:2). The gift and office of teaching is also emphasized in Ephesians 4:11–12 and Romans 12:6–7. Teachers are colaborers with God. God, in his infinite wisdom, has chosen to work through imperfect vessels to teach others of his grace. Regardless of one's knowledge or spirituality, all believers can learn more about God from other believers. All believers are our teachers.

The illumination of the Holy Spirit does not exempt the believer from studying God's Word. A teacher should not share the attitude of those who simply open their Bibles and "let the Holy Spirit tell them what it means." Paul encouraged Timothy to diligently study the Scripture (2 Tim. 2:15). God does his part, but he also expects us to do ours. Pinnock said that it is presumptuous to study Scripture without total dependence on the Holy Spirit. But to expect the Holy Spirit to instruct us apart from God's Word is "sub-Christian fanaticism."[5]

Christian education, says Zuck, "is a cooperative process, a venture involving both the human and the divine."[6] May we be ever faithful in our study and dependent upon him for our understanding. As Charles H. Scott wrote:

---

4. John F. MacArthur, Jr., *Charismatic Chaos* (Grand Rapids: Zondervan, 1992), 95.
5. Clark H. Pinnock, *Biblical Revelation* (Chicago: Moody, 1971), 216.
6. Zuck, 37.

Open my eyes, that I may see
Glimpses of truth Thou hast for me;
Place in my hands the wonderful key
That shall unclasp and set me free.
Silently now I wait for Thee,
Ready, My God, Thy will to see,
Open my eyes, illumine me, Spirit divine.[7]

HIS WORK IN THE TEACHER

The Holy Spirit works in the learning process by helping teachers understand the content, the learner, and the appropriate methods. Most importantly, the Spirit helps the teacher to walk a Christlike life.

Content. The Holy Spirit authenticates that what we read in Scripture is the Word of God. In his *Institutes of the Christian Religion,* John Calvin writes:

> The same Spirit, therefore, who has spoken through the mouths of the prophets must penetrate our hearts to persuade us that they faithfully proclaimed what had been divinely commanded. . . . Until he illumines their minds, they ever waver among many doubts! . . . Let this point therefore stand: that those whom the Holy Spirit has inwardly taught truly rest upon Scripture, and that Scripture indeed is self-authenticated; hence, it is not right to subject it to proof and reasoning. And the certainty it deserves with us, it attains by the testimony of the Spirit. For even if it wins reverence for itself by its own majesty, it seriously affects us only when it is sealed upon our hearts through the Spirit.[8]

The Holy Spirit also helps the teacher understand the meaning and application of Scripture. Billy Graham asserts, "That the writers of the Old and New Testament were inspired by the Holy Spirit is one part of the story. In addition, He illumines the minds and opens the hearts of its readers. We find spiritual response to the Word of God."[9]

The prophet Jeremiah describes the illumination in this way, "Thy words were found and I ate them, and Thy words became for me a joy and the delight of my heart; For I have been called by Thy name, O Lord God of hosts" (Jer. 15:16, NASB).

Learners. The Spirit also helps the teacher understand the needs and interests of his students. This understanding was a marvelous characteristic of Jesus' teaching. He knew the deepest needs of those whom he sought to save. Whether it was the woman at the well (John 4:7), the woman caught in adultery (John 8:3), or Zaccheus (Luke 19:2), Jesus knew each of their inner motivations, fears, and desires. Teachers should understand and love people. Yet this is impossible without the Holy Spirit. Since the fall in the Garden of Eden, people have been unable to love others uncon-

---

7.   Charles H. Scott, "Open My Eyes, That I May See," hymn in *New Baptist Hymnal* (Nashville: Broadman, 1991), hymn 502.

8.   John Calvin, *Institutes of the Christian Religion,* ed. John McNeil, trans. Ford Lewis Battles (Philadelphia: Westminster Press, 1960), Book one, chapter 7, sections 4 & 5, 79–80.

9.   Billy Graham, *The Holy Spirit: Activating God's Power in Your Life* (New York: Warner Books, 1978), 65.

ditionally. However, Jesus made it possible for us to love others with the same kind of love that God loved us. Jesus declared, "I have made you [the Father] known to them, and will continue to make you known in order that the love you have for me may be in them and that I myself may be in them" (John 17:26). Teachers who understand the emotional, psychological, physical, social, and spiritual needs of their pupils will be far more effective than those who don't.

Methods. The Holy Spirit also helps teachers to use effective and appropriate teaching methods. We speak of "bathing" our lessons in prayer. We should pray, asking the Spirit to help us use the right methods for the group we are teaching. Zuck states, "A teacher working in tune with the Holy Spirit will seek to use the best educational techniques and tools available."[10]

Christlike Life. Teachers should exemplify the truth they teach. They should be models of Christlikeness. This can only happen when teachers submit themselves to the Spirit of God. As teachers walk in the Spirit (Rom. 8:4; Gal. 5:16–17) and grow in their relationship with Christ, they provide examples of what Christ can do in the lives of his followers. Paul admonished his students to follow his example (1 Cor. 11:1–2; 2 Thess. 3:9) as he followed the example of Christ. Only the Spirit of God can enable us to be the examples we need to be.

Figure 3.1 represents the Holy Spirit's work through the teacher. In order for a teacher to be effective, he should know his content, his pupils, and the appropriate methods to employ. Furthermore, he should walk in the Spirit so that his life is a testimony of God's grace. The Holy Spirit enables the teacher to understand God's Word, to discern the needs of the pupils, and to select the right method for the age group he is teaching. The Divine Teacher's Aide also empowers the teacher to do his work (2 Cor. 3:5–6).

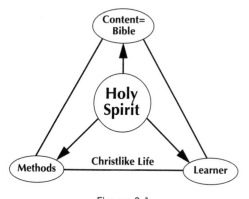

Figure 3.1

---

10.   Zuck, 40.

HIS WORK IN THE LEARNER

The Holy Spirit works in the life of the learner as he convicts of sin (John 16:7–8), regenerates the sinner (John 3:3, 5–6; Titus 3:5), indwells the believer (1 Cor. 6:19), seals (Eph. 1:13b), baptizes (1 Cor. 12:12–13), issues gifts (1 Pet. 4:10), fills (Eph. 5:8), and comforts (John 14:16).

The Holy Spirit produces spirituality (Rom. 8:1–13; 1 Cor. 3:1–4; Gal. 5:19–21), growth (2 Cor. 3:18; Eph. 1:17–19; 1 Pet. 2:1–2; 2 Pet. 3:18), maturity, and effective ministry (1 Cor. 3:18; 2 Tim 1:16; 1 Pet. 4:12).[11]

One purpose of the Holy Spirit is to warn believers against error (1 John 2:26–27). Christians should not simply trust the words of any human teacher. Each learner must rely upon the presence of the Holy Spirit to discern the difference between good and evil, between truth and error (1 Cor. 2:14; Heb. 5:14).

Works through Developmental Processes. One misconception of the role of the Holy Spirit in the teaching ministry is that he works in some magical way against all natural processes. While the Spirit may perform supernatural works, he normally works through the developmental processes. Jesus experienced these same maturation processes. Scripture records that "Jesus grew in wisdom and stature, and in favor with God and men" (Luke 2:52).

In the words of the psalmist, we are "fearfully and wonderfully made" (Ps. 139:14). We are complex beings. While there are many facets to our being, these facets do not operate independently of one another. Just as God is one, man is also one. Our spiritual growth is affected by our physical, mental, and emotional growth. We live in a fast-paced society that expects everything to happen immediately. There are some things that cannot be rushed, and spiritual growth is one of them. Even the greatest teacher knew his disciples were not ready to learn certain truths (John 16:12). We cannot expect a preschooler to have the faith of an adolescent. Nor can we expect a teenager to have an adult faith. God made us to grow in increments, through stages of life. Paul alludes to this natural process when he describes new Christians as babes that begin with the milk of the word and progress to eating the meat of the word (1 Cor. 3:2). Each stage of life provides new challenges that act as catalysts for growing in our faith.

A teacher should understand the natural developmental processes of students in order to meet their spiritual needs. For example, younger youth may look like adults, and at times talk and act like adults, but they do not have the experiential base of adults. They have difficulty in verbally expressing their feelings and emotions. That is why such methods as art, drama, or creative writing are used to help youth express their thoughts and feelings. Children before the third grade think literally, not abstractly. It is inappropriate to expect three-year-old preschoolers to sit in a

---

11.   C. Fred Dickinson, "The Holy Spirit in Teaching," in *Introduction to Biblical Christian Education* (Chicago: Moody Press, 1981), 121–22.

circle and listen to a teacher "talk" for twenty minutes about their sins being "covered by the blood."

The Samaritan woman at the well had a spiritual void that affected her relationships with others (John 4). The morals of the woman caught in adultery had resulted in social ostracism (John 8:3). Zaccheus's height and occupation had an impact on his social and spiritual life (Luke 19:2). The children who came to Jesus needed attention and a sense of value (Matt. 19:14). The five thousand needed physical replenishment before they could receive more teaching (Mark 8:19). The man at the pool of Siloam needed physical healing before he could receive social and spiritual healing (John 9:7). Teaching should be viewed as a holistic ministry. Effective teachers are aware of all the dynamics at work in the life of his or her pupils. Figure 3.2 illustrates the relationships of these various facets.

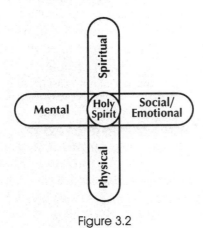

Figure 3.2

Our spiritual development is affected by the physical, social/emotional, and mental dimensions of our being. The Holy Spirit is at work through all of the processes of life to help us be what God wants us to be. As colaborers with the Holy Spirit, we need to understand the developmental processes of our learners in order to meet their faith needs.

Works through the Experiences of Life. The Spirit uses the experiences of life to communicate spiritual truths. Each experience of life provides an opportunity for faith to grow. The wilderness was a training ground for the Israelites, preparing them for the promised land. Each day provided the Israelites with new opportunities to learn obedience to God. Life is like the wilderness experience. God is continually teaching us what he would have us be and do.

HIS WORK THROUGH OTHERS

Learning doesn't take place in a vacuum. Everyone, in essence, is our teacher. We learn through the divine experiences of others. As Vogel states, "Human beings become faithful by living in a community of faith and by discovering what it means to claim its stories and values as their own."[12] The apostles shared their experiences and stories with the early Christians. Acts 2:42 reports, "They devoted themselves to the apostles' teaching and to the fellowship, to the breaking of bread and to prayer." These new Christians became partners with the apostles, fellow sharers of the gospel story (Phil. 1:5). Teachers in the early church encouraged believers to "not give up meeting together, as some are in the habit of doing, but let us encourage one another" (Heb. 10:25). Christian education is not a solo experience but the fellowship of others who have begun the journey.

As the proverb states, "Iron sharpens iron, so one man sharpens another" (Prov. 27:17). We are called to encourage each other's faith (Rom. 1:12). Cole states, "their story, yours, mine—it's what we all carry with us on this trip we take, and we owe it to each other to respect our stories and learn from them."[13]

The Holy Spirit has endowed the body of Christ with the variety of gifts necessary to accomplish his work. It is imperative that the church employ this diversity in the teaching ministry. While this may sound easy, just how is it done?

HELPING OTHERS DISCOVER
AND USE THEIR SPIRITUAL GIFTS

One of the most important responsibilities of a church leader is to discover, develop, and use the spiritual gifts present in the body of Christ. Yet there is much confusion and doctrinal error taught about this work of the Holy Spirit. This is nothing new. Paul wrote to the church at Corinth to correct several problems in the church, including the self-aggrandizement of some members over spiritual gifts.

Most New Testament teaching on spiritual gifts is found in three key chapters: Romans 12, 1 Corinthians 12, and Ephesians 4. Other important passages are 1 Corinthians 13–14, 1 Peter 4, 1 Corinthians 7 and Ephesians 3. Modern scholars disagree on the number of gifts mentioned in Scripture. Theodore Epp lists eleven, Ryrie fourteen, Walvoord fifteen, and Stedman sixteen basic gifts. Gangel identifies eighteen.[14] Since no two listings of spiritual gifts are the same we can conclude that there is not an exhaustive or complete list of the charismata. In every generation of believers, God will provide the necessary gifts for the church to accomplish its mission. We know every believer has at least one spiritual gift or possibly more (Rom.

---

12.   Linda J. Vogel, *Teaching and Learning in Communities of Faith* (San Francisco: Jossey-Bass Publishers, 1991), 85.

13.   R. Cole, *The Call of Stories: Teaching and Moral Imagination* (Boston: Houghton Mifflin, 1989), 30.

14.   Kenneth O. Gangel, *You and Your Spiritual Gifts* (Chicago: Moody, 1975), 11.

12:6; 1 Cor. 12:7, 11; Eph. 4:7; 1 Pet. 4:10). A spiritual gift is a special attribute given by the Holy Spirit to every Christian at the time of salvation. It is given according to God's grace for use within the body of Christ.[15] No believer needs to feel left out when it comes to having a spiritual gift. There is no place for inferiority in the body. There is no reason for dissatisfaction with service.

In 1 Corinthians 12:4, the Greek word for gifts is *charismata*. This has the same root as the Greek word for "grace" (*charis*: compare Eng. "charity"). Spiritual gifts are freely and graciously bestowed by God as an act of his grace. Just as the believer cannot earn salvation by works, the Christian cannot work up his spiritual gifts. All the charismata have their source in the grace of God.[16] Therefore, a Christian cannot boast about his spiritual gift.

Pride and feelings of spiritual superiority were the basis for the problems in the church at Corinth. Like small children arguing over who has the biggest and best toys, the believers at Corinth were apparently boasting, "My gifts are better than your gifts." Feelings of spiritual superiority dissipate when we realize that, "all the gifts are bestowed; none is earned or merited. To identify the receiving of any gift as the evidence or consequence of total commitment is to inject works into our gospel of grace. The gifts do not constitute a measure of our maturity as Christians. All are expressions of God's grace. Since they are bestowed, they may be gratefully received but never proudly displayed."[17]

The purpose of spiritual gifts is not for personal gain. They are given for one reason—to build up the body of Christ. "Now to each one the manifestation of the Spirit is given for the common good" (1 Cor. 12:7; 14:4–5, 17–26; Eph. 4:12). Since no one person possesses all of the spiritual gifts, each person in the body is important for its proper function. We need the gifts and abilities of each other in order for the church to minister effectively in the community. While the *charismata* are given to individuals, they are given in the context of the local church.

The gifts of the Spirit focus on Christ and glorify him, just as the Holy Spirit glorifies Christ by teaching about him. "He will bring glory to me by taking from what is mine and making it known to you" (John 16:14). The gifts are meant to bring honor and glory to our Lord (1 Cor. 10:31).

The possession of a spiritual gift does not excuse a believer from performing other Christian duties. Certain activities are expected of every believer. One member in my church told me she would pray for the church's visitation program but she wouldn't attend because she doesn't have the gift of evangelism. No Christian is excused from witnessing. Because a person does not have the gift of giving does not excuse him or her from tithing. Spiritual gifts should not be confused with the roles, functions, or activities of ministry. All Christians have some responsibility for teach-

---

15. C. Peter Wagner, *Your Spiritual Gifts Can Help Your Church Grow* (Glendale, Calif.: Regal Books, 1979), 42.
16. Jack W. MacGorman, *The Gifts of the Spirit* (Nashville: Broadman, 1974), 28.
17. Ibid., 30.

ing as they mature in the faith, but not every Christian has the gift of teaching.[18] The purpose of a spiritual gift is to enable others to perform that function in the church. Those with the gift of evangelism are to teach others how to witness. Those with the gift of teaching are to teach others how to teach. Those who are gifted with administration are to enable others to administer their ministry.

Since natural talents are also gifts from God, what is the difference between a spiritual gift and natural talent? Zuck feels that spiritual gifts are the "sanctifying, enhancing, or channeling of natural abilities into the spiritual realm."[19]

DISCOVERING SPIRITUAL GIFTS THROUGH SERVICE

How then do you discover your spiritual gifts? There are a number of spiritual gifts inventories on the market, and they may be helpful for some in understanding the gifts of the Spirit. However, sometimes they simply add to the confusion. Often they are subjective and nothing more than personality or interest surveys. There are several dangers in relying upon these instruments. First, a Christian may project into the test the kind of gift(s) he would like to possess, rather than an accurate self-assessment of his gifts and abilities. We are not always our best critic. A person might, for example, justify to himself that he has the gift of prophecy, when in fact, he doesn't. Second, a person may close his mind to opportunities of service because the spiritual gifts inventory suggested he doesn't have that gift. Third, the spiritual gifts inventory sometimes wrongly serves as justification for inappropriate behavior. One church member became outspokenly opinionated after taking a spiritual gifts inventory. This Christian felt compelled to tell people what they ought to do with their lives. The member justified this brash behavior by saying, "I have the gift of discernment."

Don't expect a spiritual gifts inventory to neatly and conveniently determine your gift. This doesn't mean we shouldn't use spiritual gifts inventories in our church. However, the only real way to discover one's spiritual gift is through service. All the spiritual gift inventories in the world are worthless unless believers become involved in the life and work of the church. At the time of their salvation, some believers may know their spiritual gift. There are others who may receive their gift through a blinding light or audible voice. For most believers, discovering one's spiritual gift is a gradual process that is learned through the course of ministry experiences. Prospective Sunday school teachers have told me, "I don't have the gift of teaching." When asked, "Have you ever taught Sunday school?" They reply, "No, but I could never be a teacher." I have to bite my tongue from replying, "Try it, you may like it!" God has something great for you if you will make yourself available to him.

---

18.   Wagner, 70.
19.   Zuck, 39.

In discussing the importance of effective teachers in the church, my students have said, "The problem with our teaching ministry is people teaching who don't have the gift of teaching." It doesn't bother me that we have people serving who may not be gifted at that responsibility. Experience is a great teacher. Through experience we can learn our spiritual gift and discover what we are not called to do. Besides, people accept teaching positions because church leaders made them aware of the need for teachers and invited them to become involved in the teaching ministry. If persons are in positions of leadership for which they are not spiritually gifted, church leaders should not criticize their willingness to serve. It is the responsibility of church leaders to help people discover their niche in the community of faith by involving them in the life and work of the church.

It is through service that the members of the body have an opportunity to affirm the gifts they see operating within us. The church has the responsibility for confirming the gifts within the body. It is not the sole responsibility of the individual believer to discover his spiritual gift. James Smart writes:

> The missions, and also the ministry of the Church, have suffered severely because of the failure of the Church to take seriously the fact that, while the gifts of the ministry are from God, the recognition of them and the call to those who possess them to use them in the service of God are acts that God expects of his Church. Perhaps if a larger number within the Church knew themselves called to the ministry of the Word that belongs to *all* believers, the Church's task of recognizing the special gifts of preaching and teaching would not be so difficult as it is and the call to these special ministries would not be allowed to remain so purely individual a matter.[20]

The gifts are given to edify the body. Therefore, the members of the body should have the final word in confirming your gift. Wagner states, "If you think you have a spiritual gift and are trying to exercise it, but no one else in your church thinks you have it—you probably don't."[21] You may know what your spiritual gift is before the church does, but if you exercise that gift, in time the church will confirm it. This is the essence of the practice of laying on of hands. "Do not neglect your gift, which was given you through a prophetic message when the body of elders laid their hands on you" (1 Tim. 4:14). The laying on of hands is the recognition by the church that God is working in that individual to perform a certain task.

In one of my churches, a man wanted desperately to serve God, so we gave him an adult Sunday school class to teach. I had never seen anything like this. He took a vibrant class of fifteen people, and in just a few short weeks only three people, including himself, were attending. We then gave him the job of department director. In just a matter of weeks, the opening assembly had dwindled from sixty down to a handful. People were coming late or talking in the hallways to miss the opening assembly he led. He then said he would like to help us in the outreach ministry. He

---

20. James D. Smart, *The Teaching Ministry of the Church* (Philadelphia: Westminster Press, 1974), 30.
21. Wagner, 131.

suggested several ways in which our process could be improved and then developed a system that enabled the church to be more accountable for our church prospects. We made him our director of outreach. He had found his niche in the body of Christ. His gift of organization and administration enabled our church to be more effective in reaching people for Christ.

While finalizing our yearly roster of church committee members, a young woman told me she no longer wanted to serve on the long-range planning committee. We had asked her to serve on this committee to represent the growing segment of our congregation of adults with young children. I asked her if she would like to serve on another committee. She replied, "I'm not sure, but I really enjoy helping people." We were able to place her on the benevolence committee, where she was able to lend her expertise and passion to meet the needs of our church family and community. She became our Mother Teresa. The motto, "If at first you don't succeed, try, try again" applies also to spiritual gifts. We discover our gifts through service.

Joy in Service. You know you are using your spiritual gift when there is an inner fulfillment and motivation to serve. Findley Edge says that a Christian who is using his spiritual gift has a "eureka feeling," an inner motivation that says, "This, really, is what I had rather do for God than anything else in the world."[22] There is a joy that comes when one is using the spiritual ability that God has given him. A person also knows he is using his spiritual gift when it produces blessings, when it is effective.

Spiritual gifts must be developed. They don't arrive in full bloom. With the spiritual gift comes responsibility to develop the gift. "Do not neglect your gift[s] . . . give yourself wholly to them, so that everyone may see your progress" (1 Tim. 4:14–15; 2 Tim. 1:6). We are encouraged to learn how to use our spiritual gift to edify the body.

Don't become so preoccupied with discovering your gift that you fail to see the opportunities around you to minister. In one of my classes I was discussing that discovering one's gift is a process that may take years. A student approached me after class. With tears running down her face, she said, "Last week my pastor told me I had no business being in seminary if I didn't know my spiritual gift." All are not struck with a blinding light telling us what our spiritual gift is. That should not paralyze us. Preoccupation with finding your spiritual gift is really another form of narcissism. The problem is not that people are ignorant of their spiritual gift, but that people are unwilling to serve when the opportunity arises. Through a sense of inner joy, the affirmation from God's people, and effectiveness in service, God makes his children aware of the their gifts.

---

22.   Findley Edge, *The Greening of the Church* (Waco: Word Books, 1971), 141.

THE GIFT OF TEACHING

The gift of teaching is mentioned in three out of the four major passages in Scripture dealing with spiritual gifts (Rom. 12:7; 1 Cor. 12:28–29; Eph. 4:11). The person with this gift has the ability to discover and communicate to others the truth he has been taught by the Holy Spirit. Kenneth Gangel states, "There seems to be a clear implication of study, mental and verbal skills, and reliance upon the Holy Spirit in the ministry of teaching."[23]

All believers have some responsibility for teaching as they grow in their faith. However, those with the gift of teaching have the unique ability of equipping others to teach. They are teacher trainers. No Christian can exempt himself from the teaching ministry of the church. Parents are called to teach. Deacons have the responsibility to teach. Older women should teach younger women. Mature Christians should teach new Christians. All Christians are to share their faith story with others.

CONCLUSION

We have much to learn about the role of the Holy Spirit in the teaching/learning process. Learning is a cooperative effort between the human and the divine. The Eternal Counselor works through the developmental growth process to help learners understand the Word of God. He helps teachers minister to the needs of learners. The Spirit of Truth warns believers of doctrinal error. The Spirit bestows gifts that enable the church to accomplish its mission. The Holy Spirit is indispensable in the teaching/learning process. For the church to reach the world for Christ and see his glorious power in operation, we must submit ourselves to the Divine teacher. As Andrew Murray writes, "Each time you come to the Word in study, in hearing a sermon, or reading a religious book, there ought to be as distinct as your intercourse with the external means, the definite act of self-abnegation, denying your own wisdom and yielding yourself in faith to the Divine teacher."[24]

The success of the teaching ministry of the church is not dependent upon efficient organizations, new programs, modern teaching methods, or the latest technology. The power of the teaching ministry is dependent upon our faithful obedience to the teaching of the Holy Spirit. In the words of Eliza Hewitt, our prayer should be:

> More About Jesus let me learn,
> More of His Holy will discern;
> Spirit of God my teacher be,
> Showing the things of Christ to me.[25]

23. Gangel, *You and Your Spiritual Gifts*, 71.
24. Andrew Murray, *The Spirit of Christ* (London: Nisbet & Co., 1888), 221.
25. Eliza E. Hewitt, "More About Jesus," hymn in *New Baptist Hymnal* (Nashville: Broadman, 1991), hymn 600.

FOR FURTHER STUDY

1. Write an essay on the role of the Holy Spirit in teaching.

2. Describe the Holy Spirit's ministry of illumination. Does the illumination of the Holy Spirit negate the need for studying? Why or why not?

3. Describe the relationship *between* the Holy Spirit, teaching methods, biblical content, pupils, and the teacher.

4. Why must a Christian teacher study human growth and development? Why isn't it enough to simply depend on the Holy Spirit and explain the Word of God clearly?

5. How does the Holy Spirit use the experiences of life to teach us?

6. How did you discover your spiritual gifts? How can the church help believers discover and utilize their spiritual gifts?

SUGGESTED READING

Dickinson, C. Fred. "The Holy Spirit in Teaching," in *Introduction to Biblical Christian Education*. Chicago: Moody Press, 1981.

Gangel, Kenneth O. *You and Your Spiritual Gifts*. Chicago: Moody, 1975.

Hemphill, Kenneth S. *Spiritual Gifts: Empowering the New Testament Church*. Nashville: Broadman Press, 1988.

———.*Minor, Minor on the Wall: Discovering Your True Self Through Your Spiritual Gifts*. Nashville: Broadman Press, 1992.

MacGorman, Jack W. *The Gifts of the Spirit*. Nashville: Broadman, 1974.

Smart, James D. *The Teaching Ministry of the Church*. Philadelphia: Westminster Press, 1974.

Swindoll, Charles R. *Flying Closer to the Flame*. Dallas: Word, 1993.

Torrey, R. A. *The Person and Work of the Holy Spirit*, rev.ed. Grand Rapids: Zondervan, 1974.

Vogel, Linda J. *Teaching and Learning in Communities of Faith*. San Francisco: Jossey-Bass Publishers, 1991.

Wagner, Peter C. *Your Spiritual Gifts Can Help Your Church Grow*. Glendale, Calif.: Regal Books, 1979.

Walvoord, John F. *The Holy Spirit*. Grand Rapids: Zondervan, 1965.

Zuck, Roy B. "The Role of the Holy Spirit in Christian Teaching," in *The Christian Educator's Handbook on Teaching*. Wheaton, Ill.: Victor Books, 1988.

———. *The Holy Spirit in Your Teaching*. rev. ed. Wheaton, Ill.: Victor Books, 1984.

CHAPTER 4

THE BIBLE AS CURRICULUM

—NORMA HEDIN

While attending a friend's baptism into a church of another denomination, my family entered the foyer with our Bibles firmly in hand. As we approached the sanctuary, one of the greeters commented: "You must be visitors; you brought your Bibles." We looked around to discover that indeed we were the only ones with Bibles. As we joined our friends, we were given worship folders with the Scripture printed inside, along with a list of doctrinal beliefs of the church. One of those beliefs is that the Word of God, its teachings and its study, is central to the church. It was interesting that in a church claiming to center itself around the Word we were so conspicuous in carrying our Bibles.

Obviously, not all denominations agree on the place or the use of the Bible in the "curriculum" of the church. But evangelicals rally around the central role of the Bible in the teaching ministry of the church. Historically and practically, the Scriptures have provided the content for their curriculum in the church.

What do we mean by "curriculum"? The word *curriculum* literally means a "race-course." Traditionally this "course" was viewed as the body of content to be covered in the educational process. More contemporary usage suggests the activity of the student as he "runs through" various experiences that comprise the content.[1]

As we apply this to study of the Bible, curriculum may be defined as *student activities related to scriptural content that are implemented by Christian leadership to bring students closer to maturity in Christ*. It is obvious from this definition that curriculum is more than the printed materials acquired from a publisher. Curriculum includes all

---

1. Lois E. LeBar, *Education That is Christian* (Wheaton, Ill.: Scripture Press, 1989), 254.

of the activities under the direction of the church. What is commonly referred to as "curriculum" is actually a curriculum plan—the plan for those learning activities to take place. A curriculum plan includes not only the printed resources, but also all of the activities related to the use of those resources.

Curriculum plans for church education have not always been available; nevertheless, the Bible, as the focus or content of curriculum in the church, has been the norm throughout our history.

THE PLACE OF THE BIBLE IN CURRICULUM

HEBREW EDUCATION —"INDISPENSABLE FOUNDATION"

The instruction of man began as early as his encounter with God in the Garden of Eden (Gen. 2:16ff). From that time onward God communicated to man, either directly through spoken words or through various other means, such as tablets of stone (Exod. 24:12), dreams (Gen. 37:5ff), writing on the walls of palaces (Dan. 5:5–6), or through human prophets. The instructions came to be identified as laws, commands, statutes, or ordinances. The words of God as recorded in written form became the Word of God and as compiled became our Bible.

Some of the earliest commands were related to the teaching of the Law or Torah, particularly in family life. The familiar passage in Deuteronomy 6 relays the importance of teaching the Law to children: "And these words, which I am commanding you today, shall be on your heart; and you shall teach them diligently to your sons and shall talk of them when you sit in your house and when you walk by the way and when you lie down and when you rise up. And you shall bind them as a sign on your hand and they shall be as frontals on your forehead. And you shall write them on the doorposts of your house and on your gates" (vv. 6–9 NASB).

Hebrew parents were to instruct their children in the content of the law and instruction was to take place in every activity of daily living. This content and its application became the indispensable foundation for future religious education. However, for the Hebrew there was no separation of religious education and secular education. Education was for life and this life was a religious life.

The teaching of the law was centered in the home and was performed by the parents. Additional teaching was eventually introduced through priests, sages, and prophets, and through such experiences as provided by the tabernacle in the wilderness, feasts, fasts, festivals, and the Temple. All of these experiences had their foundation in the law and became the content for Hebrew religious education.

Education outside the immediate family setting arose sometime during the Babylonian Exile. The term *synagogue*, originally referring to the assembly of persons for instruction and worship, was later applied to the actual building. The content of teaching in the synagogue followed the previous pattern of instruction for the Hebrews and focused on the law or Torah. Judaism as we know it rests in the

Talmud which was created roughly between 100 B.C.E. and 500 C.E. The major portion of the Talmud did not come into existence until after the destruction of the Temple in 70 C.E.[2] The Talmud is formed by the *Mishrah* or *Review of Oral Torah* and the other half is additional commentary called the *Gemara* which utilized the *Mishrah* as its source. The Talmud was used in addition to the Torah and the prophets for religious instruction. The children were taught the Pentateuch between the ages of six and ten. Pupils aged ten to fifteen were instructed in the Mishnah. After age fifteen instruction came from the Talmud.[3]

Elementary and secondary schools arose around 75 B.C.E. These schools used the Scripture and Talmud as the curriculum to teach the children to read and write. The main objective of the elementary school was to teach the Hebrew Scriptures. After a student was taught to read he then began to memorize large portions of Scripture.[4] These synagogue schools, elementary, and secondary schools were the educational institutions during the time of Jesus.

EARLY CHRISTIAN EDUCATION—"CONSUMMATION IN JESUS CHRIST"

As a pupil and as a teacher, Jesus learned and taught the Scriptures. Although there is no evidence that he received formal training, he set the example and taught those who would lead the Christian church. Jesus is the Master Teacher and as our model filled his teaching with Old Testament Scripture. He was particularly skillful at taking the Scriptures and interpreting them in light of his ministry. For example, as the risen Christ joined the disciples on the Emmaus road, "beginning with Moses and all the Prophets, he explained to them what was said in all the Scriptures concerning himself" (Luke 24:27).

Following Jesus' example, the early Christian churches, recognizing the consummation of the Word in Jesus Christ, used the Old Testament Scriptures as foundational for teaching, then added the Christian interpretation of the Jewish Scriptures, the teaching of the central facts of the gospel, the individual Christian's confession of personal faith, the oral transmission of the life and sayings of Christ, and ethical instruction to their "curriculum."[5]

THE MIDDLE AGES—THE CHURCH AS AUTHORITY

Three movements within the church made use of the Scripture during the Middle Ages. The *catechetical* schools used the Scripture for instruction of new converts and those destined for the clergy. *Monastic* education, although based in oriental as-

---

2.   Leo Trepp, *Judaism: Development and Life*, 3d ed. (Belmont, Calif.: Wadsworth Publishing Co., 1982), 218.

3.   William A. Poehler, *Religious Education Through the Ages* (Minneapolis, Minn.: Masters Church and School Supply, 1966), 100–103.

4.   C. B. Eavey, *History of Christian Education* (Chicago: Moody Press, 1964), 64–65.

5.   Charles A. Tidwell, *Educational Ministry of the Church* (Nashville: Broadman Press, 1982), 38.

ceticism and Greek dualism, contributed to the preservation of sacred literature through the copying of manuscripts and preservation of books. *Cathedral* schools employed study of the Scriptures to train religious leaders. The audience of these schools was almost exclusively religious leaders; as a result, the masses were almost totally ignorant of the Bible and its teachings. The church played an increasingly important role in education as it began to increase in control. However, the role of the Bible as subject matter in the schools decreased as the school curriculum introduced such subjects as grammar, rhetoric, geometry, music, and astronomy.[6]

By the end of the Middle Ages, the great universities began to emerge and Christendom was said to be sustained by three great powers or virtues: the priesthood, the secular authority, and the universities. God and the Bible no longer comprised the central focus of life.[7]

EARLY MODERN AGE—"IN THE HANDS OF LAYMEN"

It is overly simplistic to pinpoint a single cause of the Reformation. But one key circumstance is identified by Eavey:

> Luther, as well as Wycliffe, Huss, Zwingli, and Calvin, revolted against the human authority of the church and the pope and against the collective judgment of the church. They substituted for these the authority of the Bible and the right of individual conscience and judgment. . . . The new theory of individual judgment and responsibility made it important that every person be able to read the Word of God, be enlightened in respect to church services, and order his life in accordance with real understanding of what God required of him.[8]

The emphasis on every person's right to read the Word of God resulted in the Bible being placed in the hands of laymen. This necessitated the education of the masses in order to make their possession of Scripture valuable. The men named above, as well as others, carried out true reform by stressing education based on Scripture. While the Reformation stressed revelation, the Renaissance stressed human reason, and the combination of the two changed education in the church.

As the New England colonies were formed, new schools neglected to separate religious instruction from secular education. The *New England Primer*, regarded by many as the most important literary molder of the founders of the republic, came from the educators of New England. Eighty-five percent of the book was made up of selections from the Bible.[9] The establishment of Harvard College in 1636, and the Middle Atlantic colleges of Princeton, University of Pennsylvania, Rutgers, and others in the 1700s reveals the importance of prayer and Scripture reading. Students

---

6. Eavey, 101–5.
7. Lewis Joseph Sherrill, *The Rise of Christian Education* (New York: Macmillan Co., 1944), 260.
8. Eavey, 145.
9. Tidwell, 49.

at these colleges were required to read Scripture and give evidence that they had profited from its reading.[10]

THE MODERN ERA—"RISE OF THE SUNDAY SCHOOL"

The most significant event that ushered in the modern era of religious education is considered by most to be the birth of the Sunday school movement. Although Bible teaching on Sundays had been conducted on the American continent for some time prior to 1780, no significant movement was generated until Robert Raikes started his school in Gloucester for the purpose of instructing boys in reading, writing, arithmetic, and spelling.[11] The Sunday school movement in the United States began in 1785 with William Elliot, on his plantation. It was later located in the Methodist Oak Grove Church building in Accomac County, Virginia. The first denominational Sunday school is claimed to have been established at the Broadway Baptist Church of Baltimore, Maryland in 1804.[12]

Originally begun as an agency of social betterment to reform society, the Sunday school's use of the Bible as a text was as a means of influencing and "moralizing" the character of the poor, and thereby "improving the social fabric."[13] It later evolved into a much more religious-oriented program as churches incorporated this teaching time into their schedules. In describing the Sunday school, Frost makes the following statement, "For sake of emphasis it may be said the work of the Sunday school is threefold: First, teach the Scriptures; second, teach the Scriptures; third, teach the Scriptures."[14] The Sunday school movement, with its emphasis on Scripture, continued to grow until around 1916 when it experienced decline due to liberalism, lack of unity among evangelicals, and theological differences between liberal and evangelical groups.[15] Additionally, a turning away from the Bible as the primary text contributed to this decline. The Uniform Lesson Series implemented some major changes in the 1920s under the influence of liberal theologians and educators such as John Dewey. This move was from Bible-centered lessons to experience-centered lessons.[16]

The establishment of the National Sunday school Association in 1945 by leading evangelical Christian educators was the beginning of a positive turnaround in Sunday school literature. But complaints against the Sunday school have continued to include the lack of focus on the Bible.

---

10.   Eavey, 197.
11.   J. M. Frost, *The School of the Church* (New York: Fleming H. Revell, 1911), 8–9.
12.   Tidwell, 52–53.
13.   Jack L. Seymour, "A Reforming Movement: The Story of Protestant Sunday School" in D. Campbell Wyckoff, *Renewing the Church and the CCD* (Birmingham: Religious Education Press, 1986), 7–8.
14.   Frost, 47.
15.   Eavey, 266–67.
16.   Ibid., 285–88.

CONTEMPORARY PERSPECTIVES

The Sunday school serves as the Bible teaching arm of the Baptist church. Although the Bible is the curriculum for all of the church's activities, most view Bible study as being confined to the Sunday school hour. So what is the current place of the Bible in the curriculum?

In a study reported in *Christian Education in the Year 2000*, Marion Brown and Marjorie Prentice asked one hundred Southern Baptists the following question: "Why do you come to Sunday school?" Of those questioned, 98.8 percent answered that they come to learn more about the Bible. When asked why they attend a particular class, 93.5 percent said because the teacher knows the Bible.[17] The inference is that Bible study continues to be important to those who attend Sunday school and may be of even greater importance in the future.

Although historically it appears that we may have moved away from the proper use of the Bible in curriculum, most evangelicals strongly attest to the central place of the Bible in the church. It is the textbook of the Sunday school. Charles Tidwell states that the Bible is "the foundation, not only that it is the principal text, but also in that it is the standard by which all of a church's educational ministry should be appraised. Ignorance of the Bible is a bane to the church and to the world. Knowledge and practice of it are a blessing to all."[18]

Why is it so important for the Bible to be the textbook in Sunday school? Colson and Rigdon in *Understanding Your Church's Curriculum* address several questions regarding the Bible's relation to Christian education. In answer to the first question, "What is the Nature of the Bible?" they relate the following:

- The Bible is the record of God's self-revelation. It provides the history of the Christian faith from creation to Jesus Christ and presents the gradual unfolding of God's purpose for man.

- The Bible is the repository of God's redemptive message for the world. The good news of Jesus Christ, which could have been lost or distorted, has been preserved in the pages of the Bible.

- The Bible is inspired by God. God's Word presents truth which could never have been realized with our own finite minds.

- The Bible has been providentially preserved. God himself has presided over the process of preservation that makes available the accurate Word.

- The Bible is God's gift to his church. The church and God's Word are inseparable as the church is dependent on the Word.

---

17.   Marion E. Brown and Marjorie G. Prentice, *Christian Education in the Year 2000* (Valley Forge, Pa.: Judson Press, 1984), 48.

18.   Tidwell, 124.

- The Bible furnishes the only authoritative guidance for Christian life and work. This is the evangelical view that rejects the word of man or the creeds of the church as being authoritative.

- The Bible brings men to Christ.[19]

Additionally, they discuss the "place" of the Bible in the curriculum. As the *source* of Christian teaching, the Bible must be presented as the Word of God so that pupils will know it is intended to speak to them. As a result, the learner will come to hear the voice of God personally speaking to him and will respond. As the *norm* for Christian teaching the Bible becomes the standard by which all Christian teaching is judged. And as the *instrument* for Christian teaching, the Bible is viewed as the chief tool in the teaching process, used by the teacher, the learner, and the Holy Spirit.[20]

Although people and situations change, because the nature of the Bible remains constant, its place in Christian teaching must remain intact. But that does not mean that those constant truths cannot meet the needs of a changing society. In a discussion of the Bible's relevance, Colson and Rigdon state, "The Bible deals vitally and authentically with humanity's persistent life needs. . . . It is at the point where an eternal reality of the gospel intersects with a persistent life need of the learner that true Christian learning takes place. In such learning needs are met, and a person is changed. Such is the relevance of biblical truth."[21]

Educators debate the centrality of content in curriculum as opposed to that of personal experience. Although personal experience is of extreme importance in learning, that experience must be held up to the light of God's Word. Christian teaching has at its center the Living Word, Jesus Christ, as revealed in the written Word, the Bible. Memorized and recited Bible facts do not necessarily transform lives. But Bible facts translated into truths for living and then applied to personal experience create the environment for true learning.

This type of teaching and learning, however, cannot be left to chance. It will not automatically happen. Teachers must make provision for including experience in the curriculum that relates to the truths of the Bible. Experience occupies an essential though secondary place in the Christian curriculum.

Most evangelicals agree wholeheartedly about the place of the Bible in the curriculum of the church; however, it appears that we have given little thought to the way the Bible is actually used in the curriculum.

---

19. Howard P. Colson and Raymond M. Rigdon, *Understanding Your Church's Curriculum* (Nashville: Broadman, 1981), 104–5.
20. Ibid., 105–6.
21. Ibid., 107.

THE USE OF THE BIBLE

It is one thing to assert that the Bible is our textbook. It is quite another to transmit that assertion into practice. If you were to visit various classes on a typical Sunday morning you might be surprised to find that very little true Bible study is taking place. You may observe a "teacher" talking endlessly to students with glazed eyes, or groups of people animatedly discussing Friday night's football game, but not necessarily quality Bible study. That is why Sunday school was described in the 1970s by *Life* magazine as being the "most wasted hour of the week." These observations may be translated into the following concerns as voiced by Christian educators.

BIBLICAL IGNORANCE—"WE DON'T UNDERSTAND"

Even though we have attempted to improve Bible teaching, it appears that our efforts may have been quite futile. James Smart clearly articulates this concern: ". . . the church school, after a century and a half of almost exclusive concentration upon Bible study, cannot and does not claim to have produced a church that is capable of understanding and using the Bible. . . . Nothing is more difficult to find in a congregation than people who have an intelligent grasp of the Scriptures as a whole and a knowledge of how to get at their meaning, either for themselves or for anyone else."[22]

This criticism is echoed by parents and pastors who sense that the evangelical Sunday school does not even achieve the minimum it set out to do—to teach the Bible. Lack of basic biblical knowledge among children and teens as well as adults is evidenced in various research studies in which groups are asked simple Bible knowledge questions and are unable to respond correctly. Parents complain that their children are "playing" rather than learning. Pastors and staff members are concerned that even after years of church membership, the majority of church members remain spectators rather than participants. The "not doing" follows the "not knowing." It seems to be an affront to those who struggled during the Reformation to get the Bible into the hands of the laymen that the laymen are now so uninterested in its contents.

Several factors may contribute to the lack of interest and participation in Bible study. One of these is the way the Bible is studied in Sunday school. The fragmented approach of many periodicals appears to study a group of verses that does not take into account the context of the passage. This makes the Bible seem disjointed. As a result, students neglect to grasp the Bible as a whole, but rather examine only isolated snippets arranged around subjects.

As a result, publishers receive criticism regarding the issue of printing the text in periodicals. If the text is printed, then the passage is taken out of its context and the

---

22. James D. Smart, *The Teaching Ministry of the Church* (Philadelphia: Westminster Press, 1976), 132.

student doesn't have to bring his Bible; if it isn't printed, then those without Bibles cannot follow along in the reading. Consequently, based on one rationale or another, publishers make the decision whether or not to print the passage. Their decision may be influenced by such letters as this one quoted by James Smart:

> Dear Sir:
> I am writing to protest the omission of the printed Scripture passages from the last issue of the teachers' quarterlies. We down here want you to know that if you can't print the Scripture in the quarterlies, we can't use your quarterlies. Our teachers are busy men and women, and when they go to prepare a lesson for Sunday, they can't be wasting time hunting up the Scripture passages in a Bible.[23]

An additional reason for biblical ignorance may be that many students are overwhelmed by the outward appearance of the Bible. With close to one million words written in ancient times with ancient images in an ancient context, the erroneous implication is that a person in today's context cannot understand. In addition, the arrangement of the books are such that chronology or logic do not appear to play a great part. And, once inside a particular book, the various literary forms and sheer strangeness of thought forms create confusion. A friend shared his experience of witnessing to a coworker who then began to read her Bible. After a few days of reading the Old Testament she expressed her frustration. His response was, "The Old Testament is hard to understand. Get out of the Old Testament and into the New." Unfortunately, even many of our church members feel a similar frustration.

Reading and studying the Bible is not an easy task. However, because it is God's Word, the task is made easier through the aid of the Holy Spirit. Learners must be taught that Bible study can and should be done and then they must be taught how to study God's Word for themselves. As they become more comfortable with personal Bible study, then they will overcome the difficulties as God's Word becomes real to them. But biblical ignorance cannot be erased until laypersons become Bible students.

SPIRITUAL IMMATURITY—"BIBLE BASEBALL"

Students who are ignorant of the Bible are consequently undeveloped in their spiritual lives. This development or "maturity" is the goal of Christian education.

Paul writes to the church at Ephesus about the need for maturity (Eph. 4:11–13). This spiritual maturity is a process that grows out of knowledge and application of Scripture, both within the context of Bible study and outside in the context of the world. Although we have no control over the lives of learners outside of Sunday school, we do have some control over their learning experiences during Sunday school. Lois LeBar identifies a concern from within the church walls: "Instead of nurturing toward maturity, we often play Bible baseball with our classes on Sunday

---

23. Smart, 74.

morning. We try to warm them up by throwing Bible words at them and asking them to toss them back to us. When the game begins, we pitch factual questions at them. But when they go home and take off their 'Sunday togs' they're the same people underneath. They haven't experienced the presence of the Lord."[24]

We must provide experiences within the church that lead learners toward spiritual maturity. Although memorizing Scripture is important, the learner must go beyond the memorized Word to the doing of God's Word. Within the context of the church, teachers can utilize activities such as role play, case studies, or small group discussion to help learners practice applying Scripture to life situations. The teacher can also assist the learner in applying biblical knowledge outside the classroom by giving assignments and allowing students to report on their progress week by week. God's Word is not learned merely to be repeated, but to change the person. Maturity is the process of weeding out the old self and nurturing the new self so that the selfish sinful nature is replaced by the godly redeemed self. This process does not happen in forty-five minutes on Sunday but must spill over into every day in between.

Spiritual maturity is evidenced in the lives of learners as they exhibit love for one another (1 Tim. 1:5), as they make consistent moral choices (Heb. 5:14), as they display theological stability, and as they serve in the Christian community (Eph. 4:11–14). Until these characteristics are exhibited in the lives of learners, the teacher's task is not complete.[25] In order for these things to happen in the teaching ministry, teachers must be equipped in leading learners to maturity.

UNTRAINED TEACHERS

A recent book in the field of Christian education states that the number one concern among Christian educators is the recruitment and retention of teachers.[26] Because of this continuous struggle to find enough teachers, hasty recruitment yields positions filled with temporary teachers who neglect to prepare because of the transient nature of their commitment. The other struggle addresses the teacher who has been teaching for decades and yet refuses to secure further training because of her years of experience. Either situation produces the same result: untrained teachers.

These unprepared teachers pose a problem for the educational ministry of the church because in choosing not to be trained, they are choosing to be less effective. The teacher is the key to the educational process. Training provides opportunities for growth in teaching skills. It has been said that teachers teach the way they have been taught. As I informally survey classes each semester, I find that "the way they

---

24.   LeBar, 149.
25.   Michael S. Lawson, "Biblical Foundations for a Philosophy of Teaching," in Kenneth O. Gangel and Howard G. Hendricks, *The Christian Educator's Handbook on Teaching* (Wheaton, Ill.: Victor Books, 1988), 66.
26.   John R. Cionca, *Solving Church Education's Ten Toughest Problems* (Wheaton, Ill.: Victor Books, 1990), 11.

have been taught" is a mixture of preaching the lesson, reading a verse and telling what you think it means, or talking about what happened during last night's party. If teachers are teaching this way, and if we are to grow in our educational ministry, then teachers must consciously make a choice to break out of the mold of "the way we were taught" and be different in their teaching.

Most curriculum plans provide teaching helps for those who are interested in variety in teaching. But most, particularly Southern Baptists, also assume that the lay leadership using the materials will be trained in their use. Consequently, if a person is simply handed a periodical in the hallway without further assistance, they must struggle alone in determining how to use it. Training is not a luxury; it is a necessity. If we are to fight the biblical ignorance and spiritual immaturity in our churches, then we must begin with equipping our teachers.

GRADING—"MAKE SURE THEY'RE READY"

The audience of the Bible is adults. It is written by adults for adults. However, that does not mean that it cannot be used with all ages. The challenge is determining what parts of the Bible are appropriate for children of various ages and, in addition, how the Bible can be used as the text in addressing the developmental tasks of learners as they move from one stage to another.

Opinions vary among educators as to what a child can learn when. One group believes that children should not be taught abstract concepts (including spiritual concepts) until they have reached later stages of childhood. Others adhere to the position that the roots of spiritual knowledge can begin to grow as early as the preschool years. It is important that the Bible be handled wisely with children so that they do not have to unlearn something they have misunderstood as a child. Grading allows the student to learn stories and truths that are appropriate for his stage of development. Inappropriate use of the Bible can cause harm in the life of a child. Colson and Rigdon warn: "The mere fact that the Bible is "taught" to little boys and girls does not guarantee sound spiritual results. It can be taught in ways that will give children twisted concepts, in ways that will instill fear instead of trust, in ways that will generate a dislike for spiritual things instead of love."[27]

Teaching the Bible without considering a child's level of development creates the possibility that if the child learns something he does not understand, then he may be given the impression that the Bible is something he cannot understand. Grading gives the opportunity to provide appropriate lessons to certain age groups without the necessity of perverting the Bible in order to make it usable with younger children. As Smart describes, "grading simply means that we do not try to make the child take any step in his pilgrimage into the Bible until he is ready for it."[28] The

---

27.   Colson and Rigdon, 112.
28.   Smart, 148.

purpose of teaching the child the Scriptures is not merely that he may have knowledge, but that he may come to have faith in the God revealed in the Scriptures.

CURRICULUM RESOURCES

In my encounters with teachers I occasionally find some who, for one reason or another, have chosen to write their own curriculum plans. While it is a rare person who undertakes such a task, there are those who feel that available resources are not adequate for their needs. Others may feel sufficiently overwhelmed by the choices already available. The issues to be addressed are: whether to use resources at all, whether to write your own, or whether to choose from those available.

A Sunday school teacher who commits to teach week after week will be hard to recruit unless he or she is given quality materials from which to teach. It would be wonderful if all of our teachers were trained in Greek and Hebrew, educational psychology, and curriculum design, but reality prevents the realization of such a dream. So the option of no resources is not really an option.

Writing your own curriculum plans is an alternative that takes significant commitment on the part of the writer. Most churches feel that with so many choices available, time can be better spent on other tasks. The concern with teachers who write their own curriculum is whether the writer is appropriately trained in biblical exposition and in curriculum design; if not, the weaknesses may outweigh the advantages.

Southern Baptists, as well as other denominations, have chosen to produce their own curriculum plans. Three options are provided for adults, based on several factors. The Bible serves as the foundation and the focus for all the lessons, and the learning activities focus on understanding and application.

Other evangelical publishers also declare that the Bible is central in their curriculum plans. The factors to consider in evaluating curriculum plans are detailed in chapter 16.

Curriculum plans and materials are viewed as aids in studying the Bible and in drawing from it lessons for life. Many teachers prefer an approach that moves through an entire Bible book, making applications to life that grow out of the text and context. Others like a variety of approaches to Bible study: book studies, personality studies, or topical studies. Preferences can be considered as one makes decisions about curriculum plan needs.

CONTENT VERSUS METHODOLOGY

Although as educators it may seem ridiculous to pit content against methodology, some controversy does exist. Secular education experiences shifts from one emphasis to another, and not without influencing Christian education. The 1970s brought an abundance of innovations in education that focused on methodology. Students schooled in those years were guinea pigs for experiments such as programmed instruction, interactive learning, open classrooms, and discovery learning. Reactions to consequent low student achievement scores resulted in a return to more "traditional" learning couched in firm discipline and hard work.

Christian education, trailing behind secular education, was influenced by these shifts as well. Sunday school curriculum designed in the early 1980s gave evidence of more innovative methodology, sometimes interpreted as being at the expense of content. In current design, emphasis is again being placed on content. Current revisions in Southern Baptist materials emphasize a focus on the Bible, particularly more Bible exposition for teachers.

As stated above, the Bible is the textbook of the Sunday school, but that does not mean it must be dryly read and choked down on Sunday morning. An episode of "The Cosby Show" shows Cliff Huxtable reacting to the ill-presented news of the engagement of his third daughter, Vanessa. His thoughts, as expressed to the new son-in-law to be, were framed in a long discussion related to eating steak. He describes a big, juicy steak, cooked to perfection on the grill. The steak is then served on a garbage can lid, his point being that no matter how tasty the food, its appeal can be spoiled by the presentation. Vanessa had "dumped" the news of her engagement on her parents in an unappealing way creating a negative reaction. In a similar manner, the wonderful contents of the Scriptures, if presented in an unappealing manner, can produce nonproductive reactions in students.

CONCLUSION

Christian heritage provides the foundation for the central place of the Bible in religious education. From the Garden of Eden to the present, God's Word, in its myriad forms, has been communicated to man and has fashioned the heart of Christian teaching. The Bible must remain as the central focus of our education in the church.

The various concerns related to the Bible as curriculum, although valid to some extent, do not take into account the fact that Christian teaching has played a significant part in the spiritual development of many people. Church leaders, seminary professors, and godly laypersons attest to the church's role in spiritual development. This growth is a direct result of the strength of Bible teaching coupled with the "text people" who live the biblical lifestyle.

The fact is that many Sunday schools do teach people the Bible. Numerous Christians were first introduced to the Bible in Sunday school. Robert Dean addresses the positive aspects of Sunday school's influence. "We may pay so much attention to Sunday school pupils who learn almost nothing that we overlook others who do develop some Bible skills. Rather than lamenting how little Bible insight many people get in Sunday school, why not recognize how much less there would be without Sunday schools?"[29] Although there is always room for improvement in any situation, many of our churches are equipping teachers to teach; many teachers are adequately preparing and using resources available; and many students are being transformed by the truths of God's Word that are taught in the context of the church.

Dean makes an additional observation regarding the purpose of the Sunday school which acknowledges the volunteer nature of the teacher in the church: ". . . the Sunday school should not be expected to provide educational experiences that requires a specially trained professional. Rather than focusing on what the Sunday School cannot do, why not be grateful for what it does accomplish: lay involvement in Bible study, fellowship, ministry, and evangelism?"[30]

Rather than focus exclusively on the negative, let us focus on those positive examples of godly men and women who are committed to excellence in teaching and who adequately prepare themselves and their lessons. Rather than lament over the ineffectiveness of the past, let us rejoice that the future holds opportunities for better educational experiences in the church. And let us cling to the Bible as essential to all of those experiences.

FOR FURTHER STUDY

1. Imagine that a person is visiting your church for the first time. How would that person perceive the importance of the Bible to your church?

2. Why do you think adults attend Sunday school? Survey the adult classes in your church and compare the results with your own perceptions.

3. Evaluate your church's use of the Bible in teaching. What evidences do you see of biblical ignorance, spiritual immaturity, and untrained teachers?

4. Describe a biblical concept or story that might be inappropriate for young children. At what age do you think this concept could appropriately be taught?

5. How has Christian teaching influenced your spiritual development? What are some practical suggestions growing out of those experiences?

---

29.   Robert J. Dean, "Tradition Can Be Good: The Evangelical Sunday School" in *Renewing the Sunday School and the CCD*, ed. D. Campbell Wyckoff (Birmingham: Religious Education Press, 1986), 121.

30.   Ibid.

SUGGESTED READING

Colson, Howard and Rigdon, Raymond M. *Understanding Your Church's Curriculum*. Nashville: Broadman Press, 1981.

Eavey, C. B. History of Christian Education. Chicago: Moody Press, 1964.

Harris, Maria. *Fashion Me a People: Curriculum in the Church*. Louisville: Westminster/John Knox, 1989.

LeBar, Lois E. *Education That is Christian*. Wheaton, Ill.: Victor Books, 1989.

Pazmino, Robert W. *Foundational Issues in Christian Education*. Grand Rapids: Baker Book House, 1988.

Roehlkepartain, Eugene C. *The Teaching Church*. Nashville: Abingdon Press, 1993.

Smart, James D. *The Teaching Ministry of the Church*. Philadelphia: Westminster Press, 1976.

Wilhoit, J. *Christian Education and the Search for Meaning*. Philadelphia: Westminster Press, 1961.

CHAPTER 5

THE DISCIPLE: CALLED TO LEARN

—DARYL ELDRIDGE

> In the same way, any of you who does not give up everything he has cannot be my disciple (Luke 14:33).

Growing up I noticed our religious practices were different from those of my neighborhood friends. They practiced infant baptism. We believed one must be old enough to understand the significance of accepting Christ before being baptized. They ate fish on Fridays. We ate fried chicken. They sprinkled. We dunked. We didn't smoke, drink, dance, or chew, and (as the jingle goes) we didn't go out with people that do. We were Baptists.

Our name suggested a distinctive belief—baptism by immersion. Baptism is the church's symbolic act by which persons are drowned and brought back to new life, incorporated into the body of Christ, infused with the mind and character of Christ, ordained for ministry, and empowered by the Holy Spirit to be a sign and witness to the gospel in the world.

Still, two facts need to be faced. First, almost two thousand years after the life, death, and resurrection of Jesus, the vast majority of the world's population has not accepted the gospel. Second, after almost two thousand years of performing baptisms in the church, the lives of the baptized are not significantly different from the lives of the non-baptized. Fact two explains fact one, but the root of the problem lies in an inadequate understanding of discipleship.

We seek to lead people to "accept Christ as Savior." After individuals have done this, we suggest that they grow in the Christian life. This practice in our churches gives the impression that whether the new convert grows or not is optional. Many evidently choose not to grow. Discipleship, however, is not an option for the Christian. As James Carter states: "As Christians we do not have a choice about whether we will be disciples. We become disciples for Jesus Christ when we accept him as personal Savior. The only choice we have is the kind of disciple we will display, whether we will be good disciples or bad, or a mixture of the two."[1]

Disciple is the Holy Spirit's favorite word to describe the followers of Christ. The writers of the Gospels and the Book of Acts use the term disciple over 250 times. The Greek word for disciple is *mathetes*, which means "a student" or "a learner." It denotes one who follows another's teaching.

A disciple is a person who submits to the instruction and authority of another. The word *mathetes* always implies a personal attachment with a person who shapes the learner's life.[2] Practically speaking, disciple is a synonym for a Christian. Luke writes that the disciples were first called Christians at Antioch (Acts 11:26b).

In 2 Timothy 2, Paul uses three metaphors for a disciple. He likens the learner to a soldier, an athlete, and a farmer. Because of my involvement in sports, I have a great appreciation for those who pay the price to become successful at their game. Skill development is a continual process involving the following elements: commitment, training, and conditioning. Champions do not overlook any one of these elements. We will examine the life of the disciple by looking at each of these.

COMMITMENT

No athlete becomes a champion on half-hearted commitment. There is a price to pay for athletic success. Winning requires an athlete's full energy. I went to college on a basketball scholarship. Each September, our coaches took us through a running routine to get us in shape for the season. On Mondays we ran several one mile races. On Tuesdays we ran 440 yards. On Wednesdays we ran 220 yards. The coach expected us to beat the previous time. If we didn't, we had an additional segment to run. There was always the temptation to hold back, to beat the previous time by a split second. Coach would yell, "Eldridge, are you giving 110 percent?" More than once I wanted to say, "Coach, I'm drenched with sweat. I'm dying out here. I've got the best times today. Besides, aren't you aware that it is impossible for anyone to give more than 100 percent?" How I stacked up to everyone else was not the concern of my coach. Nor the amount of energy I had expended. He wanted to know if I was giving my best. Commitment is an unalterable condition for discipleship (John 14:1–6, 10–12). Christ calls us to radical allegiance and consistent

---

1.   James E. Carter. *Following Jesus* (Nashville: Broadman Press, 1977), 7.

2.   Gerhad Kittel, ed., *Theological Dictionary of the New Testament*, vol. 4 (Grand Rapids: Eerdmans, 1967), 441.

obedience.[3] "If anyone would come after me, he must deny himself and take up his cross and follow me. For whoever wants to save his life will lose it, but whoever loses his life for me will find it" (Matt. 16:24–25).

DENY SELF

Commitment means that a person has abandoned spirit, soul, and body to the Almighty God. As Bonhoeffer states, "When Christ calls a man, he bids him come and die."[4] Commitment to Christ requires a denial of self which is different from self-denial. "It consists not simply in the abandonment of something that one cherishes, but rather in the repudiation of his right to cherish it."[5] The popular meaning of self-denial is to deny things to oneself. This leads to asceticism and self-mortification. The denial required by Christ is the denial of self itself. Ernest Best makes this contrast: "The opposite is for a man to affirm himself, to put a value on himself or on his position before God or his fellows, to claim his rights, not just as someone who has special rights, but the very right of being a human being."[6]

Disciples seek the desires of God before their own desires. Jesus displayed this action of self-denial as he prayed, "Not my will but thine be done." As Jesus was in the Garden of Gethsemane, he was "engaged in a struggle between his will and the will of God."[7]

By following the example of Jesus, one must practice the denial of self. "It means to say no to our own desires, appetites, ambitions, and pleasures."[8] Seeking to do the will of God should take priority over the will of oneself. The daily activities of life need to be carried out in a fashion pleasing to the Father. "To deny self is to refuse to take any longer the road which leads to one's own ease, advancement, or popularity, if these conflict with the straight and narrow road to Calvary. It means to surrender sovereignty over one's own life, and to accept the Lordship of Christ."[9]

Athletes place their lives into the hands of a coach. For his team to be successful, a coach must have the undivided loyalty and trust of his players. Jesus also expects his players to be loyal. Robert Coleman writes: "Jesus expected the men He was with to obey Him. They were not required to be smart, but they had to be loyal. This became the distinguishing mark by which they were known."[10]

---

3. Lucien Coleman. *Why the Church Must Teach* (Nashville: Broadman Press, 1984), 24–25.
4. Dietrich Bonhoeffer. *The Cost of Discipleship* (New York: Macmillan Publishing Co., 1949), 7.
5. Merrill C. Tenney, *Roads a Christian Must Travel: Fresh Insights into the Principles of a Christian Experience* (Wheaton, Ill.: Tyndale House, 1979), 58.
6. Ernest Best. *Disciples and Discipleship* (Edinburgh: T & T Clark, 1986), 8.
7. Paul Powell, *The Complete Disciple* (Wheaton, Ill.: Tyndale House, 1979), 113.
8. Ibid.
9. Tenney, 54.
10. Robert Coleman. *The Master Plan of Evangelism* (Old Tappan, N.J.: Fleming H. Revell Co., 1963), 50.

There can be only one head coach. When the coach calls a specific play, the players cannot second guess him and call a different play. Success is dependent on all the athletes carrying out the play exactly as the coach had taught them in practice. In the same way, disciples cannot be above their master. To do so is to play god. "There are two philosophies we may follow. We can choose to deny ourselves or we can choose to deify ourselves. We can become our own gods. We can govern our own lives. Or we may abdicate the throne of our lives and let Jesus Christ be Lord. The choice is ours."[11]

TAKE UP YOUR CROSS

The cross is an instrument of death and a symbol of sacrifice.[12] Realizing the symbolism of the cross is important to comprehending the essence of Christ's command. The Romans used the cross to execute convicted criminals. Jesus Christ shed his innocent blood on a rugged cross so that we might live. "Jesus' use of the word cross in this passage suggests that if we are going to be his disciples we must follow him with absolute loyalty and that we are ready to die for Him if necessary."[13] "Taking up the cross is the voluntary assumption of that responsibility which awaits one when he agrees to walk with Christ. . . . It is the sacrifice which alone can make one fit into the will of God. It may not be pleasant, but it means that one accepts the price of a ministry that can be exercised only by the cross. As the cross becomes the supreme manifestation of Jesus' dedication and compassion, so it does for the disciples."[14]

In basketball there is an expression, "Give up your body." It refers to a defensive player stepping in front of an offensive player and taking the charge, possibly causing pain and injury to the defensive player. This act of sacrifice and love for the team results in his team getting the ball. Champions suffer pain and pay the price in order for their team to receive the glory of winning.

FOLLOW ME

Commitment to Christ requires following him. When Jesus called Peter and Andrew he said: "'Come, follow me, . . . and I will make you fishers of men.' And at once they left their nets and followed him" (Matt. 4:20).

The twelve disciples Jesus chose to accompany him were an interesting lot. They were uneducated, impulsive, lacked faith, and slow to learn. "Yet Jesus patiently en-

---

11.   Powell, 114.
12.   Ibid., 7.
13.   Ibid., 112.
14.   Tenney, 59.

dured these human failings of his chosen disciples because in spite of all their short-comings they were willing to follow Him."[15] Others expressed interest in joining Jesus' band, but they were unwilling to make the commitment required by our Lord. "Then a teacher of the law came to him and said, 'Teacher, I will follow you wherever you go.' Jesus replied, 'Foxes have holes and birds of the air have nests, but the Son of Man has no place to lay his head.' Another disciple said to him, 'Lord, first let me go and bury my father.' But Jesus told him, 'Follow me and let the dead bury their own dead'" (Matt. 8:19–22).

This sounds hard, but Christ makes it clear that there is no place on his team for those who are unwilling to follow him. Some conclude the cost is too great, that God needs us to carry out his plan and therefore we are doing him a favor by committing our lives to him. Henrichsen reminds us that following Christ is a privilege. "In discipleship we are not doing God a favor. He is doing us a favor. It is important that the disciple grasp this important concept. However, Jesus warns us to weigh the cost and weigh it well, for discipleship will cost us something. It will cost us our lives. But the results are infinitely greater than the cost, so much greater that one would be foolish to turn down such an offer."[16]

I had the privilege of playing for a nationally ranked basketball team that traveled across the United States, participated in tournaments, and made it to the nationals. I am even more privileged to be on God's team, under the leadership of his son, Jesus Christ. He doesn't need me. There are far more talented players. But by his grace, Christ calls people like you and me to an intimate relationship with him. "When Jesus called men and women to follow Him, He offered a personal relationship with Himself, not simply an alternative lifestyle or different religious practices. . . . Discipleship means the beginning of a new life in an intimate fellowship with a living Master and Savior."[17]

GOAL ORIENTED

Commitment is futuristic, motivated by what can be. Every good athlete has a goal. For some it may be to win the next game. For others it might be to "turn professional," or "to go to nationals." The apostle Paul expressed his commitment in the following way: "But one thing I do: Forgetting what is behind and straining toward what is ahead, I press on toward the goal to win the prize for which God has called me heavenward in Christ Jesus" (Phil. 3:14).

The past can cripple an athlete's future success. Past failures cloud an athlete's confidence in his ability to win. Past successes can deceive athletes by making them

---

15.   Robert Coleman, 55.

16.   Walter A. Henrichsen, *Disciples Are Made, Not Born: Making Disciples Out of Christians* (Wheaton, Ill.: Victor Books, 1974), 30.

17.   Michael J. Wilkins, "Surfers and Other Disciples," in *Discipleship Journal*, 10.

believe they do not need to prepare for the next competition. Concentrating on the past results in future failure. A favorite truism of coaches is, "Quitters never win, and winners never quit." Quitters will look at the past and say, "What is the use, I never win." Winners do not concentrate on the past, they focus on the task before them. No matter how far behind they are, no matter how difficult the circumstances may be, they give their best to the cause.

You may remember the Olympic speed skater, Dan Jansen, who barely missed a bronze medal in the 1984 Olympic games. In the 1988 Olympics in Calgary hopes were high that he would bring home the gold. Jansen had won the world title that year. Who could possibly stop him? During the '88 Olympics, Dan's mind was on his dying sister, who expired before his event. The world pulled for him to win the two races as a memorial to his sister. In both the 500 meter and the 1000 meter, Dan fell. Everywhere he went, the media asked him about the two falls. Jansen's coaches brought in a sports psychologist, Dr. Loehr. Dan was confused about his failures in Calgary. In the 1994 Olympics in Lillehammer, Dan again slipped on a turn and missed a medal. The 1000 meter sprint was his final chance for an Olympic medal. He remembered the words of Loehr, "You can go down, but make sure you come back up."[18] Jansen came back to win the 1000 meter sprint and set a new world record.

We all fall. That is okay. But what we do after the fall is what is important. Disciples get up with dignity and complete the race. I believe that is what the apostle Paul had in mind when he said, "forgetting the past." You cannot worry about yesterday's defeat or glory over yesterday's victory. You have to get ready for the next game. Disciples savor victory at the end of the season.

We must not only forget the past, but faith pilgrims have to "press on toward the goal." Goals help us focus on what is important. In the midst of training and conditioning it is easy to forget the purpose of the workouts. Disciples focus their sights on Jesus Christ, the author and finisher of our faith (Heb. 12:1–2).

TRAINING

A person may be totally committed to a sport, but unless the athlete follows with a thorough training regimen he or she will not reach his or her physical peak. Every champion spends years perfecting his or her physical abilities under the leadership of a skilled coach. Even superstars like Michael Jordan and Steffi Graf require the direction of a trainer/coach to improve their game. Discipleship also requires more than commitment. As Coleman writes, ". . . the term embraces the concepts of repentance, radical conversion, and submission to the lordship of Jesus Christ. But it

18.   Dan Jansen and Jack McCallum. *Full Circle: The Dan Jansen Story.* Condensed in *Readers Digest,* November 1994, 240.

also implies lifelong enrollment in the school of Christian learning, for the essence of discipleship is learnership. A disciple who disdains learning is no less paradoxical than a cowboy who won't go near horses."[19]

Jesus said, "Take my yoke upon you and learn from me, for I am gentle and humble in heart, and you will find rest for your souls" (Matt. 11:29). The yoke was a symbol of submission, obedience, and service. It was a means to harness power and direct the energy of an animal. The yoke guides or steers the beast of burden. "To take the yoke of Christ upon us means that we submit to His leadership and to His lordship."[20] The yoke symbolizes the disciple's willingness to come under the guidance of the teacher. In other words, the disciple is "teachable." The disciples of Jesus lacked many attributes necessary for potential leaders. Yet, they possessed the one quality Jesus required. "One might wonder how Jesus could ever use them. They were impulsive, temperamental, easily offended, and had all the prejudices of their environment. In short, these men selected by the Lord to be His assistants represented an average cross section of the lot of society of their day. Not the kind of group one would expect to win the world for Christ. Yet Jesus saw in these simple men the potential of leadership for the Kingdom. They were indeed 'unlearned and ignorant' according to the world's standard (Acts 4:13), but they were teachable."[21] It is only as we yield to Christ and get under his yoke that we can learn of him.[22]

Training disciples involves three steps. The learners *observe*, *practice* what they have learned, then *teach* others.

OBSERVATION

Students of the rabbinical tradition came to the synagogue and heard their teachers. By contrast, Jesus called his disciples to follow him. His classroom was comprised of the roads, fields, and hills of Judah and Samaria. Christ's disciples were to do more than hear his words. They were to observe his life. The disciples saw how Jesus reacted to a violent storm. They watched as he ministered to the rich, the troubled, the sick, and the oppressed. They observed him on the mountaintop and they saw him emotionally spent. They watched as he commanded the attention of the crowds and they saw him in the homes of friends. They observed him perform a miracle at a wedding and cry at the death of a loved one. In short, they saw his faith in action.

Christ challenged his students to be intellectually honest (Matt. 6:12). Our Lord also challenged the status quo and encouraged his disciples to do the same. "You have heard it said. But I say to you . . ." were common words of Christ. When the

---

19.   Lucien Coleman, 30.
20.   Powell, 8.
21.   Robert Coleman, 23–24.
22.   Powell, 11.

Pharisees and common man questioned Jesus' messianic claims, Jesus asked them, "Who do people say I am?"; "Who do you say I am?"

One mark of good students is that they ask questions. They are intellectually curious. Jesus' disciples were no exception. They asked the Master teacher questions and they discussed what his teachings meant. The following are a few examples of their desire to learn:

Matt. 13:10	Why do you speak to the people in parables?
Matt. 13:36	Explain to us the parable of the weeds.
Matt. 15:12	Do you know the Pharisees were offended?
Matt. 15:15	Explain the parable to us.
Matt. 16:7	They discussed this among themselves.
Matt. 17:10	Why then do teachers of the law say Elijah must come first?
Matt. 17:19	Why couldn't we drive it out?
Matt. 18:21	How many times should I forgive my brother?
Matt. 19:27	What then will there be for us?
Matt. 24:3	Tell us, when will this happen?

Paul writes, "be imitators of me" (Eph. 5:1). Before one can imitate a behavior the person has to observe the behavior. Simply watching someone, however, does not make one a skilled learner. Listening is not learning and telling is not teaching. The learner is to process what he sees. There are three questions learners should ask in their educational pilgrimage: "What did I learn?"; "What does it mean?"; and "How can I use it?" Learners are keen observers who process what they see and hear.

PRACTICE

It is not enough to observe faith and to contemplate its meaning. Disciples are to practice what they know to do. This is what Jesus meant when he said, "He who has ears, let him hear" (Matt. 11:15). A disciple not only listens but does what the teacher says to do. A disciple is receptive to the teaching of the Spirit.

> The talmid of the Rabbinical schools is primarily a student. His chief business was to master the contents of the written Law and the oral Tradition. The finished products of the Rabbinical schools were learned biblical scholars and sound and competent lawyers. The life of a talmid as talmid was made up of study of the sacred writings, attendance on lectures, and discussion of difficult passages or cases. Discipleship as Jesus conceived it was not a theoretical discipline of this sort, but a practical task to which men were called to give themselves and all their energies.

> Their work was not study but practice. Fishermen were to become fishers of men, peasants were to be labourers in God's vineyard or God's harvest field. And Jesus was their Master not so much as a teacher of right doctrine, but rather as the master-craftsman who they were to follow and imitate.[23]

Imitation requires seeing the behavior and then practicing it. Learning is putting feet to ideas. It is trying out faith in the real world. It is being obedient to the commands of our Lord. Scripture records when Jesus had instructed his disciples, they "did as Jesus said" (Matt. 21:6). The Great Commission tells us to teach our disciples to *obey everything* Christ commanded. Jesus said, "If you love me, you will obey what I command" (John 14:15). Followership means practicing what he preaches. After the Sermon on the Mount, Jesus said, "Not everyone who says to me, 'Lord, Lord,' will enter the kingdom of heaven, but only he who does the will of my Father who is in heaven" (Matt. 7:21). The Apostle James writes, "Do not merely listen to the word, and so deceive yourselves. Do what it says" (James 1:22).

In college, we had some tremendous basketball fans. They would come to all of our games and some even watched our practices. These spectators were acquainted with every aspect of our game. They could converse with us about the strategy we were going to use in next week's game. They knew our plays. They talked about the sport but they were not capable of walking on the court and playing with us. The skills we were developing could not be learned by observation. So it is with faith. Spiritual growth does not occur by observing spiritual giants. It is the result of practicing our faith. God calls us to his team. He does not want us to be spectators or to warm the bench. He wants us in the game. With his leading we can become spiritually mature, but we must practice what we have learned from him. As the advertisement says, "Just do it!"

TEACH OTHERS

The final step in the training process is for the learner to teach others what he or she has learned. Educators call this "third-person teaching." One person teaches someone (the second person) who then teaches a third person. Paul expresses it this way: "And the things you have heard me say in the presence of many witnesses entrust to reliable men who will also be qualified to teach others" (2 Tim. 2:2).

Asking disciples to teach others accomplishes three things. First, the disciple learns by teaching. How often have you heard a teacher say, "I learn more than my students." Expressing an idea in a way that others can understand increases the teacher's comprehension. When I was a teaching fellow, my professor would give me opportunities to teach when he was out of town. Although I had taken the course

---

23.   T. W. Manson, *The Teaching of Jesus* (Cambridge: Cambridge University Press, 1963), 239–40.

and I thought I knew the material, it was while teaching that I really learned the subject.

Second, third-person teaching crystallizes a person's beliefs. It is important that disciples own their faith. Faith cannot be second hand. The disciple needs to know that he believes what he believes because he believes it and not because his parents, teachers, or friends believe. Some religions require older adolescents to do two years of missionary work. Part of their experience involves sharing their faith with others. In defending what they believe, their faith is strengthened. Students who teach others about their faith are less likely to leave the faith for other religions.

Third, requiring disciples to teach others multiplies the impact of the teacher (2 Tim 4:12). Our Lord did not want his teaching to end with his twelve disciples. His worldwide, eternal enterprise was dependent upon his disciples "getting it and getting it right" while the Teacher was still with them.[24] After Christ was rejected in his hometown of Nazareth, he traveled from village to village teaching. The disciples reached a point in their development that they needed to teach others what they had learned. He sent them off in pairs to share the Good News of his coming (Matt. 6:7–13). When the disciples returned they "reported what they had done and taught" (Matt. 6:30).

Disciples are not simply to learn about Christ. The goal of discipleship is not production but reproduction. Ken Hemphill writes, "To become mature believers we must not only become producing members of the body of Christ but also reproducing members. The goal of every believer should not only be involved in ministry, but also training others to be ministers. In other words, everyone should strive to reproduce themselves by discipling others in the body of Christ."[25]

The disciple observes, practices what he has learned, and then teaches others the things of God. Through this three-step process, disciples train new believers in the faith. Disciples who are fully mature will train others in the faith.

CONDITIONING

I will not forget watching the television sportscast on the night that Nolan Ryan, a pitcher for the Texas Rangers, pitched his seventh no-hitter. After this spectacular performance sportscasters asked Ryan how he was celebrating the no-hitter. He replied that he was going to the locker room, climb on a stationary bicycle, and begin pedaling toward his goal of eighteen miles before calling it a day. Few baseball players are in the professional league at the age of thirty-four, much less forty-four. He had done it all. He had nothing to prove. He had already broken several professional records. Ryan demonstrated greatness that night, not on the baseball field in front

24.   Lucien Coleman, 25.
25.   Ken Hemphill. *The Antioch Effect* (Nashville: Broadman, 1994), 204.

of forty thousand people, but in the privacy of the workout room. True success is the result of a disciplined life.

While commitment and training are necessary to improve the skills of an athlete, winning the crown requires conditioning. Some athletes have natural talent and achieve moderate success because of their innate abilities. Those who make it to the top have learned the meaning of "paying the price." Conditioning can be done only by the athlete. No one else can run the laps, lift the weights, and control what an athlete eats and drinks. Training helps sharpen skills. Conditioning provides strength and stamina. I have watched talented players get beat, not because they did not have the moves or the skill. They lost the match because they grew weary and could not play at that level of performance for the entire game even though they were far superior to their opponents in many areas.

The word discipline is a derivative of disciple. Discipline refers to behaviors that are taught, practiced and celebrated within a community. We live in a society where people lack discipline. We think we can be virtuous without practicing the virtues. We want instant health and weight loss without the discipline of exercise and dieting over the long haul. We want to wear the uniform without paying the price of conditioning. Richard Foster exclaims, "Superficiality is the curse of our age. The doctrine of instant gratification is a primary spiritual problem. The desperate need today is not for a greater number of intelligent people, or gifted people, but for deep people."[26]

There is a slang phrase among athletes: "No pain, no gain." The apostle Paul referred to the discipline required of Christ's followers when he wrote, "Do you not know that in a race all the runners run, but only one gets the prize? Run in such a way as to get the prize. Everyone who competes in the games goes into strict training. They do it to get a crown that will not last; but we do it to get a crown that will last forever. Therefore I do not run like a man running aimlessly; I do not fight like a man beating the air. No, I beat my body and make it my slave so that after I have preached to others, I myself will not be disqualified for the prize" (1 Cor. 9:24–27).

I ran track in my first year of high school. Our conditioning program involved running 330 yards and walking 110 yards, then running another 330 yards until we had run 6–8 quarter-miles. The coach had observed my times in the 330 and thought I had potential for running the 440. I had always thought of myself as a short distance runner, a sprinter, not a marathon runner. I had never run the 440 in competition and I hated to run anything over 220 yards. It so happened that our two 440 yard runners on the varsity team could not run at a track meet. Because of my fast 330 yard times, the coach asked me to run in their place. I was thrilled that the coach would ask me, a freshman, to dress out for the varsity team. On the day of the race, I got into the starting blocks, and when the gun sounded I took off like a jack

---

26.   Richard J. Foster. *Celebration of Discipline* (San Francisco: Harper & Row, 1978), 1.

rabbit. I turned around the first turn and things were going so well that I kicked it into high gear. "This is easy," I said. I had it made. The ribbon was mine. The crowd went wild as I pulled away from the pack. People stood and cheered as they watched the stadium clock. I was on a record-setting pace at the 330 mark. Suddenly I felt as if I had run into a brick wall. My legs slowed and I could barely catch my breath. In just seconds all the runners passed me. I finished last. I felt humiliated. I learned that day why 440 yard sprinters train by running long distances and lift weights to get ready for a race. Conditioning is the price for athletic success. Conditioning involves not only an aerobic exercise and strength program, but also an appropriate diet. Champions have a disciplined life. When preparing for the Olympics athletes monitor their calories, fat grams, and carbohydrates. Steroids and other drugs may not be used to enhance performance. Winners say no to things that will not help them achieve their goals. They are not willing to take short cuts that might jeopardize their career.

A disciple learns that you cannot say no unless there is a bigger yes burning deep within you. When temptations come, disciples refuse immediate gratification so they might win the prize. A disciple is not "one who is under some external pressure and is forced to live a certain way. The motivation of the disciple is not external, but from within."[27] The ability of the disciple to say no, comes from "a deep love for the Father and His desire for His children."[28]

In the spiritual realm, conditioning involves the inward disciplines of meditation, prayer, fasting, and study. The depth of an individual is not discovered in the public arena, but rather in quiet solitude, where the disciple meets God. Neglecting the inner life results in a failed public life. Eventually, like my humiliating 440 race, the spiritual conditioning of the disciple is revealed. Unfortunately, in recent days we have witnessed several well-known Christian leaders humiliate themselves and the church because of moral or ethical failure. Gifted speakers and writers who could command the attention of thousands were disqualified because they lacked the strength of character resulting from a neglected private life.

Conditioning is not a program; it is a lifelong process. Nolan Ryan did not begin a strenuous personal exercise program when he turned forty. His entire career reflected a disciplined regimen. In the same way, discipleship is not a program, but a lifelong process. Discipleship is not a notebook that one completes. It is not a group of people to whom you regularly attend. It is not a certificate you can hang on the wall and say, "I've been there, I've done that." Discipleship is a lifestyle. It is living each day as Christ would live it.

---

27.   LeRoy Eims, *What Every Christian Should Know About Growing* (Wheaton, Ill.: Victor Books, 1983), 75.
28.   Hemphill, 197.

THE PRIZE: GOD'S APPLAUSE

By this time you may be thinking, "Is all this self-discipline, sacrifice, and hard work worth it?" Do you feel like sitting back and watching the game, choosing to be a spectator rather than a participant? Friends tell me a marathon runner experiences fatigue around the eighteenth mile. The body is screaming at the athlete to stop. To complete the twenty-six mile endurance contest the runner has to push through the pain and fatigue and focus on the finish line. My coaches would frequently bark, "When the going gets tough, the tough get going." Character is forged in the crucible of adversity. James the apostle writes, "Consider it pure joy, my brothers, whenever you face trials of many kinds, because you know that the testing of your faith develops perseverance. Perseverance must finish its work so that you may be mature and complete, not lacking anything" (James 1:2–4). The apostle Paul seemed to thrive on pain and suffering. He writes, "I delight in weaknesses, in insults, in hardships, in persecutions, in difficulties. For when I am weak, then I am strong" (2 Cor. 12:10). The disciple digs deep into his soul and finds the source of strength to take the next step. Paul uses this image when he writes: "Therefore, since we are surrounded by such a great cloud of witnesses, let us throw off everything that hinders and the sin that so easily entangles, and let us run with perseverance the race marked out for us. Let us fix our eyes on Jesus, the author and perfecter of our faith, who for the joy set before him endured the cross, scorning its shame, and sat down at the right hand of the throne of God. Consider him who endured such opposition from sinful men, so that you will not grow weary and lose heart" (Heb. 12:1–3).

Christians are not free from life's problems and difficulties. They endure pain and suffering like everyone else. How do we keep going when the going gets tough? Stephen Covey defines happiness as "the fruit of the desire and ability to sacrifice what we want now for what we want eventually."[29] The disciple is future-minded. He looks beyond the present difficulties and focuses on the finish line. Those who have gone before us line the course, applauding us to finish the race. Jesus Christ is at the finish line cheering us on. He is waiting to place a crown on our head and to tell us, "Well done, good and faithful servant!" (Matt. 25:21).

Athletes spend hours in training, conditioning their bodies and enduring pain to obtain a perishable crown. My twelve-year-old son is in a bowling league. He has received many trophies, patches and pins for his winning performances. These will one day rust, rot, and be thrown in the trash. Christ's disciples run for the applause of heaven and the imperishable crown of righteousness. May we agree with Paul who writes, "I have fought the good fight, I have finished the race, I have kept the faith. Now there is in store for me the crown of righteousness, which the Lord, the

---

29. Stephen Covey. *The 7 Habits of Highly Effective People* (New York: Simon and Schuster, 1989), 48.

righteous Judge, will award to me on that day—and not only to me, but also to all who have longed for his appearing" (2 Tim. 4:7–8).

FOR FURTHER STUDY

1. Write a paper that describes the attributes of a disciple. Or, design a stained glass window that conveys symbols of the relationship between Christ and his disciples (cross, yoke, vine, etc.).

2. What Christian made a significant contribution to your spiritual growth? What do you remember about him or her? What qualities does he or she possess that you would like to emulate?

3. How important is practice in the training process? How can we employ this principle in our discipleship training programs?

4. We recognize in the great commission the command to witness and we encourage all Christians to adopt a witnessing lifestyle. Do we recognize the same command to teach and equip all believers to do this? React to this question and suggest ways it could be done in the local church.

5. What elements should be included in a spiritual conditioning program? Develop a lesson plan to teach others in the classical spiritual disciplines.

SUGGESTED READING

Bonhoeffer, Dietrich. *The Cost of Discipleship*. New York: Macmillan Publishing Company, 1949.

Bruce, Alexander Balmain. *The Training of the Twelve*. New York: A. C. Armstrong and Son, 1894.

Carter, James E. *Following Jesus: The Nature of Christian Discipleship*. Nashville: Broadman, 1977.

Coleman, Lucien. *Why the Church Must Teach*. Nashville: Broadman, 1984.

Coleman, Robert E. *The Master Plan of Evangelism*. Old Tappan, New Jersey: Fleming H. Revell Co., 1968.

Eims, LeRoy. *The Lost Art of Disciple Making*. Grand Rapids: Zondervan Publishing House, 1978.

Hemphill, Ken. *The Antioch Effect*. Nashville: Broadman, 1994.

Henrichsen, Walter A. *Disciples Are Made Not Born*. Wheaton, Ill.: Victor Books, 1974.

Hughes, Milt. "The Disciple Maker's Handbook," *The Student*. (February 1991):3.

Hull, Bill. *The Disciple Making Pastor*. Old Tappan, N.J.: Fleming H. Revell, 1988.

_____. *The Disciple Making Church*. Old Tappan, N.J.: Fleming H. Revell, 1990.

Manson, T. W. *The Teaching of Jesus* (Cambridge; Cambridge University Press, 1963), 239–40.

Powell, Paul W. *Dynamic Discipleship*. Nashville: Broadman, 1984.

Southard, Samuel. *The Imperfect Disciple*. Nashville: Broadman Press, 1972.

Tenney, Merrill C., *Roads a Christian Must Travel*. Wheaton, Ill.: Tyndale House Publishers, 1979.

Trueblood, Elton. *The Company of the Committed*. New York: Harper & Row, 1961.

Wilkins, Michael J. "Surfers and Other Disciples," in *Discipleship Journal*. 62:8–14.

CHAPTER 6

THE CHURCH'S ROLE IN TEACHING

—WILLIAM A. "BUDD" SMITH

> Hear, O Israel: The LORD our God, the LORD is one. Love the LORD your God with all your heart and with all your soul and with all your strength. These commandments that I give you today are to be upon your hearts. Impress them on your children. Talk about them when you sit at home and when you walk along the road, when you lie down and when you get up (Deut. 6:4–7).

> Therefore go and make disciples of all nations, baptizing them in the name of the Father and of the Son and of the Holy Spirit, and teaching them to obey everything I have commanded you. And surely, I am with you always, to the very end of the age (Matt. 28:19–20).

Just before Christ ascended into heaven, he gathered his disciples around him and gave them their "marching orders." Most of us interpret this as his institution of the missionary enterprise—and it is that. However, on closer observation, one realizes that much more is involved in what has become known as the "great commission." Without a doubt, one of the most prominent words in this passage is the word "teaching." Jesus is calling the church alongside himself into a divine enterprise requiring a lifetime of investment. Teaching is a commitment to relationship—a relationship with the Lord, a relationship with one another, and a relationship to a world of lost people.

As we have seen in previous chapters of this book, reflected in this call is the very nature of a teaching God. From the beginning of the Old Testament we see God teaching his people. Jesus came primarily in the role of teacher as he approached his own ministry. And now he calls the church into the ministry of teaching and promises to be present with his people through the person of the Holy Spirit.

89

The mission of the church is to be carried out primarily through the process of Christian education, for we are to "go teaching." Therefore, the very nature of Christian education is obviously missionary for we are to "teach all nations." The content of this mission, then, is resident in Christ himself, for "baptizing them" indicates securing total submission to him as Savior and Lord. But the mission is not over at this point. The statement "teaching them to observe all that I commanded you" calls for a lifelong process of growing in discipleship and Christian action. It is more than merely "winning" them! And like the apostle Paul, every disciple is continually "pressing toward the mark" (Phil. 3:14).

If the church then is to be all that Christ called it to be, we cannot escape the role of teaching. This role is not only filled by church leadership, but is the responsibility and privilege of every church member. The church of Jesus Christ is a teaching church!

CONTEXT FOR TEACHING AND LEARNING

Following World War II, the western world seemed to abandon much of its previous interest in the study of sociology and group or social influences on the development of persons in the teaching and learning context. This reflected many of the fears of dehumanization, loss of self-determination, and loss of control over the world in which people found themselves. The world had experienced a fearful taste of what social control and manipulation could look like and the impact it could have. There was a radical shift in interest toward psychology and the study of the individual in the teaching and learning process.

Individualism became the order of the day, from education to business. The "me age" that was born is still alive and well and has had more impact on the way we approach teaching and learning in the church than we are aware. Such thinking deals with the individual as though there is nothing beyond the individual and that he or she is subject to the fate of his or her own intrinsic operations. This kind of thinking leaves the impression that understanding all human behavior, including the teaching and learning process, begins and ends with the individual. I hope that you will immediately recognize some obvious problems that this philosophy can cause for healthy growth of an individual within the context of the church.

Erik Erikson, among others, began to build some bridges between psychology and sociology.[1] "His views on the connections of the self-concept and identity, in the form in which he elaborated them, included a sense of the blending of social, cultural, and historical forces in the individual's strivings for a place in his society."[2]

---

1.   Erik Erikson, "Identity and the Life Cycle," *Psychological Issues*, vol. I, No. 1 (1959): 120.
2.   Grace Ganter and Margaret Yeakel, *Human Behavior and the Social Environment* (New York: Columbia University Press, 1980), 32.

There is nothing wrong with recognition of the individual within itself (a process we would encourage), but it is often dangerous to do so to the neglect of the relational context of that individual, including the impact that each has on the other.

THE SIGNIFICANCE OF CONTEXT

Curriculum developers (those who attempt to write curriculum plans) and curriculum implementors (those who attempt to teach curriculum plans) are constantly working within the framework of the elements of curriculum design. Two of these elements are "content" and "context." These elements are complicated and difficult to understand. I will attempt to explain them with the analogy of baking a cake. Keep in mind that all analogies break down after a point.

First, let me stretch the analogy to include the concepts of curriculum and curriculum design. There is always a difference between the recipe for a cake (how the cake *should* look when it is finished) and the cake itself (how the cake *actually* looks when it is finished). The same is true of a curriculum plan (how the teaching and learning process *should* happen) and curriculum (what *actually* happens in the teaching and learning process as a result of the plan).

The content of a curriculum plan is similar to the list of ingredients for a cake recipe. In a Sunday school lesson, the content includes the Bible passage for that lesson, the commentary from the lesson quarterly, additional commentary from other resources, the personal commentary of the teacher and the learners, maps, charts, visual aids, etc.

The context of a curriculum plan is similar to the oven where a cake is baked. In a Sunday school class, it includes the personal relationships of the class members, the general theological perspective of the group, the impact of the culture or subculture within which the members live, the historical setting, the size of the group, the worldview of the group, how the group perceives the teaching and learning process, the size and shape of the room, the lighting and temperature of the room, the time of day, and many other atmospheric conditions.

Let's look at one more concept before leaving the cake-baking analogy. That concept is "model." In the analogy, we said that the pan used for baking a cake is a part of the context. But what is the shape and size of the pan? There are square pans and round pans. There are shallow pans and deep pans. There are large pans and small pans. There are pans shaped like hearts, and even cartoon characters. To a great extent, the shape and size of the pan determines what a cake will look like when it is finished. In the same way, the models we choose in both the curriculum planning and curriculum implementing processes will determine, to a great extent, what learning will look like. Models will be explained a little later in this chapter.

FORMULA

Curriculum plan	=	Recipe for baking a cake.
Curriculum	=	Actual baked cake which is the result of the recipe.
Content	=	All the ingredients that should go into the cake.
Context	=	The total atmosphere within which the cake is baked. It consists of the amount of heat, the type of heat (electric, gas, etc.), the pan used, the length of cooking time, the degree of temperature, the humidity at the time of cooking, the altitude, and other atmospheric conditions.

THE CHURCH AS CONTEXT

Modern individualism has influenced us so much that we easily forget that Christian identity is not developed in an isolated vacuum. Rather, it is developed within the context of a vital, living, cooperative body of believers growing toward the goal of Christian education or, in other words, growing in the person of Christ. Paul described this growth as follows: "Just as each of us has one body with many members, and these members do not all have the same function, so in Christ, we who are many form one body, and each member belongs to all the others" (Rom. 12: 4–5).

At this point I want in no way to negate the content of Christian education, for that is absolutely vital to the teaching and learning process. In fact, I have often been frustrated that we have become masters of the "how" of methodology and forgotten the "what" of teaching. What good is it to teach well if you have nothing to teach?

On the other hand, the teaching and learning process is so often focused on the individual mastering the content of curriculum that it loses sight of the cultural setting or context within which learning takes place. For the church, that curriculum context is the life and work of the church, both gathered and scattered. It is the relational one-to-another process at work. It is the milieu for Christian growth and development, where the content of the gospel is both taught and caught. More often than not, the "caught" part of the content depends primarily upon the context. Therefore, the context not only becomes the place of teaching but often the teaching itself. Jesus not only came teaching but he was the teaching. He implied the same of us when he said: "You are the light of the world. A city on a hill cannot be hidden. Neither do people light a lamp and put it under a bowl. Instead they put it on its stand, and it gives light to everyone in the house. In the same way, let your light shine before men, that they may see your good deeds and praise your Father in heaven" (Matt. 5:14–16).

Understanding the church as an organism and the progressive development of "Christ-life" in the believers helps us realize that Christian education must deal with individuals in the context of the church. Jesus' example in choosing twelve to be with him is reflected in the biblical injunction that believers not forsake gathering themselves together (Heb. 10:24).

Teaching and learning in the church must deal with the conglomeration of all members as we develop a ministering relationship with one another. When we express our faith in ministry to one another and to others around us, we powerfully alter both individual and collective identity and behavior. Thus, learning is caught!

A MODEL SHIFT

Models are operational processes or formalized ways of doing things. Any time people are functioning, operating, or relating within a group context for any extended period of time, models are at work.

My grandmother had a definite philosophy of education, although she probably could not have given it a formal name. In fact, I'm not really sure she would have agreed that she had a philosophy. Yet, if someone with a background in philosophy, who had been around her for some time, would soon identify a formalized type of philosophy. Grandmother might even have been categorized in one of the major schools of philosophical thought. I will not attempt to identify her philosophy here, but the point is—she had one! And we all have one!

The same could be said of theology, educational psychology, and other disciplines. People often adopt operational processes without being aware of formalized categorizations. The same can be said of models. What kinds of models do we adopt within the church? What causes us to adopt those particular models? What difference do the models we choose make to the context?

SOME MODELS WE USE

We have already mentioned the fierce individualism that often prevails in much of western society. When we live in a world where individualism dominates many areas of life including politics, public education systems, and business systems, it is easy to see how we can so readily incorporate that same ideology into the life of the church.

Individualism has long dominated the corporate world. This is evident in the fierce need to succeed and the incessant drive to reach the top. Individualism promotes the leadership of a few and the followship of the many. It promotes decisions made at the top of the corporate ladder that later float down toward the bottom. Not a few church staff members have likened themselves to the CEOs of large corporate structures. Language such as "my church," or "In order for me to be a successful minister I must . . ." are strong indicators of this kind of thinking.

It is alarming to study the average length of tenure of church staff members. Ministerial staff move from one congregation to another approximately every twenty-two months. Can one possibly learn all the names of the people in a church in that length of time? Does God really change a "call" on an average of every twenty-two months? Or are some churches and staff members emulating a secular model of success and individualism?

Not only staff members but also church members reflect this societal influence. I have visited people looking for a church home who say, "We really are shopping around for a church that can meet our needs," or "We want a church where we enjoy the preaching, or music, or . . ." It seems they are looking for a place where they feel good or where their own individual needs can be met by someone else. Rarely do you find someone looking for the place where God can use them and their family in a way that will best benefit the Kingdom of Christ. Seldom do you hear, "We are looking for a place where we can best fulfill God's call on our lives through service."

Too frequently the measure of a church's success is based on the size of the membership, programs, or financial condition. James Smart, in *The Teaching Ministry of the Church*, has suggested that "Numbers are deceptive. The strength of a church lies, not in the magnitude of its membership or in the extent of its financial resources, but rather in the measure in which it is fulfilling its nature and destiny as the Church of Jesus Christ."[3] The problem is that this is much more difficult to measure. When we begin to check our "stock report," we may discover that we have adopted a corporate model for our church. It is interesting to note, as we shall discuss later in this chapter, that many corporations today have discovered major problems with the old corporate models. They are now looking for new approaches that will better meet the needs and aims of both the corporation and its employees.

Education systems are also dominated by individualism. It can be seen in the determined craving of learners to be first in the class or have top grades at the expense or use of others, with no apparent regard for the consequences. When you look at the structure of the operation, you often find one leader in front of a class with numerous followers, all in rows, frantically taking notes. The measurements of success are already determined by those in leadership and the evaluation of success is handled in the same way. If you finally pass, someday you may move up the ladder of the system to be part of the leadership. The structure of the organization also reflects numerous rooms filled by persons who are strictly graded by age or accomplishment.

It does not take much effort to see school structures in the way we do church. We even call it Sunday "school." Is it possible that we have difficulty getting some peo-

---

3. James Smart, *The Teaching Ministry of the Church* (Philadelphia: Westminster Press, 1954), 96.

ple involved in church life because they see it simply as school and they are tired of school?

I am not calling for an eradication of the grouping and grading procedures in the educational programs of our churches—in fact, far from it. But I would ask, "Is it always necessary to be so strict with the procedures to the extent that we will allow no flexibility?" And I would also ask, "Do we want all of the programs and activities of the church to reflect the school model of grouping and grading?"

Recapturing the Model. We suggested earlier that a model shift sometimes occurs. When you adopt a particular model or multiple models, you set up a posture of the context within which learning takes place. And, as we also said earlier, often as much, or more, is learned (caught) from the model itself as from its content. Models, by the way, are not always consciously adopted. Often we just drift into them without much thought. What is the New Testament model for teaching and learning in the context of the church?

We tend to think of Christianity as individualistic. It is, to some extent. Most of us recognize the necessity of a personal relationship with Jesus Christ. However, a careful examination of the Scriptures reveals a major concern for the individual within the community of faith. And it is here that we must ask, "What is the dominant model presented in that community of faith?" Consider these examples:

- "This, then, is how you should pray: 'Our Father in heaven, hallowed be your name'" (Matt. 6: 9).

- "My prayer is not for them alone. I pray also for those who will believe in me through their message, that all of them may be one, Father, just as you are in me and I am in you. May they also be in us so that the world may believe that you have sent me" (John 17:20–21).

- "Just as each of us has one body with many members, and these members do not all have the same function, so in Christ we who are many form one body, and each member belongs to all the others" (Rom. 12: 4–5).

- "Because you are sons, God sent the Spirit of his Son into our hearts, the Spirit who calls out, 'Abba, Father.' So you are no longer a slave, but a son; and since you are a son, God has made you also an heir" (Gal. 4: 6–7).

- "'I will be a Father to you, and you will be my sons and daughters, says the Lord Almighty'" (2 Cor. 6:18).

- ". . . and you are all brothers" (Matt. 23:8).

The whole Bible, particularly the New Testament, indicates that God has established a relationship with his people in such a way as to manifest a family model. Jesus always referred to God as his Father, and told his disciples, along with us, to address him the same way. He reminded them that their relationship to one another was that of brothers and sisters. The apostle Paul and other New Testament writers describe the church as a family. We frequently use this word when we refer to the church, but have we perhaps adopted so many other models that it is difficult to see people as family members? If nowhere else in all of society, we need to recapture the family model in the context of the church. But what kind of family?

THE FAMILY MODEL

The word *family* conjures up many and varied images. That unit of the society we used to call the family is in real trouble today (see Fig. 6.1). When addressing this issue in his book *The Frog in the Kettle*, George Barna says, "What has happened is that the traditional family unit—the working father and a mother who stays home to care for the two children—has been replaced by a different type of household. In 1960, this stereotypical family type represented 60 percent of all households; today, it reflects just 7 percent of our households."[4] He went on to say, "Presently, one out of four households consists of a single parent with one or more children. The trends indicate that of all the children born in 1990, six out of ten will live in a single-parent household for some period of time before they reach the age of 18."[5] Vast changes have taken place in what sociologists have called the nuclear family or the primary family unit.

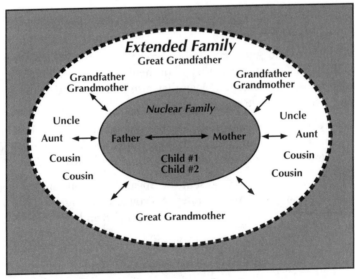

Figure 6.1

Just as alarming is what has happened to the extended family—that group comprised of grandparents, uncles and aunts, great-grandparents, great-uncles and aunts, and a host of cousins. This extended family is almost a thing of the past except

4.   George Barna, *The Frog in the Kettle* (Ventura, Calif.: Regal Books, 1990), 66.
5.   Ibid., 67–68.

for some isolated pockets within our society. And the impact of this loss is far greater than we may imagine.

Some of you may be saying right now, "Oh, he's about to call for the establishment of some kind of improbable, sociological "Jurassic Park." This, however, is not
the case. I live in the real world and am very much aware of what has happened and
is happening to the people who make up our churches.

I am, however, suggesting that we should not ignore some alarming trends that
are dramatically changing the way Christian education happens in most of our
churches. I also suggest that we find some creative ways to recapture a healthy family model for teaching and learning that has been slipping away, almost impercep-
tibly, for some time now.

If the family model is a good picture of what we perceive as a New Testament,
biblical model and if some things have been better taught and caught in a traditional
family structure in the past, we might need to stop and consider, "What will we be
giving up if we let it slip away?" Are there some vital kinds of learning that depend
greatly or even totally upon a context using a good family model? Can Christian education afford to abandon the family model? These are not easy questions to answer.

"AFFECTIVE" CHANGE AND THE FAMILY MODEL

Several different taxonomies have been developed to classify the learning process.
One of the best and most precise systems of classification was developed by Benjamin
Bloom of the University of Chicago, along with a committee of college and university
examiners from various other colleges and universities. They divided learning into
three domains—cognitive, affective and psychomotor.[6] They gave most of their attention to the cognitive and affective domains, suggesting that higher education concerned itself very little with the development of psychomotor skills.[7]

The cognitive domain was defined as "those learning objectives which deal with
the recall or recognition of knowledge and the development of intellectual abilities
and skills."[8] Six major classes for this domain were developed as follows: knowledge,
comprehension, application, analysis, synthesis, and evaluation.[9] Bloom and the
others went on to suggest that the cognitive domain "is the domain in which most
of the work in curriculum development has taken place and where the clearest definitions of objectives are to be found phrased as descriptions of student behavior."[10]

---

6.   Benjamin S. Bloom, ed. *Taxonomy of Educational Objectives: Handbook I* (New York: David McKay
Company, 1956), 7.
7.   Ibid.
8.   Ibid.
9.   Ibid.
10.   Ibid.

I would assert further that this is the domain where most formal education (including Christian education) has spent its greatest time and effort. It is much easier to measure results in this domain.

The second domain, and certainly the more elusive of the two, is the affective domain. It is defined as "objectives which describe changes in interest, attitudes, and values, and the development of appreciations and adequate adjustment."[11] Teachers may neglect this domain because it is "difficult to describe the behaviors appropriate to these objectives since the internal or covert feelings and emotions are as significant for this domain as are the overt behavioral manifestations."[12]

David Krathwohl, Benjamin Bloom, and Bertram Masia developed a sequel to the *Taxonomy of Educational Objectives* that concentrated exclusively on the affective domain. They developed five classes for this domain: receiving, responding, valuing, organization, and characterization.[13]

They suggest that one of the keys to learning in this domain is the learner's willingness.[14] The level of valuing as "the ascribing of worth to a phenomenon, behavior, object, etc. The term 'belief' describes quite well what may be thought of as the dominant characteristic here."[15]

IMPLICATIONS FOR THE CHURCH

It is my own conclusion that the implications of the affective domain for Christian education are more far-reaching than we are usually willing to explore. In the affective domain we deal with the active will of the learner and seek the voluntary commitment of the learner. As an educator, I have long been aware that just because I am committed to the subject of the day does not mean that my students are. And, in a much greater sense, as a Christian, I am aware that just because I am committed to Christ does not mean that those who are learning from me will have the same commitment.

It is very difficult to teach commitment! Maybe a better way of saying this is that it is very difficult to lead someone else to a point of commitment. One must always be aware that learners exercise active wills of their own. Jesus honored this principle when he encountered the rich young ruler (Matt. 19:16–22). How difficult it must have been to let him walk away, but Jesus knew that commitment must be voluntary. It can't be forced. Jesus respected the free will that God gave to man and woman from the time of creation.

---

11.   Ibid.
12.   Ibid.
13.   David Krathwohl, Benjamin Bloom, and Bertram Masia, *Taxonomy of Educational Objectives: Handbook II* (New York: David McKay Company, 1964), 35.
14.   Ibid., 181.
15.   Ibid.

The difficulty of leading others to commitment often frustrates educators, causing them to avoid altogether the affective domain and the whole area of influence. Many times we take the position, "Just give them the information and let them make up their own minds." As we said earlier, we can readily determine a student's grasp of cognitive material. Commitment is not so easily measured. What, then, can we do or even attempt to do? Are we stuck with the "you can lead a horse to water, but you can't make him drink" syndrome? I certainly hope not. We can greatly nurture the climate for affective learning by giving more attention to the context in which this kind of learning occurs.

ARE THERE SOME CLUES?

We need to understand better the nature of the affective domain. Much of what is learned in this domain is the caught part of learning, even though the taught part is essential for the catching to take place. And the process often takes place over a long period of time. The learner's struggle in the affective domain cannot take place in a vacuum. It is a relational process. There must be room for exposure to new, different, and conflicting ideas. There must be a safe atmosphere where learners can struggle with the ideas of others while at the same time have room to struggle within themselves.

Only a few years ago in the traditional family setting, the caught part of learning had a much better chance of happening. Not only does a stable nuclear family unit lend itself to this process of learning, but perhaps in a much larger way, a stable extended family and community become the fertile context essential for affective learning.

When I was a child growing up on a small farm in Kentucky, I was part of the more than one-third of the population in this country who lived on a farm. These farms were surrounded by small farming communities made up mostly of shopkeepers. Today, only a little over two percent of the population still lives on the farm. This is a major sociological shift that has resulted in many major changes.

When most people were farmers, parents both lived and worked at home. Even most of the shopkeepers lived in or near their work. To a large extent the community was often made up of the extended family members. Our farm joined my grandfather's farm, which joined my uncle's farm, and so on. The community was made up of people who knew me personally and whom I knew personally. We were all involved in each others' lives. The people I saw at church also went to school with me, or worked in the grocery store where we shopped, or pumped gas for us at the local filling station.

What does this have to do with affective learning? We said earlier that learning of this type needs an acceptable amount of time to happen. Specifically, it needs time for the learner to reflect on values and relationships. One does not memorize values! One does not program commitments!

What is the key? In an extended family community, each member becomes a mirror which reflects a value system similar to that of the nuclear family. Obviously, each person will not possess the same values as the others but most people will hold to a similar basic value system.

When I was a child, my parents would attempt to teach me something of value or lead me to make an affective commitment. I did not always "buy in" to their instruction. I would go up the road to my grandfather's farm where I knew I would get an impartial hearing. As my grandfather would talk, he would become a mirror of the values my parents were trying to teach. I had heard the instruction again from another perspective and from someone else whom I loved and trusted and who was significant to me. Often that did the trick. But I needed a place where it was safe to question so that when I came to a conclusion it was my own. How many times I have said to myself, "I heard it, I heard it, and then finally, I heard it!"

WE ARE NOT ALONE

The church is not alone in the rediscovery of the family model. We mentioned earlier in this chapter that some corporations are discovering the family model and making changes.

Ichak Adizes is the developer of a diagnostic and therapeutic methodology for helping companies with organizational and cultural change. He has helped a significant number of major corporations with their problems. Adizes suggests that "team-building exercises are important because most of the problems identified in a diagnosis are not problems that are easily solvable by individuals."[16] He is trying to help a company identify its mission by asking, "Where is this company going?" He suggests that "this involves 'we' as a team, rather than departments working individually with a staff unit integrating the final product into a corporate mission. This is a visualization process where 'we' jointly discover what it is that 'we' as the company want to do, so that when finalized, 'we' support it and 'we' know that it can be accomplished."[17]

This team building process changes attitudes in people and promotes a sense of competence in those who are involved. People are free to talk about problems without fear of being persecuted or blamed. The focus is on what is wrong, what must be solved, and how to do it, rather than who did it wrong, when it was done wrong, and why someone did it wrong. All the members of the group become responsible for analyzing and diagnosing the problems, and they see the possibility that prob-

---

16.   Ichak Adizes, *Corporate Lifecycles: How and Why Corporations Grow and Die and What to Do About It* (Englewood Cliffs, N. J.: Prentice Hall, 1988), 308.

17.   Ibid., 310–11.

lems can be solved. It becomes a family process of discovering what is wrong and a family responsibility to fix it.[18]

Businesses need to discover the family model—not the kind of family in which one person makes all the decisions, but the old farming-family model in which everyone had an investment in the stock of the enterprise.

Cottage industries are also changing the face of modern business. Because of the computer and other new technologies, many people are able to work at home. They may go to the office only, for special events. Some have suggested that this reflects a desire for isolation. I see it as an expressed need to be at home and with the family more. It is much like the old farming community where small children could be present and play around parents while they did their work. It is amazing how much communication takes place in that kind of atmosphere. What can be done with the hour or two hours that most people spend driving to and from work each day is also amazing. This time can now be directed toward the family.

Another interesting modern occurrence is what is happening in housing. Planned communities are springing up around the country. Some of these communities are built around what is called a "common." This area belongs to the community and makes up a common backyard to every house. All the children in the neighborhood play in the same backyard. The people who live there even think of the neighbors as family members—like having brothers and sisters and cousins and grandparents. There are more than eighty of these developments already in place in our country.

THE CHURCH AS AN EXTENDED FAMILY

If corporations and housing planners are seeing the need for extended family, how much more should churches rediscover the model that has belonged to us from the beginning? How much more should every child who walks into the church building find surrogate aunts, uncles, grandparents, and even parents? This is especially important for children who live in single-parent homes, and for the parent who is single and needs the guidance of an older parent who may live several states away. It is important to older people who may only see their grandchildren once or twice a year. It is important to all of us. Lyman Coleman, in his *Serendipity Series*, asks the question, "If you needed someone at 3:00 A.M. for a real life or death situation, who would you call?"[19] Unfortunately, for many of us the answer would be "nobody." The church must recapture the extended family model. The extended family is the context where the "stuff" of affective learning takes place.

---

18. Ibid., 312ff.
19. Lyman Coleman, *Serendipity Series*, available through Word Books, Waco, Texas, and through Serendipity House, Scottsdale, Pennsylvania.

One of the most exciting little books I have read in a long time is *A Patchwork Family* by Mark and Mary Frances Henry. In the introduction they state that our whole society is on the move. Many forces in this mobile society are pulling the family apart. They suggest that the church may be the one place where we can counter some of these trends. They call for intergenerational groupings of people in all the programs of the church if possible. They also recognize the need to create an atmosphere where the "caught" part of learning can take place.[20] I'm not sure that many churches will soon be ready to change the structure of Sunday school and probably not many of the other programs either; but surely intergenerational groupings can find a meaningful place in our educational structures.

WHAT CAN WE DO?

Just a few simple suggestions, and then we must leave the rest of the creativity up to you. It is a family problem after all, and you must be a part of the solution.

Try to make your fellowships intergenerational. Recreational experts have taught us that much can be learned through playing together. The people who play together learn together. And most of this learning is "caught."

Churches can plan family retreats and camp outs with activities in which all family members can participate. I have been on many family retreats where there were separate activities planned for men, women, and children. Nothing "family" ever happened.

Churches can also plan intergenerational mission trips and choir trips. It is amazing what is learned when we are working side by side toward a common goal or mission. People who work together learn from one another.

Let me encourage you to plan intergenerational worship experiences. It is wonderful to see what happens when children observe their parents leading in worship for the first time. It is also fantastic to discover what we can learn from the innocent and pure leadership of children in worship. Can I learn from my child? Certainly!

Churches can provide informal social experiences that are intergenerational. Deaf children have some difficulty learning language because they cannot practice their language by listening to others who are actively engaged in conversation. In the same way, the child who never gets to listen to others talk and discuss ideas and values and attitudes will have difficulty doing reflective thinking when encountering new ideas.

Now you are on your own. Keep going. You can do it. Get a group together and have a brainstorming party. Be sure to make it an intergenerational group.

If plants need a climate that allows them to draw nutrients from the soil and water and light from the sky in order to grow and be healthy, how much more do

---

20.   Mark and Mary Frances Henry, *A Patchwork Family* (Nashville: Broadman, 1978), i–ii.

learners need a context that is fertile for the development of affective learning? I hope you caught that!

SUMMARY

The teaching and learning functions of the church included in the missionary mandate in Scripture include a lifetime commitment to involvement in relationships—with the Lord, with other Christians, and also with the lost. In the context of community, individuals are to mature in discipleship and Christian action.

It is the task of the church to overcome the prevailing influence of the world, clearly demonstrated in business functions and education, which emphasizes individualism and striving for success at any cost. The church, through Christian education, must provide opportunities for relational processes in a context where the content of the curriculum may be caught as well as taught, so that authentic learning can occur.

The biblical model for education is the family, and the church can find creative ways to recapture a healthy family model. This can be achieved through the learning process when there is an emphasis on affective learning, rather than the more prevalent bent towards cognitive processes. The affective domain deals with changes in interests, attitudes, and values and concerns the will of the learner and a voluntary commitment to values. It is possible to nurture the climate for affective learning through attention to context, the arena in which learning is both caught and taught. This nurture involves a lifetime process of interaction, struggle, and change. This is the heart of Christian teaching and learning.

In earlier times, education took place within the extended family. In the context of family relationships, opportunities were provided to discuss, process, and evaluate ideas and their meaning. It was in this atmosphere of love and freedom that members developed a personal value system.

While the secular world is considering the family paradigm, the church has an even more pressing need to do so. It will need to find creative ways to foster intergenerational learning and compensate for the changes in family structures. The church must find new ways to broaden its vision and to create a climate for affective learning to occur. This context must include family activities in learning and worship and through church events and functions.

FOR FURTHER STUDY

1. Research biblical terms that describe the church as a community of faith. How do the phrases "family of God," "household of faith," "bride of Christ," and "the body of Christ" highlight the relational aspects of Christian education?

2. Discuss in small groups whether you agree or disagree with the author that today's church leaders are likened to CEOs of large corporate structures. What should be the model for Christian education in the church?

3. Prepare a research paper on the teaching ministry of the early church. How is the approach to Christian education of the early New Testament church similar to or different from the modern church?

4. Form a panel and discuss how today's church emphasizes individualism rather than corporate responsibility in the teaching ministry.

5. Form a think tank and discuss ways in which the church can utilize more intergenerational learning experiences.

SUGGESTED READING

Bausch, W. J. *Storytelling: Imagination and Faith*. Mystic, Conn.: Twenty-Third Publications, 1984.

Boys, M. C. *Educating in Faith: Maps and Visions*. New York: Harper & Row, 1989.

Groome, T. H. *Christian Religious Education*. New York: Harper & Row, 1980.

Hendrix, John and Lela Hendrix. *Experiential Education, Christian Education: How to Get Your Church Started*. Nashville: Abingdon Press, 1975.

Henry, Mark and Mary Frances Henry. *A Patchwork Family*. Nashville: Broadman, 1978.

Osmer, R. R. *A Teachable Spirit: Recovering the Teaching Office in the Church*. Louisville: Westminster-John Knox Press, 1990.

Seymour, J. L., and D. E. Miller, eds. *Contemporary Approaches to Christian Education*. Nashville: Abingdon, 1982.

———. *Theological Approaches to Christian Education*. Nashville: Abingdon, 1990.

Shotwell, Malcolm. *Creative Programs for the Church Year*. Valley Forge, Pa.: Judson Press, 1986.

Vogel, Linda J. *Teaching and Learning in Communities of Faith*. San Francisco: Jossey-Bass Inc., 1991.

Westerhoff, J. H., III. *A Pilgrim People: Learning Through the Church Year*. New York: Harper & Row, 1984.

———. *Living the Faith Community: The Church that Makes a Difference*. Minneapolis: Winston Press, 1985.

White, James W. *Intergenerational Religious Education: Models, Theory, and Prescription for Interage Life and Learning in the Faith Community*. Birmingham: Religious Education Press, 1988.

CHAPTER 7

THE FAMILY'S ROLE
IN TEACHING

—WILLIAM A. "BUDD" SMITH

Train a child in the way he should go, and when he is old he will not turn from it (Prov. 22:6).

My son, keep your father's commands and do not forsake your mother's teaching (Prov. 6:20).

Children, obey your parents in the Lord, for this is right. "Honor your father and mother"—which is the first commandment with a promise—"that it may go well with you and that you may enjoy long life on the earth." Fathers, do not exasperate your children; instead, bring them up in the training and instruction of the Lord (Eph. 6:1–4).

THE AMERICAN FAMILY TODAY

"The Cleaver's don't live here anymore." So George Barna introduces his book, *The Future of the American Family*. And it is true. The close extended families, the pristine, safe neighborhoods, stable jobs, and peaceful homes of earlier days have almost disappeared from American life.[1] The typical American family no longer exists. According to one report, only 7 percent of the population fits the profile of a typical nuclear family. Other sources say that less than 10 percent of the families in the United States are "traditional" in the sense that the father works and the mother

---

1. George Barna, *The Future of the American Family* (Chicago: Moody Press, 1993), 17.

stays at home.[2] Because of these changes, the time parents spend with their children has declined approximately 40 percent since 1965.[3] Before they reach the age of eighteen, two out of three children born this year will live in a single-parent household.[4]

America now boasts the highest divorce rate in the world. Despite some minor fluctuations, the pattern of ruptured marriages has remained constant during the eighties and into the nineties.[5] In the 1940s divorce was not a common choice. Today the divorce rate shows that over half of married families are split apart from reasons ranging from incompatibility and unfaithfulness to boredom and indifference. Statistics show that more than two out of three remarriages will end in divorce. Compared to the traditional family of three decades ago, today's families do seem broken.

However, families today do not fall into a set stereotype. A typical family of the nineties could have a single working parent, two parents who work, stepparents with combined families, or an extended member of the family caring for children.[6] In the 1930s, less than 20 percent of women in the United States worked outside the home. Today over 58 percent of the mothers with children under the age of six leave to go to work each day. The traditional family concept of the father who works outside the home and the mother who stays at home and cares for the children is an exception in today's society.

Evidence exists to show that the family is in the midst of a fundamental transition. The coming decade promises to bring even more sweeping changes in the way we think about the family. Those transitions will substantially impact the future of our nation, the strength of our religious institutions, and our fulfillment as individuals. Barna suggests: "Although it sounds trite, the truth remains that America's future is in the hands of its parents. The importance we attach to parenting, the tangible support provided to parents in their vital task of nurturing young people, and the success parents experience in bringing up their youngsters will greatly influence the destiny of our nation."[7]

However, Barna also believes there is cause for hope. Despite the hostile forces arrayed against it, the traditional family can yet make a comeback. He says: "Traditionally, one of the most important sources of stability has been our enduring faith in family. Despite the monumental social changes of recent times, we continue to maintain the belief that when all else fails, the family will be there to help pull us

---

2. David Blankenhorn, Steven Bayme, and Jean Bethke Elshtain, eds. *Rebuilding the Nest* (Milwaukee: Family Services of America, 1990), 11.

3. Gary Bauer, "The Facts on the Family," in David J. Gyertson, *Salt and Light* (Dallas: Word Publishing, 1993), 188.

4. Barna, 23.

5. Ibid., 65.

6. Robert and Debra Bruce, *Reclaiming Your Family* (Nashville: Broadman & Holman, 1994), 8.

7. Barna, 112.

through. Regardless of whether that expectation is realistic or not, the peace of mind provided by such a notion still eases the anxiety of many Americans."[8]

The sanctity of the home and the importance of family life remain dominant values in American society. A 1989 Massachusetts Mutual Life Insurance Company investigation of family and family values found that "family is the central element in the lives of most Americans" and that "the values Americans call 'family values' are the most important values to most Americans."[9]

Religion is also vitally important to most Americans, but Christian values no longer hold the position of prominence and influence that they did in the past. While the majority of Americans still describe themselves as "religious," the meaning of that term has changed. The Search Institute recorded that 65 percent of Americans are members of a church or synagogue, but only 40 percent report attending worship services on a regular basis.[10]

A survey taken by The George Gallup International Institute found that 95 percent of teens believe in God, but only 29 percent report having experienced the presence of God, and less than half "believe it is very important to have a deep religious faith."[11]

Regardless of societal changes, family and religion still seem to be closely related. Americans who consider religion to be "the most important influence in their lives, and those who receive a great deal of comfort from their beliefs," also report closer family bonds than those placing less importance on religion.[12] A study conducted by the Search Institute on forty-seven thousand teens revealed that teens credit their parents as being the most vital influence on their faith.[13]

Eugene Roehlkepartain brings it all into perspective when he states: "Suppose your church included 100 families. And suppose those families reflected the population of the United States. Here's what your church would look like:

- It would have about 321 parishioners, reflecting an average family size of slightly more than three people.

- Fewer than ten of the families would be "traditional"—intact marriage, father working outside the home, mother not, at least two children.

---

8. Barna, 18.

9. Mark Mellman, Edward Lazarus, and Allan Rivlin, "Family Time, Family Values," in Blankenhorn, Bayme, and Elshtain, eds., *Rebuilding the Nest* (Milwaukee: Family Services of America, 1990), 73–74.

10. Search Institute, "What Congregations Offer," *Search Institute Source 8* (February 1992), 2.

11. George H. Gallup International Institute, "The Religious Life of Young Americans," (Princeton, N.J.: George H. Gallup International Institute, 1992), 11–27.

12. Ibid., 8.

13. Eugene C. Roehlkepartain and Peter L. Benson, "Youth in Protestant Churches," *A Search Institute Report* (Minneapolis: Search Institute, 1993), 24.

- Fifty-nine of the families would be married couples. Of these, 29 would have children under age 18. Well over half of these families would have two working parents.

- Eight families would be single-parent families—seven of them headed by a mother.

- Twenty-three adults would live alone.

- Two unmarried couples would live together.

- The remaining eight households would have some other living arrangement."[14]

This picture is a far cry from the idealistic portrait of the traditional nuclear family. It is even further removed from the concept that God intended for the family. But this is the milieu in which the family and church are called to exist and to minister.

A BIBLICAL PERSPECTIVE

In the beginning God created man and woman and blessed them with children. The family became the nucleus for a world that would be constantly changing. The roots of family life are deeply embedded in Hebrew thought and life described in the Old Testament. In Genesis, God says in reference to his covenant with Abraham: "For I have chosen him, so that he will direct his children and his household after him to keep the way of the LORD by doing what is right and just, so that the LORD will bring about for Abraham what he has promised him" (Gen. 18:19).

The ancient Hebrews took their role in the religious education of their children seriously. The home was the central teaching agency for the Hebrew children and education was natural, informal, and included all aspects of life. The home was the context where the family encountered God. Parents were to be preoccupied with God and they were to educate their children to do the same. In the context of loving warmth, acceptance, and communication, the family became an educational tool for teaching a child about his relationship with God.

Children were taught by example. They learned about their covenant relationship with God and their responsibilities to that covenant as the parents led in rituals of worship. As the family prepared for the Sabbath, observed the feasts and festivals, touched the portions of Scripture over the doorposts, and memorized Scripture, they learned the meaning of a personal relationship with God.

The Shema, which is foundational to all Hebrew or Jewish belief, speaks not only to the nature of God but to the importance and place of education. Jesus called the first statement the first and greatest command: "Hear, O Israel: The LORD our

---

14.   Eugene C. Roehlkepartain, *The Teaching Church* (Nashville: Abingdon Press, 1993), 167.

God, the LORD is one. Love the LORD your God with all your heart and with all your soul and with all your strength" (Deut. 6:4–5).

Immediately following is the instruction for parents to be responsible to instruct their children in God's law: "These commandments that I give you today are to be upon your hearts. Impress them on your children. Talk about them when you sit at home and when you walk along the road, when you lie down and when you get up. Tie them as symbols on your hands and bind them on your foreheads. Write them on the door frames of your houses and on your gates" (Deut. 6:6–9). This command is repeated in Deuteronomy 11:19.

Gene Getz draws three conclusions for parents from Deuteronomy 6:4–7:

1.   Parents need more than head knowledge about the Bible.

2.   Effective teaching in the home must also involve more than a period of instruction.

3.   The Word of God must permeate the total atmosphere of the home.[15]

God considered the family to be so fundamental that he incorporated the duty of children toward their parents in the Ten Commandments: "Honor your father and your mother, so that you may live long in the land the LORD your God is giving you" (Exod. 20:12). God shows repeatedly that a child learns respect for and obedience to authority, including ultimately the authority of God, by learning to obey his parents. That is the emphasis in Leviticus 19 where God connects obedience to parents with the repeated statement of his very being: "I am the Lord." The Creator and Ruler of the universe is the source of all authority.

Although the young child would not comprehend the meaning of many of these teachings and commandments, as he grew older and questioned his parents, they were given the opportunity to help him grasp the true meaning of the Law.

In the future, when your son asks you, "What is the meaning of the stipulations, decrees and laws the LORD our God has commanded you?" tell him: "We were slaves of Pharaoh in Egypt, but the LORD brought us out of Egypt with a mighty hand. Before our eyes the Lord sent miraculous signs and wonders. . . . But he brought us out from there to bring us in and give us the land that he promised on oath to our forefathers. The LORD commanded us to obey all these decrees and to fear the LORD our God . . . And if we are careful to obey all this law before the LORD our God, as he has commanded us, that will be our righteousness" (Deut. 6:20–25).

Moses' instructions to the elders of Israel just prior to the last plague in Egypt included the following exhortation: "Obey these instructions as a lasting ordinance for you and your descendants. When you enter the land that the LORD will give you as he promised, observe this ceremony. And when your children ask you, 'What does this ceremony mean to you?' then tell them, 'It is the Passover sacrifice to the

---

15.   Gene Getz, "The Role of the Home in Childhood Education," in Roy E. Zuck and Robert E. Clark, eds., *Childhood Education in the Church* (Chicago: Moody Press, 1975), 466.

LORD, who passed over the houses of the Israelites in Egypt and spared our homes when he struck down the Egyptians.' Then the people bowed down and worshiped" (Exod. 12:24–27).

Joshua also emphasized to God's people the important educational role of the family in the spiritual nurture of children. After the Lord miraculously enabled the Israelites to cross the Jordan River and enter the land of Canaan, their new leader placed a mound of stones at the spot to provide parents with another opportunity for teaching. Joshua issued this command to the twelve tribes: "Go over before the ark of the LORD your God into the middle of the Jordan. Each of you is to take up a stone on his shoulder, according to the number of the tribes of the Israelites, to serve as a sign among you. In the future, when your children ask you, 'What do these stones mean?' tell them that the flow of the Jordan was cut off before the ark of the covenant of the LORD. When it crossed the Jordan, the waters of the Jordan were cut off. These stones are to be a memorial to the people of Israel forever" (Josh. 4:5–7).

The leaders of Israel anticipated that children would ask questions as they participated in commemorative religious ceremonies. Hebrew children learned primarily through teaching in the family that God is omnipotent, merciful, gracious, and mindful of those who fear him, a redeemer of his people.[16]

The mother was to teach the children while performing her household duties. Mothers were to obey dietary restrictions and other household restrictions so that their children would be familiar with these laws. The mothers also related stories of the patriarchs and other national heroes and of the acts of God in Hebrew history.

Hebrew fathers considered teaching children their most important task. Fathers encouraged their children to memorize and repeat without error the Mosaic law and oral traditions.

Hebrew family education also placed demands upon the child. The call to obedience was reflected in the command, "Honor your father and your mother, so that you may live long in the land the LORD your God is giving you" (Exod. 20:12). Later the Scripture urged, "My son, keep your father's commands and do not forsake your mother's teaching" (Prov. 6:20).

The experiential and practical education demanded by the Hebrews was expressed in religious feasts and festivals. Sabbath observances (not just the Sabbath Day, but also the Sabbath and Jubilee years) taught about creation as well as responsibility and stewardship toward God. Children learned about the Exodus and God's grace and provision for his people through the family's annual observance of Passover. The Feast of Tabernacles recalled the Hebrew wilderness experience. The expiatory ritual of the Day of Atonement taught the people about God's continuing mercy, justice, and deliverance.[17]

---

16.   Kenneth O. Gangel and James C. Wilhoit, eds. *The Christian Educator's Handbook on Spiritual Formation* (Wheaton, Ill.: Victor Books, 1994), 290.
17.   James E. Reed and Ronnie Prevost, *A History of Christian Education* (Nashville: Broadman Press, 1993), 48.

These celebrations taught the people (especially the children) to relive or reexperience to some degree these important events in their national history. The feasts and festivals included informal conversation with family members. "As the child asked questions about the meaning of the ceremonies, the parents' answers were to be informative and instructive."[18]

In addition, teachings such as what we find in Proverbs 22:6, "Train a child in the way he should go, and when he is old he will not turn from it," refer to spiritual nurture in the home. In this verse the parent/teacher observes yet another dimension to his responsibility of teaching in the family. The parent is to guide the development of the child, so enabling him to contribute to the Lord's work from his own sphere of ability and expertise.[19]

Similar indications in the New Testament reveal the important role of the family in the spiritual education of children. Paul notes the significant role of parents when he writes to Timothy, "I have been reminded of your sincere faith, which first lived in your grandmother Lois and in your mother Eunice and, I am persuaded, now lives in you also" (2 Tim. 1:5). It is probable that Timothy was won to the Lord through the teaching ministry of his grandmother and mother who, besides sharing their own faith with him, exposed him to the sound doctrine of God's Word: "And how from infancy you have known the holy Scriptures, which are able to make you wise for salvation through faith in Christ Jesus" (2 Tim. 3:15).

The Scriptures reveal that from the earliest days of God's people, the family has had more than simply physiological (procreative) and sociological (integrative) purposes. A key element in the biblical purpose of family is educational (communicative), an element through which the child is brought to grips with the reality of God and his Son Jesus Christ and the ministry of the Holy Spirit. The child learns about God and how he may know God through faith primarily in the context of family. (For more explanation about the family as a context for learning along with the church, see the section "The Church as Context" in chapter 6 "The Church's Role in Teaching" in this book.)

In addition, the child learns how he should behave in society as a representative of God and God's people. Parents enjoy the greatest privilege and bear the greatest responsibility for the spiritual education and development of their children.

The early church had its beginnings in the homes of converts. On several occasions Paul sent greetings "to the church that meets at their house" (Rom. 16:5, 1 Cor. 16:19, Col.4:15, Phil. 1:2). God in his creative purpose has designed that the home shall have the central responsibility for teaching religion to the young. Both the church and the home must recognize this and act and work accordingly.

Paul exhorts parents to raise their children in the discipline and instruction of the Lord (Eph. 6:4). Parents are not to exasperate or to frustrate their children. Rather,

18. Ibid.
19. Gangel, 293.

they should nourish them as they raise them lovingly and caringly. This kind of loving and caring nourishment includes discipline, and discipline requires guiding and correcting children as they develop.

THE UNIQUE INFLUENCE OF THE HOME

Religious education depends upon the home more than any other social institution, including the church. The home is important because Christian education is not institutional; it happens in the daily exchange of the life of the family and is transmitted by intimate relationships.

The family is the ideal setting for religious education for several reasons. It is a small group setting which allows a child to learn to live with a few people in such a way as to learn how to live in the larger community. The home is the best place for social training because it requires that the child live in a setting of give and take. It exists for people, is maintained for people, and its methods and standards are determined by the needs of people. Spiritual values are cherished in the Christian home. The worth of each family member is determined by the very fact that he exists and is a part of the family and not by some material measurement.

Healthy families develop loyalty which is a quality necessary for adherence to spiritual principles and values. Participation in a family is always costly. It requires self-denial, service to others, and sacrifice. These qualities are taught, caught, lived out, and refined in the context of a Christian family. In the end, the family becomes a microcosm of the kingdom of God. The family is the basis for a child's understanding of the fatherhood of God and the brotherhood of man.

The primary task of the family is the support and growth of each member as well as the group as a whole. It is this experience of family that gives us our first sense of who we are and how we relate, and it is the primary basis of our understanding of and interaction with God.

There is no automatic way to pass on the Christian faith, but parents can prepare the foundation for faith. The Christian faith is not something to be added to a child's life after infancy, but rather it grows out of the concrete and abstract experiences of the early years within the context of the family. Babies naturally trust their parents as powers beyond themselves. This is not just a matter of the cognitive (taught), but also a matter of the affective (caught), and is the basis for a future trust in God. Learning to trust parents is an important factor in the healthy development of children. It is this affective factor that is more likely to lead to faith than all of the cognitive teaching given in early years.

The influence provided by the home is what Ron Taffel calls the "empathic envelope."[20] This envelope includes both a sense of belonging and the values and ex-

---

20.   Ron Taffel, *Parenting by Heart* (New York: Addison-Wesley Publishing Company, 1991), 7.

pectations in the home that provide a boundary between the family and the outside culture. Regardless of age, economic standing, or family stability, the most successful parents have one thing in common: they attempt to provide for their children an empathic envelope. The empathic envelope is like a container around the family and makes it unique. In successful families the empathic envelope derives from three basic qualities: compassion, consequences, and communication. Taffel says, "Theoretically, as the parent, you are in charge of this container. It is made up of your values, your expectations, and your ways of being with your children. It is the feeling you get visiting someone else's house and immediately experiencing the difference between your family and theirs: the values, the kind of language that is allowed, the habits and rituals that they have. Every family just feels different."[21]

FAMILY CONTEXT TEACHING

It has been said that the foundation for a child's life is laid in the very early years and most of the building of that life occurs in the years before adulthood. Parents, therefore, carry the major responsibility for the physical, emotional, moral, and spiritual growth of their children. Some of this is accomplished through intentional teaching while much of it comes through nonverbal or family context teaching.

When our son would do something that went against the moral standards of our family, I would often practice the "Perry Mason" approach: the presentation of the infraction, the prosecution, the conviction, and the punishment phase. This was usually all done in a very methodical way. However, on one occasion, he came running through the house with baseball equipment hanging all over him only to run into a table breaking my wife's grandmother's vase. Before I knew what I was doing, I was chasing him through the house yelling at the top of my voice. Suddenly I realized what I was doing. I was, by my very emotional response, teaching him that "things" were more important than "moral values." I had shown immense passion over the broken vase. That was not what I wanted my son to catch. Needless to say, as a parent, I had some value mending to do. Family context teaching refers to the moral and spiritual climate, or absence of such a climate in the home. If God is not mentioned, children are unlikely to gain a concept of him. Parents are the ones who give a picture of who God is. Dorothy Nolte shows that much teaching frequently takes place without words, but simply by imitation:

> If a child lives with criticism, he learns to condemn.
> If a child lives with hostility, he learns to fight.
> If a child lives with pity, he learns to feel sorry for himself.
> If a child lives with ridicule, he learns to be shy.
> If a child lives with jealousy, he learns to hate.

---

21. Ibid., 7.

If a child lives with shame, he learns to feel guilty.

If a child lives with encouragement, he learns to be confident.

If a child lives with tolerance, he learns to be patient.

If a child lives with praise, he learns to be appreciative.

If a child lives with acceptance, he learns to love.

If a child lives with approval, he learns to like himself.

If a child lives with recognition, he learns to have a goal.

If a child lives with sharing, he learns about generosity.

If a child lives with fairness, he learns justice.

If a child lives with honesty, he learns what truth is.

If a child lives with security, he learns to have faith in himself.

If a child lives with friendliness, he learns that the world is a nice place to live in.[22]

To parent children as God parents us, we must have a living relationship with God and a firm foundation in the Bible. Our lives must be a living testimony to our faith, as set out in Deuteronomy 6:5–9. Children learn from stories and the story they will know and remember is the story enacted in front of them. If one wants to know what a child is learning about the spiritual and moral dimensions of life, look at the examples around them. The sixth chapter of Deuteronomy is a reminder of the importance of parental modeling in everyday life. Parents need to take time to evaluate and to establish the values that they want to communicate in their homes. Harry Lucenay suggests that the list might include "a deep personal commitment to Christ, reverence for God, respect for others, self-esteem, self-control, self-discipline, honesty, responsibility, love, kindness, perseverance, and patience."[23]

Parents need to involve themselves and their families in ministry events that describe in picture language to their children the meaning of the Christian faith. Parents need to share in the fellowship of the church where they can find support in their struggles from other parents and can find other models of living faith for their children. Finally, parents need to parent their children as gifts from God, unique and of great worth. In this way, they parent their children as God parents them. They are a living demonstration of the love of God.

Parents serve as a model relating to other human beings. Along with siblings and other extended family, parents also model what it means to be male and female. Other concepts, such as the obligation of the stronger to help the weaker, the younger to respect the elderly, and the merits of sharing within the family, are all learned in the home.

These same persons also provide the models for relating to the physical world. In the home, the child learns how to treat animals, how to care for plants, and how to use material resources. Even more significantly, these role models influence attitudes towards self, others, God, church, the Bible, and the created order. These at-

---

22.   Dorothy Nolte, "Children Learn What They Live," *Scouting Magazine* (April, 1964), 31.

23.   Harry Lucenay, *Families Planning for Bible Study and Worship* (Nashville: Convention Press, 1991), 12.

titudes continue to shape the child more profoundly than the words taught by parents.[24]

TEACHING THROUGH SITUATIONS

Parents are with their children at every developmental stage of life and are therefore present to make the most of teachable moments in the lives of their children. Teachable moments are shared experiences between parent and child in which applications of biblical principles or insights are made. These very incidents of everyday life are part of the child's first curriculum. The Scriptures exhort parents to use all the opportunities presented to them to teach their children the commandments of God: "When you sit at home, and when you walk along the road, when you lie down and when you get up" (Deut. 6:7). Every day brings new opportunities for parents to teach and train their children in the way of the Lord.

Most parents find it helpful to know what is normal for each stage of development for their children. Knowing what to expect, parents can prepare themselves. Understanding a child's development provides a perspective on behavior that helps parents see the larger picture instead of being caught up in a whirlwind of self-doubt and overreaction to what may be an important, but passing, phase of development. Since no two children develop in the same way, parents need to understand their individual children as well what most children are like. Children inform parents about themselves. Parents need to listen, observe, and ask questions. These situations can become teachable moments.

Unique family situations provide teaching opportunities. Some children have unique needs, such as those in single-parent families or blended families. A single-parent family unit is formed either through the death of a marriage partner, divorce, separation, or desertion. It also occurs when an unmarried person becomes a parent through giving birth, adoption, or fostering. In addition to the regular needs of their age group, children of single-parent families have unique needs.[25] Children of blended families face their own unique issues of establishing new relationships and learning to communicate.[26] As conflicts or concerns arise, parents can use the situations to teach values and instruct their children in biblical living.

Additional teaching situations arise when families relate to those outside the family unit. Relating to other families or community needs teaches principles of reaching out to meet the needs of others. Passing on outgrown coats and shoes to others, or taking food to a family experiencing loss becomes a process of teaching the principles of sharing and giving through situations.

---

24. Eugene Chamberlain, *Today's Children* (Nashville: Convention Press, 1993), 39–40.
25. *Parenting by Grace* (Nashville: Convention Press, 1987), 36.
26. Ibid., 40.

Parents need to live out their faith, modeling what the children are taught. The key to being an effective model for children is personal commitment. Children have a better opportunity to grow in integrity and biblical morality when they not only hear about those values but see them practiced in the lives of their parents.

FORMAL TEACHING

The home has been rightly called a laboratory. A laboratory is where the student learns by actual experience. The *koinonia* of the New Testament is best reflected in the Christian home where family members learn by experience to bear one another's burdens and so fulfill the law of love.

Family devotions provide an avenue for formal teaching. Unfortunately, this practice is significantly lacking in many families. The skills of Christian discipleship—prayer, worship, Bible reading, and witnessing—can be learned only by doing them. No school can provide this sort of laboratory experience. Children need to see their parents actively and earnestly involved in prayer, not just routinely asking a blessing at mealtimes. The child must also actively be taught to pray and how to pray. In family gatherings and in the person-to-person sharing around the meal table, the spiritual heritage of past generations and the current mission of Christ's people are shared, experienced, and learned.

The goal of parents as they seek to nurture and educate their children is to provide them with Christian experience and Christian values by which they can make life decisions and face the issues of their own lives. More than any other institution, the family is responsible for teaching core values. Families are spiritual entities, "held together not only by bloodline, name, lineage, tradition, address, photo album, or legal documents, but primarily by love, pride, recognition, affinity, memory, and responsibility."[27]

Teaching in the home often results from children asking questions. Formal religious teaching in the early years should be done by answering these questions. If topics are not raised by the child, they seldom should be addressed. Answers should not go beyond what is actually being asked. The answers a child receives will shape his understanding of the world, develop his attitudes toward other people, and teach him how to handle disappointment and conflicts. His future depends upon the pictures he forms in childhood. For this reason, parents should be cautious about how they answer, never making up answers that will later cause confusion, and never telling the child a lie.

Parents also cultivate faith and spirituality in children by providing opportunities for ritual. Family devotion time can develop the habit of worship and serve as ritu-

---

27.   Bruce D. Lockerbie, "The Drama of the America Family," *Vital Speeches of the Day* 59 (June 1, 1993), 495.

alistic experiences. The modern family spends too little time together and opportunities for family worship are few.

One of the most important tasks a parent can perform is that of priest. The privilege of praying for their children should not be neglected, for it holds the greatest power and influence available to parents. It is not enough that parents pray for their children when they are alone, they should also pray in the presence of their children and with their children.

SUMMARY

Parents do not receive practice in the art of Christian parenting. They learn by observing others or by reflecting on their own experiences in childhood. Society is all but void of models for raising children. Conventional family norms rooted in religiously based moral principles have been replaced by the transient values of a popular culture.

The decision to live a godly life ultimately rests with the individual, but parents have an enormous opportunity to influence their children in a positive way. By living a consistent Christian life, modeling a deep religious faith, and providing opportunities for Christian worship and experience in the home, parents can contribute to the religious development of their children. Even in the midst of a changing society, parents are still the most influential forces in the lives of their own children. "As Christian parents, we have opportunities each day to listen, build up, and teach biblical truths. We can guide our children to view life with hope and optimism, and encourage our children to become the best they can be. Remember, however, that what we think each day, how we react to parenting situations, and what we say to those around us—all govern our perspective on life. Parenting expectations and attitude determine the path your child will take. As you become more aware of the attributes of techniques into your lifestyle."[28]

THE CREED OF THE CHRISTIAN HOME

I BELIEVE in the Christian home, established by God, honored by our Lord Jesus Christ, blessed by the Holy Spirit, and entrusted to human parents.

I BELIEVE in family worship, in family Bible reading, in family prayer, and in family participation in church, Sunday school, and prayer hour.

I BELIEVE in family love by parental demonstration of God's love in human relationships in which love for one another is fostered and encouraged.

---

28. Bruce, 129.

I BELIEVE in family loyalty, in which family relationships are held to be the highest of all human responsibilities with each member supporting the other.

I BELIEVE in family honesty in which parents communicate to their children with integrity and where children learn to be open and honest with their parents.

I BELIEVE in family goals which encourage each member to do his very best, resulting in a Christ-honoring home that is a witness to the community.

I BELIEVE in family fun, an interplay of recreation where time is taken to do things together resulting in refreshment, satisfaction, and fulfillment for all.

I BELIEVE in the Christian home as the cradle of character, the strength of the community, the sanctity of the nation, the hope of the world, and the keystone of all society.

GOD GRANT us Christian homes like these.[29]

FOR FURTHER STUDY

1. What evidences of changing family structures do you see in your church or community? Do you sense that these changes are inevitable? If so, what are the implications for ministering to families in the future?

2. Discuss how the church can address the area of parents as teachers in homes where there is no Christian parental influence. How can the church "family" teach values to children from broken homes?

3. Although the "family is the ideal setting for religious education," do you think that the majority of Christian families are instructing their children in religion? If not, why? How can the church assist families in knowing how to teach in the context of the family?

4. Describe some examples of teaching situations within the home. What events or situations might arise in the context of the family that may lend themselves to teachable moments? What are some ways to instruct children through these situations?

5. Design a plan for training parents to lead a devotional/prayer time with their families. Compile a list of resources to aid them in their efforts.

SUGGESTED READING

Barna, George. *The Future of the American Family*. Chicago: Moody Press, 1993.

Blankenhorn, David, Steven Bayme, and Jean Bethke Elshtain, eds. *Rebuilding the Nest*. Milwaukee: Family Services of America, 1990.

Bruce, Robert and Debra. *Reclaiming Your Family*. Nashville: Broadman & Holman, 1994.

---

29.   Robert Gray, "The Creed of the Christian Home," *Parents and Children* (Wheaton, Ill.: Victor Books, 1986), 647.

Campbell, Ross. *How to Really Love Your Child*. Wheaton, Ill.: Victor Books, 1977.

————. *How to Really Love Your Teenager*. Wheaton, Ill.: Victor Books, 1981.

Curran, Dolores. *Who, Me Teach My Child Religion?* 4th rev. ed. Minneapolis: Winston Press, 1982.

Gangel, Kenneth and Elizabeth. *Building a Christian Family*. Chicago: Moody Press, 1987.

Kimmel, Tim. *Legacy of Love: A Plan for Parenting on Purpose*. Portland: Multnomah, 1989.

Lucenay, Harry. *Families Planning for Bible Study and Worship*. Nashville: Convention Press, 1991.

Parenting by Grace. Nashville: Convention Press, 1987.

Taffel, Ron. *Parenting by Heart*. New York: Addison-Wesley, 1991.

CHAPTER 8

THE PASTOR AS TEACHER

—RICK YOUNT

> It was [Christ] who gave some to be . . . pastors and teachers, to prepare God's people for works of service, so that the body of Christ may be built up until we all . . . become mature, attaining to the whole measure of the fullness of Christ (Eph. 4:11–13)

What is the role of the pastor?[1] Some say the pastor is primarily a prophet, proclaiming the Word of God. Others say a shepherd, nurturing and protecting the church. Still others say a leader, managing and administrating the work of the church. Each has its importance, but church leaders must balance all three if congregations are to grow in a healthy way (see chapter 9). Yet underlying all these roles is the fundamental calling of the pastor: to "equip the saints for works of service." This was, as we saw in chapter 2, Jesus' primary ministry role while on earth, and it remains his continuing task through the Holy Spirit.

But the random noise of secular success models threatens to drown out the steady heartbeat of teaching. John Brady recently stated the problem well:

> In North Carolina 70 percent of the Baptist churches have been declining for ten years.[2] The problem is the result of a failure to do what the church was de-

---

1. In February 1992, I taught a Doctor of Ministry seminar in educational psychology. My aim was to help my students apply fundamental principles of the teaching-learning process to a pastor's role as teacher in a local church. The class consisted of pastors Robert Carter, John Brady, David Hixon, Steve Washburn, Dennis Suhling, Rick Atkinson, and missionaries David Borgan, Alvin Gary, and Virgil Suttles. Their final assignment was to write an exegesis of Ephesians 4:11–16 in light of educational principles discussed in the course. While the outline of this chapter is mine, their insights concerning the "pastor as teacher" were invaluable and are referenced throughout.
2. Bobby Stafford, Memo to Associational Missions Development Directors, March 29, 1992.

signed to do. The church must actively bring the truth of God's Word and the needs of people together, so that God's Spirit may bring the new life needed. This sounds simple. So, what's the problem?

The church is sick. This results from what Dallas Willard calls the "Great Omission from the Great Commission."[3] The third command of the Great Commission "teaching them all things whatsoever I have commanded you" has been omitted from serious application by the modern church. There are grand plans for evangelization and stewardship but rarely is anything but lip service paid to discipleship.

The Great Commission calls the church to make disciples. Disciples cannot be disciples unless they are taught the disciplines of the Christian life. The great omission leaves the Great Commission task half done. John Wesley saw this problem. "It was a common saying among Christians of the primitive church 'The soul and body make a man; the spirit and discipline make a Christian; implying that none could be real Christians without the help of Christian discipline."

In recent years the church has done what it seems to do best—follow the world's lead. The pastor may be more directed by a business suit than a shepherd's heart. The CEO's power more the goal than the teacher's vision of changed lives. The models we are following seem drastically out of balance with the biblical model for church life. In Ephesians 4:11–16 we find a clear statement of the biblical model for church life.[4]

It is this biblical model of the pastor-teacher that we seek to develop in this chapter. But this chapter is not for pastors only. Any minister who teaches in a Christian context must also pastor those whom he teaches. Every staff member is called to be a pastor-teacher. Every Sunday school teacher. Deacon. Organization leader. Committee chair. Christ has gifted the church with pastor-teachers to prepare others for kingdom service. And teaching is at the very heart of this process.

PAUL'S VIEW OF TEACHING

Paul was a teacher at heart. The great teacher Gamaliel thoroughly trained Paul in Rabbinic Law[5] (Acts 22:3). After Paul was converted, but while he was still a virtual unknown, Barnabas personally brought him to Antioch from Tarsus. There they "met with the church and taught great numbers of people" (Acts 11:26).

Paul's emphasis was on "living in Christ." We find the key to Paul's teaching in his thoughts concerning Jesus Christ, aptly expressed by his frequently repeated

---

3.   Dallas Willard, *The Spirit of the Disciplines: Understanding How God Changes Lives* (San Francisco: Harper and Row, 1988), 15.

4.   John Brady, "The Pastor as Teacher," D.Min. Seminar in Educational Psychology, April 5, 1992.

5.   Not only did Paul know the Old Testament as a devout Jew might know it, he was a trained rabbi and he knew the Old Testament as a rabbi knew it. He knew not only the Old Testament; he also knew the special traditions of the rabbis. William Barclay, *The Mind of St. Paul* (London: Collins Clear-Type Press, 1958), 13–14.

phrase "in Christ."[6] Jesus taught that true life grows from living in union with him (John 15:1–8). Paul expressed the same truth: "Christ in you, the hope of glory" (Col 1:27). Thus, teaching that is Christian must have Christ at its center.

Though Paul taught large crowds (Acts 13:42–45; 17:12–13), he was personally interested in converts. The personal notes at the end of his letter to the Romans show the concern and care that Paul had for those whom he brought to the Lord: Priscilla and Aquila, Epenetus, Mary, Andronicus and Junias, Ampliatus, Urbanus, Stachys, Apelles, Aristobulus, Herodion, Narcissus, Tryphena and Tryphosa, Persis, Rufus, Asyncritus, Phlegon, Hermes, Patrobas, Hermas, Philologus, Julia, Nereus, and Olympas (Rom. 16:3–15). "[I warn] each of you night and day with tears" (Acts 20:31). His missionary journeys were much more than traveling gospel shows. As F. B. Meyer wrote, "All the fruit [Paul] gathered was hand-picked. He was more fond of the hand-net than the sieve."[7] His aim was to draw, to win, to establish, to equip, and to mature converts one by one.

Paul discipled new converts and selected a few men to train more extensively for the ministry. John Mark, Silas, Titus, and Timothy are all prominent examples of Paul's personal touch. Other coworkers with Paul include Tychicus, Onesimus, Aristarchus, Justus, Epaphras, Luke, and Demas (Col. 4:7–14).

By teaching through personal example, Paul did far more than tell converts how to live. He showed them how to live a Christ-centered life and encouraged them to imitate him. To the Corinthians he said, "I urge you to imitate me" (1 Cor. 4:16). To the Philippians, "Join with others in following my example, brothers, and take note of those who live according to the pattern we gave you" (Phil. 3:17).

Paul taught in a variety of situations: in the synagogue, by the riverside, in prisons, in the marketplace, on a hilltop, in a school, from a staircase, in a council chamber, in the courtroom, on shipboard, and in a public dwelling in Rome. He taught in public and private and from house to house. In the groups he taught were Hebrews, Greek, Romans, barbarians, friends, enemies, and strangers. There were philosophers, soothsayers, orators, jailers, prisoners, slaves, the sick; soldiers and sailors; women, devout, honorable, and industrious; rulers, magistrates, governors; a king and a queen. His life was one teaching experience.[8]

Paul established churches as teaching stations. He expected believers to reach and teach others. Paul wrote to Timothy, "And the things you have heard me say in the presence of many witnesses entrust to reliable men who will also be qualified to teach others" (2 Tim 2:2).

Paul sent "teaching letters" to churches in which he discussed the current situations in the churches and gave specific advice in dealing with them. Particularly,

---

6. Richard Longnecker, *The Ministry and Message of Paul* (Grand Rapids: Zondervan, 1971), 89.
7. F. B. Meyer, *Paul: Servant of Jesus Christ* (London: Lakeland Press, 1968), 131.
8. Carl Collins, Jr., *Paul as Leader* (New York: Exposition Press, 1955), 104.

his last letters contained specific directions for organization, government, and worship.[9]

Paul was a deep thinker and philosopher. Before being trained by Gamaliel in rabbinical law, it is probable that Paul attended the University of Tarsus, in his home town (Acts 9:11). This school surpassed all other universities of its day in the study of philosophy and educational literature.[10] His writings certainly reflect his depth of thought, so much so that even the apostle Peter admits that some of Paul's writing is hard to understand (2 Pet. 3:15–16).

Paul was a practical problem solver. Though he was a philosopher and deep thinker, Paul was no abstract theoretician, weaving an obscure intangible religious philosophy. His teaching and his writings provided specific, practical, realistic, and functional advice for living "in Christ." His topics covered a large number of subjects: unity in the church, reliance on the Spirit, serving Christ, renouncing immorality, advice on marriage and family relationships, the proper use of liberty and spiritual gifts, bearing one another's burdens, Christian stewardship, living like Christ, deacons, widows, apostasy, and discipline.

Paul emphasized the work and power of Holy Spirit. He wrote that the Holy Spirit sets us free from sin and death (Rom. 8:2), gives us righteousness, peace and joy (Rom. 14:17), sets us apart for God's use (Rom. 15:16), justifies us in the name of Jesus (1 Cor. 6:11), brands us as God's own (Eph. 1:3), helps us know God better (Eph. 1:17), reveals the mystery of Christ (Eph. 3:4–6; Col 1:27), gives joy (1 Thess. 1:6), helps to guard sound teaching (1 Tim. 1:13–14), and is the agent by which the Father washes and renews us (Titus 3:3–6).

Paul emphasized prayer. Because of his conviction concerning the power and work of Holy Spirit, he believed any training program would be incomplete without prayer. Paul prayed faithfully for his trainees (Phil. 1:3–8; 1 Thess. 3:9–10).

Finally, Paul stressed spiritual growth. He was more interested in the spiritual growth or maturity of the church than he was in mere numbers. This chapter's focal passage reinforces repeatedly the importance of maturity over mere size. This is the essence of Paul's Ephesian treatise on church growth. The remainder of the chapter analyzes the role of pastor-teachers in promoting spiritual growth in congregations.

THE PASTOR-TEACHER

GENERAL QUALIFICATIONS

Paul expected believers to "live a life worthy of the calling" they had received (Eph. 4:1; see also Col. 1:10). Their faith was not some appendage to add to their

---

9. Arthur Leacock, *Studies in the Life of St. Paul* (New York: International Committee, 1964), 6–12.
10. Robert E. Speer, *Studies of the Man Paul* (New York: Fleming H. Revell Company, 1947), 19–20.

own system of values and lifestyle. "You are not your own; you were bought at a price. Therefore honor God with your body" (1 Cor. 6:19–20). Believers are to be "completely humble and gentle; be patient, bearing with one another in love" (Eph. 4:2), not arrogant, not mean-spirited, not hot-tempered. We are to bear with, or in today's language, "put up with" other believers in love.

Believers are to "make every effort to keep the unity of the Spirit through the bond of peace" (Eph. 4:3). Struggle to keep peace. Wrestle with the forces that would divide believers into camps. Warfare among believers never comes from Holy Spirit but is always of the flesh (Gal. 5:19–23). This unity belongs to the body or the community of believers (Eph. 4:4), and is based on our unified hope in Christ: "one Lord, one faith, one baptism; one God and Father of all, who is over all and through all and in all" (Eph. 4:5–6).

What is the purpose of our unity? To use our personal ("to each one of us," v. 7) gifts ("grace") together, so that we will no longer live like "Gentiles" or hardhearted, sensuous, ignorant pagans (see vv. 17–19).

Since believers are expected to live in a way that is worthy of the Lord, to be humble, gentle, patient, forbearing, loving, peaceful, and united, their leaders should reflect these characteristics even more. "Not lording it over those entrusted to you, but being examples to the flock" (1 Pet. 5:3).

THE PASTOR-TEACHER IS A MEMBER OF A TEAM

Paul says that Christ gave four kinds of gifted leaders to the church: apostles, prophets, evangelists, and pastors and teachers. Missionary David Borgan gives an excellent description of each of these leaders.[11]

> Apostle means "one sent out." Originally Jesus sent out the Twelve—eleven of whom were eye-witnesses of the resurrection. But the New Testament records others who were also sent out into pioneer work. He first gives "some apostles"—not the Twelve, but apostles like "the apostles Barnabas and Paul (Acts 14:14) who are sent forth to plant the Gospel for the first time in a place.[12] The modern term from the Latin translation of *apostolos* is "missionaries," ones who are sent out with the specific purpose of establishing new churches . . . .

> [Prophet means] "Speakers for God and Christ." [This involves] not only foretelling but forthtelling the truth of the Gospel. Robertson writes, "Prophets are needed today if men will let God's Spirit use them, men moved to utter the deep things of God."[13]

---

11. David Borgan, "The Pastor as Teacher," April 5, 1992.
12. Dale Moody, *Christ and the Church* (Grand Rapids: Eerdmans, 1963), 93.
13. A. T. Robertson, *Word Pictures in the New Testament*, vol. 5 (Nashville: Broadman Press, 1931), 174.

[Evangelist means] "Bearers of the Good News." Those who have the gift of calling others to Christ. "These men traveled from place to place to preach the Gospel
and win the lost (Acts 8:26–40; 21:28) . . . . The apostles and prophets laid the foundation of the church, and the evangelists built upon it by winning the lost to Christ."[14]

The term "pastors and teachers," our focus in this chapter, requires more analysis. Are "pastors and teachers" one group or two? Guthrie and Motyer write, "The
construction of the phrase pastors and teachers with one definite article covering
both words suggests that there were two functions shared by the same individuals
whose chief task is described in Acts 20:28. These men would be local congregational leaders in charge of established churches brought into existence by the preaching
of the apostles and others."[15]

Curtis Vaughan writes that "pastors and teachers" constitute one office with a
dual function. The two functions are combined in one person.[16] Marcus Barth
notes that "Often the word *and* has the meaning 'that is' or 'in particular' and indicates that the 'shepherds' and 'teachers' are viewed as one common group, i.e.,
'teaching shepherds.'"[17] Pastor John Brady continues, "This connects Paul's teaching with the instructive God of the Old Testament who David called 'my Shepherd.' Our Lord's example gave Paul a key to the health of the church, a teaching
shepherd. Therefore the biblical model for leadership in each congregation is the
pastor/teacher."[18]

Pastor Steve Washburn notes that the term "pastor" (*poimen*, "to protect")[19] refers
to the shepherding role of the minister. Jesus is the model (John 10:11). "As shepherds
of Jesus' flocks, pastors are to love and nurture and meet the needs of their congregations."[20] Also, pastors are to be "able to teach" (1 Tim 3:2). Again, Jesus is the model.
Washburn further writes, "It is enormously significant that the only time the term
pastor is used to describe the spiritual gifts given to undershepherds of the churches,
it is directly connected to the gift of teaching: 'pastors and teachers.'"[21]

Pastor David Hixon reflects his understanding of Paul: "The pastor's primary
role according to Ephesians 4 is not to be preacher, or an evangelist, or a counselor.
His primary responsibility is to equip or to prepare God's people to do the work.
The church needs to grow and mature through the ministry of the laity and not primarily through the works of the paid staff."[22]

---

14.   Warren W. Wiersbe, *Be Rich: Are You Losing the Things that Money Can't Buy?* (Wheaton, Ill.: SP
Publications), 101.
15.   D. Guthrie and J. A. Motyer, *The New Bible Commentary: Revised* (Grand Rapids: Eerdmans,
1970), 116.
16.   W. Curtis Vaughan, *The Letter to the Ephesians* (Nashville: Convention Press, 1963), 91.
17.   Fritz Rienecker, *Linguistic Key to the New Testament*, trans. and ed. Cleon L. Rogers, Jr. (Grand
Rapids: Zondervan, 1980), 531.
18.   Brady, "The Pastor as Teacher," April 5, 1992.
19.   Robertson, 537.
20.   Steve Washburn, "The Pastor as Teacher," April 5, 1992.
21.   Ibid.
22.   David Hixon, "The Pastor as Teacher" April 5, 1992.

Pastor Richard Atkinson writes, "'Feeding the sheep' means teaching them, nurturing them, equipping them. The very nature of the pastor's role is that of a teacher."[23] Missionary Alvin Gary summarizes the role of the minister, the pastor-teacher, as one who "protects and instructs" the flock under his care.[24]

A. T. Robertson underscores the importance of the teaching function of the pastor-teacher: "It is a calamity when the preacher is no longer a teacher, but only an exhorter."[25] Borgan emphasizes the importance of this truth for new pastors:

> New preachers tend to identify themselves more with the first three ministries (apostle, prophet, evangelist) than they do with the title of teacher. The most significant biblical insight in this passage for new pastors is how it clearly identifies the pastoral ministry as a teaching ministry. In fact, in small churches a pastor has almost total responsibility for Christian teaching in areas of salvation, baptism, and classes for new Christians and new members. . . .
>
> American Christianity has compartmentalized church work into pastoral ministry and religious education departments. Pastors should not look down upon their biblical title of "teacher." Jesus called Himself a teacher (John 13:13) . . . Pastors need to become more like Christ in developing their teaching expertise as well as their pastoral talents. The practical application of this should include learning principles and methods of expert teaching throughout a pastor's career.[26]

THE GOAL OF THE PASTOR-TEACHER

What do pastor-teachers do? Why does Jesus give pastor-teachers to the church? Paul says the pastor-teachers are to "prepare God's people for works of service" (Eph. 4:12a). To "equip the saints" (KJV). The word "prepare" means "to mend, to complete, to fit out, to make one what he ought to be."[27] It is used in Matthew 4:21 to refer to mending nets. Pastor Robert Carter writes "the pastor-teacher sees the goal of his ministry to be, not teaching a great lesson to people, but teaching people to be great."[28]

Teaching people to be great in what way? The focus of equipping is "works of service (*diakonia*)." Literally, the word means "waiting at tables." The term came to mean any discharge of service in genuine love for the benefit of the Christian community.[29] The Lord's call to every believer is to serve him and others. Each believer has gifts given by the Lord to enhance the work of the church. Human nature's call,

23.   Rick Atkinson, "The Pastor as Teacher" April 5, 1992.
24.   Alvin Gary, "The Pastor as Teacher" April 5, 1992.
25.   Robertson, 174.
26.   Borgan, "The Pastor as Teacher," April 5, 1992.
27.   E. Y. Mullins, *Studies in Ephesians* (Nashville: Sunday School Board of the Southern Baptist Convention, 1935), 96.
28.   Robert Carter, "The Pastor as Teacher," April 5, 1992.
29.   *Theological Dictionary of the New Testament*, ed. Gerhard Kittel and Gerhard Friedrich, vol. 2, trans. and ed. Geoffrey W. Bromiley (Grand Rapids: Eerdmans, 1964), 87.

however, is to personal convenience and personal comfort. The pastor-teacher lives in the gulf between the Lord's will and individual human wills in the church. He calls out the called and equips them to use their gifts effectively. As James Smart says, "The pastor who refuses to get involved in the personal aspects of teaching is like a farmer who simply scatters seed and refuses to do anything else to encourage a successful harvest."[30] But this task has many obstacles, as I'll discuss later.

And what is the result of preparing or equipping God's people for works of service?—"so that the body of Christ may be built up" (Eph. 4:12b). The body of Christ is the church (Col. 1:18, 24). But what does "may be built up" mean? Does this mean numerical growth, helping the church to get bigger? Not primarily. The term has the meaning of edifying (Rom. 14:19; 1 Cor. 14:5), or strengthening (Rom. 15:2; 1 Cor. 14:26), or benefiting (Eph. 4:29). The result of this may certainly include numerical growth, but the emphasis is on strengthening, benefiting, and edifying the church body. Washburn writes passionately on this point:

> We are asked to consider the effectiveness and efficiency of a body that develops and grows proportionately [1 Cor. 12]. Such a body is able to handily and happily do everything it is asked to do. Conversely, we are asked to consider the effects of a body where some parts do not develop, or where they underdevelop. The picture in our mind is that of a sadly deformed body that is unable to perform even the most simple of tasks, no matter how often or how passionately we may plead with it to do so.
>
> Any pastor who devotes himself primarily to church growth, or new buildings, or increasing budgets, or improved administration, or even to sermonizing, to the neglect of preparing God's people to do their works of service will soon find himself in a sadly deformed church body that is unable to perform even the most simple of church tasks, no matter how often or how passionately he may plead with them to do so.
>
> But as a pastor-teacher focuses on preparing God's people through instructive and applicable preaching, through teaching and discipling that develops member gifts, and through one-on-one counseling that encourages members and helps them become what God intended them to be, then the marvelous revelation that unfolds before his eyes is that of a strong, proportionate, evenly developed, beautiful body of Christ growing and building itself up, able to hear and respond to pastoral leadership, handily and happily doing the work of the ministry. . . .
>
> What is a pastor supposed to do? He is to prepare God's people for works of service. If this one simple truth were embraced by many struggling pastors, it would transform their ministries.[31]

One major stumbling block for contemporary pastors is the fear of losing control over the congregation. As one pastor remarked, "Someone has to be in charge. It might as well be me!" Following society's values, pastors may seek, like powerful corporate executives, to pull to themselves all the power they can in order to effect their wills over their congregations. Brady writes, "The model of the teaching shepherd seeks to empower the disciple to follow Christ and to be involved in discipling

---

30.   James Smart, *Teaching Ministry of the Church* (Philadelphia: Westminster Press, 1954), 83.
31.   Washburn, "The Pastor as Teacher," April 5, 1992.

others. Often power has been carefully guarded as something that cannot be shared. 'If you share, then you have less.' This is a false assumption. Empowering another enhances the one who empowers."[32]

How long? How long do we focus on church maturity? Do we focus on preparing God's people in ministry at the beginning, and then use our equipped members to do what's really important: big crowds, budgets, staffs and prestige? No. Paul says we are to focus on equipping the saints "until we all reach unity in the faith and in the knowledge of the Son of God" (Eph. 4:13a). The pastor-teacher's goal is for "the whole congregation [to] believe the same thing in and about the Son of God."[33] Paul's term "knowledge" (*epignosis*) does not refer to mere information about him. It stresses the experiential knowledge of knowing Christ by being yoked with him ("Take my yoke upon you and learn from me" Matt. 11:29) and living in union with him (John 15:4–5). This was Paul's passion for himself (Phil. 3:12–14), and, as we see here, the church at large.

Notice that a significant part of this experiential knowledge comes to individuals by participating in the body, living in community with each other. The focus of this entire passage is the unity and community of the church. Believers will not develop fully as long as individuals hold to a "me and Jesus" piety. Jesus taught us to pray "Our Father," not "My Father."

The focus of this development is spiritual maturity: "and become mature." Paul uses this same term to mean "full-grown" in his letter to the Colossians: "We proclaim him, admonishing and teaching everyone with all wisdom, so that we may present everyone perfect (*teleios*) in Christ" (Col. 1:28). Paul had no thought of church size or numerical growth rate in his plea for the Ephesian church to grow. His emphasis was the maturity of the body which comes as believers are equipped in ministry and united in their faith and knowledge of Christ.

How mature? How mature must the church become? How long do pastor-teachers teach and equip? When can pastor-teachers move on to other matters—"attaining to the whole measure of the fullness of Christ" (Eph. 4:13b). Paul's goal for the church was nothing short of the maturity of Jesus Christ. When the body is united and as mature as the Lord Jesus, then the work of pastor-teachers is complete. Atkinson reflects that the ". . . purpose of the pastor's teaching role is to 'build up' the body of Christ. . . . The pastor is to so nurture and equip the members that [the church] grows as a unified body until it measures up to Christ's standard. This is a continuing process since the church cannot achieve perfection here on earth."[34]

Our present obsession with numerical growth rates and "ten more next Sunday" has dangerous implications for church maturity. When evangelism outruns discipleship, converts' growth in the Lord is stunted. A church filled with carnal Christians cannot fulfill its mission. The church entered the Dark Ages when

---

32. Brady, "The Pastor as Teacher," April 5, 1992.
33. Suhling, "The Pastor as Teacher", April 5, 1992.
34. Atkinson, "The Pastor as Teacher," April 5, 1992.

Constantine made Christianity the state religion of Rome. As hundreds of thousands of soldiers marched along a river bank, priests baptized them into the church by using trees to fling water over them. This provided great numerical growth for the church, but had nothing to do with biblical faith or spiritual maturity. Numerical growth does not necessarily equate with spiritual growth. Spiritual growth is the result of members of the body of Christ serving God through their spiritual gifts. As Atkinson points out, "It is the pastor's responsibility to lead church members to discover their service gift or gifts in order for the church to carry out her ministry."[35] This is not to denigrate evangelism or to retreat from the task of reaching the whole world for Christ. The fact is, though, that the world will be reached only by equipped and mature churches.

Paul's emphasis was maturity, not numerical growth. The result of Paul's personal teaching in Ephesus was missionary activity throughout the region which established churches in Hierapolis, Colossae, and Laodecia.[36] And Paul's emphasis on maturity so changed Asia Minor that some two hundred years later, the pagan temples were largely empty because the pagans had become Christians. The emphasis is growing up in Christ; the effect is healthy numerical growth. To reverse this order, to place emphasis more on numerical growth than the maturing of the church, is to open the church to strife, division, and ruin. Today's emphasis on giving the baby boomer worship consumer what he wants would invite a rebuke from Paul, who wrote to Timothy,

> Preach the Word; be prepared in season and out of season; correct, rebuke and encourage—with great patience and careful instruction. For the time will come when men will not put up with sound doctrine. Instead, to suit their own desires, they will gather around them a great number of teachers to say what their itching ears want to hear. They will turn their ears away from the truth and turn aside to myths. But you, keep your head in all situations, endure hardship, do the work of an evangelist, discharge all the duties of your ministry (2 Tim 4:2–5).

THE RESULTS OF THE WORK OF THE PASTOR-TEACHER

What happens in a congregation that grows according to Paul's pattern? "Then we will no longer be infants, tossed back and forth by the waves, and blown here and there by every wind of teaching and by the cunning and craftiness of men in their

---

35.   Atkinson, "The Pastor as Teacher," April 5, 1992.

36.   "[In the synagogue in Ephesus], in the cool and shadowed interior, [Paul's] congregation sits on little stone benches. Timotheus and Titus and Priscilla have brought them hither. Most of the listeners are Jews, such as have not been frightened away by his strange doctrine, but have, on the contrary, found in it consolation and strength and hope. Some of them have already accepted baptism. There are Ephesians among the listeners, but there are also visitors from towns nearby, merchants who, having heard strange reports of a wonderful message, have come to hear for themselves. They come from Colossae, from Laodecia, and from Hieropolis. What they have heard they will carry forth from Ephesus, even as they carry their merchandise; and as they sell the latter, they will distribute the former. They will found new congregations and churches of believers, which will grow into one great organization with the church of Ephesus as its center." Sholem Asch, *The Apostle* (New York: G. P. Putnam's Sons, 1943), 515–16.

deceitful scheming" (Eph. 4:14). Believers will put away the instability, fickleness, and gullibility that mark the immature. When Paul says we will "no longer be infants," he is attacking the "fickleness of children's volatile moods, shifting like a kaleidoscope, dazzled by the first glittering bauble or flimsy distraction that catches their eye."[37] Such infants are "tossed back and forth by the waves," unstable in their thinking and believing. They are "blown here and there by every wind of teaching," fickle in their convictions and confused by false teaching. They are gullible, swallowing fraudulent claims and deceptive promises by the "cunning and craftiness of men in deceitful scheming." The term "cunning" (*kubia*) refers to playing with dice, trickery, or fraud. This deception is intentional and designed by evil men.[38] "Craftiness" (*panougria*) literally means "readiness to do anything"[39] and implies a trap ("unable to trap him," Luke 20:26, NIV) or being "led astray" (2 Cor. 11:3). "Deceitful scheming" (*methodeia*) has the positive meaning of "handling according to plan," but came to mean "handling craftily, overreaching, deceiving."[40] Paul uses the same term in chapter 6 when he writes "Put on the full armor of God so that you can take your stand against the devil's schemes" (Eph. 6:11). Gary writes,"Pastors who use their gift for instructing the flock in truth and who emphasize discipleship in their ministries will provide protection from heretical teaching. They will help church members examine truth, become settled in the truth, and hold fast to the truth."[41]

Hixon writes, "Many of our people are seduced by false teachers because we, as pastors, have not done our job in growing them up in Christ Jesus. Discipleship is the key to avoiding an infantile ministry."[42]

Suhling believes ". . . the goal of the teacher is spiritual maturity in the believer. If this is not achieved, then the result will be that the believer will be like one who is foolish and inexperienced when it comes to doctrine and practice. Indeed, the immature believer will be like a cork tossed about on rough water[43] or a weathervane at the mercy of a hard uncertain wind[44] when it comes to believing the right teaching."[45]

Washburn summarizes Paul's thrust in this way: "[There is a] popular new approach to churchmanship that strives to appeal to the baby boomer church-shoppers by offering the most exciting and joyous worship product in the community

37. E. K. Simpson, "Commentary on the Epistle of the Ephesians," in *Ephesians and Colossians*, 11–157. *NICNT*, vol. 9 (Grand Rapids: Eerdmans, 1980), 98.
38. Hixon, "The Pastor as Teacher," April 5, 1992.
39. *Greek-English Lexicon of the New Testament and Other Early Christian Literature*, 2nd English ed., Revised and augmented by F. Wilbur Gingrich and Frederick W. Danker from Watler Bauer's 5th ed. (Chicago: University of Chicago Press), 613.
40. TDNT, 5:102.
41. Gary, "The Pastor as Teacher," April 5, 1992.
42. Hixon, "The Pastor as Teacher," April 5, 1992.
43. James Moulton and George Milligan, *The Vocabulary of the Greek New Testament Illustrated from the Papyri and Other Non-Literary Sources* (Grand Rapids: Eerdmans, 1974), 332.
44. *Greek-English Lexicon*, 659.
45. Suhling, "The Pastor as Teacher," April 5, 1992.

market. Laboring to tickle the fancy of the worship experience consumer may fill a pastor's church with warm bodies, but it does little to foster commitment, involvement, and true discipleship."[46]

So what alternative does Paul offer? What is the option? "Instead, speaking the truth in love, we will in all things grow up into him who is the Head, that is, Christ" (Eph. 4:15). Here's the clincher. Here's the definitive word from Paul on church growth: to "grow up into him." Leonard Griffith explains the difference between growing and growing up. "Academic learning leads to knowledge, but not necessarily to maturity. Some adults with high IQ's remain psychologically children. This is the difference between "growing" and "growing up." Is the church seeking only to grow or is it growing up?"[47]

Atkinson notes that this

> . . . may seem idealistic since so few churches have attained such maturity. What may by implied is that too few pastors function as teachers. Whether by misguided expectations of church members or his own misinterpretation of his pastoral role, pastors are not fulfilling their calling as equippers of the saints. By directing qualitative attention to discipleship, a pastor's teaching ministry in the church can lead the church to attain the Lord's intended purpose for his Body, that is, unity and spiritual maturity. . . . Spiritual maturity is the natural result of a biblical understanding of the role of the pastor as teacher.[48]

Gary warns that spiritual growth in the church is hindered if the pastor-teacher is too crowd-oriented. "The pastor should follow Jesus' example of focusing on small groups, and giving in depth training. Jesus never took pride in huge crowds that followed him. He emphasized quality over numbers."[49]

Churches grow up into Christ by "speaking the truth in love" (Eph. 4:15a). The truth that Paul refers to is the gospel, but "speaking the truth" involves much more than saying religious words. Believers cannot speak the truth until they know the truth experientially (*epignosis*). Believers cannot speak the truth effectively until they exercise it in daily living, solving problems biblically. The writer of Hebrews chided his readers on this very point: "We have much to say about this, but it is hard to explain because you are slow to learn. In fact, though by this time you ought to be teachers, you need someone to teach you the elementary truths of God's word all over again. You need milk, not solid food! Anyone who lives on milk, being still an infant, is not acquainted with the teaching about righteousness. But solid food is for the mature, who by constant use have trained themselves to distinguish good from evil" (Heb. 5:11–14).

Those who personally know the Lord and have applied his Word to their lives are well-qualified to speak the truth. But how should the truth be spoken? What

---

46.   Washburn, "The Pastor as Teacher," April 5, 1992.
47.   Leonard Griffith, *Ephesians: A Positive Affirmation* (Waco: Word Books, 1975), 87.
48.   Atkinson, "The Pastor as Teacher," April 5, 1992.
49.   Gary, "The Pastor as Teacher," April 5, 1992.

shall be the manner of our speaking? Paul says believers are to "speak the truth in love." Suhling comments, "Teaching the believer is not a matter of teaching facts in a cold manner. The truth must be modeled and bathed in the warm embrace of Christ-like love."[50]

There are some who know the truth, but have no love. They tend to be mean-spirited, dogmatic, angry people who use "the truth" like a weapon to intimidate others. They have confused personal arrogance with confidence in the Lord. There are others who love, but have little appreciation for "the truth" as objective reality. They tend to be happy-go-lucky, compliant people who just want everyone to be happy and contented. They cannot understand why anyone would want to fight over something as cold and inflexible as "objective truth." They have confused fleshly compromise with the Lord's harmony.

Paul says the truly mature in the Lord speak the truth in love. They speak the truth warmly, carefully, patiently, kindly. They love with integrity, honesty, and sincerity. Warm, not harsh. Caring, not hurting. Lifting, not condemning. This was the manner of Jesus' teaching, fulfilling the prophecy of Isaiah: "A bruised reed he will not break, and a smoldering wick he will not snuff out" (Isa. 42:3; Matt. 12:20). Jesus spoke the truth with love and so should all those who carry his name. Albert Barnes underscored the importance of the balance between truth and love. "[One] has done about half his work in convincing another of error who has first convinced him that he loves him; and if he does not do that he may argue to the hour of his death and make no progress in convincing him."[51] The result, as we have already noted, is that "we will in all things grow up into him who is the Head, that is, Christ" (Eph. 4:15).

And finally, Paul concludes, "From him the whole body, joined and held together by every supporting ligament, grows and builds itself up in love, as each part does its work" (Eph. 4:16). The body grows because of Christ ("from him"). The body strengthens itself ("grows and builds itself up") by being held together, unified. This is an ongoing process. How is this accomplished? By having "each part of the body function properly in its own sphere."[52]

The pastor-teacher must focus on building relationships among the members of his congregation. These relationships, says Brady, "must be genuine relationships built on honest loving communication that builds a team that works together."[53] Washburn writes, "As the pastor-teacher focuses himself on preparing God's peo-

---

50. Suhling, "The Pastor as Teacher," April 5, 1992.

51. Albert Barnes, *Barnes on the New Testament: Ephesians, Philippians and Colossians* (Grand Rapids: Baker Book House, 1949), 82.

52. Robertson, 539.

53. Brady, "The Pastor as Teacher," April 5, 1992.

ple individually, lovingly, encouragingly, the body of Christ that he serves will build 'itself' up into the fullness of Christ our Lord."[54]

THE CHALLENGE OF THE PASTOR-TEACHER

Paul finally described the challenge that pastor-teachers face as they endeavor to fulfill their task: hardened Gentiles. These pagans had hardened their hearts toward God, causing them to be separated from life in him. They could not fathom what life in the Lord might mean, because they had been darkened in their understanding (Eph. 4:18). Because they had lost all sensitivity for spiritual things, they indulged themselves in every kind of sensual impurity. But their indulging did not satisfy them, so they became lost in an ever-increasing cycle of continual lust for more (Eph. 4:19). "So I tell you this, and insist on it in the Lord, that you must no longer live as the Gentiles do" (Eph. 4:17).

The community where you serve or will serve as pastor-teacher is populated with the same kind of sensual, self-serving Gentiles that lived in Ephesus. American culture is Greek in that Americans tend to compartmentalize their lives into separate areas: home and family, work, school, recreation, friends. American Christians add the compartment of "church," but many fail to see the connection between what they say and do at church and the other compartments of life. These carnal Christians have not yet grown into a biblical mind-set in which the Lord is at the center of life—where all of life revolves around him. So, just as in Corinth and Ephesus, sexual perversion, violence, abuse, and petty power plays face pastor-teachers at every turn. False teachers, magicians, and mesmerizers feed on the church, often from within the body itself. Greek compartmentalization is common in churches, dividing the body into self-serving blocks of power—Sunday school, missions, music, age groups, deacons, committees, and special interests. Pastor-teachers who emphasize unity of the whole body can be perceived as self-serving. The logic of turf protectors[55] goes like this: "Leaders who won't promote my interests over the interests of other groups are really acting against me." If many lay leaders fall prey to this line of reasoning, there is no way pastor-teachers can succeed. They are always seen as self-serving by one group or another. This fragmentation literally pulls leaders to pieces as each part demands attention and promotion over the others, and attacks leaders when their demands are not satisfied. The church grows increasingly unteachable as Satan builds a wedge between pastor-teachers and the body. This is why the writer of Hebrews cautioned the church, "Obey your leaders and submit to

---

54.   Steve Washburn, "The Pastor as Teacher," April 5, 1992.
55.   "Turf protectors" are leaders who use whatever power they have to promote their agenda, their organization, their committee, their class—to the detriment of others and the fragmentation of the church. Some do this unintentionally and may consider themselves nothing more than committed workers. Others use their organizations as a means of promoting their own ego and widening their influence.

their authority. They keep watch over you as men who must give an account. Obey them so that their work will be a joy, not a burden, for that would be of no advantage to you" (Heb. 13:17).

This is in no way a license for pastor-teachers to lord it over the body. Jesus' directive stands: "You know that the rulers of the Gentiles lord it over them, and their high officials exercise authority over them. Not so with you. Instead, whoever wants to become great among you must be your servant, and whoever wants to be first must be your slave" (Matt. 20:25–27).

Peter further underscores this principle: "Be shepherds of God's flock that is under your care . . . not lording it over those entrusted to you, but being examples to the flock" (1 Pet. 5:2–3).

When leaders function as true pastor-teachers rather than self-serving tyrants, and when the congregation submits to the leadership of the pastor-teacher rather than assuming ill motives behind every move, then the body is free to progress. But such an ideal state is seldom achieved for very long. Satan "prowls around like a roaring lion looking for someone to devour" (1 Pet. 5:8b). Misunderstandings, rumors, and malicious perceptions persist even under the best pastor-teachers. Therefore, Peter warns us to be "self-controlled and alert" (1 Pet. 5:8a).

So, as with the Ephesians, Paul tells us to "put on the full armor of God, so that when the day of evil comes, you may be able to stand your ground, and after you have done everything, to stand" (Eph. 6:13).

CONCLUDING REMARKS FROM PASTORS

The pastors and missionaries in the recent Doctor of Ministry educational psychology seminar made significant discoveries in their study of the ministry of the pastor-teacher in Ephesians 4. Many of these have been shared in this chapter. Below are some concluding comments made by several class members. These are shared in lengthy quotes because you need to hear the heart of these experienced pastors.

David Hixon:

> We want our congregations to respond and often we want them to change their system of values. This can only happen through a long-term commitment to the teaching of individuals. The pastor who follows the steps of Jesus must be willing to commit to years of service with the same people.
>
> My suggestions for doing this are:
>
> 1. Make sermons didactic as well as prophetic.
>
> 2. Consider the needs of congregation in preparing sermons.
>
> 3. Clearly explain biblical concepts and practical applications.

4. Model the attitudes and values you wish to convey.

5. Build relationships with your congregation and live out the truth together.

6. Focus on Christian actions to be done as a result of preaching.

7. Help the congregation to discover answers for themselves.

8. Use small groups, when possible, for discussion and participation.

9. Focus on individuals within the congregation.

Let us not wake up one day to discover with regret that our years of labor were invested in vain because we neglected the ministry of teaching and discipling our congregations. God will hold us accountable for their lack of understanding and lack of spiritual growth which will result from our failure to train them as we should.[56]

Dennis Suhling:

The major thrust of these passages is clear. The pastor must be prepared to teach the Word of God clearly and accurately. The life and growth of a local congregation very much depends on it. The unity and harmony of a local congregation will be maintained only as the teacher or teachers equip the saints for the work of service. Ultimately this causes the spiritual growth of the individual in Christ and it causes the physical and spiritual growth of the congregation as a whole.

It is my observation that all too many churches have pastors who are not willing to pay the price to not only teach the Scriptures, but train the saints to do the work of ministry.

Unity is attained because the saints are equipped. This means more than just lecturing. Jesus not only lectured; he put the disciples into real life situations to test what they learned. As with Christ, pastors must be more concerned with building great men and women of God than building great churches. Indeed, as this passage teaches, as the individual comes to maturity in Christ the church will grow both in numbers and spiritually. Each believer must understand that they are important to God and to every other member. If one ligament is weak and can no longer hold, the whole body suffers!

Finally, this passage has a real sense of reaching goals. In the beginning of Jesus' ministry, He expressed the goal for the next three years of his life (Luke 4:18–21). On the cross he proclaimed, "it is finished." In Ephesians 4:11–16 the goal of the pastor and teacher is clearly outlined: to teach others, Christ in you the hope of glory![57]

John Brady:

There are several hindrances to the discipling process:

56.   Hixon, "The Pastor as Teacher," April 5, 1992.
57.   Suhling, "The Pastor as Teacher," April 5, 1992.

1. The demand that the process quickly produce the product. But the complexity of human learning insures that no strict timetable can be followed.

2. Church expectations that the pastor be the one who gets things going. A congregation should work more like a family than a corporation.

3. Contrast between authority and leadership. Often pastors assume authority that hurts the discipling process. This type of authority demands obedience to the person in authority and undermines the process of empowerment because the goal is not maturing the disciple. On the other hand, leadership inspires the person to follow but places the burden for the growth on the disciple who must choose to follow. Franklin Segler draws the contrast:

   "Servant leadership enables, persuades, encourages, and unites God's people (*laos*) to fulfill the mission to which He has called them. Authority leadership deceives, intimidates, denigrates, and divides God's people, thus hindering the free and willing ministry their giftedness could make possible."[58]

   This does not mean that the Christian is under no authority. It means that authority supremely belongs to God and he exercises it through his living Word (Christ), his written Word (Bible) and his Holy Spirit who guides and teaches his people. The teaching shepherd lets the authority work in his life and thus inspires others to do the same.

4. Deadening effect of ritual. Religious ritual comes when we quit living in the power of the Spirit and start living by our own strength. This turns off the discipling process.[59]

ARE ALL MINISTERS PASTOR-TEACHERS?

This chapter has focused on those called by God to be undershepherd, or pastor, of a local congregation. But there are lessons here for any who are called to lead or teach in the church—whether they be vocational or lay ministers, ordained or not.

Ministers of education are called to work with churches' educational programs. But the effective minister of education will minister as a pastor-teacher, protecting his educational flock and teaching workers at all levels of leadership how to use their gifts more effectively. Ministers of music, youth, children, counseling, or recreation can all benefit from Paul's view of the pastor-teacher. Our first calling is to minister: to protect and instruct. Then comes our area of specialization.

All leaders in the church—deacons, Sunday school teachers, committee chairs, or program directors—would serve more effectively if they saw themselves as pastor-teachers of the groups they lead. The church grows stronger as lay pastor-teachers learn how to give and take with other leaders in the church. As each leader emphasizes the whole above his or her own small area, he or she becomes a "supporting ligament" that helps the whole to be built up (Eph. 4:16). Turf protectors

---

58. Franklin Segler, "Theological Foundations for Ministry," *SwJT* 29 (Spring 1987), 15.
59. Brady, "The Pastor as Teacher," April 5, 1992.

care only for their own areas and use whatever means to build them up, even to the detriment of other areas and the whole. This is the work of the flesh ("selfish ambition, dissensions, factions," Gal. 5:20) born in the heart of Satan to hinder the Lord's work through his churches.

In light of the rampant "me-first" philosophy in our society, the greatest challenge facing pastor-teachers today is helping lay leaders understand the destructiveness of self-serving turf, and leading believers to love one another in the practical day-to-day life of the church.

SUMMARY

Paul laid out the character, the work, and the fruit of the pastor-teacher—as to character, becoming like Christ; as to work, enabling believers to minister by winning them, protecting them and instructing them; as to fruit, spiritual maturity in learners particularly and in the church at large.

And so we complete Paul's treatise on healthy church growth, the goal of the pastor-teacher. Healthy church growth can be defined as: believers, equipped to work together in the ministry, carrying out the great commission, reaching their world for Christ, and "teaching them to obey everything" Jesus commanded (Matt. 28:20). It also involves churches living out the truth of the gospel in loving ministry and devoid of petty strife or division, because leaders and those being led are growing together into Christ.

A navigator guides an ocean liner to a distant port and back again by taking bearings from the North Star. The ship never reaches the star, but it does reach home safely. So Paul has given us a North Star for pastor-teachers to navigate congregations toward healthy church growth. We may never reach the ideal he has given us. But by properly charting our course, we can avoid the shallow reefs of immaturity, the storms of sensuality, and the tidal waves of conflict and division. Thus, we can make our way safely home, becoming congregations that possess the qualities of Jesus, sharing those qualities in ministry with one another, the local community, and the world at large. Oh, Lord Jesus, make it so!

FOR FURTHER STUDY

1. What is your reaction to the description of the pastor-teacher given in this chapter? How does Paul's model of the pastor-teacher compare to "secular" models of leadership?

2. Discuss the importance of perseverance in the ministry of the pastor-teacher. How is perseverance related to the pastor-teacher's goal?

3. Compare your view of teaching to Paul's view of teaching. How would others describe your teaching?

4. What will your ministry look like in ten years if you follow your current pattern of leadership? What suggestions from the pastors quoted speak to your need to grow as a pastor-teacher?

SUGGESTED READING

Barclay, William. *The Mind of St. Paul*. London: Collins Clear-Type Press, 1958.

Browning, R. L. *The Pastor as Religious Educator*. Birmingham: Religious Education Press, 1989.

Dobbins, Gaines S. *A Ministering Church*. Nashville: Broadman, 1960.

Forsyth, Nathaniel F., ed. *The Minister and Christian Nurture*. Nashville: Abingdon, 1957.

Glen, Stanley J. *The Recovery of the Teaching Ministry*. Philadelphia: Westminster Press, 1960.

Hull, Bill. *The Disciple Making Pastor*. Old Tappan, N. J.: Fleming H. Revell, 1988.

Shelp, Earl E. and Ronald H. Sunderland. *The Pastor as Teacher*. New York: Pilgrim Press, 1988.

CHAPTER 9

THE GOAL OF CHRISTIAN TEACHING: CHRISTLIKENESS

—RICK YOUNT

> Brothers, I do not consider myself yet to have taken hold of it. But one thing I do: Forgetting what is behind and straining toward what is ahead, I press on toward the goal to win the prize for which God has called me heavenward in Christ Jesus. All of us who are mature should take such a view of things. And if on some point you think differently, that too God will make clear to you. Only let us live up to what we have already attained (Phil. 3:13–16).

To be like Christ. What a goal! Strong but gentle. Just but loving. Truthful but merciful. Demanding but accepting. No one has blended the rod and the staff so well. Even Paul, given to religious devotion as much as any man of his time, fully committed to the exalted Christ who saved him and called him as an apostle to the Gentiles, strained to grow toward Christlikeness. We are in a journey, says Paul. I'm more like the Lord today than yesterday. I press on to be more like him tomorrow. But in the process, Paul says, live up to what you've attained.

To lead others to be like Christ. What a calling! Christian teachers are far more than transmitters of lessons from quarterly to class. Our calling is to help learners grow toward Christlikeness. Paul writes of Christ: "We proclaim him, admonishing and teaching everyone with all wisdom, so that we may present everyone perfect in Christ. To this end I labor, struggling with all his energy, which so powerfully works in me" (Col. 1:28–29).

Oh, we'll spend plenty of time with commentaries and notes and illustrations and stories and examples. But the end product of our teaching in Christ is nothing short of Christlikeness in our learners. How do we begin? How do we proceed? How do

141

we know if we're making progress? These are the issues of the chapter before us. My prayer is that it will challenge you to the very core of your calling as a teacher and minister. We'll begin with three common approaches to teaching that hinder growth in Christ.

TEACHING APPROACHES THAT HINDER GROWTH TOWARD CHRISTLIKENESS

The following three approaches to teaching the Bible hinder growth in the Lord because they put the emPHAsis on the wrong sylLAble. Teachers who use these approaches may neglect the life issues of learners, very real and practical issues that lie at the heart of transforming teaching. The message of this chapter will be clarified if we dispense with these approaches in the beginning.

CENTERED ON THE LESSON

Some teachers frequently talk about "the lesson." A lesson refers to the assigned passage of study and accompanying commentary for a given Bible study session. Teachers study the lesson in preparation for teaching. For some, this means reading over the quarterly on the way to church. For others, studying the lesson means spending hours in commentaries, gathering additional information about the passage. For still others, it means rehearsing one of the suggested teaching plans. But all of these teachers view Christian teaching as presenting the lesson. They talk of "good lessons" and "bad lessons," referring to the packets of facts contained in the teachers' quarterly they feel obliged to talk through.

Too much emphasis on the lesson can mislead teachers. Review Jesus' emphasis in chapter 2: the people we teach are more important than lessons. Overemphasis on the lesson crowds out the real life issues bombarding our learners.

> John taught a young married class. Suzie came into the classroom just as the session began. As John moved into his introduction, Suzie began to weep quietly to herself. John noticed her distress and said, "Suzie, is there something wrong?"
>
> Suzie quietly said, "No, nothing."
>
> John believed her, and went on with his lesson!
>
> Toward the end of the session, Suzie became more visibly distressed. Tears streaked her cheeks. Now even a man knows there's something wrong when a woman has tears running down her cheeks! So he said to her, "Suzie, I can see you're upset this morning. Would you like to tell us what's wrong? Is there anything we can do?"
>
> Suzie summoned her courage and said in a broken voice, "Tom and I had our first fight this morning! He wouldn't come to church with me. And I don't know what to do!"

John thought for a moment and said, "Gee, Suzie, I wish we had time to discuss this—but I have five more verses to cover." Which he then proceeded to do. The lesson that morning was entitled "Ministry One Toward Another."

Five more verses on "Ministry One Toward Another." He had more concern for his lesson than for Suzie. The folks in his class would have learned far more about ministry if he'd put aside those five verses and helped the class minister to Suzie and Tom. He could have easily picked up the five verses the next Sunday. Teaching that's focused primarily on the lesson will not be focused on learners. The result? The teacher actually hampers the learners' spiritual growth.

CENTERED ON THE TEACHER

It is natural for teachers to give attention to what they will do in class. How will I begin? What verses will I explain? What questions will I ask? What assignments will I make? How will I explain this term? How will I challenge the class to put the Bible into action?

Take a moment to read back through these questions. As you read, circle the "I" words. Too much emPHAsis on the teacher sylLAble. Begin here, yes. But teachers must move beyond their personal concerns to the concerns of the learners in the class. What do *they* need to consider as you begin a session? What verses do *they* need to have explained? What questions will reveal *their* understanding? What assignments will help *them* put Bible principles into practice? What will challenge *them* to carry these truths into their workaday world?

There is a darker side to this sylLAble. Teachers who focus primarily on themselves inevitably become self-centered. A good lesson is the one I like. A bad lesson is one I don't like. I teach what interests me. I tell my stories. I give my explanations. Please don't ask questions because it takes my teaching time. I have my soapboxes to parade. Don't embarrass me. Don't challenge my views. You sit still while I instill. If the lighter side of teacher-focus hinders growth, the darker side will literally drive people away.

Joan's approach to teaching was the same—Sunday after Sunday. She would call on a class member and ask, "Will you read verse one?" After the member read, she would ask, "What do you think that verse means?" After a few stumbling remarks from the member, Joan would say, "Okay, here's what the quarterly says . . ." and proceed to give her view. This procedure was followed around the room, one person per verse, until she ran out of time. "All right, that's all our time today. See you next Sunday, and bring a friend!"

One day a visitor came to class. When it came her turn to read a verse, she read from the Revised Standard Version, the only Bible she had. Joan had studied from the King James, and had planned to talk about one of the words in the text. But the word wasn't in the Revised Standard Version! (The concept was there, but the RSV used a different word to express it.) Joan panicked. What will I do? I'm not prepared to talk about that word! I'm so embarrassed! But what came out of her mouth was, "Oh, somebody with the good kind of Bible read that verse for us."

The visitor never returned. And the class slowly withered under her self-centered teaching.

Joan cared more about herself than this lady visitor. She was more worried about being embarrassed than embarrassing someone else. Had she prepared properly, she could have discussed the concept behind the "word"—whether from King James or Revised Standard. Teaching that's focused primarily on the teacher will not be focused on learners. The result? Hampered spiritual growth in the class.

CENTERED ON OPINION

How do we move away from teacher-focus toward learner-focus? We need to involve learners more: ask questions, use small groups to do Scripture searches, call for testimonies and personal experiences. But there are dangers here as well. Unless the answers to our questions are biblically correct, unless the learning in the small groups is evaluated from a biblical point of view, unless the personal experiences are grounded in the truth, Bible study may deteriorate into sharing opinions. Human voices may well drown out God's voice. Class opinion may influence learning more than God's Word.

There is definitely a place for personal sharing in Bible study, as we'll discuss shortly. Sharing testimonies and opinions helps learners remove their religious masks and become more real. But if our goal is growing to be like the Lord, we cannot stop there. There is more to Bible study than discovering what the passage "means to me." Walt Russell[1] makes the distinction between the "meaning of the text" (What does it mean?) and the "relevance of the text" (What does it mean to me?). Many teachers confuse these two questions. Russell uses the following dialogue to underscore the problem:

Teacher: So Paul says in verse 14 that, because of his chains, others have been encouraged. What do you think he means?

Learner 1: Oh, I know. Paul's writing a letter, right? So this is a chain letter, like the one I just got!

Learner 2: No, no, you're missing the point! I'm a chain smoker, and God is speaking to me through this to tell me I am to encourage other chain smokers!

Learner 3: Well, it reminds me of that Aretha Franklin song, "Chain of Fools." Maybe Paul means we're fools for Christ!

Teacher: Ummm . . . those are . . . very interesting insights . . . But do you think Paul could simply be referring to his prison chains, in Rome?

Learner 2 to Learner 3: I told you this Bible study wasn't about practical living.

Learner 3: "R-E-S-P-E-C-T" is another Aretha song that ministers to me.[2]

---

1.   Walt Russell, "What It Means to Me," *Christianity Today* (October 26, 1992), 30–32.
2.   Ibid.

Teaching that's focused primarily on opinion will not be focused on the truth that learners need to navigate their real-life issues. The result? Hampered spiritual growth in the class.

Do we need to focus on the meaning of Scripture? Of course. But too much focus on the lesson can hinder spiritual growth. Do we need to give attention to how we will teach? Of course. But too much focus on the teacher can hinder spiritual growth. Do we need to focus on the thoughts and experiences of our learners? Of course. But too much focus on opinion and personal experience can hinder spiritual growth.

How, then, do we teach so that our learners will grow in the Lord? What can we do to lead our learners toward Christlikeness? The answers can be illustrated in the triad of human life.

THE TRIAD OF HUMAN LIFE

The three intersecting circles represent three areas of human life. Each circle is independent of the other two. Each circle can be any size. Figure 9.1 represents an ideal balance: all three circles are the same size, and all three intersect equally. The three areas of human life represented by this triad are what I think, how I feel, and what I do. Let's look at each of these.

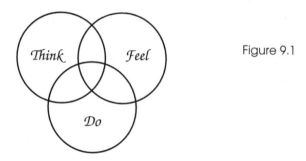

Figure 9.1

WHAT I THINK

The first circle represents the rational side of life: knowing, conceptualizing, problem-solving, analyzing, synthesizing, evaluating. Without a clear focus on "correctly handl[ing] the word of truth" (2 Tim. 2:15), we open ourselves and our learners to deception and delusion.

John 3:16 says "For God so *loved* the world that he gave his one and only Son, that whoever believes in him shall not perish but have eternal life." What did God do when he loved the world? And who is the world that he loved? What does it mean to *believe* in his Son? What kind of life do we obtain through this belief? And what does *eternal* add to this life?

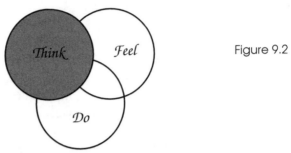

Figure 9.2

Jesus said, "Do not judge, or you too will be judged" (Matt. 7:1). What did Jesus mean by "judge"? Are we not to have an opinion? Are we to go through life without evaluating our teachers and preachers? No. John writes, "Dear friends, do not believe every spirit, but test the spirits to see whether they are from God, because many false prophets have gone out into the world" (1 John 4:1). So what did Jesus mean?

I grew up singing the hymn "Come Thou Fount of Every Blessing." I love that hymn, even the second verse, which begins with "Here I raise my Ebenezer." But it wasn't until I began interpreting our worship services for deaf people that I ever asked myself what an "Ebenezer" is! The answer is found in 1 Samuel 7:12 where Samuel builds an altar of thanksgiving to God and names it "Ebenezer, saying, 'Thus far has the LORD helped us.'" The second phrase of the hymn captures this very meaning: "hither by Thy help I'm come." I've always loved to sing the hymn, but until I studied the meaning of the words I didn't understand what I was singing!

If our learners are to grow in the Lord, they must go beyond simplistic facts and pat answers. They must go beyond words to meanings. For unless these learners understand what Paul meant when he wrote under inspiration of Holy Spirit, they will never make proper application of God's message to their own lives. We will not grow up into Christ (Eph. 4:15) without a clear understanding of what God's Word means.

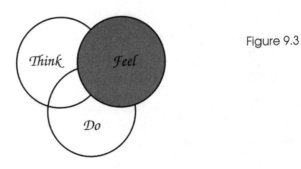

Figure 9.3

The second circle represents the emotional or affective side of life: feelings, attitudes, values, and priorities. If the rational represents what we think (our "head"), we might consider the affective representing what we value (our "heart"). Actually, the biblical use of "heart" involves the entire triad: mind, emotion, actions, and will. But often the Bible uses the term heart to refer to the affective elements of life. "A happy heart makes the face cheerful, but heartache crushes the spirit" (Prov. 15:13) refers to feeling happy or depressed.

Several passages refer to proper values or commitments. "Only be careful, and watch yourselves closely so that you do not forget the things your eyes have seen or let them slip from your heart as long as you live. Teach them to your children and to their children after them" (Deut. 4:9). "From your heart," not "from your head." The command was for Israel to value what the Lord had done. Or, another, "I have *hidden your word in my heart* that I might not sin against you" (Ps. 119:11). The writer had made a commitment to live by God's Word. Finally, John writes, "Blessed is the one who reads the words of this prophecy, and blessed are those who hear it and take to heart [i.e., value] what is written in it, because the time is near" (Rev. 1:3).

Still other passages use the term "heart" to refer to proper priorities in living. "Whatever you do, work at it with all your heart, as working for the Lord, not for men" (Col. 3:23). Or another, "But if from there you seek the LORD your God, you will find him if you look for him with all your heart and with all your soul" (Deut. 4:29). Or another, "There is, however, some good in you, for you have rid the land of the Asherah poles and have set your heart on seeking God" (2 Chr. 19:3). Then again:

> Hilkiah and those the king had sent with him went to speak to the prophetess Huldah. . . . She lived in Jerusalem, in the Second District.
> She said to them, "This is what the LORD, the God of Israel, says: Tell the man who sent you to me, 'This is what the LORD says: I am going to bring disaster on this place and its people—all the curses written in the book that has been read in the presence of the king of Judah. Because they have forsaken me and burned incense to other gods and provoked me to anger by all that their hands have made, my anger will be poured out on this place and will not be quenched.'
> Tell the king of Judah, who sent you to inquire of the LORD, 'This is what the LORD, the God of Israel, says concerning the words you heard: Because your *heart was responsive* and you humbled yourself before God when you heard what he spoke against this place and its people, and because you humbled yourself before me and tore your robes and wept in my presence, I have heard you, declares the LORD. Now I will gather you to your fathers, and you will be buried in peace. Your eyes will not see all the disaster I am going to bring on this place and on those who live here.'"
> So they took her answer back to the king (2 Chron. 34:22–28).

If our learners are to grow in the Lord, we must help them personalize Bible truths. They must move from doctrine to lifestyle. For unless these learners value what Jesus said, they will never put his words into practice. We do not grow up into Christ (Eph. 4:15) without personal commitment to live according to God's Word.

WHAT I DO

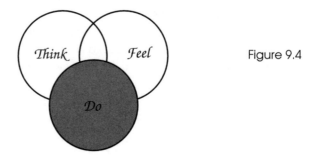

Figure 9.4

The third circle represents the behavioral or action side of life. We may have the greatest understanding of "love," but do we love? We may value missions but do we support missions with our time, talent, or money? We can believe "with all our hearts" in forgiveness, but do we forgive? What I do with my life, what I do in my life, is a window of who I am. Jesus said, "Watch out for false prophets. They come to you in sheep's clothing, but inwardly they are ferocious wolves. By their fruit you will recognize them. Do people pick grapes from thornbushes, or figs from thistles? Likewise every good tree bears good fruit, but a bad tree bears bad fruit" (Matt. 7:15–17). Furthermore, "Make a tree good and its fruit will be good, or make a tree bad and its fruit will be bad, for a tree is recognized by its fruit" (Matt. 12:33).

Jesus underscored the importance of doing this way: "Therefore everyone who hears these words of mine and puts them into practice is like a wise man who built his house on the rock. The rain came down, the streams rose, and the winds blew and beat against that house; yet it did not fall, because it had its foundation on the rock. But everyone who hears these words of mine and does not put them into practice is like a foolish man who built his house on sand. The rain came down, the streams rose, and the winds blew and beat against that house, and it fell with a great crash" (Matt. 7:24–27).

The day I realized what Jesus was saying in this passage, I got down on my knees and asked his forgiveness for the many times I had "taught the Bible" but never given a hint to my learners how they might live out its precious truths. I was sending them out as fools, not wise.

What is the work of the pastor-teacher? "To prepare God's people for works of service, so that the body of Christ may be built up" (Eph. 4:12). Preparing involves teaching people to think correctly (head). Preparing requires personal commitment to the task (heart). But the proof, the verification, the witness, the confirmation that true preparation has been made is in the service, in the ministry, in the doing of what God has called his people to do.

THE DISTORTION OF IMBALANCE

The problem, of course, is that we are called to prepare *people*. People do not come to us prepackaged and preequipped to serve. They do not come spin-balanced and ready to roll. Every person tends toward one of the three elements of the triad. Some emphasize the rational, others the emotional, and still others the behavioral. But imbalance in life, just as in wheels, causes vibration and eventual breakdown. Let's look at the consequences of imbalance.

Intellectualism. Learners who emphasize the rational over emotional or behavioral elements are thinkers. They like theologically sound hymns rather than foot-tappin' choruses. They prefer factual and conceptual questions over personal ones. They tend to like well-organized lectures more than group discussion—particularly if the group emphasizes people's feelings and personal experiences more than the Scripture.

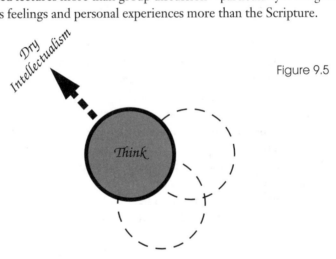

Figure 9.5

The problem with this emphasis is that it can result in a Bible study which is purely academic. When we focus on the rational to the exclusion of the emotional and behavioral, we open ourselves to a dry, impersonal, abstract head knowledge that makes little or no difference in our lives. It is one thing to understand honesty, but quite another to be honest. One thing to understand the plan of salvation, quite another to be saved. One thing to understand Matthew 28:19–20, quite another to support and engage in missions. Bible knowledge, doctrinal understanding, Christian principles, and spiritual concepts will lead to spiritual pride unless we integrate them into our own lifestyles (1 Cor. 8:1–3).

Emotionalism. Learners who emphasize the emotional over rational or behavioral elements are feelers. They focus on feelings, attitudes, values, and personal experiences. They prefer free-wheeling discussions over structured lectures. They enjoy giving testimonies and hearing the testimonies of others. They are easily bored with explanations of terms or historical background; they're eager to move into personal application.

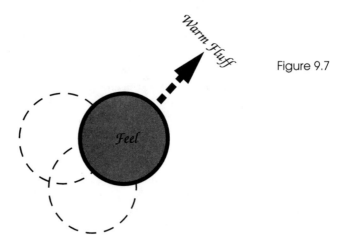

Figure 9.7

The problem with this emphasis is that it can result in a Bible study that is purely subjective. The Bible means what it means *to me*. "What does it matter what I believe so long as it feels right?" What feels right, however, may not be right. My self-centered speculations about what Jesus meant may not be what he meant. When we focus on the emotional to the exclusion of the behavioral and rational, we open ourselves to deception and delusion.

Burnout. Learners who emphasize the behavioral over rational or emotional elements are doers. They prefer to be involved in various activities and projects, mission programs and organizations. Their study tends toward the utilitarian—"What are we going to do with this? How can we use it?"

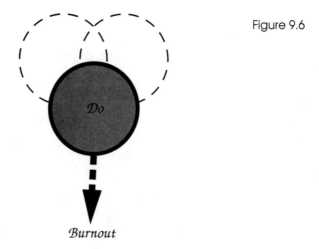

Figure 9.6

The problem with this emphasis is that it can result in an approach to Bible study that leads to busyness, overwork, and eventually, exhaustion. Without understanding the why of ministry, without personally owning the ministry, we simply go through the motions until we burn out and give up.

So here is our dilemma as teachers and teacher-trainers: an effective teaching ministry requires thinking, but too much focus on thinking leads to a cold, idealistic intellectualism. An effective teaching ministry requires positive feelings toward the class, the content, and the teacher, but too much focus on feelings leads to mindless, sentimental, impractical fluff. An effective teaching ministry requires doing, but too much focus on doing leads to mindless, unfeeling ritual.

What's the answer? The answer to this dilemma is to balance the rational, emotional, and behavioral elements of our own Christian growth as teachers as well as our teaching. Develop biblical concepts, embrace Christian values, engage in spiritual activities. Proper understanding provides the foundation for biblical values and ministry. Personally embraced biblical values inject life into biblical exegesis and practice. Christ-centered ministry builds the bridge between Bible study (concepts and values) and the world of people in need.

THE TRIAD OF JESUS THE TEACHER

Jesus reflected this triad of rational, emotional, and behavioral elements in his ministry. Jesus was a prophet (Matt. 13:57; Matt. 21:11; Luke 24:19; John 6:14), proclaiming the kingdom of God. He used stories and illustrations to explain the kingdom of heaven. He represented God the Father to the people and proclaimed the Word of God. As prophet, Jesus focused on the objective element of faith.

Jesus was a priest (Heb. 3:1; 4:14). He loved people and gave his life for others. He healed their sicknesses and calmed their fears. He ministered to them. He moved among the people and lifted them to the Father. As priest, Jesus focused on the subjective element of faith.

Jesus was king (Mark 15:2; Luke 23:3; John 18:37; Acts 17:7). He chose twelve apprentices and trained them for action (Matt. 10). He sent his followers into the whole world to "make disciples of all nations, baptizing them . . . and teaching them to obey everything I have commanded you" (Matt. 28:19–20). He is our Leader, our Lord. He calls us to action (Matt. 5–7; John 17:20) and taught that our fruit (actions) exhibits our roots (concepts, values) (Matt. 7:16–17). Our spiritual wisdom is shown in how we practice his words—not by how well we understand them or value them (Matt. 7:24–27).

Jesus demonstrated in his teaching ministry and life, the balance we raise as our standard. He is our model, our guide, and our helper as we seek to emulate this balance in our own life and ministry.

The External Influence of the Teacher

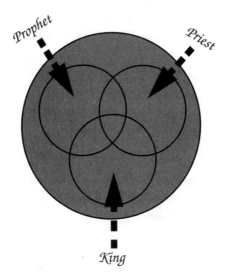

Figure 9.8

THE CHRISTIAN TEACHER'S TRIAD

How do we provide a learning environment that permits balanced growth in the rational, emotional, and behavioral elements of life? How do we help learners think? Or feel? Or put into practice? Here are some practical suggestions.

HELPING LEARNERS THINK

A little boy sat in his Sunday school class listening to his teacher intently. She asked, "What is gray, has a furry tail, and stores nuts for the winter?" The little boy thought for a moment and then said, "Well, it sounds like a squirrel—but I'll say Jesus Christ." He was not being irreverent. He was doing his best to answer the teacher's question. And it seemed to him that "Jesus Christ" was the answer to most of her questions.

How can we help our learners to think clearly? We will do well if we focus on the meaning of concepts, ask questions, pose problems, and share examples. Let's look more closely at each of these.

Concepts versus words. Take a moment and write down eight definitions of the word "run." (It will mean more to you if you stop reading and do this exercise first.) Here are some sentences which use various meanings of the word "run":

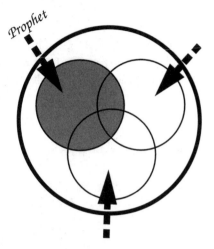

Figure 9.9

- Johnny runs (moves swiftly) to second base.

- Judy runs (manages) her business well.

- Tim runs (operates) the printing press well.

- Jane has a run (defect) in her hose.

- Peter's team scored a run (score) in the second inning.

- Water always runs (flows) downhill.

- The congressman ran (campaigned) for office.

- Fido was kept in a nice dog run (an outdoor enclosure).

The word is singular: "run." The meanings are multiple: move swiftly, manage, operate, and reflect the concepts referenced by the word "run."

Earlier in this chapter I asked you several questions about Jesus' statement, "Do not judge, or you too will be judged" (Matt. 7:1). Jesus was condemning the nagging, carping, censorious spirit of the Pharisees and religious leaders of his time. He was saying that when we live with a judgmental spirit, we will be criticized by others. Citizens of the kingdom are to avoid the hyper-critical, judgmental spirit of religious bigotry. It is not enough to say, "Jesus said, 'Don't judge.'" Unless you explain what Jesus meant by judge, you leave your learners to define the word for him. Their definition of "judge" may not agree with Jesus' definition.

Here is the danger of focusing on words rather than concepts. What do the words mean? One day a seminary student of mine led the class in a Bible study on the fruit of the Spirit (Gal. 5:21–22). He explained "joy" this way: "Joy is another one of the fruits of the Spirit. Joy is the kind of joy that only God can give. It's the kind of joy we'll experience in heaven. Ohhhh. The joy of the Lord is wonderful!"

Sorry. But this student didn't have a clue about the meaning of "joy." He talked about it, said nice words about it, said the words with deep feeling. But in terms of explanation, his words were empty.

Joy is similar to the concepts of fun, pleasure, and happiness. In fact, some Christians mistakenly believe that biblical joy means fun or happiness—most wouldn't use pleasure as a synonym for joy because it's a worldly term. All of these terms are emotional. The distinction is that joy is unrelated to life circumstances; fun, pleasure, and happiness are all tied to the circumstances of life. I discover joy in the dark times of my life when I depend on the Lord rather than on circumstances. As I lean on him, he produces a sense of overwhelming joy by his Spirit.

Focus on Bible meanings, concepts, and principles. Don't stop with knowing words. You may be reading your own definitions of these words into Scripture, and then reading out of Scripture your own ideas. This is eisegesis (reading into) rather than exegesis (reading out of) and it is heresy!

Questions versus answers. You will help your learners think by asking more questions and giving fewer answers. When you give an answer, it may be little more than noise in the air because your learners haven't invested any brainpower in it. In one ear and out the other. Forgotten by Monday lunch. But when you ask a question, you drive learners into the Bible for answers. You confront them with a dilemma: they must process facts, develop concepts, relate those concepts to your question, and formulate an answer. Along the way they may develop questions of their own— a sure sign that thinking is taking place! How do they answer? Mold their responses into clear understanding. Help them discover God's answers to your questions. Ask more questions and give fewer answers.

Posing problems versus giving reasons. You will help learners think more by posing problems than by giving reasons. Giving five reasons why Christians ought to forgive will do less to develop an understanding of "forgiveness" than confronting them with problems that can be solved by a forgiving spirit. "Here's a case study. Based on our study this morning, how would you handle it?" Listen to their answers. Correct misunderstandings. Suggest alternatives. Lead the class to see the relevance of "forgiveness" in a contemporary situation.

Examples versus facts. Love is patient, kind; it does not envy, boast; it is not proud, rude, self-seeking, easily angered; it keeps no record of wrongs; does not delight in evil but rejoices with the truth (see 1 Cor. 13:4–6). These are the facts of love. What do they *mean?* What is an example of patient, kind? Illustrate envy and boasting. Explain proud, rude, self-seeking, and easily angered. How might I keep a record of wrongs? Why would anyone delight in evil, and what is the truth that I am to rejoice with? Even with the modern New International translation, we must clearly explain the meanings of the biblical words. But even more so with the King James which uses language unfamiliar to most people today. "Charity suffereth long, and is kind; charity envieth not; charity vaunteth not itself, is not puffed up, Doth not behave itself unseemly, seeketh not her own, is not easily provoked, thinketh no evil; Rejoiceth not in iniquity, but rejoiceth in the truth" (1 Cor. 13:4–5 KJV).

Whatever translation of Scripture we use, we must focus on correctly translating the words on the page so that the Word, the message, comes through clearly. Paul said it this way: "Do your best to present yourself to God as one approved, a workman who does not need to be ashamed and who correctly handles the word of truth" (2 Tim. 2:15).

HELPING LEARNERS FEEL, RESPOND, AND VALUE

One day years ago I was having a cup of coffee with a pastor acquaintance, listening to him tell about his ministry with children's church. He told me of a ten-year-old boy who had come forward during the invitation to get some help. When they retired to a room for counseling, the boy began sharing his story. His parents were getting a divorce, he had no friends at school, his grades were bad—he just didn't know what to do. The pastor responded something like this, as I recall his story, "Son, I really don't care to hear about your problems. Do you know that you are a lost sinner? Do you know that if you die tonight without Jesus, you'll spend eternity in hell?" The boy, according to the pastor, looked at him with ever-widening eyes. His mouth fell open and tears ran down his cheeks. Then he stood and ran out of the church. "So I guess I put the fear of God in him!" was the pastor's conclusion.

I never think of that boy without praying that the Lord will send someone to share the love of Jesus with him. For you see, the pastor was doctrinally correct. But he had not one ounce of care, concern, or compassion for the heartfelt needs of this ten-year-old boy.

Do you remember "Joan" and her "Oh, somebody with the good kind of Bible read that verse for us." This statement in no way served to create an atmosphere of openness, warmth, and trust in the class. So how do we create such a climate? We will make good progress toward emotional warmth in the classroom if we focus on sharing ourselves, sharing the experiences of class members, accepting them as they are (while helping them grow), using humor appropriately, and building trust. Let's look at each of these more closely.

Personal experiences versus wooden stories. An effective way to begin a Bible study session is to tell a story related to the subject. Our teaching materials provide suggestions for doing this: "Joan is a single mother. . . ." and the like. These are good suggestions, but not necessarily the best material for your class. Fictitious testimonies, contrived case studies, and artificial anecdotes may do little to warm up your class. They are wooden, stilted, forced—no matter how good they are—because they are not related to the life experiences of you or your class.

Far better are stories that come from your experiences or the experiences of class members. All of us have experiences of success and growth and victory in the Lord. As these experiences are shared, to the glory of God, the class is warmed by his pres-

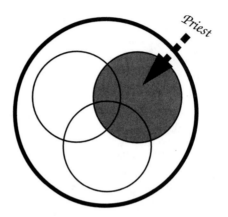

Figure 9.10

ence and our praise of him. Use the suggestions to direct your thoughts to living stories of the class—and use these as a way to lead the class to ready their hearts and minds for God's Word.

Earn the right versus put on the spot. Teachers do not have the right to call on learners to confess their sins in front of the group. This "group confession of sin" was a primary tactic in brainwashing our military prisoners in both the Korean and the Vietnamese Wars. Christian teachers "prepare God's people for works of service, so that the body of Christ may be built up" (Eph. 4:12). It is not for us to tear down our learners through guilt, but to correctly handle God's Word (2 Tim. 2:15). The Holy Spirit convicts people of sin (John 16:8), not teachers. And yet the natural tendency is to put learners on the spot. A seminary student of mine began his ten-minute MicroTeach exercise this way: "Okay, how many of you haven't had a daily time of prayer and Bible study this week (pause)? Just lift your hands (uncomfortable pause). Well, now I know that in a class this size there's someone who hasn't had a regular time of Bible study and prayer this week. Remember, God is watching and he knows who you are (angry pause)." Finally, a young man in the back of the room bowed his head and slowly lifted his hand.

The student teacher then proceeded to talk about quality quiet times. He had no right to do this. It humiliated the learner. It angered the class. It certainly killed any sense of openness toward the student teacher.

If the student had earned the right to ask that question by sharing his own struggles with having a daily quiet time, there would have been no problem. Look at the difference: "This past week I've not spent time in prayer and Bible study as I normally do. I mean, things have gotten so busy and hectic—and I've let them push my devotional time aside. Any of you struggling with this problem? (several heads nod in agreement). Let's see what we can discover that will help us give top priority to the Lord."

Such an approach increases openness. It warms the class because "we have a common struggle" and "we're working together" to find answers from God's Word. Share of yourself before you ask others to share. Earn the right.

Acceptance versus judgment. We discussed Jesus' command, "Judge not, lest ye be judged," earlier in the chapter. Jesus was condemning the carping, nagging, nit-picking censorious spirit of the Pharisees. We need to pray through our own attitudes toward those we teach or we will move in this same direction. "Oh, my people never want to pray." Or, "I can't get anyone in my class to answer a question." Or, "Projects? Are you kidding?! I can't get anyone to do anything in my class!"

Hmmmm. I wonder if these teachers tell their classes these things! The disciples failed in many ways, but Jesus forgave them, loved them, and continued to teach them. Accept those you teach where they are. Then love them and teach them and allow them to grow in the Lord. Some will take longer than others. The commitment level of a few may never please you. But that is not our concern. Our concern is to be faithful in our loving ministry toward those whom we teach. If your focus is on acceptance rather than judgement, openness and warmth will grow in your class or church.

Humor versus solemnity. Paul was a great Christian philosopher. His writings are deep and often hard to understand. Even Peter had trouble understanding him sometimes! (2 Pet. 3:16). But for Paul, the evidence of Christ in our lives was not philosophical reasoning or theological expertise, but the joy and gratitude we have from the indwelling Christ.

- "Be joyful in hope, patient in affliction, faithful in prayer" (Rom. 12:12).

- "For the kingdom of God is not a matter of eating and drinking, but of righteousness, peace and joy in the Holy Spirit" (Rom. 14:17).

- "May the God of hope fill you with all joy and peace as you trust in him, so that you may overflow with hope by the power of the Holy Spirit" (Rom. 15:13).

- "Convinced of this, I know that I will remain, and I will continue with all of you for your progress and joy in the faith" (Phil. 1:25).

- ". . . being strengthened with all power according to his glorious might so that you may have great endurance and patience, and joyfully giving thanks to the Father, who has qualified you to share in the inheritance of the saints in the kingdom of light" (Col. 1:11–12).

- "Do not be anxious about anything, but in everything, by prayer and petition, with thanksgiving, present your requests to God" (Phil. 4:6).

The Bible is a solemn book, with a solemn message. We must approach Scripture and its study with reverence. But this reverence differs from the stoic, stern, dispassionate logic of the false teachers Paul wrote against in Colossians. Where the Spirit is free to produce fruit, there is joy (Gal. 5:22).

The super-serious has little warmth. The super-silly has little depth. But the proper use of humor can both warm up and settle down a class. Humor can enhance the openness of class members, not just to one another, but to God's Word as well. People who honestly laugh together can also honestly share together, or pray together, or weep together (see Rom. 12:15). If you can use humor naturally, you will find an effective technique for building openness in the classroom.

One last word on humor. Be sure that the humor is positive and uplifting. Avoid crude or vulgar jokes, stories with double meanings, and even lighthearted pranks or gags. Humor is wrong when it denigrates others, or demeans the sacred task at hand. "Nor should there be obscenity, foolish talk or coarse joking, which are out of place, but rather thanksgiving" (Eph. 5:4).

Trust versus guilt. One last suggestion on improving the warmth of a class is to avoid guilt and strengthen trust. Guilt is a strong motivator. Perhaps that is why so many immature leaders use it. It produces quick results but undermines the glue that holds human relationships together, trust.

B. F. Skinner conducted many experiments in which he taught rats to run mazes. In some cases he used a positive reinforcer, food. In others he used punishment, electric shock. He found that electric shock motivated the rats to learn the maze faster than food. But the shock also taught the rats to fear the maze. Eventually, the rats refused to move, regardless of the degree of shock applied, even to the point of death.

Guilt is like an electric shock to the personality. Whether in a Sunday school class, seminary class, or congregation, it produces quick results, but leads to fear. Such motivational techniques are toxic to learners. Where do you find Jesus, the Lord of lords, teaching this way? "For God did not send his Son into the world to condemn the world, but to save the world through him" (John 3:17). Where do you find Paul, strong personality that he was, teaching this way? Paul counters his enemies in Corinth, who claimed he was strong in his letters but weak in person (2 Cor. 10:10), by saying, "In fact, you even put up with anyone who enslaves you or exploits you or takes advantage of you or pushes himself forward or slaps you in the face. To my shame I admit that we were too weak for that!" (2 Cor. 11:20–21a).

Rather, Paul loved the church at Corinth, and grieved over their problems: "For I wrote you out of great distress and anguish of heart and with many tears, not to grieve you but to let you know the depth of my love for you" (2 Cor. 2:4). By his clear teaching and firm but loving exhortation, Paul led the church at Corinth away from her problems and into a more focused relationship with Christ.

Trust grows among people as they live and work and pray together, as they share needs together, as they forgive one another. Paul underscored this social element of the Christian faith:

> But now you must rid yourselves of all such things as these: anger [fury toward another], rage [settled hatred toward another], malice [wishing harm on another],

slander [demeaning another's character], and filthy language [abusive talk] from your lips. . . .

[But] . . . clothe yourselves with compassion [soft-heartedness toward others], kindness [kind actions toward others], humility [right thinking toward others], gentleness [tenderness toward others] and patience [long-suffering with others].

Bear with each other [put up with each other] and forgive whatever grievances you may have against one another. Forgive as the Lord forgave you. And over all these virtues put on love [caring for others in need], which binds them all together in perfect unity.

Let the peace of Christ rule in your hearts, since as members of one body you were called to peace. And be thankful. Let the word of Christ dwell in you richly as you teach and admonish one another with all wisdom, and as you sing psalms, hymns and spiritual songs with gratitude in your hearts to God.

And whatever you do, whether in word or deed, do it all in the name of the Lord Jesus, giving thanks to God the Father through him" (Col. 3:8–17).[3]

If we were to take Paul's words as marching orders for our classes, the level of trust among the members of the classes would increase dramatically.

HELPING LEARNERS DO

Years ago I taught a Sunday school class for deaf college students. One day I met one of the members of my class on campus and, after a few minutes of conversation, asked him what discoveries he'd made during our study the previous Sunday. "Ohhh," he said, "that was a long time ago." Yes, I agreed. This was Wednesday and our study was Sunday, but what did he get out of the study? "Well, ummmm, we were studying the Old Testament, right?" Well, no, actually, we studied a passage out of Ephesians. "Ephesians! That's right! I remember now!" So what did he discover? What did he learn? "Ohhhh, well, I don't remember. That was a long time ago!" I had spent five or six hours preparing to teach. I had given the presentation all I had. Now, on Wednesday, he couldn't remember the first thing about what we'd studied. What a discouragement!

How can we help our learners put what they learn into practice? Let me suggest two general ways and then focus on a third specific way to do this. The first general way is to engage learners in thinking through concepts and implications of Scriptural truth. We discussed this under "Helping Learners Think." Learners cannot transfer truths from classroom to life unless they clearly understand those truths. Solving real-life problems in class, based on the Scripture study, is an excellent way to build bridges into the daily lives of learners.

The second general way to lead learners to put truth into practice is to lead them to value Scriptural truths and their implications. We discussed this under "Helping

---

3.   All bracketed words inserted into biblical quotations are added by the author.

People Feel, Respond and Value." When learners see for themselves the value of biblical truth, they are far more likely to use it in facing situations in their own lives.

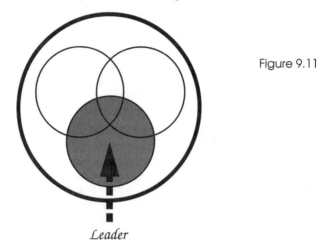

Figure 9.11

Leader

The third and most specific way to encourage learners to put biblical truths into practice is by way of assignments. Assignments can vary in their intensity and scope: selected verses to read, specific questions to answer, projects to do, journals to keep, words to analyze, and the list goes on. By giving an assignment to be done outside of class, you prompt learners to think of Sunday school (and the content of the study) during the week. You share part of the teaching responsibility with learners as they share the results of their study the following Sunday. Assignments can be done individually, in pairs, or in groups of various kinds. By giving learners things to do during the week, you give them the opportunity to learn from the Lord on their own.

Be sure to use these assignments in your class discussion next time. Provide time for learners to share what they did and what the Lord taught them. Do not chastise learners who forget the assignment—toxic teaching, remember? Simply focus on the results of the learners who remembered. Let them shine by sharing what they learned during the week. This will encourage all the learners to do the assignments in the future. Consistent bridge-building between Sunday school class and the real life of learners pays rich dividends for Christian growth!

THE CENTER OF THE TRIAD

The Christian teacher provides an environment for healthy, balanced growth by emphasizing thinking and valuing and by doing activities. Furthermore, he or she sets the example as a thinking, committed doer of the Word. There is another element of Christian growth that far outweighs all that we've discussed up to this point. You'll notice in figure 9.12 that the three circles form a small triangle in the center of the triad. We might consider this triangle as the will, the ego, the "I" of the per-

Figure 9.12

sonality. Those without Christ determine the course of life for themselves: what *I* think, what *I* value, what *I* choose to do. This I-centered view is a philosophy called existentialism, and has been a central force in American thinking for three decades now. Any outside authority—parent, teacher, government, church, Bible—that attempts to bow me to its views impinges upon my personhood and makes me less human. I must define myself by making choices. The nineteenth-century Russian Christian, Dostoyevsky, once wrote, "If God did not exist, everything would be permitted." This is exactly the beginning point of existential philosophers like Nietzsche and Sartre: "God does not exist, so everything is permitted. Make your choices." John Randall, a more recent existentialist, wrote, "Man should place their faith in man himself—in man's infinite possibilities . . . [as well as in] a realistic recognition of man's finite limitations."[4] By contrast, Paul wrote, "The man without the Spirit ["natural man" KJV] does not accept the things that come from the Spirit of God, for they are foolishness to him, and he cannot understand them, because they are spiritually discerned" (1 Cor. 2:14).

When we accept Jesus Christ as our Lord and Savior, he takes up residence within us (Col. 1:27). The struggle of spiritual growth centers on who will be in charge. If *I* continue to reign, determining what *I* think, what *I* value, and what *I* do, there will be little perceptible difference between my way of life and one who isn't saved. Paul suffered this battle and described it this way:

> I know that nothing good lives in me, that is, in my sinful nature. For I have the desire to do what is good, but I cannot carry it out. For what I do is not the good I want to do; no, the evil I do not want to do—this I keep on doing. Now if I do what I do not want to do, it is no longer I who do it, but it is sin living in me that does it.
>
> So I find this law at work: When I want to do good, evil is right there with me. For in my inner being I delight in God's law; but I see another law at work in the members of my body, waging war against the law of my mind and making me a prisoner of the law of sin at work within my members. What a wretched man I am! Who will rescue me from this body of death? Thanks be to God—through Jesus

---

4. John Herman Randall, Jr., "What Is the Temper of Humanism?" *The Humanist* (Nov/Dec 1970): 34.

> Christ our Lord! So then, I myself in my mind am a slave to God's law, but in the sinful nature a slave to the law of sin.
>
> Therefore, there is now no condemnation for those who are in Christ Jesus, because through Christ Jesus the law of the Spirit of life set me free from the law of sin and death (Rom. 7:18–8:2).

Who will be on the throne in my life? Do I call the shots or do I humble myself under the gracious hand of the Lord? Spiritual growth comes as I learn to surrender my life to him. Jesus said, "If anyone would come after me, he must deny himself and take up his cross daily and follow me" (Luke 9:23). Deny self. This is anathema to existentialists. It is the destruction of all they hold most sacred: the exalted free choice of an individual to do as he or she judges right. Not much has changed. Three thousand years ago, the writer of Judges noted, "In those days Israel had no king; everyone did as he saw fit" (Judg. 17:6). One need only read today's newspaper to learn the result of everyone doing as they "see fit." Rampant divorce, child abuse, rape, murder, gang violence, suicide, drugs, pornography, and so on *ad nauseam*.

By contrast, as we give over the control of our lives to the Spirit of Christ, he gives us power to become all we were created to be. Spiritual growth is learning how to let Jesus be Lord, not just in my theology but in my life. Paul said it this way: "I have been crucified with Christ and I no longer live, but Christ lives in me. The life I live in the body, I live by faith in the Son of God, who loved me and gave himself for me" (Gal. 2:20).

The most important thing we can do to help our learners grow in the Lord is to teach them to depend on him. Let's see how.

CHRIST, THE CENTER OF THE TRIAD

As we have seen, the key to spiritual growth is surrender. Jesus is the Way. Jesus is the Truth. He is the Life (John 14:6). But he does not force his way into our lives, nor does he dominate us. "I stand at the door and knock. If anyone hears my voice and opens the door, I will come in and eat with him, and he with me" (Rev. 3:20). He gives us the freedom to invite him in or lock him out. As we invite him to lead us, to teach us, to mold us into what he desires, he helps us think and feel and do according to his will.

CHRISTian THINKING

Paul spent three years in Ephesus (Acts 19) preaching and teaching. One of his converts was Epaphras, a prominent man from Colossae, city in the Lycus Valley about a hundred miles to the east. Epaphras returned home and ministered to the church there (Col. 1:7). Later, after Paul was imprisoned in Rome, Epaphras visited him and shared a growing concern: Greek ideas of "mystery" and secret "knowl-

The Internal Influence
of the Teacher

Col. 1:9–10   Rom. 12:15

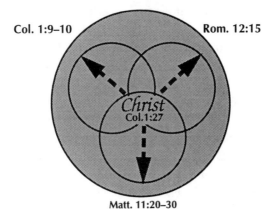

Figure 9.13

Matt. 11:20–30

edge" and special "wisdom" were undermining the faith of the Colossians in Christ. In his letter to the Colossians, Paul uses these very terms to refocus their minds on the Lord.

> For this reason, since the day we heard about you, we have not stopped praying for you and asking God to fill you with the knowledge of his will through all spiritual wisdom and understanding. And we pray this in order that you may live a life worthy of the Lord and may please him in every way: bearing fruit in every good work, growing in the knowledge of God, being strengthened with all power according to his glorious might so that you may have great endurance and patience, and joyfully giving thanks to the Father, who has qualified you to share in the inheritance of the saints in the kingdom of light (Col. 1:9–12).

Col. 1:9–10

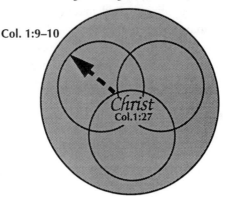

Figure 9.14

The knowledge Paul prays for the Colossians to have is not secretive, special head knowledge (*gnosis*), which puffs us up with pride (1 Cor. 8:1), but an intimate heart knowledge (*epignosis*) of the Lord's will which comes through our relationship with him. As we walk with the Lord, he teaches us what his will is. In the context of Bible study, Jesus teaches us what the Bible says. Further, the Lord helps us understand what Scripture means. If I rush to understand Scripture on the basis of my interpretation, rather than to learn the writer's meaning, I may read my own thinking into Scripture rather than read God's thinking out of it. As I walk with the Lord day by day, he leads me into a proper understanding of Scripture, just as he did with the disciples on the road to Emmaus (Luke 24:13, 32). Further, the Lord helps us put his teachings into practice. We've already noted that Jesus declared this as wisdom (we'll talk more about this under "CHRISTian Doing" below). From knowing to understanding to doing. Doing begets broader knowledge, which begets deeper understanding, which begets more effective doing. All of this under the direction of the Lord who lives within and teaches us. And this cycle of knowing, understanding, and doing results in a change of thinking. I think less like my culture, my background, and my upbringing—and begin to think more like the Lord himself. "Do not conform any longer to the pattern of this world, but be transformed by the renewing of your mind. Then you will be able to test and approve what God's will is—his good, pleasing and perfect will" (Rom. 12:2). How do our learners renew their minds? By knowing what the Bible says, understanding what the Bible means, and putting it into practice—as Jesus leads.

CHRISTian FEELING

The affective component of the personality is important in spiritual growth because so much revolves around openness, values, priorities, and commitments. And yet, many Christians have emotional problems and value defects just like unbelievers: hatred, anger, instability, harshness, insecurity, bitterness, selfishness, and the like. Scripture underscores the importance of progression in removing the negative and growing in the positive. Love, not hate. Forgiveness, not anger. Steadfastness, not instability. Gentleness, not harshness. Courage, not insecurity. Sweetness, not bitterness. Generosity, not selfishness. And so on. Paul underscored this to the Romans. Watch for the focus on priorities and values, and compare them to the "natural behavior" of people.

> Be joyful in hope, patient in affliction, faithful in prayer. Share with God's people who are in need. Practice hospitality.

> Bless those who persecute you; bless and do not curse. Rejoice with those who rejoice; mourn with those who mourn. Live in harmony with one another. Do not be proud, but be willing to associate with people of low position.

As we walk with the Lord, he teaches us within each day's struggle how to put off the negative and put on the positive. He shows us that seeking his values produces positive results, not only in our own lives but in the lives of those around us. His priorities, not mine. His values, not my society's.

CHRISTian DOING

Much of what we've discussed regarding thinking and feeling, understanding and valuing, flows into doing. We've discussed "doing" all along. It is difficult to properly understand Scripture, yet fail to act on it. Likewise, it is difficult to be committed to scriptural values, yet not live them. This is part of the natural balance of Christian growth. Therefore, as I grow in understanding of and commitment to the Lord, my actions also change. Old habits die; new habits grow. How do we refine

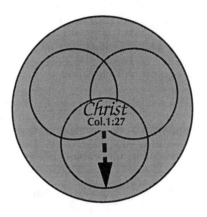

Figure 9.15

Matt. 11:29–30

those habits? How do we learn the skills of spiritual living as Jesus lives within us and teaches us? Here is his own illustration of the process: "Take my yoke upon you and learn from me, for I am gentle and humble in heart, and you will find rest for your souls. For my yoke is easy and my burden is light" (Matt. 11:29–30).

First, let's define terms. "Take" denotes a voluntary action. I can take the yoke or I can leave the yoke. "Yoke" refers to a wooden bar that ties two oxen together. Two oxen can pull a load more easily than one, and the yoke ties them together. "My" refers to whose yoke it is. The yoke Jesus is calling us to accept is his yoke. Not my parents' nor my pastor's nor my friends'. The yoke of the Lord is my ministry—what does the Lord want me to do? All believers are gifted (Eph. 4:7) in order to help strengthen the church (Eph. 4:12). Where should I serve? What should I do? "Take my yoke," Jesus says.

What kind of yoke is it? That's all church people talk about—work, work, work. Why should I give up what I want in order to do what the Lord wants? Because his yoke is the place where we find real refreshment ("rest"). Remember when Jesus was talking to the woman at the well? The disciples had gone to town for food. When they returned, they urged him to eat. He said, "I have food to eat that you know nothing about" (John 4:32). Had he gotten food somewhere else? No, Jesus' food was "to do the will of him who sent me and to finish his work" (John 4:34). In the same way, when we take on Jesus' yoke, we have abundant life.

Further, Jesus himself teaches us how to pull in his yoke ("learn from me"), not learn about Jesus, but learn from Jesus. Just as a steady plow horse is hitched to a colt to teach the colt how to pull, so we hitch ourselves to the Lord and learn from him how to minister.

Is his yoke harsh and cutting like the yoke of the law? Does it irritate and chafe? No, his yoke is "easy," comfortable, and his burden is "light," easy to be carried. Jesus the carpenter had carved yokes for oxen and had custom fit the wooden beams to the shoulders of the animals. So too, he custom fits our ministry to who we are. When we are in his will, when we are pulling with him, when we are doing at his direction, there will be no burnout. For in his yoke, there is rest.

My first lesson in ministry yokes came with the call into deaf ministry. The Lord helped me learn sign language and understand deaf culture. I had no one in my family or background who was deaf, but he gave me a heart for deaf people. Through my years of working with deaf people, Jesus taught me things about teaching, and listening, and communicating that permeate my efforts. Now my yoke is the seminary classroom. I sense it every time I step into the room; it is confirmed every time I leave. To teach, equip, shape, challenge, mold, and learn from young ministers is an indescribable joy. The Lord's yoke leads to fulfillment and joy.

INDIVIDUAL LEARNERS

The Lord lives within each believer. As we give him freedom to guide our thinking, values, and actions, he grows us to be like him. Over time, we begin to reflect biblical concepts, priorities, and behaviors. The world can see the difference that true spiritual maturity makes. Jesus said, "By their fruit you will recognize them. Do people pick grapes from thornbushes, or figs from thistles? Likewise every good tree bears good fruit, but a bad tree bears bad fruit" (Matt. 7:16–17). And what, specifically, is this fruit? "The fruit of the spirit is love, joy, peace, patience, kindness, goodness, faithfulness, gentleness and self-control. Against such things there is no law. Those who belong to Christ Jesus have crucified the sinful nature with its passions and desires. Since we live by the Spirit, let us keep in step with the Spirit" (Gal 5:22–25).

Figure 9.17

Loving, not hateful. Joyful, not bitter. Peaceful, not bickering. Patient, not angry. Kind, not selfish. Faithful, not fickle. Gentle, not harsh. Self-controlled, not impulsive. We allow the Spirit to produce this heavenly fruit as we put and keep Christ on the throne of our lives.

THE CHURCH AS A WHOLE

Beyond the joy of personally growing in Christ and teaching others to grow in him stands the challenge of moving an entire congregation in the direction of Christlikeness. As more individuals in the church focus on him, grow in him, and reflect him in their lives and work, so the church as a whole begins to reflect him. "Christ in you"—whether we speak of individual believers or the church at large—is our "hope of glory" (Col. 1:27).

FINAL WORDS

The goal of Christian teaching is Christlikeness in our learners. The teacher helps by balancing thinking, feeling, and doing components in the classroom, and leading learners to depend on the Lord day by day. We, of course, cannot produce Christlikeness. Only the Lord can teach us how to live as he does. But we are instruments in the Master's hand. We can cooperate with him in the process, or we can do things our own way and fail.

In the end, those who honor Jesus as Teacher and Lord, who teach as he teaches them, who love as he loves them, will be the teachers who influence others toward

Figure 9.18

Christlikeness. May God richly bless you as you spend your life pursuing this won-drous task. "Only let us live up to what we have already attained" (Phil. 3:16).

FOR FURTHER STUDY

1. Of the three"teaching approaches that hinder growth" (pp. Teaching Approaches that Hinder Growth Toward Christlikeness–145), which best describes you? Which least describes you?

2. Are you predominately a thinker, a feeler, or a doer? What evidence supports your evaluation? What dangers do you risk in focusing only on this "natural" emphasis?

3. Think of persons you know who fit the areas other than your own. That is, if you see yourself as a "thinker," think of a "feeler" and a "doer." How do you relate to them? What conflicts have you had?

4. Where do you need more emphasis: helping people think, feel, or do? What specifically will you do to strengthen these areas?

5. How are you allowing the Lord to shape your thoughts? Your emotions and values? Your actions?

6. What was your greatest discovery in this chapter?

SUGGESTED READING

Augsburger, Myron S. *Called to Maturity: God's Provision for Spiritual Growth*. Scottdale, Pa.: Herald Press, 1960.

Barclay, William. *The All-Sufficient Christ*. Philadelphia: Westminster Press, 1961.

Carter, Steven and Julia Sokol. *Lives Without Balance*. New York: Villiard Books, 1992.

Maston, T. B. *Why Live the Christian Life?* Nashville: Thomas Nelson, 1974.

Nee, Watchman. *Not I But Christ*. New York: Christian Fellowship Publishers, 1974.

Shelley, Bruce and Marshall Shelley. *The Consumer Church: Can Evangelicals Win the World Without Losing Their Souls?* Downers Grove, Ill.: InterVarsity Press, 1992.

Part Two:
Preparation for Teaching

CHAPTER 10

HOW TO STUDY THE BIBLE

—TERRELL PEACE

Bible study is similar to exercise; we know that we need it but many of us have a hard time doing it. In 2 Timothy 2:15 we read, "Do your best to present yourself to God as one approved, a workman who does not need to be ashamed and who correctly handles the word of truth." God calls believers to a lifetime study of his Word. Unfortunately, many Christians fail to get the most of their study because they have not learned how to study the Bible effectively.

It is not unusual for Bible students to drift repeatedly to the same favorite passages. This piecemeal approach does not encourage a systematic exploration of the Bible. Bible students should seek to study all of God's Word.

Some students become dependent on commentaries, Bible handbooks, and Sunday school literature for knowledge of the Scriptures. Knowledge of the Bible should not be secondhand. Studying God's Word by reading commentaries is like reading Cliff notes and not the book. If your best friend wrote you a letter, would you ask someone else to read the letter and write his or her interpretation of it?

There is nothing wrong with consulting Bible study resources, but we must start with reading the real thing. As a result of the nature of Scripture (2 Tim. 3:16) and the nature of the Holy Spirit's ministry (1 John 2:27), it is possible for Christians to understand the Bible.

Too often believers approach Bible study with little expectation of discovering truth. Study God's Word with the excitement of an explorer. Enter each encounter expecting God to teach you about himself (John 16:13–15). Anticipate what new horizons of knowledge God will open.

Richard Warren suggests five principles for getting the most out of your Bible study:

1. The secret of dynamic Bible study is knowing how to ask the right kinds of questions.

2. Dynamic Bible study involves writing down what you have observed and discovered.

3. The ultimate goal of dynamic Bible study is application, not just interpretation.

4. Dynamic Bible study means that God's Word must be studied systematically.

5. In dynamic Bible study you never exhaust the riches in any one passage of Scripture.[1]

This chapter presents suggestions for your Bible study with the prayer that you become a diligent student of God's Word. I encourage you to study Scripture systematically, fully, and with great expectation.

TYPES OF BIBLE STUDY

Like other matters in life, we need a balanced approach to Bible study. If we look only at the "big picture" in studying the Scripture we can overlook very important details. If we concentrate exclusively on a verse by verse method, we may draw conclusions that are inconsistent with the context. If we study academically and not devotionally, it is easy to forget the role of the Holy Spirit in personal application. By using a variety of methods, Bible students can avoid these pitfalls. Studying particular words, doctrines, Bible characters, or other topics can deepen our appreciation for God's Word and our commitment to be obedient to it. Your choice of methodology is determined by what you are trying to achieve. Richard Warren explains twelve proven Bible study methods:

1. *Devotional.* Designed for personal application by meditating on Scripture and asking the Holy Spirit to show you how to apply it.

2. *Chapter Summary.* Read a chapter of a Bible book several times and then summarize the central thoughts contained in it.

3. *Character Quality.* Choose a character quality you would like to work on and cross-reference Scriptures that examine this quality.

---

1. Richard Warren, *12 Dynamic Bible Study Methods for Individuals or Groups* (Wheaton, Ill.: Victor Books, 1981), 13–17.

4. *Thematic.* Identify a theme. Write out several questions you would like to have answered about this theme. Record your answers.

5. *Biographical.* Research a Bible character. Make notes on attitudes, strengths, weaknesses. Apply what you have learned to your own life.

6. *Topical.* Collect and compare all the verses you can find on a particular topic. Organize your conclusions into an outline that you can share with another person.

7. *Word Study.* Select a key word in the Bible. Find out how many times it is used. Find out the original meaning of the word.

8. *Book Background.* Study how history, geography, culture, science, and politics affected what happened in Bible times. Use Bible reference books to increase your understanding of the Word.

9. *The Book Survey Method.* Read an entire book of the Bible through several times and write a general overview of the book. Make notes on the content.

10. *Chapter Analysis.* Engage in an in-depth look at each verse of the chapter.

11. *Book Synthesis.* Summarize the contents and main themes. Make an outline of the book. Use this method after using the Book Survey and Chapter Analysis methods.

12. *Verse by Verse Analysis.* Select a passage or verse and examine it in detail finding cross-references and paraphrasing each verse. Record possible applications.[2]

The purpose of this chapter is not to give an exhaustive description of these methods, but to deal with Bible study primarily as it relates to the teaching ministry of the church. Therefore, we will concentrate on the two major categories of Bible study: the Synthetic Study and the Analytic Study.

SYNTHETIC BIBLE STUDY

Sometimes we want to get an overview of a Bible book or gain insight into the purpose of the writing. This is accomplished by the synthetic approach. The key to getting a good overview of a lengthy passage of Scripture is to read the entire book or passage without stopping to examine specific details. If possible, read the book at one sitting. With a shorter book, read it several times at one sitting.

Use only paper, pencil, your mind, and the Holy Spirit in these initial readings of the book. Using commentaries and other study tools early in the study may cause you to lose the broader perspective you are seeking. As you read and record your

2. Ibid., 27–28.

impressions, try to be sensitive to book-long themes or ideas. Consider the following questions as you read.

- Is there a stated purpose for the book?

- Is there a dominant or recurring theme?

- Are certain words, phrases, ideas, or names repeated throughout the book?

- What feelings does the writer seem to have? Is he happy? Sad? Angry? Triumphant?

- Why does the writer feel this way?

- Is the content primarily inspirational, historical, or instructional?

- Is there an obvious structure or pattern in the writing?

- What have I learned by reading the book?

After reading the book (or lengthy passage) repeatedly, taking notes, and answering questions about its writer and content, it's time to summarize. One way to see if we understand what we are reading is to state briefly what that author is saying. Anybody can use many words to explain an idea. It takes a better grasp of the material to explain it correctly in a few words.

First, try to summarize the book's message in a single paragraph. Limit yourself to two or three sentences. Next, trim your summary down to one sentence that states the essence of the book. Now, try to think of a short phrase that communicates what the book is about. Finally, come up with a short title that accurately describes the writing.

Next it is time to look at several commentaries and Bible handbooks. Compare your evaluation of the book's meaning with that of others. Your wording does not have to be the same as any of these other references. You may want to reexamine your findings if you have a completely different idea of what the book is about.

You may be asking yourself at this point, "Why didn't I just read a commentary and save myself all that work?" There are several good reasons for this effort. First, you have exposed your mind and spirit to the Word of God through your repeated reading and study. You are likely already reaping spiritual benefits of which you may not even be aware. You also will know God, which is more exciting than knowing about him. You have made the Scripture yours and that is much more valuable than secondhand knowledge.

You have also created a valuable tool for further Bible study. We discussed earlier some dangers of studying verses or words without understanding the background of the book. With the skills gained through a synthetic study, you can examine the details of any passage without fear of misinterpreting Scripture. Synthetic skills can serve as a check for your analytical studies.

ANALYTIC BIBLE STUDY

Sometimes it is necessary to study all the internal intricacies of a passage. For this kind of study to take place, an organized, deliberate method must be used to analyze each verse, paragraph, and phrase. This is known as an analytic approach to Bible study. Once we have gained insight into the meaning of a lengthy passage using a synthetic approach, we can probe more deeply into a shorter segment with greater confidence. We deal most often with only a few verses of Scripture at a time. Personal Bible study, preparation for teaching, and sermon preparation usually involve only a chapter or several verses of Scripture. Still, these preparations require a detailed study of the content. The key components of an effective analytic study are simple but crucial to a proper understanding of Scripture.

1. Observation—"What does it say?"

2. Interpretation—"What does it mean?"

3. Application—"How can I use it?"

Observation. Observation takes time and effort. It needs to be done carefully to assure proper interpretation and application of Scripture. We should know what a verse really says before we decide what it means. Otherwise, doctrinal errors can occur. A classic example is the misinterpretation of Matthew 16:18 that Peter is the father of the church. Even a quick look at the Greek reveals the verse does not say this. The word for Peter is petros, a stone. The word for rock is petra, large stone or bedrock.[3] Christ used Peter's name as a picture of strength. Christ was saying that upon this strong faith he would build his church.

This example of interpretation does not imply that a knowledge of Greek and Hebrew is necessary to study the Bible. Today we have many excellent translations of Scripture. The finest scholars in the world have translated these new versions from the best manuscripts available. These translations can help us understand what a verse says, especially if we use several translations in our study.

Good observation involves several commitments. The first is a commitment to a proper attitude toward observation. We must develop a persistence to observe what Scripture says. Time and effort in God's Word requires this attitude. We must also commit ourselves to employing good reading skills. We must read the verses thoughtfully, repeatedly, and reflectively. It takes time to make good observations. It is also necessary to read imaginatively and purposefully so we see the atmosphere, humor, and other factors hidden between the lines. Purposeful study is important to understanding a passage.

Observation also calls for a commitment to ask the right questions. Who, what, why, where, and when are helpful tools in understanding a passage of Scripture.

---

3.   W. E. Vine, *An Expository Dictionary of New Testament Words* (Old Tappan, N.J.: Fleming H. Revell Co.,1940), 3:302.

Book or Passage:	
Stated Purpose:	
Dominant Theme?	
Repeated Words?	
Repeated Phrases?	
Repeated Ideas?	
Repeated Names?	
Repeated Others?	
Feelings of Writer? (Happy? Sad? Angry?)	
Reasons for Feeling?	
Content? ❏Inspiration ❏Historical ❏Instructional ❏Other? _____	
Structure or Pattern?	
What Did You Learn?	
Paragraph Summary:	
Sentence Summary:	
Phrase Summary:	
Descriptive Title:	

Figure 10.1

These questions help us probe deeply into the Scripture and give us clues to its meaning. Commit to examine structural relationships based on the different literary devices. Knowledge of the following literary devices can enhance our powers of observation.

- *Comparison* is the association of like things. Similes are comparisons using the words *like* or *as*. James 1:6 says, "He who doubts is like a wave of the sea, blown and tossed by the wind."

  Sometimes comparisons are implied. These are called metaphors. James uses this device effectively in comparing the tongue with fire (James 3:6).

- *Continuity* is the reiteration of exact terms or consistency expressed by the repeated use of similar terms, phrases, or ideas. In John 14:15–24, Jesus stated the connection between our love for him and our obedience to his commands four times.

- *Centrality* is the use of a pivotal, crucial event or statement to organize an idea. Jesus used this device when he asked, "Who do you say that I am?" and Peter replied, "You are the Christ" (Mark 8:29).

- *Contrast* is the association of opposites used to point out essential relationships. What are more direct opposites than life and death? These contrasting images are used by Paul to instruct us to be dead to sin and alive to Christ (Rom. 6:1–14).

- *Climax* refers to the arrangement of ideas to progress from the lesser to the greater, either in importance or intensity. An example of this device can be found in Romans 2:17–29. Paul began by discussing the Jews' pride in the law and circumcision. Next, he argued the relative value of Jews who did not keep the law and non-Jews who did. He concluded with what must have been a thunderbolt to most Jews in verse 29: "No, a man is a Jew if he is one inwardly; and circumcision is circumcision of the heart, by the Spirit, not by the written code."

- *Interrogation* is the employment of a question to clarify or enhance a discussion. In Romans 6 and 7, Paul used a series of questions to build his argument.

  "Shall we go on sinning so that grace may increase?" (Rom. 6:1). "Shall we sin because we are not under the law but under grace?" (Rom. 6:15). "Is the law sin?" (Rom. 7:7).

- *Interchange* is the exchange or alternation of certain elements, ideas, or phrases. An example of this special kind of repetition is found in John 15 where Jesus alternates between telling his disciples what they can do if they abide in him and the results of not abiding (John 14:15–24).

- *Hyperbole* is a literary device we use quite often in our conversation. Does the following statement sound familiar? "If I've told you once, I've told you a thousand times . . ."This is a hyperbole. A hyperbole is a deliberate over-statement used to emphasize an idea or relationship. In Matthew 5:29, Jesus used an overstatement to drive home the awfulness of sin. "If your right eye causes you to sin, gouge it out and throw it away." Hyperbole does help get the point across!

Finally, observation requires a commitment to focus on terminologies used in the passage. The use of unusual terms, connective terms, figurative terms, or repeated terms may give significant insight into what the author of a passage is saying. Ultimately it may help understand what the author means. Knowing what a passage says is a prerequisite to knowing what it means.

Interpretation. "He will cover you with his feathers, and under his wings you will find refuge; his faithfulness will be your shield and rampart" (Ps. 91:4).

This verse says God will cover us with his feathers and wings. Does this mean God has feathers and wings? The obvious answer is no. It means that God will protect us and shield us like a hen would shield her brood. The large step from what the verse says to what it means is the step from observation to interpretation. Interpreting Scripture is the subject of entire books and courses. We will examine just a few of the major principles.

- The Principle of Clearest Meaning

    Unless there is some reason not to do so, take the simplest, most straight-forward, most easily understood meaning of a passage of Scripture. This means that we are to take a literal interpretation, while recognizing descriptive, figurative, and prophetic uses of language. Use easily understood passages to interpret difficult passages.

- The Principle of Scripture Interpreting Scripture

    This principle reminds us to look at all the Bible says on a subject. Let Scripture interpret Scripture. Matthew 5:22 taken alone could be misinterpreted to mean that God will give us anything we ask for. If we believe strongly enough, he will do it. Other Scriptures, such as James 4:3, 1 John 5:14–15, must be considered in interpreting Matthew 5:22. Yes, the Bible does tell us that we need to pray in faith. It also tells us we need to pray with pure motives and to pray for those things that are in God's will.

    Also included in this principle is the rule to always interpret a verse in context. Do not pull a verse out and look at it alone. Look at the surrounding verses to get a sense of what the author is trying to communicate on a larger scale. This principle applies to a single verse or passage that seems contradictory to the clear meaning of the whole of Scripture. The unity of the Scriptures should cause us to look carefully at a disparate interpretation.

- The Principle of the Accommodation of Revelation

  We know God speaks to us through human language. (That's good, since it is the only kind we understand!) This means that an infinite, eternal, absolute God communicates infinite, eternal, absolute truth to us in finite, temporal, human terminology. In no way does this change the truth we read. As we interpret Scripture, we must recognize that we don't know everything.

- The Principle of Historical Propriety

  When interpreting Scripture we need to ask, "Would people of that time and place understand this interpretation?" The key to interpretation is understanding what people in the historical context understood. Avoid "reading into" a passage more than the author intended. We still must recognize the possibility of prophetic types of interpretation. For example, the Book of Revelation can be interpreted by the events of the first century. However, it also refers to events yet to come.

  At this point in a Bible study, students have difficulty differentiating between interpretation and application. When there is a disagreement you may hear, "That's your interpretation." Or, "I interpret that verse in a different way." Such statements leave the impression that there is much latitude in interpreting Scripture. This is not so. We either understand what a verse means and interpret it correctly or we do not. However, we do have freedom in personal application. Each of us has different needs and we apply God's truth differently in our lives.

Application. Although a Scripture passage may be applied in several ways, this does not mean that *any* application is correct. An application must be consistent with what the passage says and means. There are a few basic guidelines that will help you apply the truth of God's Word in a meaningful and consistent way.

- Understand the principle involved. The worst misapplications of the Bible take place when someone tries to obey a biblical command without considering the biblical principle behind the command. Once we understand the principle, we can apply the truth of Scripture in a way that is consistent with the context in which we live. This principle is foundational to the rest of the guidelines.

- Understand the historical and cultural connotations. The Bible was not written in a vacuum. Real people, living in real places, experiencing real pain and pleasures wrote the Bible. The books of the New Testament were written close to two thousand years ago. So it should come as no surprise that the ideas and practices contained in the text are foreign to our time and culture.

  The Book of Philemon is a letter from the apostle Paul to a Christian slave owner. Slavery was a part of that culture. This is not a justification for owning slaves today. Drinking wine, foot washing, anointing with oil, and many other practices were part of the New Testament culture. We should cautiously apply New Testament practices to our culture by applying principles, not form.

Does this mean all biblical truth is culturally biased? Absolutely not. The Old Testament and the New Testament condemn adultery and homosexuality, and they are still unacceptable to God. God's moral standards are not subject to change. If a passage has obvious cultural overtones, does that mean the message is not applicable to our time and situation? Again, absolutely not. Refer to the first guideline. Ask, "What principle is taught in this passage?" Admittedly, separating cultural biases from biblical truth is not always a simple task. In fact, it can be difficult. If we are to keep the eternal truth of God vibrant and meaningful, we must be willing to undertake this task.

• Understand the use of descriptive and figurative language. This guideline points to the importance of the whole Bible study process: observation, interpretation, then application. "You have heard that it was said, 'Do not commit adultery.'" But I tell you that anyone who looks at a woman lustfully has already committed adultery with her in his heart. If your right eye causes you to sin, gouge it out and throw it away. It is better for you to lose one part of your body than for your whole body to be thrown into hell. And if your right hand causes you to sin, cut it off and throw it away. It is better for you to lose one part of your body than for your whole body to go into hell" (Matt. 5:27–30).

Imagine the applications that might be drawn from this passage without correctly interpreting the verses or considering the figures of speech (hyperbole, in this case)! Again, if we return to the idea of discovering the principle in the passage, we avoid many incorrect applications.

CONCLUSION

If you consistently employ the principles presented in this chapter you will realize several benefits. First, you will be more confident in your teaching or preaching, because you will have thoughtfully and carefully studied the Scriptures in preparation for your presentation. Second, you will develop a deep reservoir of biblical knowledge that will be useful in other areas of ministry. More importantly, you will develop the understanding and ability to help others discover the riches of God's Word for themselves.

FOR FURTHER STUDY

1. Choose a book and do a synthetic Bible study, as outlined in this chapter. For a first attempt, it would be advantageous to pick a somewhat short work. Let me suggest Philemon or perhaps Philippians.

2. Test your powers of observation. Read Acts 1:8 and John 3:16 as if you are reading them for the very first time. Record at least ten observations (no interpretations) for each verse. Remember, you are only describing what the verse is saying.

3. Using Mark 11:27–12:44, list and describe all the literary devices you can find.

4. Evaluate several Bible study resources such as study Bibles, concordances, Bible dictionaries, atlases and maps, translations, special Bibles, commentaries, and other resources, including computer Bible software. Develop a list of resources for new teachers.

5. Design an experiential learning experience that equips teachers to use Bible study resources. Include a lesson plan and teaching materials.

6. Use a minimum of four Bible study resources to develop a background study of this week's Sunday school lesson.

SUGGESTED READING

Cate, Robert L. *How to Interpret the Bible*. Nashville: Broadman Press, 1983.
Fee, Gordon D. and Douglas Stuart. *How to Read the Bible for All Its Worth*. Grand Rapids, Mich.: Zondervan Publishing House, 1982.
Henrichsen, Walter A. *Understand: A Straight Forward Approach to Interpreting the Bible*. Colorado Springs, Colo.: Navpress, 1976.
———. *A Layman's Guide for Interpreting the Bible*. Grand Rapids, Mich.: Zondervan Publishing House, 1978.
Jensen, Irving L. *Enjoy Your Bible*. Wheaton, Ill.: Harold Shaw Publishers, 1992.
———. *Independent Bible Study*. Chicago: Moody Press, 1976.
Lea, Thomas D. *How to Study Your Bible*, Survival Kit 3. Nashville: Convention Press, 1989.
Warren, Richard. *Twelve Dynamic Bible Study Methods*. Wheaton, Ill.: Victor Books, 1986.

TOOLS FOR BIBLE STUDY

A Sample Experiential Learning Experience

Goal: The student will demonstrate an understanding of how to use Bible study resources by:

1. Explaining how to use various Bible study tools.

2. Using a commentary, Bible concordance, and Bible dictionary to develop biblical background material for a given passage of Scripture.

Before the Session:

1. Obtain a hand tool (hammer, pliers, screwdriver, etc.).

2. Set up the learning labs (study Bibles, translations, special Bibles, Bible dictionaries, concordances, commentaries, Bible atlases, other sources) with all of the necessary resources. (These are listed in the Bible Study Resource Sheet.)

Activities:

1. Creating learning readiness. Display a hand tool (screwdriver, hammer, pair of pliers, etc.) Ask: What is this? What is it used for? State: Just as there are tools to do certain jobs around the house, there are also tools for studying God's Word. Today we will be looking at how to use these tools. State the goal and indicators for the session.

2. Learning centers. State that in this session you will be receiving hands-on experience with various Bible study resources. Hand out the list of "Bible Study Resources." State: As you come to each learning center, you will need to read a description of that resource from the information sheet, then complete the assignment at each center.

3. Divide the class into eight groups. (If you have a smaller group, let them go through the learning centers individually.) Move from group to group assisting them if they have any difficulty.

4. Assignment: Ask each class member to use at least three of the Bible study resources to develop a background study of this week's Sunday school lesson.

SUGGESTED BIBLE STUDY RESOURCES

1. Study Bibles

A good study Bible contains in addition to the text itself, marginal references, maps, a limited Bible dictionary, a system of marks to help in pronunciation of names, and a concordance. All of these features you will need to learn to use effectively.

Thompson Chain Reference, Kirkbridge

NAS Ryrie Study Bible, Moody

Disciples Study Bible, Broadman & Holman

Life Application Bible, Tyndale

NIV Study Bible, Zondervan

Experiencing God Study Bible, Broadman & Holman

2. Various Translations of the Bible

    Every teacher should own and use at least two translations of the Bible.

    New American Standard Bible

    New International

    New Century Version

    Amplified Bible

    King James Version

    New King James Version

3. Special Bibles

    The Living Bible

    The Cotton Patch Version of Matthew & John, Jordan

    The Message New Testament, NavPress

4. Bible Dictionaries

    A Bible dictionary is a volume containing a vast amount of information about Bible words, Bible subjects, characters, historical background, archaeology, and other similar matters. It also has an article on each book of the Bible, telling about the author and message, and gives an outline of its contents.

    Unger's Bible Dictionary

    Holman Bible Dictionary

    Zondervan Pictorial Bible Dictionary

    Vines Complete Expository Dictionary of Old & New Testament Words

    Anchor Bible Dictionary (6 vols.)

5. Concordances

    This lists the main words found in the Bible. It tells where they are used and gives a portion of the sentence in which they appear.

    Young's Analytical Concordance

    Strong's Exhaustive Concordance of the Bible

    New American Standard Bible Exhaustive Concordance

6. Commentaries

    The purpose of a commentary is to explain the meaning of the Scripture. Usually the best commentary is one devoted exclusively to one book of the Bible. However, it is well to begin with a one-volume commentary that covers the entire Bible. One-volume commentaries include:

    The Teacher's Bible Commentary, Broadman

    The New Bible Commentary, Eerdmans

    The One Volume Bible Commentary, Macmillan

    Multi-volume commentaries include:

    The Daily Study Bible, Barclay

    Layman's Bible Commentary, John Knox Press

    New American Commentary Broadman

7. Maps and Atlases

    Atlas of the Bible Lands

    Holman Concise Bible Atlas

    The Moody Atlas of Bible Lands

8. Other Helpful Books

    Holman Bible Handbook, Holman

    The Canon of Scripture, F. F. Bruce

    A Survey of the New Testament, Gundry

    Understanding the Old Testament, Anderson

    Biblical Backgrounds, Broadman

    How to Interpret the Bible, Cate

    Pronouncing Bible Names, Severance

    Manners and Customs of the Bible, Zondervan

CHAPTER 11

PLANNING TO TEACH

—RICK YOUNT

> Be very careful, then, how you live, not as unwise but as wise, making the most of every opportunity, because the days are evil (Eph. 5:15–16).

In our last chapter we discussed ways to study a Bible passage in preparation for teaching. "So, what's left to be done?" you may ask. You've analyzed the text. You've defined key concepts. You've outlined the verses. What more should teachers do—could teachers do—than walk into their classrooms and talk through their notes?

The simple answer is "plenty." Analysis of a text is the beginning point of preparation, but effective teaching is far more than talking through one's study notes. What are the needs of your learners? How will this passage speak to them? What do you want to happen as a result of this study? How will you prepare the hearts and minds of your learners to receive a word from the Lord? What kinds of activities will you use to establish knowledge, or deepen understanding, or change attitude, or stimulate Christian action? How will you know if you've achieved what you planned to do? How will you bring the session to an effective conclusion? How will you prepare learners for next week's study? How will you evaluate what you did or didn't do, in order to become more effective as a Christian teacher?

The Amplified New Testament renders the phrase "redeeming the time" this way: "Making the most of the time—buying up each opportunity." We have so much more to accomplish in teaching than saying religious words or telling Bible stories. Paul warned us that the days are evil. We must use every tool at our disposal to make the most of every teaching opportunity. Proper preparation prevents poor performance. Lord Jesus, help us learn how to prepare more effectively to teach your Word and help your church to grow up into you.

How do we make the most of our teaching time? How do we buy up each opportunity for Bible study that transforms the lives of teachers and learners alike? You will find the key to this puzzle in the lesson planning process. A lesson plan reflects the care and planning that a teacher has made, in cooperation with the Holy Spirit, for what will happen in a particular Bible study session. In the process of planning, teachers open themselves to the Word of God and the illumination of God over a period of time. The teacher who merely fills time without a clear vision of where he is taking the class will waste a great deal of that time. Let's examine five key ingredients to an effective lesson plan:

THE INSTRUCTIONAL OBJECTIVE: "SET UP A TARGET"

When I was ten, my folks gave me a bow and arrow set for Christmas. Living in El Paso, Texas at the time, I was able to head out to the backyard—it was a balmy sixty-five degrees—and shoot my arrows. I set up a target on a box in front of a stone wall and shot my first arrow. I missed the target and the box, hit the fence, and split the arrow down the middle. I didn't want to break any more arrows, so I made up a new game in which I shot my arrows straight up in the air, and made my foot a moving target—trying to get it as close to the impact point as possible—without being hit, of course. The result was that I never learned how to shoot an arrow. Skills require targets. Shoot at the target, miss the target, adjust your aim. Shoot, miss, adjust. Eventually we master the skill. When I began teaching Sunday school, I found myself doing the same thing. I "shot" the Bible up into the air, and anywhere we landed by the end of the class was the Lord's will. While God can bless even these misguided efforts, I did not develop skill as a teacher because I had no target to hit, no way to evaluate what I had accomplished.

A properly prepared instructional objective provides a target for teaching. This target is something concrete to aim for—a place to end up—at the conclusion of the session. Detailed lesson planning will fill in the gaps with what you will do during the session, but setting up an instructional target clarifies your purpose. You have already begun to "redeem the time."

IMPORTANCE OF THE LEARNER

An instructional target underscores the importance of the learner, who is the most important ingredient in the Bible teaching-learning process. The Pharisees of Jesus' day put the observance of the Sabbath above the people who observed it. They criticized Jesus for healing on the Sabbath, because healing is work and work is forbidden on the Sabbath. But Jesus put the observer above the observance: "The Sabbath was made on account and for the sake of man, not man for the Sabbath"

(Mark 2:27, Amplified). The learner is the key ingredient in the learning experience. What will the learner be able to do at the end of your teaching that he could not do before? What impact will you make on the individuals sitting in your class? How have they been changed? In writing an instructional objective, you are planning ahead of time, with prayerful dependence upon the Lord to lead you, what your learners should get from your teaching.

TYPE OF LEARNING DESIRED

Instructional targets differ according to the emphasis you desire in a given lesson. We can identify four major emphases in teaching: knowledge, understanding, personal response, and purposeful action.

Knowledge. Knowledge refers to the learner's ability to identify or recall information given to him.

Learners will demonstrate knowledge of . . .

- John 3:16 by quoting it from memory.

- Paul's first missionary journey by identifying from a list of Asian cities the names of the cities he visited.

Understanding. Understanding refers to the learner's ability to explain, illustrate, or describe—in his own words—biblical concepts or principles he has studied. The learner who understands has moved beyond the words and grasped the meaning of the words.

Learners will demonstrate understanding of . . .

- John 3:16 by explaining in their own words the terms "loved the world," "believeth in him," and "everlasting life."

- the armor of God (Ephesians 6) by explaining how truth is a "belt," salvation is a "helmet," faith is a "shield," and the Word of God a "sword."

Personal Response. Personal response refers to the learner's willingness to share a personal experience or opinion related to the topic being discussed. Values, priorities, and commitments develop out of the integration of truth and personal experience.

Learners will demonstrate appreciation for

- John 3:16 by giving a testimony in class about his life before and after he was saved.

- Paul's first journey by sharing an experience in missions.

Purposeful Action. Purposeful action refers to the learners' ability to use what they have learned in class or during the week.

- Learners will demonstrate understanding of the armor of God (Eph. 6) by developing appropriate responses to case studies involving spiritual warfare (Problem-solving).

- Learners will demonstrate appreciation for Paul's first missionary journey by working in one of our church's mission projects over the next month (Commitment).

The outcomes of knowledge and understanding belong to the "Cognitive circle" in chapter 9. The personal response outcome belongs to the "Affective circle" in chapter 9. Purposeful action belongs to the "Behavioral circle" (skillful doing) but also flows out of the cognitive (problem-solving) and affective (commitment to act) domains in chapter 9.

By setting up targets, teachers focus the entire lesson planning process to a specific end. Lecture, discussion questions, and dialogue are all focused on hitting the target. This redeems the time.

LEARNING READINESS: "PRIMING THE PUMP"

One of my summer responsibilities as a child was to draw water for the chickens. My grandfather had an old pump handle water pump. Before it would pump water out of the ground, I had to pour water into the top of the pump. This was called priming the pump. The last responsibility of anyone drawing water was to fill the bucket so the next person could prime it and draw water. If there was no water to put into the pump, it could not draw water out of the ground.

Teachers make a dangerous assumption when they walk into a classroom thinking their students are ready to learn. The individuals seated before them have their hearts and minds on a hundred different personal interests, and they may not be at all ready to focus on the things of God. Jesus said, "Do not give dogs what is sacred; do not throw your pearls to pigs" (Matt. 7:6). Your class is not ready to study spiritual truth when they walk into the room. Their pumps need priming. And this is what the learning readiness section of a lesson plan does. Here are some guidelines to follow in designing learning readiness activities.

REMEMBER YOUR OBJECTIVE

It does not help the learning process to begin your session with a class discussion of last week's football game or the morning's headlines (unless that discussion can lead directly into the passage being studied). Discussion for discussion's sake is not the point. The intention of pump priming should be to focus hearts and minds on a central issue that will prepare the way for the learning activities which follow. Here are some examples drawn from the objectives we stated above.

1. *Objective:* Learners will demonstrate knowledge of Paul's first missionary journey by identifying the names of the cities he visited from a list of Asian cities.

   Suggested learning readiness: Hang a large map of the Middle East and Asia Minor on the front wall. This can be drawn by hand on several sheets of newspaper. Identify each of the major cities in Asia Minor with a large dot. Have the names of the cities written in large print beside their respective dots. Be sure to include all the cities Paul visited on his first missionary journey. Then ask the class to trace the route Paul took on this first journey. (The Bible study will retrace the route and emphasize major events that took place on the journey.)

2. *Objective:* Learners will demonstrate understanding of John 3:16 by explaining in their own words the terms "loved the world," "believeth in Him," and "everlasting life."

   Suggested learning readiness: Write the following words on the chalkboard as learners come into class: "love," "world," "believe," "everlasting," "life." (You've already begun to focus attention.) As the class begins, ask learners to define each of these terms in light of John 3:16. (The Bible study will analyze these terms in light of John 3:16 and parallel passages.)

3. *Objective:* Learners will demonstrate appreciation for Paul's missionary journey by sharing an experience in missions with the class.

   Suggested learning readiness: Write the words "Experiences in Missions" on the chalkboard and share a personal experience you've had in a mission project or on a mission trip. Emphasize the impact the experience had on your life. (The Bible study will focus on Paul's journey and the experiences class members have had in mission work.)

4. *Objective:* Learners will demonstrate understanding of the armor of God (Eph. 6) by developing appropriate responses to case studies involving spiritual warfare (problem-solving).

   Suggested learning readiness: Write the following words on individual pieces of blue poster board: "belt," breastplate," "shoes," "shield," "helmet," and "sword." Write these words on pieces of yellow poster board: "truth," "righteousness," "gospel," "faith," "salvation," "Word of God." Tape these words randomly on the front wall of the classroom. At the beginning of class, have learners match them up. (The Bible study will focus on the meanings of the pieces of spiritual armor.)

AVOID GIMMICKS

Avoid gimmicks that might shock, frighten, or offend learners. You will certainly get attention by using sudden loud noises (firecrackers, air horns), "pretend" rude comments and abusive remarks, or embarrassing skits. Youth ministers seem to be particularly fond of such tactics because of the perceived need to grab teenagers by the throat before they're taught. But shock will do more to disrupt learning than to enhance it.

BUILD A BRIDGE TO BIBLE STUDY

Plan carefully for the transition from learning readiness to Bible study. The learning readiness section should lead naturally into the study portion of the teaching plan.

> (Knowledge of Paul's first journey): "We've traced Paul's first missionary journey on the map. Now let's open to Acts 13 and dig a little deeper into what happened along the way."

> (John 3:16 transition): "We've written your definitions for 'love,' 'world,' 'believe,' 'everlasting,' and 'life' on the board. Open your Bibles to John 3:16. We're going to use this verse and other passages to define these terms and focus on what the verse means."

> (Appreciation for Paul's first journey transition): "My experience taught me so many things about the Lord, but the apostle Paul had many such experiences. Let's look at some of them. Meanwhile, think of experiences you've had in missions action that you'd like to share later."

> (Understanding the armor of God transition): "We've matched up the pieces of armor and spiritual characteristics. Open your Bible to Ephesians 6 and check our work. Did we match them all correctly? (After checking and making changes if needed:) We're going to look at each of these spiritual characteristics today and learn exactly what they mean."

If the pump has been primed correctly, your learners will be eager to get into the Scripture to find answers, clarify meanings, or share the experiences of Bible personalities. In just a few moments, you have focused the attention of your class on the very issues you've targeted. You've made a major step toward "buying up the opportunity" you've been given to teach.

BIBLE STUDY: "HAUL THE FREIGHT"

I had a friend in high school who spent a great deal of his time polishing his candy-apple red 1949 Ford pickup. It had chrome wheels and dual chrome exhaust pipes. He spent most of his time caring for that truck. One day I asked him what kind of load it would carry. "Carry?! Carry?! I don't use this truck to carry anything! I carry it on a trailer when I take it to car shows." What good is a truck if it doesn't haul the freight? What good is a lesson plan if it doesn't convey the deep things of God in a way that learners can understand them?

The Bible study section is the heart of the lesson plan. It is here that the text is analyzed, concepts are explained, applications made, values investigated, attitudes confronted, and lifestyles questioned. Yet for many teachers, this section calls for little more than conveying information. It is amazing that many teachers give years to gathering information, and only minutes to planning a strategy for conveying it effectively. For these individuals, teaching is nothing more than telling what one knows. "The more one knows, the better teacher he is."

No, the essence of teaching is conveying experience, understanding, and attitude to learners in a way that changes their lives. Here is where you haul the freight—don't be satisfied to merely polish the truck! Let's consider how to organize the Bible study section and what teaching methods are most appropriate.

ORGANIZATION

Organization of the Bible study section can take one of several general forms. Let's consider verse-by-verse study, group study, key concepts study, and personal response.

Verse-by-verse study. Teachers explain each verse in the assigned passage. This is by far the most common approach in youth and adult Bible studies. Perhaps this is because the lesson commentary provides information on the passages in this way. You must take care not to lose the learners' interest. Pepper your explanations with questions. Answers will tell you whether the learners correctly understand your explanations. In general, follow this procedure when teaching a verse-by-verse study: Explain the verse or verse fragment; ask a question about your explanation; and then, correct any misunderstandings. Enliven your explanations with illustrations, personal examples, and practical applications.

Example: Trace Paul's first missionary journey from Antioch and back, verse by verse. Focus attention on each city and its associated events as you go.

Small group study. Break the class into several groups of three to five persons. Give members a question or list of questions and let them study the assigned passage to find answers. This allows the Bible to speak to them as they dig out the answers for themselves. Plan about half your teaching time for group work and half for class discussion on their answers. You will have the opportunity to clarify meanings and correct misunderstandings during the group discussion. You must take care to avoid having the groups merely "pool their ignorance"—that is, to base present answers on past learning. Give a brief background study of the passage and explain key terms before sending the groups into the Scripture to find answers.

Example: Read Acts 13–15 and answer the following: Who was the leader of the first missionary journey at the beginning? Who was the leader at the end? When did this change in leadership occur? Why? How did the older, established leader react to the new leader? Who deserted the team? What was the reaction of the two leaders to this "quitter"? Which of the two reacted more like you would? What key discoveries did you make in these three chapters?

Key concepts study. Organize your material around the key ideas in an assigned passage. In Revelation 1 we have the twin pictures of Jesus as Lord-judge and as friend. In Galatians 5 we have a contrast between flesh-works and Spirit-fruit. Separate the related key concepts in a given passage and help learners analyze them.

Example: A study of the fourth chapter of Ephesians might focus on verse fifteen: "speaking the truth in love, we will in all things grow up into him who is the Head, that is, Christ." Organize the Bible study section around these four concepts:

- Speaking the "truth": Christians should live lives of integrity.

- Speaking "in love": Christians should live lives of mercy.

- Speaking "the truth in love": A fusion of the two. Not callous conviction; not sentimental fuzziness; loving with integrity; speaking truth mercifully.

- Growing up into Christ: The result of balancing truth and mercy is spiritual growth. Compare with Proverbs 3:3–4.

Personal response. Organize the Bible study around the personal experiences of class members. This approach is the most unstructured of any discussed so far. It is also the best way to involve learners in the class discussion. Focus attention on positive testimonies that illustrate the principle you are teaching. If you are discussing prayer, ask learners to share times they've prayed effectively. Avoid asking them to confess their failure to pray. If you're discussing tithing, ask for testimonies on good experiences in giving. You must take care to anchor the sharing of personal experiences to the Bible passage(s) being studied. Otherwise, the Bible study can cease to be a Bible study and become group therapy. But this kind of positive sharing can be a real boost to living out the teachings of the Bible.

Example: After surveying the first missionary journey of Paul, ask class members to describe mission activities and projects they have personally experienced. (Remember the learning readiness for this comes from a personal testimony of the teacher. Earn the right to ask members to share by sharing yourself first.)

Let's look at several sets of teaching principles that relate to the four teaching emphases we've been discussing.

TEACH SO THEY'LL REMEMBER

Teaching for knowledge requires more than telling learners about the Bible. When you set up a target of knowledge, you desire your learners to remember the essentials of what you teach. If your learners do not remember from one week to the next what you've taught, then you are not establishing knowledge. You are merely transmitting information. Here are some suggestions to enhance your learners' memory.

Advance organizers. The newsprint map of the cities of Asia Minor suggested under the discussion of learning readiness is an example of an advance organizer. An advance organizer tells the learner at the beginning of class what information will be covered in class.

Tell the class your objective for the day. "At the end of the class today, you will be able to list the pieces of the armor of God from memory." Or, give a short self-graded quiz over the major points of the session. Or, write out an outline of the key points on poster board and tape it to the front wall of the class. Each of these objectives helps learners get an overall picture of the material.

Structure. Learners remember the material much better when it is organized and presented in a clear manner. Emphasize major points as you go along. Use verbal markers to separate one topic from another: "Okay, we've seen how the disciples avoided Paul when he came to Jerusalem. Now let's see how and why they eventually accepted him." Review the section on "organization" for specific suggestions.

Sequence. Learners do better when your material seems to be "going somewhere." Sequence your presentation logically from point to point. Help learners visualize the sequence much like a series of snapshots telling a story.

Active review. The learner will remember key points better if you use "active" review throughout the Bible study section. Have learners repeat key points from memory throughout the session. This is more effective than passive review, in which you repeat the key points for your learners. Enhancing recall requires some measure of drill and practice. ("All right, let's say these together.") Keep the drills short to avoid monotony. Space them out over the session rather than doing them all at one time. Memory of items is increased when your learners concentrate on remembering part of a list, then relax a while to discuss items in the list, then remembering another part of the list, and so on.

TEACH SO THEY'LL UNDERSTAND

It is important for learners to know what the Bible says. But you must carry them beyond the mere recall of biblical facts. Unless they understand what those facts mean, they will not be able to live them in a consistent way. Many of your learners "know the Bible," but do they understand what the Bible means? They may know the answers to a lot of religious questions. But do they understand those answers? If they don't, you are simply playing "Bible trivia" with them. This will fill time, but it will not redeem the time. Here's how to enhance understanding.

Simple to complex. Begin with simple, single concepts. Then move to more complex principles which meld these concepts. The "key concepts" organization on page 194 follows this sequence. First explain the meaning of speaking "the truth." Few would object to that idea. Then explain the meaning of speaking "in love." Again, few would have a problem with that idea. But when you put the phrase together, "speaking the truth in love," you present a principle that will be new to many of your learners. People can speak truthfully (often losing their tempers). And they can speak lovingly (often ignoring the truth of wrongdoing). But to do both at the same time is a complex concept to teach!

Concrete to abstract. Begin the session discussing things that your learners are familiar with: their experiences, opinions, or ideas. These are tangible, concrete things known by your learners. Then move to Bible words (knowledge), Bible meanings (concepts), and finally to eternal principles. Each stage moves the learner farther from his own tangible reality into greater levels of abstract thinking. Jesus' parables are excellent examples of this sequence. He began with tangible things his hearers knew about: wind, sheep and goats, treasure. Then he moved them to consider how these things reflected the Kingdom of God.

Examples and non-examples. Clarify concepts by using examples of what the concept is and examples of what the concept is not. For example, in a session on *agape* love, you want to separate *agape* love from other kinds of love your learners know about. What kind of love *is agape* love? What kinds of love is it not? Both kinds of comparisons are important. Contrast agape love with *eros* (lust) and *phileo* (brotherly affection). This removes the emotional and affectionate aspects of our English word "love" from *agape*, which means "doing good to others." We are not commanded to "like" everyone, but we are commanded to *agape* them—do for them in their best interest. In a similar way, "Christian joy" should be contrasted with concepts it is often confused with, such as happiness, pleasure, and fun.

When you set up a target for understanding, ask yourself again and again, "How do I explain this?" "What examples are there of this?" "What confuses people about this concept?"

Ask questions. Clarify the meaning of concepts by asking questions. By far the most important part of teaching for understanding is being able to ask the right question at the right time. The kind of question you ask is critical.

You should avoid rhetorical questions. Do not ask a question and then answer it yourself. When you use rhetorical questions, you actually condition learners not to answer. Then when you ask a question you want your learners to answer, you may wonder (often in cold silence) why no one responds! The reason is you've taught your learners to wait for you to answer your own questions. Rhetorical questions reduce participation and hinder thinking. Much of the lag time between question and class response is due to learner uncertainty. They simply do not know whether you really want them to answer or not. Once they see you really want them to answer, then they begin thinking about your question. My rule is simple: Never ask a question unless you want a learner to answer it. If you will consistently apply this rule in your teaching, you will discover the lag time between question and response will dramatically decrease.

You should also avoid leading questions. Do not ask questions that have obvious answers. Such questions bore learners and stifle their interest in the study. "Do you see that Paul is saying that we should . . ." (Of course!) "Do you understand that

Jesus is teaching us to . . ." (That's what you just said!) It is better to explain what the passage means than to ask leading questions.

You should avoid simplistic questions. Avoid yes/no questions. "Was Jesus Jewish?" "Was the apostle Peter married?" "Did Cain kill Abel?" "Was Barnabas the one who helped Paul in Jerusalem and Antioch?" These factual questions extinguish the thinking process.

You should use conceptual questions. Focus learner attention on meaning. "John describes Jesus' eyes as 'like a blazing fire' (Rev. 1:14). What does this mean?" Or, another: "In Colossians 3:8–15, Paul lists some characteristics that Christians should take off and others we should put on. How are these characteristics related?" Or another: "Jesus says, 'Let your light shine before men, that they may see your good deeds and praise your Father in heaven' (Matt. 5:16). He also says, 'Be careful not to do your acts of righteousness before men, to be seen by them' (Matt. 6:1). Is this a contradiction?"

Your questions should probe for real understanding. Probing questions cause learners to "dig deeper" for answers. Go beyond initial responses to get at the heart of what learners understand. Ask for more detail.

For example, ask, "How can we go out this week and *agape* the people we meet?" A learner says, "Be kind to people."

Probe: "Okay. How would you do that?" The learner thinks a moment and says, "Well, I'd be nice to people."

This is still too vague. You are looking for some specific action the learner will take.

Probe: "So, how exactly will you be nice to people?"

The learner thinks a little more. Then, as if a light snaps on, he says, "I know! I could visit my friend who's in the infirmary!"

"Excellent! You've got the idea! Someone else have a suggestion?"

Agape is an action. Loving people in Jesus' sense of the word involves doing specific things for people in specific need.

Learners organize the material better so that they can answer your questions. This reorganization of material enhances understanding.

You may sometimes need to redirect questions. Probing questions can cause discomfort for learners. You can make learners feel as if you are harassing them if you continue to probe too long. Redirect the question by asking the entire class for an answer. Let's say that the learner in the example above shows signs of embarrassment at your question, "So, how exactly will you be nice to people?" He stammers ("uhhhh . . . uhhh . . . uhh"), he looks at the floor, he pats his leg. "Class, what specifically can we do to be nice?"

Clarify meanings by problem-solving. When you present your class a problem or dilemma related to the subject you're studying, you will get a clear view of how well the class members do or do not understand. Problems will be approached differently by individual learners. Priorities and values will be reflected in the decisions the class makes. These procedures take you as close to "real-life events" as you can get inside a classroom. Let's look at examples of the statement response, the situation response, and the case response.

First, the statement response. Write a statement on the chalkboard before class begins. At the beginning of the class, give learners time to analyze and then respond to the statement. Write down the responses for use later in the session.

Second, the situation response. Rather than giving the class a statement to react to, provide them a situation they might face. The closer the situation fits the learners' real world, the better. This is because relevant situations help learners integrate Bible teachings with their own views.

Third, the case response. Case studies bring together multiple truths or principles into one problem. A "statement" focuses on Bible study concepts. A "situation" focuses on learner actions. Both are helpful in promoting understanding. Yet they are limited because they usually aim at a single truth or principle. A case study reflects real life issues better than statements or situations because they are more complex.

There may be more than one correct answer to a given case because learners will approach it in different ways. Some may approach the case with rational coldness. They have light but no warmth. Others may approach the same case with irrational emotion. They have warmth but no light. Cold light and warm darkness fail to solve the case biblically. We need both light and warmth. Learners discover the values and ideals of others as they solve the case. Blind spots in thinking are revealed. As learners share their solutions, each gains experience in looking at the situation from perspectives other than his own. All these elements make good case studies an effective tool for learning to solve problems.

TEACH SO THEY'LL PERSONALLY RESPOND

Securing personal responses from your class depends on how free learners feel to share experiences, opinions, or feelings. There must be an atmosphere of freedom and openness in the classroom, or learners will keep their ideas and experiences to themselves. As we have seen, learner ideas and experiences are essential to your goal of "redeeming time" and helping them grow. The more you can involve your learners in the session—the less detached and isolated they are—the better you can teach them. How do we improve the openness of our classes? How do we help learners become personally involved? Let's look at these two vital aspects of Bible study.

Improve openness. In order to help members remove their masks and share personal experiences with others, you must build an atmosphere of trust and acceptance within your class. You might want to review the affective circle in chapter 9 as you consider these methods.

You can improve openness by using subjective questions. Subjective questions allow the learner to share personal opinions related to the passage. They do not require specific factual knowledge of the Bible passage, nor do they depend on the learner's ability to think clearly or logically. The intention of the question is to "open up the learner"—to see how the learner is feeling or thinking within himself. Here are some examples of subjective questions.

- "Jesus forgave Peter for his betrayal during the trial (John 17). How would you have reacted if you had been in Peter's place?"

- "What experiences of forgiveness have you had?"

- "God gave Moses an 'impossible task.' Have you received God's call to what seemed an impossible task? How did you respond? What happened?"

Questions such as these move into the hearts as well as the minds of learners. These do much more to build an interactive environment than factual questions that call for specific answers. "Can anyone name the twelve disciples?" "Someone tell me who Saul was. No, no, the other one." "What was David's wife's name? The second one." "Where was James when he wrote Revelation? Oh, I meant John!" Teachers who use too many factual questions will reduce their students' willingness to contribute in class.

Another way to improve openness is to ask questions of the whole group rather than of one individual. Calling a learner's name before asking a question puts the "chosen one" on the spot. Furthermore, since you have already decided who will answer, the other learners in the group do not need to think about the question. This limits their thinking. Asking questions of the whole group gives each member an opportunity to think and allows anyone to share.

You must earn the right to ask questions that may lead to the sharing of personal experiences. You have no right to ask your learners to share personal experiences if you are not willing to do so. Earn the right to call for personal experiences of others by sharing one of your own first. However, this is not a license to put your every experience on display before a captive audience. Share an appropriate experience in order to prepare the way for your learners to share their experiences.

You will want to focus on positive experiences. A common mistake of inexperienced teachers is to ask students to share failures rather than successes. "When was the last time you had an opportunity to share your faith but didn't?" You will do more for class openness and trust if you only call for positive experiences. "Who is willing to share a time when you told someone about the Lord?" Such experiences focus learners' thoughts on the redeeming work of Christ.

Learners may well share times of failure as they feel more comfortable in the class; this sharing can be a wonderful display of openness in a class. But do not ask learners to share their failures in front of the group. ("Confession before the group" is an important part of Communistic brainwashing.) The sharing of personal experiences in the class, over time, helps members learn from each other and develops an atmosphere of trust and acceptance.

Handling wrong answers. Give attention to how you respond to wrong answers. When a learner answers your question, it shows that he has developed enough confidence to risk being wrong. Take care to handle an inadequate or incorrect answer sensitively. If you react in a way that belittles or humiliates him, he will immediately "put his mask up." You will certainly lose several weeks as you try to win back his trust. And you may lose the chance to teach him altogether!

How, then, do we respond when a person answers wrongly or shares an opinion that does not reflect clear biblical thinking? Support the person and deal with the answer. Throw the answer to the class for analysis. Defend the learner's willingness to share if others criticize him, but guide the class to see what the Bible says. Or respond yourself. "I see what you're saying but I have a problem with that. It seems to me that Paul is saying (express the idea in other words). How do you react to that?"

When members begin to argue, defend the right of all to speak their minds. Keep the discussion on the issues involved. Defuse negative emotions as much as possible.

We do not give up the truth of God's Word in order to placate the feelings of people (2 Tim. 4:1–5). At the same time, we do not condemn or ridicule God's people in the name of truth (John 3:17–18). We teach the Truth by patiently leading them to compare their own conceptions with those of the Bible. This requires trust and openness. Nothing hampers openness in the classroom more than harsh, judgmental, humiliating responses to incorrect answers. By contrast, loving responses affirm the learner, correct the answers, and teach both biblical content and Christian behavior at the same time.

Avoid a harsh or negative attitude. When you present a negative, dominating spirit, you build psychological walls between yourself and those who disagree with you. You hinder learner participation. And you may well destroy your opportunity to teach. Immature teachers believe they are "standing strong" for their convictions. "If they'd get right with God, they'd agree with me!" Such egotistical attitudes destroy the fragile atmosphere that is required to help learners grow.

Model desired attitudes and behaviors. Real changes in the lives of your learners come not from the words you speak but the life you live. Subjective learning is more "caught from the teacher" than "taught by the teacher." As you prepare to teach, ask the Lord to show you how to live what you are planning to say. Aspire to narrow the gap between the biblical ideal and your way of living. Your struggle toward Christlikeness can be a living example to your class members.

Work with small groups. Learners feel less threatened in a group of four than they do in a group of fourteen or forty. There are always learners in a class who seldom raise a question or make a comment. They do not have the confidence to speak up in the larger group. But when placed in the small groups, they are less anxious and are more willing to share.

Further, only one person can speak at a time in an intact class. When you divide the class into smaller groups, more learners are involved in sharing because more than one person can speak at once. The result is greater freedom for sharing and participation by more learners.

Learners are worthwhile individuals. Whether your learners agree with you or not, whether they are pleasant or not, they are individuals for whom Christ died. They are worthy. They are valuable. Treat them as precious jewels. You may "lose the battle" today, but ultimately "win the war" if you persevere in loving the individual.

Consider Jesus' treatment of the Samaritan woman, the Roman centurion, Matthew and Zacchaeus the tax collectors, and Nicodemus the Pharisee. Treat your learners as Jesus would. God has brought your learners into your class. You are a steward of those whom you teach. You will find that "love covers over a multitude of sins" (1 Pet. 4:8). A teacher who loves his students overcomes many deficiencies in style or technique.

TEACH SO THEY'LL RELATE

The building of relationships among your class members depends on what kind of opportunities you give them to work together. The greatest drawback of lecturing is that learners focus on the teacher, not on one another. Give your learners occasions for bridge-building among themselves. We have already discussed advantages of using small groups. Consider the variety of groupings that you can use.

Vary group size. Groups can consist of pairs, triads, quads, or quints (2, 3, 4, 5). You can divide the class in halves, thirds, or fourths. Each size grouping is different. Each has its own best use. Use larger groups of five or six when you want learners to review several weeks of Bible study. They need "more heads" for remembering content and principles of application. Use smaller groupings when you are asking for students to share personal experiences, discoveries, or problems.

Vary group type. In an adult couples' class, one could have husband-wife pairs, or men-only/women-only groups, or randomly mixed groups. Each kind of group produces its own kind of learning outcome.

The husband-wife pair allows couples to use their knowledge of each other. These classroom efforts might strengthen their relationship at home.

Men-only/women-only groups demonstrate the different viewpoints of men and women toward issues in our society. "So God created man in his own image, in the image of God he created him; male and female he created them" (Gen. 1:27). Men and women differ but both are created in God's image. As you lead your class to explore differences of perspective in light of Scripture, you contribute to a richer understanding of issue, Scripture, and relationship.

Random groupings build relationships in the class as members work together on a common task. Since the groupings are random, the combinations of members differ from assignment to assignment.

Plan gatherings outside the classroom. Relationships will remain tentative if the Sunday school classroom is the only place your learners meet. Mission projects, church work days, or a cup of coffee after church will build bridges fast. Plan occasional social events in homes, at the church, or "out on the town" that get members together during the week.

While socializing does not occur during the Bible study section of the plan, it does relate well to the goal of building *koinonia* in the class. Worthwhile Christian ministry does not occur among strangers. If the members of your Sunday school class are to minister to one another, it will happen as they grow in their mutual relationships. You can "redeem the time" for the process by including a variety of grouping procedures in your lesson plan.

TEACH SO THEY'LL DO THE WORD

Jesus made it clear that learning and action go together. "Go and do thou likewise" accompanied his teaching. It should accompany ours as well. The problem-solving activities and removing-the-mask techniques already discussed are excellent ways to get learning out of the classroom. But how, specifically, can we coax learners into action? By assigning activities to be done during the week. These assignments can be given to individuals, groups, or to the class at large. Here are some suggestions.

Individual assignments. When one of your learners shows special interest or talent, suggest a project that will allow him to use this interest or talent. He will learn more on his own. And he can share what he learns with the class as well. Let's say one of your members likes geography. Ask her to draw a map of the unfamiliar area the class is studying. Another might enjoy language study. Assign him a list of words from soon-to-be-studied passages. He can dig into commentaries and be prepared to share his findings in class. Others may have talents for drama or music or poetry. They can direct mini-plays or write songs or poems to share in class. This variety enhances the study. But the focused attention of learners on passages and places, on words and scripts, deepens their commitment to God's Word.

Use sensitivity and patience in suggesting projects for your learners. If you encourage too little, the assignment may never be attempted. If you encourage too much, the assignment may seem like a requirement rather than a privilege. Weave the talents of your members into the class, as they are able to do and willing to do.

Group assignments. From time to time, ask a group of three or four learners to work together on an assignment. They will teach one another in a relaxed setting outside of class. Their presentation to the class will add variety to the hour. It gives the group members a sense of belonging and usefulness in the class. Further, this is an ideal way to involve members who are hesitant to accept an individual assignment.

Class assignments. From time to time suggest a general assignment for the whole class to do. This might be a list of questions to answer. It might be a test or reaction scale to fill out. It might be a list of key words to define in preparation for a brainstorming session. Or a case study to analyze. Or a spiritual diary to keep for the week. These kinds of assignments bind the class together in doing common tasks which will improve their understanding of the Bible. Do the assignments yourself! You give the proper example to the class by doing this, but more, you make yourself part of the whole group.

Use assignments in class. When you give an assignment to be done during the week, be sure to plan time in the next session to discuss the assignment. Learners will quickly realize that the assignments are not important if you don't do this.

What is the benefit of this emphasis on outside work to Sunday school? To the learners? To you?

- Recognizes and develops the gifts of learners.
- Increases interest in personal Bible study.
- Increases enthusiasm for the Sunday school hour.
- Reduces teacher study time as learners share in teaching.
- Increases the variety of learning experiences.
- Encourages learners to explore biblical topics in more detail.
- Builds rapport between teacher and members through sharing.
- Develops teaching skills in learners.
- Helps shy members to become more involved with others.
- Expands the Sunday school "hour" into the week.
- Furnishes resources for future learning through increased sharing.
- Reduces dependence on the teacher. Increases independent study.

CHOOSING BIBLE STUDY ACTIVITIES

We've concentrated on the complexities of the Bible study section of a lesson plan. How do you decide what to do in the Bible study section? Here are some suggestions to help you determine what learning tools to use when.

Class history. What kinds of teaching experiences is your class used to? Do not try to do too much too fast. Don't make drastic changes quickly. Build trust first. Classes that are accustomed to lecture (and no participation) will not like being asked questions and may rebel at the suggestion of group work. Classes that are accustomed to free-wheeling discussion will not like to be lectured to and may resent that you are trying to structure the class by way of questions or comments. Learn from your learners! Then move them gradually and gently into better methods of learning.

Class preferences. What do class members respond to best? If the class enjoys group discussion, use this while integrating more explanation and "meat." If the class prefers lecture, use this while integrating more participatory activities.

Choose new approaches wisely. What new approach can you use without creating undue anxiety or resistance? The class has had testimonies before. Why not record answers to a central question at a Wednesday night supper and play the answers for the class. The class has participated in discussions as a class. Is it time to try using small groups to extend this participatory approach? Build on new approaches that are well received. Stretch the class just as you might stretch a muscle—with slow, gradual movements.

It is better to lead learners gently into new learning experiences than to shock them with an unfamiliar experience or class arrangement. If you plan to use a "new approach" (new to your class, at least), how will you prepare class members for it? "This week we focused on (content) by analyzing the passage as a class. Next week, let's work together in smaller groups to insure everyone a chance to participate."

Choose appropriate activities. You've set up a target for your learners to hit. Select the kinds of activities that will help them hit it. If you're afraid the activities will be unacceptable to your learners, then you've set up a target that you cannot hit. Set up a realistic target for your learners and then plan activities in line with that target.

Watch for "the fire." In time, one of your class members will "catch fire." A discovery made. An experience had. A lesson put into practice with positive results. Interest is ignited. Enthusiasm recharged. Move the class in this learner's direction by emphasizing his experience.

Be patient and move gradually. As one and then another of your learners catch the excitement of life-changing Bible study, you will be given greater freedom to do new things in class. Be cautious. Do not go too far too fast. Be patient with learners who aren't excited and don't seem to care. They may come around (think of the disciple Thomas) or they may not (think of the disciple Judas). Be faithful and continue to plant the seed.

HIT THE TARGET?

The Bible study section ends when your learners (or at least some of them) hit the target you've set up. If your target is knowledge, can they identify or recall what you've said they would? If your target is understanding, can they explain or give examples of the concepts you've taught? If personal response, have they engaged in sharing their experiences related to the study? If purposeful action, have they shared ways they can put the study into practice during the week?

If not, why not? Was the target too small? Did you fail to plan your time correctly? Did you use inappropriate methods? Did something unexpected happen in class? Each time you evaluate a session, you gain priceless help for your next teaching plan.

THE CONCLUSION: "TIE IT UP IN A BOW"

The objective has been accomplished. You now conclude the session by summarizing or leading the class to summarize what has happened. The way you draw your session to a close is as important as anything you've done so far. It is your last chance to "redeem the time" for your learners. Remember, "all's well that ends well." Here are some suggestions for ending well.

AVOID TOTAL CLOSURE

People want to close discussions and end learning activities in a satisfactory way. They want to find solutions to problems you've raised. Educators call this tendency closure. It is frustrating for learners to be left hanging in the middle of an unresolved problem or guessing at what the point of the study was supposed to be. On the other hand, you create a sense of finality or ending to the session when you bring the class to total closure. This is not good because you want the learning and experiences to follow your learners into the week. Therefore, draw the session to a close without coming to total closure. Here's how to do it.

REVIEW MAJOR POINTS

Briefly review the key discoveries of the session. You can do this passively (teacher review) if time is short or lead the class to actively review what they've learned (learner review).

INVOLVE LEARNERS

Ask learners to share their discoveries, feelings, and reactions to what they've learned from the session. If you listen carefully, you will pick up on the kinds of things that interest and satisfy your learners.

LEAD TO COMMITMENT

Ask learners to suggest ways they will act on what they've learned during the week. Write down these suggestions and review them at the beginning of the next class period (without names, of course!).

PROMPT FOR NEXT SESSION: "PLANT A SEED"

Disjointed sessions waste time. When sessions are linked Sunday by Sunday we extend Bible study time into the week and buy back time for spiritual growth. Links are established between sessions by providing learners a brief but meaningful assignment that ties into the next study.

Raise a question, pose a problem, or provide a situation analysis for learners to work on during the week. This "advance organizer" for the next session helps learners focus on Sunday school study during the week and establishes a beginning point for learning readiness in the next session.

In summary, a lesson plan consists of the following elements:

An Instructional Objective (Set Up the Target)

Learning Readiness (Prime the Pump)

Bible Study (Haul the Freight)

(Hit the Target)

Conclusion (Tie it Up with a Bow)

Make an Assignment

Plant a Seed

Using this format to structure your lesson plans will put more punch into your teaching sessions. You will accomplish much more with this approach than without it and you will "redeem the time" in a very practical way.

FOR FURTHER STUDY

1. Select a Sunday school lesson. Use the Bible passage in that lesson and develop discussion questions for each stage: Creating Learning Readiness (motivation); Guiding Bible Study (examination); and Apply to Life (application).

2. Evaluate a youth or adult Bible study class. How did the teacher encourage discussion? How was discussion discouraged? Did the teacher express appreciation for members' contributions? How?

3. Select a passage of Scripture. Write a learning objective and a learning readiness activity for the passage.

4. A class member responds to the teacher's question with a wrong answer. What are some appropriate ways for the teacher to respond?

5. Evaluate a youth or adult Bible study class. How did the teacher bring the lesson to a conclusion? Did the teacher avoid total closure? Did the teacher review major points? Did the teacher lead the class to commitment?

6. How important do you feel spiritual preparation is to an effective lesson? Ask several teachers the process they use to prepare themselves for teaching a Bible study class.

SUGGESTED READING

Arends, Richard I. *Learning to Teach*. New York: Random House, 1988.

Coleman, Lyman. *Basic Training for Leaders of Small Groups Video Series*. Littleton, Colo.: Serendipity House, 1993.

Edge, Finley B. *Teaching for Results*, Rev. ed. Nashville: Broadman & Holman, 1995.

Ford, LeRoy. *Design for Teaching and Training*. Nashville: Broadman, 1978.

Habermas, Ronald and Klau Issler. *Teaching for Reconciliation*. Grand Rapids, Mich.: Baker Books, 1992.

Jacobsen, David, Paul Eggen, and Donald Kauchak. *Methods for Teaching: A Skills Approach*. 3rd ed. Columbus, Ohio: Merrill Publishing Company, 1989.

Morgan, Norah, and Juliana Saxton. *Teaching, Questioning, and Learning*. New York: Routledge, 1991.

Pregent, Richard. *Charting Your Course: How to Prepare to Teach More Effectively*. Madison, Wis.: Magna Publications, Inc., 1994.

Sanders, Norris M. *Classroom Questions: What Kinds?* New York: Harper & Row, 1966.

Yount, Rick. *The Discipler's Handbook*. Fort Worth: Southwestern Baptist Theological Seminary, 1981–1993.

Part Three:
Lesson Planning

CHAPTER 12

TEACHING PRESCHOOLERS

—NORMA HEDIN

In 1993, Search Institute researchers asked adults and leaders to describe and evaluate their congregations' children's programs. Respondents revealed that their children's programs focused on traditional activities, such as Sunday school, Vacation Bible School, children's sermons, and children's choir. Most people surveyed believed that their churches make a positive difference in the lives of children. In fact, 85 percent of adults called their church's children's program "good" to "outstanding." They felt overall that the classes were warm and inviting and their children appeared to enjoy the programs and grew in their religious faith as a result of them.

However, the researchers also pinpointed weaknesses. The programs were not innovative enough and, in their view, congregations did not place high enough priority on Christian education for children. The study also found that teachers in children's education tend to have lower faith maturity than teachers of youth and adults.[1]

A reading tour of popular books on church growth reveals similar concerns for the need for higher priority on children's education and programs in the church:

- Boomer parents, in surprising numbers, are seriously considering returning to church for the sake of their kids.[2]

1. Eugene C. Roehklepartain, *The Teaching Church* (Nashville: Abingdon, 1993), 73–75.
2. Doug Murren, *The Baby Boomerang* (Ventura, Calif.: Regal Books, 1990), 115.

- One key reason (that the twenty-six to forty-year-old age group is reachable) is the arrival and needs of children, which seem to serve as a prime factor in bringing unchurched persons into the church.[3]

- Several studies have indicated that people identify the needs of their children as a major factor in their decision to seek a church.[4]

- Quality programs and facilities are especially important in churches reaching out for baby boomers among the successfuls. . . . The church nursery, for example, rivals in attractiveness the day-care center at the visitor's investment office or the professionally managed center down the street.[5]

- According to the Gallup Poll, the young adults, ages 18–35, comprise the fastest-growing segment of the American church population. However, many of those young adults will not remain in a church that does not have a program they feel is adequate for their children.

Analysts are not sure if young adults attend church because of their children or if they come because of the unique need that arises because they have children. Whatever the motive, it is clear that a church must have a vibrant program to teach children if the church wants to reach their parents.[6]

Parents are concerned about the needs of their children and about quality programming for children. These concerns may lead parents back to church or lead them to choose a particular church. Whether the return grows out of the children's need or the parents' need, the church faces the challenge of providing quality instruction and facilities to meet the needs of these children and parents.

Children's ministry can be divided into early childhood and later childhood. For purposes of our study, we have divided the study of teaching children into two chapters. This chapter will deal specifically with meeting the learning needs of preschoolers (birth through kindergarten), while the following chapter will focus on the learning needs of older children (first through sixth grade).

BIBLICAL FOUNDATIONS

PARENTS AS TEACHERS

Since preschoolers spend a limited amount of time at church, we will begin by noting the inadequacy of the church to do what parents were designed to do. It is

3.   Bruce Shelly and Marshall Shelly, *The Consumer Church* (Downers Grove, Ill.: InterVarsity Press, 1992), 169.
4.   Ibid., 172.
5.   Ibid., 209.
6.   Elmer L. Towns, *10 Sunday Schools That Dared to Change* (Ventura, Calif.: Regal Books, 1993), 53.

the responsibility of the parents to teach children spiritual truths in the context of daily life in the home. The biblical writings clearly instruct parents to teach their children (Gen. 18:19; Deut. 6:7; Ps. 78:5–6; Prov. 4:1–4; Prov. 22:6). The Hebrews knew that teaching about spiritual things separated from the rest of life has little meaning. The most significant teaching is sometimes intentional, sometimes casual teaching as the child grows and develops within the context of a nurturing and loving home environment. Teaching that occurs only on Sunday for an hour or two cannot possibly replace constant instruction during the walk of life. Realistically, however, we know that many parents are not instructing their children in this way. This type of teaching has been handed over to the church in many instances and thus places greater responsibility in the hands of our teachers.

One reason parents depend upon the church to carry out religious instruction is because they are unsure of their own abilities to teach their children religious things. C. Nelson Ellis suggests that "we must give first attention to the continued training of adults who are parents, so that they may grow 'in the grace and knowledge' and then, as a part of their training, help them better to perform their role of parents and teachers in the home."[7] One of the most significant aspects of preschool teaching may be that of helping parents learn how to teach their children.

While some parents simply feel inadequate, others are not interested in teaching spiritual things. The church may serve as the only spiritual teacher in the life of the child. We must support the family, but we must recognize that today's child is very different from the Hebrew child. Recent trends show that stress, divorce, abuse, and neglect are realities affecting greater numbers of children.[8] While most preschoolers may come to church with a parent or parents, an increasing number come with grandparents or caregivers. We must minister to the child of today. Our attitude must be one of willingness to love and meet the needs of children the way Jesus did.

JESUS' ATTITUDE TOWARD CHILDREN

Jesus loved children. Even after an exhausting day of travel, another encounter with the Pharisees, and unending questions about his encounter from the disciples, Jesus took time for children. "Then the little children were brought to Jesus for him to place his hands on them and pray for them. But the disciples rebuked those who brought them. Jesus said, 'Let the little children come to me, and do not hinder them, for the kingdom of heaven belongs to such as these'" (Matt. 19:13–14). When my four-year-old child first heard this story in her Sunday school class, she asked, "Why were those men so mean to the children?" I explained to her that although it

---

7. C. Nelson Ellis, *Where Faith Begins* (Philadelphia: John Knox Press, 1971), 209.
8. Louis S. Richman, "Struggling to Save Our Kids," *Fortune*, 10 August 1992, 34–40; Alice Kohn, "Shattered Innocence," *Psychology Today*, Feb. 1987, 54–63; David Elkind, *The Hurried Child* (Reading, Mass.: Addison-Wesley Publishers, 1981).

sounds like they were being mean, they probably thought Jesus was too busy to see the children and were trying to keep them from bothering him. Her response to my explanation was, "Well it still sounds to me like they were being mean!"

Maybe they were. Caught up in the excitement of Jesus' ministry, they may have been frustrated with the interruptions that children naturally bring. But Jesus himself, in a very pointed way, rebuked the disciples for trying to keep the children from him. And not only that, he then welcomed the children and the parents who brought them. He treated children and their parents with dignity and respect. He also expected others to treat them with equal respect.

Mark records that even as Jesus was teaching adults, he took time to take the children in his arms, put his hands on them, and bless them (Mark 9:36; 10:16). We can follow his lead by taking time for children and blessing them. We can acknowledge their presence, look at them, smile at them, and hug them, thus communicating God's love. If we want to follow Christ's example, we must be concerned about children as well as adults.

Jesus also used children as examples for his teaching. When the disciples were bickering and trying to assess their status in the kingdom, Jesus called a child and placed the youngster in front of them (Mark 9:33–37). He then illustrated that entering the kingdom of God requires humility like that of a child and that children are somehow numbered among those who believe in Christ. In the parallel account in Matthew 18:5–6, he also warned against causing a little child to stumble or go astray. Jesus did not ignore children as we often do in our search for truth or concern for issues. He cherished them and encouraged adults to develop some of their qualities.

PSYCHOLOGICAL FOUNDATIONS

WHAT ARE PRESCHOOLERS LIKE?

Continuing research indicates that the preschool years are the most important years in the process of development. From infancy to kindergarten, young children learn to walk, talk, socialize, categorize, express emotion, feed themselves, dress themselves, and thousands of other skills. An article in *Life* magazine describes babies as "little scientists, constantly exploring the world around them, with innate abilities we're just beginning to understand."[9] Researchers are discovering that, although limited by language in their first year, babies have a rudimentary understanding of math, a sense of the past and the future, a memory of visual sequences,

---

9.   Lisa Grunwald and Jeff Goldbert, "The Amazing Minds of Infants," *Life*, July 1993, 47.

recognition of their native tongue, and a sense of physical laws.[10] The more we research, the more we understand the amazing abilities of young preschoolers.

Theorists have studied and attempted to explain their observations of the developing child. These explanations or theories help us to understand the child and his abilities. Children actually think and learn differently than adults. Paul states this truth in 1 Corinthians 13:11, "When I was a child, I talked like a child, I thought like a child, I reasoned like a child . . ." There is a qualitative difference between the reasoning skills of children and adults. Knowing how children think and learn helps us search for ways to teach biblical truths in a way that they can understand. God has designed children in such a way that they grow and develop gradually, gaining understanding as their bodies and minds grow.

COGNITIVE DEVELOPMENT

Jean Piaget[11] provides tremendous insight into the cognitive development of children. Meticulously observing children, Piaget proposed that children move through stages of cognitive development, each stage building on prior stages. Two of these stages occur during the preschool years. During the first stage, birth through age two, he observed that newborn infants learn from the day of their birth. Through sensory input from sight, sound, smell, taste, and touch, the newborn interacts with his or her environment and begins to process that information. In addition, the infant moves, at first randomly and then in a purposeful way, learning about the effects of his movements on the environment. This *Sensorimotor Period* finds the child exploring this strange new world and developing such skills as memory and object permanence.

Piaget's second stage is the *Preoperational Stage*. From ages two to seven, the child begins to understand and use symbolic forms such as language, mental images, drawings, and make-believe to imitate those in his or her world. Other skills include categorizing information and developing ways to organize information.

We learn from Piaget that during these two early stages, there are some things that preschool children cannot do. They generally cannot see from another person's point of view. This is called *egocentrism*. It isn't that they don't want to—they simply cannot. For example, the child thinks it snows just so she can play in it. Or she thinks the sun follows her around and goes to sleep and gets up with her.

The preoperational child also cannot *conserve*. He cannot understand that the volume of something remains the same, even if its appearance changes. Piaget's classic experiment used two equal balls of clay. When one ball was rolled into the shape of a hot dog, the children believed that it contained more clay because it was

---

10. Ibid., 46–60.
11. Jean Piaget and Barbel Inhelder, *The Psychology of the Child* (New York: Basic Books, 1969).

longer. They could not conserve the fact that it was only shape, not volume that had changed.

Preschoolers also tend to concentrate on one quality of something at a time, called *centration*. They may focus on the color of an object rather than its shape. They cannot focus on two or three qualities at the same time. When you ask a child to bring you the green square and there is also a green triangle, then the preschooler may bring you a different color square or the green triangle, focusing on one quality at a time. The ability to focus on two or more qualities at the same time comes in the later preschool years.

It is this focus on only one quality that may cause concern to parents who try to find out what their preschooler learns during Sunday school. You ask Katie what she did during class and she says, "We played bubbles." The parent then asks, "But what did you learn?" and Katie keeps talking about blowing bubbles, "played bubbles outside!" The parent may begin to wonder if any teaching is going on in that class since the child can only talk about bubbles. But the child focuses on one aspect of Sunday school that was sensory related. As she matures, she will gain the ability to "decenter" and focus on other aspects of the teaching.

PSYCHOSOCIAL DEVELOPMENT

Erik Erikson[12] studied the psychosocial development of infants through later adulthood. He proposed a stage theory of personality development. This theory proposes that preschoolers move through three stages, each building on the other as the preschooler interacts with his social environment.

Basic Trust versus Mistrust lasts approximately from birth to age two. The child is totally dependent on adults in this stage and the quality of care given determines successful outcomes. If cared for, touched, held, loved, fed and kept dry, the child develops trust in caregivers. If neglected, abused or not cared for adequately, a child develops fear, suspicion, and hurt.

Autonomy verses Shame and Doubt lasts from ages two to three. This is the "I can do it" stage and finds preschoolers wanting to do everything on their own, in their own way, and in their own time. If encouraged and given adequate supervision and direction, the proper sense of independence develops. If shamed and discouraged in their attempts to be independent or forced to do things too early, then shame and doubt characterize their personality. The greatest battles at this age are feeding, dressing themselves, and toilet training.

Initiative versus Guilt, ages four and five, is the stage of those who are "into everything." They want to expand their world of experience, explore, and try out new things. They need assurance so that they will accept new challenges, explore, and

---

12.   Erik Erikson, *Childhood and Society*, 2nd ed. (New York: W. W. Norton & Co., 1963), 247–63.

ask questions. If fours and fives are rejected or punished for initiating activities, they feel guilty and afraid to try new things on their own.[13]

IMPLICATIONS FOR TEACHING PRESCHOOLERS

The child is always learning. There is much that preschoolers can know and understand. They learn about their world through smelling, tasting, touching, hearing, and seeing. As they are exposed to a number of objects and stories, they organize this information. They can also learn through movement in and acting on their environment. They need lots of room and safe places to explore and discover new things. They also can and do imitate parents, teachers, and other children. In doing so, they "try out" new behavior to see if it works and if it is acceptable.

The child is learning about God. While preschoolers are learning and processing information about their world, they also process information about God and the church. They associate the concept of God with their parents. But preschoolers can also begin to sense and understand that God loves them through their experiences with other loving, nurturing adults. These adults tell them about God, lead them to experience God and his creation, teach them about relationships, and eventually lead them to understand the words, "God loves you."

Infants form their first impressions about church from their teachers. When the physical needs of infants are met and they feel safe, they develop the confidence that when they are at church, they are safe and cared for. Mr. Jack works in our church nursery along with two other teachers. Week after week, he sits in that rocking chair and rocks babies. He talks to them, laughs with them, and tells them how special they are. By the middle of their first year, he has become a part of their world. When they have a hard time leaving mom and dad, Mr. Jack is there to comfort them. From Mr. Jack they learn that they are loved and cared for at church. Those are foundations for future learning about church.

Even very young preschoolers can understand that God made the world and the things in it. When my niece, Bethany, was two years old, we were riding in a van toward the beach. She saw in the distance a group of seagulls flying over the water. Her reaction was, "Look at the birds, mommy. God made the birds." She was beginning to make the connections between what she learned at church and home to places and things away from home. As these truths are repeated, they come to have meaning to the child, just as the words "I love you" come to have meaning.

Older preschoolers have a simple trust in God and can think of Jesus as a friend who loves them. They can learn to talk to God, to thank him, and to ask him for things they need.

---

13.   William R. Yount's book, *Created to Learn* (Nashville: Broadman & Holman) scheduled for publication in 1996, discusses all eight of Erikson's stages and their relationship to religious education.

Young children are literal and concrete in their thinking. Young children are unable to think abstractly. They tend to think of God in literal terms and cannot separate him from parents and other authority figures.[14] They are very concrete in their thinking, which limits their understanding of what they directly experience. They attempt to fit abstract concepts into their own understanding. My preschooler did this with songs. The song "Take All of Me" became "Take all the Beans." She didn't understand the concept of Jesus taking all of a person's life, but she understood beans. She gradually came to understand what the song meant, but she was in elementary school before that happened. Symbolic statements like "God is holy" or "Jesus wants to live in your heart" cannot be interpreted by the young child. Use of these phrases may lead a preschooler to believe that he cannot understand things about God. Wes Haystead tells the following story of his own child:

> One Easter Sunday we were driving home from church and I asked Andrew what his Bible story had been about. It seemed like a safe question to ask on Easter. He responded enthusiastically, "It was about Jesus in prison."
>
> I knew enough about the Bible to know stories about Paul in prison and Joseph in prison, but I hadn't heard one about Jesus in prison. After a few more questions, it suddenly became clear what Andrew had really heard. All morning long, teachers had been talking about "Jesus is risen!" They had sung songs about it, thanked God for it, told children to be glad because of it. But no one had ever stopped to explain what "risen" means. Never having heard the word before, Andrew simply did what most young children do. He substituted a word that sounded similar, and spent the whole morning wondering why everyone was so happy that Jesus was in prison.[15]

Preschoolers need security, freedom, and encouragement. Erikson helps us to see that babies need adequate care, loving adults, and kind attention at church so that proper trust can be developed. Older preschoolers need freedom to explore and experiment with their environment, a balance of firmness and permissiveness, age-appropriate activities to encourage success, and teachers with a willingness to answer questions and help them develop a sense of accomplishment.

PRESCHOOLERS AT CHURCH

HOW A PRESCHOOLER LEARNS[16]

Senses. We have already seen from Piaget that infants begin to process information from the time they are born. This processing is accomplished through interac-

---

14.   Judith Allen Shelly, *The Spiritual Needs of Children* (Downers Grove, Ill.: Inter-Varsity Press, 1982), 31.

15.   Wesley Haystead, *Everything You Want to Know About Teaching Young Children* (Ventura, Calif.: Gospel Light Publishers, 1989), 14–15.

16.   The list of basic ways that preschoolers learn is taken from Cos Davis, "How A Preschooler Learns About God" (Nashville: Baptist Sunday School Board), pamphlet.

tion with the environment. This happens through the use of senses. Children learn about their world, the world God made, through seeing the color of the blocks, smelling the banana, listening to the bells, tasting the cinnamon toast. The physical senses are the way preschoolers meet the world around them and increase their understanding of the way the world works. It also gives them the chance to relate the world to God and to express their thanks for the world God made.

Curiosity. Preschoolers are naturally curious. New objects, new smells, and new pictures all arouse the interest of children and prompt them to explore the unknown world. A variety of materials and freedom to explore leads preschoolers to strike out on their own to learn about those objects and to relate those objects and pictures to stories about God and Jesus and church.

Relationships. Relationships with people provide the most important avenue for learning for the preschool child. Teachers and parents show love for the preschooler with loving words, kind reassurances, and genuine appreciation for him and his abilities. The preschooler learns about herself and her acceptance as love is offered or withheld. Values and actions are modeled through relationships and are imitated by the preschool child. These relationships are not limited to adults only, however. Often the siblings provide the relationships for learning. One three-year-old in the nursery tackled everyone who came in the door. The mother's explanation was that it was the older sister's fault!

Repetition. Preschool children love to hear the same songs and stories and rhymes. Repetition allows for hearing something over and over, learning more details and building on previous learning. My husband and I can both repeat all the words to *Goodnight Moon* because of the many times we read that book to our oldest daughter. Our youngest daughter loves *Mr. Brown Can Moo.* Every time we read it she learns a new sound or a new word. As a teacher, you may tire of the repeated stories in the preschool curriculum. But the preschoolers love the familiar stories that become favorites.

Play and Imitation. "Play is the work of the child."[17] Anyone who has observed a room full of two- and three-year-old children knows that they are hard at work at whatever they do. Preschoolers learn about their environment and about people through their play. They pretend to teach, they care for babies, they make car noises, and they pretend to lead the singing for a church service. During play, children explore various roles and attempt to understand their world. They imitate the behavior of adults and other children. Part of their pretend play is acting out what they have seen an adult or another child do. The reactions they receive from others determine whether or not they imitate that behavior again.

Doing. Preschoolers love to do things. They learn by doing. It may take longer for a two-year-old to put on his clothes or to work the puzzle himself. But the joy in the face and voice of a child when he proudly looks at you and smiles triumphant-

---

17. Ibid.

ly and says, "Jason dood it!" reveals that lasting satisfaction of doing it himself. Satisfaction in doing will encourage him to try something the next time, thus encouraging more learning.

ACTIVITY LEARNING

Because we often connect teaching with "telling," we may be tempted to line our preschoolers up and "teach" (that is, "tell") them. Preschoolers learn from conversation with adults, but they learn very little from sitting in rows facing the teacher and listening to her talk for twenty minutes. While older children have some symbolic ability and experience to understand verbal communication more easily, the preschooler is still experiencing for the first time. You can describe the taste and smell of an orange. But you don't really know what an orange is until you have held it in your hand, smelled it yourself, and tasted its sweetness.

Preschoolers are active learners. While there are times that a short Bible story/worship time can be included in preschool teaching, the best type of teaching for preschoolers is called activity learning. It is teaching as preschoolers are involved in their play. As Kari wipes the table, you talk with her about how she is helping and that the Bible teaches us to help one another. As Kevin builds a tower with the blocks, you talk to him about what he is building and thank God for the hands he gave him so that he can build. As Paula works a puzzle of a church, you talk about coming to church and tell her that you like to go to church. As Jason and Shelby are playing in the kitchen, you tell the story of two friends, David and Jonathan, and tell them that they are being kind to each other as David and Jonathan were kind to each other.

How does this type of teaching work? First, the room is divided into learning centers. These centers may include areas for homeliving, art, puzzles, books, nature, music, or blocks. As a teacher, you plan an activity for several of the centers. The curriculum plans will give suggestions for activities in the areas. In books and puzzles, you may place two or three books and two or three puzzles related to the teaching aim for the day.

As children enter the preschool room, they are allowed to choose an activity area, and then allowed to move from activity to activity as they desire. Teachers, seated in learning centers, talk with various children about their play and activities. As children work puzzles or look at books, teachers talk with them, sing Bible songs, tell the Bible story, or share Bible thoughts. In the art area, children may paint or draw or paste pictures. As they work, teachers tell the Bible story, ask questions about their work, and thank God for their hands. In the music area, a teacher strums the autoharp. Teachers and preschoolers sing together, thanking God for ears to hear and for hands to play.

Teachers are always available to meet preschoolers' needs and give a needed pat on the back or word of praise. This approach makes use of the way preschoolers learn. Their curiosity leads them to approach a learning center. As they do an activity—cook in the kitchen or build a tower or paint a picture—the teacher converses with them, showing love and building relationships. As they pretend, children act out roles and imitate others. They may do something totally different than you had planned. John may put the pot on his head or listen to the sound of the spoon hitting the pot rather than cooking with the item. He may use his senses to listen to the sound or feel the pot on his head. Over and over again, John bangs the spoon or works the puzzle, each time learning a little more about his world.

Older preschoolers, ages three and older, may have a short worship time where they pray, hear the Bible story, and talk about the story. But these times are brief and also use active involvement as children are invited to pray, answer questions about the story, play learning games, and sing songs. Curriculum helps give suggestions for group times as well as activity learning.

CONTENT AND CURRICULUM

CONTENT

Obviously, the content of our teaching in the church is the Bible. The truths and values in God's Word are for people of all ages. However, during the child's preschool years, we are laying the foundations for future learning. We teach age-appropriate concepts and stories that speak to children. In the Southern Baptist curriculum, eight general subject areas are designated for teaching in the preschool years. "A child's initial understandings of self, family, others, church, the Bible, God, Jesus, and the natural world provide the framework for moral and spiritual development."[18]

Cos Davis summarizes these content areas:

> God—We want preschoolers to have positive feelings about people and things associated with God. We want them to associate the created world with God.

> Jesus—We want preschoolers to sense that Jesus was born, grew, belonged to a family, and was a very special person.

> Natural World—Our aim is to teach the preschooler that God made the world good and beautiful and that "thank you, God" is an appropriate response.

> Bible—We want to help preschoolers think of the Bible as a special book which tells about God and Jesus.

18. Dixie Ruth Crase, *Today's Preschoolers* (Nashville: Convention Press, 1993), 34.

Self—The biblical view of the importance of oneself should be communicated to preschoolers. Personal relationships, environment, and Bible-related activities can enhance the child's appreciation of himself as a person of worth.

Others—Preschool teachers try to help preschoolers become more aware that others are important, too. With proper guidance, the preschooler should begin to act and respond to others in appropriate ways.

Family—We desire to help preschoolers become more aware that God planned for families and to learn some ways in which families are special to them.

Church—We want preschoolers to have good experiences at church and to have positive feelings about church.[19]

Because of the developmental differences in preschoolers, the content areas listed above are adapted to meet the needs of the child. For example, in teaching about the Bible, a one-year-old would learn that the Bible is a book; twos and threes would learn that the Bible is a special book with stories about God and Jesus; fours and fives would learn that the Bible is important because it tells about God's love, it helps people to know how God wants them to live, and it tells how people have shown their love for God and Jesus.[20]

PRESCHOOL CURRICULUM

When choosing curriculum for teaching preschoolers, keep in mind the various issues we have discussed in this chapter: biblical content, awareness of the needs of preschoolers, understanding how a preschooler learns, and age-appropriate activities that make use of the way a preschooler learns. Chapter 18 discusses the evaluation and selection of curriculum materials. For preschool curriculum, you will want to focus specifically on the unique ways that preschoolers learn and teaching materials that will lead teachers to teach in a way that is conducive to the learning style and abilities of preschoolers.

LESSON PLANNING FOR PRESCHOOLERS

Lesson planning for preschoolers involves choosing or designing appropriate activities in which children participate as they move from learning center to learning center. Curriculum guides suggest a variety of activities and resources. You choose activities that include Bible conversation, Bible thoughts, Bible songs, and a Bible story being told as preschoolers play.

Plans for babies and one-year-olds include short songs, placing pictures in their beds for them to see, and age-appropriate toys, such as rattles and mobiles. For these youngest preschoolers, teachers focus on meeting their needs for food, warmth, being

19.   Davis, pamphlet.
20.   Gail Linam, *Teaching Preschoolers* (Nashville: Convention Press, 1977), 18.

PRESCHOOL LESSON PLAN
Session Title Date
Unit Teaching Aim
BIBLE LEARNING ACTIVITIES (Plan materials needed, Bible thoughts, stories, conversation, and songs for each area)
Art
Blocks
Books
Homeliving
Music
Nature
Puzzles
TRANSITION
GROUP TIME (For older twos and threes, fours and fives)
Bible story
Bible thoughts
Bible conversation
Songs
Prayer suggestions
Relaxation games
TRANSITION TO EXTENDED SESSION

Figure 12.1

held, diapering, and sleep. When they are awake, teachers sing and talk to them, using Bible thoughts such as, "You are special," "God loves you," "I love you," "Jesus loves you," "I like to come to church," and other simple thoughts that may have little meaning initially, but come to have meaning if used consistently.

Plans for toddlers, twos, and threes include learning center activities such as matching pictures, easel painting, bathing the baby doll, building with blocks, looking at the Bible, or listening to recorded sounds. As the children listen to sounds or match pictures, suggestions in curriculum guides propose conversation, songs, telling the Bible story, and simple prayers.

Older preschoolers participate in more advanced activities such as making cookies, working puzzles with more pieces, art projects, and playing musical instruments. Plans for this group include the brief large group worship time that includes such activities as prayer, songs, telling the Bible story, questions about the story, relaxation games, and learning games.

CONCLUSION

Piaget is sometimes justifiably criticized for underestimating the abilities of young preschoolers. Some preschoolers can understand more than we think they can. I have found this to be true when children are exposed to religious instruction very early on and are given the knowledge foundation for religious experiences. However, most preschoolers will not understand religious concepts as adults do. As teachers of preschoolers, we are laying the foundations for significant religious experiences later in life. Proverbs 22:6 states, "Train a child in the way he should go, and when he is old he will not turn from it." Ephesians 6:4 exhorts parents to ". . . bring them up in the training and instruction of the Lord." Though these words are primarily for parents, are they not also for the "family" of believers who likewise influence the young child? As we enter the twenty-first century, Christians are concerned about the breakdown of the family and the needs of children. It would be wonderful to return to a time of more stability in the family. But the reality is that children of today must be instructed in the nurture and admonition of the Lord. Children need God and want to know him.

Dorothy Marlow asserts that a child cannot be kept spiritually neutral.[21] Children have a natural interest in God and an inborn sense of the divine, the numinous, which must be nurtured by the family and the community. Parents and other adult caretakers will help to determine if future spiritual growth and development will be healthy or unhealthy by their actions and attitudes during these formative years.[22]

God's long-range goal is for every child and adult to obtain "the knowledge of the Son and God and become mature, attaining to the whole measure of the fullness of Christ" (Eph. 4:13). This process begins while the child is still a baby, being loved by people who love God. Just as Timothy began his learning as a young boy, children today need that same opportunity, both at home and at church.

Knowing how preschoolers learn and how much they can learn means that we cannot be satisfied with only "baby-sitting" in our churches. We must make the most of the time we have to teach preschoolers about God.

---

21.   Dorothy R. Marlow, *Textbook of Pediatric Nursing* 5th ed. (Philadelphia: W. B. Saunders Co., 1977), 613.
22.   Shelly, 34.

FOR FURTHER STUDY

1. Describe and evaluate your church's children's program. How do your responses compare to those given in the Search Institute study?

2. To what extent do you believe parents are returning to churches for the needs of their children? What does this say to your congregation in terms of its emphasis on programs for children?

3. Discuss ways you can strengthen parents in their role as teachers. To what extent are the parents in your church teaching their children regarding spiritual things?

4. Observe a preschool class in your church. Describe the activities used to teach. What evidences do you see of preschool learning: senses, curiosity, relationships, repetition, play and imitation, and doing? What content area was being taught that session?

5. Using the lesson plan sheet PRESCHOOL LESSON PLAN, select a curriculum resource for preschoolers and plan a lesson.

SUGGESTED READING

Beechick, R. *Teaching Preschoolers: It's Not Exactly Easy, but Here Is How to Do It*. Denver: Accent Books, 1980.

Clark, R. E., J. Brubaker, and R. B. Zuck, *Childhood Education in the Church*. Chicago: Moody Press, 1986.

Crase, Dixie Ruth. *Today's Preschoolers: A Profile for Teachers, Leaders and Parents*. Nashville: Convention Press, 1993.

Harrell, D. and W. Haystead, *Creative Bible Learning for Young Children, Birth Through 5 Years*. Glendale, Calif.: Regal Books, 1978.

Hildebrand, Verna. *Guiding Young Children*, 3rd ed. New York: Macmillan, 1985.

Klein, D. *How to Do Bible Learning Activities for Ages 2–5*. Ventura, Calif.: Gospel Light Publications, 1982.

Rouse, Doris, and C. Sybil Waldrop. *Moral and Spiritual Development for the Young Child*. Nashville: Convention Press.

Shelly, Judith Allen. *The Spiritual Needs of Children*. Downers Grove, Ill.: InterVarsity Press, 1981.

Strickland, Jenell, comp. *How to Guide Preschoolers*. Nashville: Convention Press, 1982.

Uland, Zadabeth. *Bible Teaching for Preschoolers*. Nashville: Convention Press, 1984.

Waldrop, C. Sybil. *Teaching Preschoolers the Bible*. Nashville: Convention Press, 1990.

———. *Understanding Today's Preschoolers*. Nashville: Convention Press, 1982.

———. *Guiding Your Child Toward God*. Nashville: Convention Press, 1985.

CHAPTER 13

TEACHING CHILDREN

—NORMA HEDIN

Upon entering first grade, children join a new world. They leave behind the dependence of the preschool years and approach a more independent time of life. Although by this time many parents have already worried about their child's development, the elementary years bring new awareness of "normal" development, mentally, socially, physically, and spiritually. Whereas the questions in the preschool years could be answered simply, the tough questions about God, death, sex, and other matters that parents thought they would never have to think about, all appear with the arrival of elementary age children. Parents readily admit that they need help answering some of their children's questions.[1]

Some parents will seek this help from the church. On a recent business trip with my husband, I was conversing with another parent regarding our children and their involvement in church. Another individual, overhearing our conversation, later asked about activities that the church offers. Although she and her husband had turned their backs on their religious upbringing and had made an intentional decision not to raise their child in the church, she was concerned that perhaps there were things that her child was missing because he was not attending church. While this parent did not necessarily see the value in religious training for herself and her husband, she did show interest in what the church had to offer her child.

Religious development is a part of the natural development of the child. Children are naturally curious about God, church, death, and heaven. Children show their

---

1.   Doug Murren, *The Baby Boomerang* (Ventura, Calif.: Regal Books, 1990), 109–10.

greatest interest in spiritual things in the elementary years. As a result, parents may bring their children to church and ask for help in religious training.

Today's children grow up in a different world than their parents grew up in. Children are touched by divorce, depression, increased mobility of families, lack of contact with extended family, abuse and neglect, suicide, non-Christian values, drugs and delinquency, and pressure to grow-up too quickly. These issues force some children to face burdens of issues beyond their developmental level and they create unrealistic expectations. "A growing number of children do not experience childhood as an idyllic time of loving and protected nurture. This discovery is very unsettling to our view of childhood in today's world."[2]

An effective teacher in the church must recognize the realities of children's lives and the unique needs that grow out of those realities. It helps to know what to expect from children at certain ages and how the differences will affect their learning.

Having already addressed the biblical foundations for ministry to children and the role of parents in the teaching of children in the previous chapter, let's move into the unique characteristics and needs of older children.

DEVELOPMENTAL CHARACTERISTICS

Each child individually develops at his own rate in his own way. However, some things we observe about children at certain ages help us identify how to address their learning needs.[3]

FIRST AND SECOND GRADE

First and second graders are slowing down in their physical growth as they develop the smaller muscles that help them to be more coordinated for fine motor tasks. They have a lot of energy but also tire easily, as they tend to overdo. Their physical needs demand that they have periods of activity that allow them to move around and use excess energy.

Mentally, this age-group varies in ability. Some will be able to read, others will not. They like to think and to be challenged to think but they are easily frustrated when they have to work too long on a problem. Whereas in the preschool years they were only concerned about the present, at this age they are able to think in terms of the past. They love to talk and are curious and generally enthusiastic. A loving

2.   Barbara Bolton, Charles T. Smith, and Wes Haystead, *Everything You Want to Know About Teaching Children: Grades 1–6* (Ventura, Calif.: Regal Books, 1987), 25.

3.   For a more detailed description of children's characteristics, see Robert E. Clark, Joanne Brubaker, and Roy B. Zuck, *Childhood Education in the Church* (Chicago: Moody Press, 1986), 125–59; and Bolton, Smith, and Haystead, 33–53.

teacher who understands a child's need to be actively involved in concrete learning experiences will help meet his or her mental needs.

Socially, first and second graders are becoming more independent. They can assume greater responsibility and enjoy choosing their learning activities. They enjoy drama and can learn much from acting out Bible stories and characters. However, they are highly sensitive, easily embarrassed, and somewhat immature emotionally. Be aware of their needs for adult approval and encourage them with praise and patience. Likewise, encourage them as they work together and be aware of their concern for justice and fairness.

The spiritual development of first and second grade children is wrapped up in their sense of fairness and justice. They are concerned about right and wrong and see things as black and white. They are becoming sin-conscious and are fascinated with God and heaven. They can understand spiritual truth in light of their own experience. Some may show interest in conversion. Because of the variety of understanding, however, individual rather than group responses should be encouraged.

Curriculum materials at this age focus on laying foundations for conversion rather than being saved. Some children will pursue a salvation experience while others will seem uninterested. Keep in mind that right words do not equal right understanding. Probe for understanding before encouraging a child's decision.

THIRD AND FOURTH GRADE

Third and fourth grade children are growing stronger physically. They enjoy team sports and other athletic activities, and they especially enjoy trying out new skills and abilities, such as soccer, jumping rope, and swimming.

Mentally, third and fourth graders continue in their eagerness to learn. Their level of mental development allows them to grasp chronology, geography, time-space concepts, and allows for greater use of the Bible in learning activities. They enjoy discussing Bible topics, personalities, and stories and are concerned with the "why" of events. They continue to develop writing and language skills, and to use those skills creatively. They memorize easily and are extremely curious. Variety is important in planning their activities.

Socially, eight- and nine-year-old children enjoy same-sex friendships. Group influence is strong and they tend to enjoy camping and "club-type" activities. They are especially sensitive to criticism and ridicule but are generally self-confident and outgoing. They are growing in their awareness of sex-appropriate behavior and need role models from male and female teachers and biblical figures. They are especially attentive to adult actions and behaviors.

Spiritually, third and fourth graders continue to expand their understanding of basic concepts studied earlier. They believe that God can hear and answer their prayers. They understand sin and the fact that Jesus died for our sins. They are increasingly aware of their need for salvation and may be interested in talking about this decision. They can also begin to form lifetime habits of Bible reading and prayer.

FIFTH AND SIXTH GRADE

Fifth and sixth grade children move into a period of rapid physical growth, following a relatively slow period of growth. They are developing fine motor coordination and boys begin to move ahead of girls in strength and endurance. An increase in appetite is evident. Body changes may bring feelings of awkwardness. Sexuality is of greater interest as well.

Mentally, fifth and sixth graders are becoming rational, logical, and reasonable. They can think and fantasize about the future. They begin to think about thinking. Their curiosity causes them to question and challenge often. They are still, however, concrete in their understanding, although they may "parrot" concepts that sound abstract.

Socially, the peer group becomes more powerful in influence, gradually replacing adult influences. These preadolescents are eager to "fit in" with their peers. They enjoy organized group activities and enjoy creating their own projects and plans. They begin to challenge authority and become increasingly critical of adults. Hero worship is strong in this age group. They admire people who do things they would like to do, people who are strong, and people who help others. These heroes are often chosen from sports or entertainment fields.

Spiritually, the fifth and sixth grader has an increased sense of responsibility toward church activities and feelings of belonging to the church. Salvation decisions are often made in this age group. They have deepening feelings of love for God and are able to seek God's guidance in decision-making.

IMPLICATIONS FOR TEACHING CHILDREN

1. Recognize the unique developmental needs of the age group you teach. Familiarize teachers with these unique needs and help them to see the implications and applications.

2. Choose curriculum materials that are appropriate for the age group.

3. Be sensitive to the child's inabilities as well as his abilities. Do not ask him to do something he cannot yet do. For example, do not ask a first grade student to read instructions to himself and do an activity. First graders vary in their reading abilities.

4. Use the growing skills of classification, chronology, and memorization to involve children in meaningful learning based on biblical content. Bible

skills activities, such as memorizing verses, classifying books of the Bible, and preparing time lines for biblical events, are excellent during the childhood years.

PSYCHOLOGICAL FOUNDATIONS

COGNITIVE DEVELOPMENT—JEAN PIAGET

The changing cognitive abilities of older children are especially significant to their learning experiences in the church. Following the sensorimotor period and preoperational stage of preschool years, children ages seven to ten move into Piaget's *Concrete Operations Stage*. During this stage, children are now able to do mentally what they could not do before. They can see from another person's point of view, thus moving out of the egocentrism of preschool years. They can conserve mentally, meaning they can consider how things work mentally once they have experienced them first hand. They can also decenter, which allows them to consider several aspects of a situation at a time, rather than focusing on only one thing. These developing mental skills bring increased mental ability to deal with concepts, particularly religious concepts.

Because seven-to eleven-year-old children can manipulate data mentally, they enjoy such activities as classifying the books of the Bible. Their new memory strategies, such as the ability to recall and rehearse, allow them to memorize more readily. Their expanding reading ability helps them to not only learn verses but also locate them in the Bible. Their sense of distance and space provides a basis for map studies.[4]

However, elementary age children are still not developed in their ability to reason abstractly. They are literal and concrete in their thinking. Object lessons are interesting but children generally don't get the point. Although they have an increased attention span (seven to fifteen minutes) they still need to move around and stay actively involved in learning.

Although thinking is concrete, the "school-age child begins to use abstract concepts to describe God."[5] Children at this age are extremely interested in God and heaven. They like to recite prayers at bedtime and mealtime. They enjoy Bible stories, although their ability to think about concepts and figure out analogies is limited. Applying principles drawn from biblical parables may be difficult. For example,

4.   Doris A. Freese, ""How Children Think and Learn," in Robert E. Clark, Joanne Brubaker, and Roy B. Zuck, *Childhood Education in the Church* (Chicago: Moody, 1986), 72.

5.   Judith Allen Shelly, *The Spiritual Needs of Children* (Colorado Springs: InterVarsity Press, 1982), 41.

> Tommy, age seven, was asked to draw his favorite Bible story. Asked to explain the drawing, he said: "This is the story of the good Americans. This guy here got mugged—he's all bloody. This guy here [walking on next hill] is the minister. He had to get to church, so he couldn't stop and help him. This guy here [in green at far right] is in the choir. He had to get to church too. These guys [in helicopters, in jet and on ground, saying, "OK"] are the good Americans. They came to help." Asked what the story meant, Tommy explained that "the Americans are always the good guys." The fact that his father was an Army officer may have influenced the military manner in which the good Americans arrived.[6]

This does not mean that we are not to teach these principles or stories to children. Children absorb information quickly and this information becomes meaningful as they mature and develop. As Shelly states:

> What a child learns about the Bible during the school years undergirds an ongoing relationship with God. Even though an eight-year-old boy may not understand all the implications of what he reads and hears, Bible stories become loved and familiar as he studies them in an atmosphere of love and acceptance. Fear of misinterpretation should not keep us from teaching the Bible to him. His relationship to God should be dynamic, personal and constantly growing. Misinterpretations will be cleared up as he matures. Moreover, part of the beauty of Scripture is that it can be understood on many levels. A child who has no concept of God's wrath over evil may still learn that God loves animals, so he saved them from the flood.[7]

Definite theological concepts do not appear to develop until later in childhood. However, a child's early impressions and awarenesses are very influential in forming the foundation for theological concepts later on.[8]

The eleven- to twelve-year-old is moving into Piaget's *Formal Operations Stage* and is developing some abstract reasoning skills. But this child still is haphazard at problem solving, falling back into concrete thinking at times. This age child may begin to articulate more clearly his or her beliefs and can describe why he believes those things.

PSYCHOSOCIAL DEVELOPMENT—ERIK ERIKSON

Having navigated Erikson's earlier three stages, elementary age children move into the fourth stage of *Industry versus Inferiority*. The child entering school is recognized for successful "producing" or performing.[9] He is evaluated on the basis of his ability to accomplish a task, particularly school work. When unable to follow

6. Ibid., 41.
7. Ibid., 44.
8. Norman Wakefield and Robert E. Clark, "Children and Their Theological Concepts," in Robert E. Clark, Joanne Brubaker, and Roy B. Zuck, eds., *Childhood Education in the Church* (Chicago: Moody Press, 1986), 349.
9. Erik H. Erikson, *Childhood and Society*, 2nd ed. (New York: W.W. Norton & Co., 1963), 255–58.

through or to perform as expected, the child may feel inferior because he somehow does not measure up to the standard.

Age-appropriate learning activities and teacher encouragement help a child to successfully negotiate this stage. Unsuccessful experiences lead to self-doubt and feelings of inferiority.

IMPLICATIONS FOR TEACHING CHILDREN

1. Use Bible stories that have one clear concept. Use visual aids to reinforce learning. Give concrete examples of concepts, such as how to show love for your neighbor or times when you can trust God.

2. Provide opportunities for students to classify, categorize, and memorize. Utilize their strengthening mental abilities in their learning activities.

3. Use frequent questions to clarify their thinking. Do not assume that the right answer equals right understanding. Ask "why" questions.

4. Use prayer even though its meaning may be vague. The ritual of prayer becomes important along with other rituals like celebration of holidays. Each exposure to these rituals deepens the child's understanding of their meaning.

5. Make sure that teachers are comfortable living out their faith. Children imitate adults and need teachers who model godly attitudes and actions.

6. Use self-competition to encourage successful completion of learning activities without comparison to other children, which leads to feelings of inferiority.

HOW CHILDREN LEARN

Doris Freese identifies several ways that children learn:

Children learn by experiencing and doing. Discovering, interacting, playing and manipulating, children experience what is around them in their world. Although developing a growing use of language, children still need to have direct experiences. Talking about things (abstract) does not give enough input for concept development.

Allow for hands-on experiences rather than just talking with children. Use visuals, videos, recordings, role playing, and dramatization that allows them to be involved in the learning process. For example, let them look up Bible verses rather than just memorize them.

Children learn by example. They learn by observing peers, siblings, parents and teachers. They try out behaviors and learn from the reactions. A child will often observe a peer talk to her parents in a certain way, then return home to try that out on her parents. The reaction of her parents will teach her the appropriate behavior.

Be aware of the behaviors and attitudes you model as a teacher. Use stories of persons who set the right example. Compliment students for their learning and appropriate behavior so that other students can observe their example.

Children learn by repetition with variation. Children enjoy reading the same books and doing the same activities over and over again. But gradually, they will begin to vary their repetitions, adding to or enlarging their activities.

Provide familiar books and use stories and concepts repeatedly. The more exposure to concepts, the deeper the understanding.

Children learn through concrete language and experiences, and they think literally and concretely. Although they can repeat correct answers, that does not mean they understand a concept. Misconceptions often occur when teachers use abstract concepts like describing Jesus as the "rock" or "the lily of the valley." Do not use object lessons with young children. They cannot understand how a lighthouse represents the Bible or rocks represent sin.[10]

CONTENT AND CURRICULUM

Sunday school has historically majored on biblical content. Content areas for teaching children build on the content areas in the preschool curriculum. As in the preschool years, we teach age-appropriate concepts and stories that speak to children. In the Southern Baptist curriculum, the content of Bible study for children addresses seven major areas.[11] Each subject area includes teaching objectives that help move away from just teaching biblical facts and knowledge to helping children apply truths appropriately in their lives:

Objective 1: Christian Conversion

To lay the foundation for a genuine conversion experience on the part of each child when he is ready and is led by the Holy Spirit.

Objective 2: Church Membership

To lay foundation for an understanding of what it means to be a church member.

---

10.   Freese, 74.
11.   Tom McMinn, *Breakthrough: Children's Sunday School Work* (Nashville: Convention Press, 1991), 136–38.

Objective 3: Christian Worship

> To help each child to know God; to develop ability to participate actively and intelligently in worship, and to find satisfaction in worship experiences.

Objective 4: Christian Knowledge and Understanding

> To help each child gain such knowledge of the Bible and Christian faith as can be related to his daily experiences.

Objective 5: Christian Attitudes and Convictions

> To guide each child in the continuing development of attitudes and appreciations that will encourage personal growth.

Objective 6: Christian Living

> To guide each child to develop and use in every day life, habits, and skills that will help him grow spiritually.

Objective 7: Christian Service

> To guide each child to use his talents and skills in ways that will help others and serve God's purpose.

Each of the areas above is addressed in an age-appropriate manner. For example, the first and second grade curriculum addresses concepts related to conversion but does not focus on a conversion experience. Later, in fifth and sixth grade, the curriculum provides a greater emphasis on conversion. In Southern Baptist churches, a child becomes a church member when he or she is baptized. Early teachings related to church membership are designed to prepare a child for that experience. Teaching in the later childhood years regarding membership is more specific.

LESSON PLANNING FOR CHILDREN

Lesson planning for children involves choosing or designing appropriate activities regarding content areas in which children actively participate. Curriculum guides suggest a variety of activities and resources. You choose activities based on the needs of your learners.

Plans usually include a Bible story, a memory verse, Bible skills activities, songs, projects or activities for groups related to the story or concept, and suggestions for application. A large group Bible study and worship time is included in each session. A sample lesson plan worksheet is in figure 13.1.

A lesson plan should include a teaching aim for the session, with all activities geared toward accomplishing that aim. Curriculum plans generally include a teaching aim and should also include some type of beginning activity. Learning begins when the first child arrives. An activity should be selected that involves each child and gives him or her something to do in relation to the lesson. For example, a be-

CHILDREN'S LESSON PLAN
Unit Title Date
Unit Purpose
Session Purpose:
Bible Story:
Bible Background Passage:
Memory Verse:
1. Beginning Activity:
Materials:
Guidance:
2. Guide Bible Study and Worship
Songs
Bible Story:
Review Bible Facts:
Pray:
Memory Verse:
Develop Bible Skills:
Apply Bible Truths:
Express Bible Learning:

Figure 13.1

ginning activity may have the children looking up verses in the Bible, working a puzzle related to the facts of the lesson, writing a story, or playing a game that introduces the lesson.

Larger Sunday school classes may be divided into several groups working on different projects. A small Sunday school may have one activity planned which is led by the teacher.

Following the beginning activity, the teacher plans a large group time that includes a Bible story and a worship time. With increased attention span, the elementary age child can participate in such a time for fifteen to twenty minutes. Be sure to actively involve children during this time, as well. Ask questions, involve them in dramatics, have them read together, hold visuals, sing, pray, look up Bible verses, and listen.

A variety of methods or learning activities is important for children. Lesson plan suggestions may include some of the following methods.

METHODS FOR TEACHING CHILDREN

Storytelling. Children are imaginative. They love stories. Bible stories, your stories, classical tales, role play, and pantomime will capture their attention and stimulate their thinking. Stories help to prepare children for the ups and downs of reality. Through Bible stories children learn about the joys and problems of human relationships. Stories of God-motivated heroes provide role models for young lives.

Dramatics. Story playing, drama, skits, role play, mime, fingerplays, and action rhymes all have value in helping children apply what they learn. As they put themselves in the shoes of other people, they begin to think and feel as other people do. Pretending is a part of children's growth and provides them with the opportunity to act out their feelings and impressions. Pretending also serves the very important function of revealing the children's thoughts to the teacher.

Questions. Questions are used by teachers as a means to stimulate interest, test knowledge, help students express their thoughts, and review past learning. Factual questions and thought questions stimulate thought and deepen understanding. Bible games make use of questions to review material.

Discussion. Discussion, or guided conversation with children, encourages students to participate in learning, share their ideas, test their knowledge, and get feedback from the teacher. Children love to talk and they love to express their ideas. Discussion gives them the chance to talk about concepts which reinforces their knowledge.

Projects. Projects help learners to "do" something related to their learning. Whether inside or outside of class, learners spend time actively involved in creating a plan and carrying it to completion. Research activities using Bible handbooks, dictionaries, maps, atlases, and books involve children in understanding and applying Bible truths.

Creative Activities. Creative writing, music activities, constructive arts and crafts, art, and mosaics are all creative activities. Creative activities bring new dimensions into learning experiences. Children become active in creating and expressing themselves. Creative activities make learning more enjoyable, lasting, and meaningful. They provide opportunities for self-expression and they instill pride in accomplishment.

Creative activities also provide a change of pace in learning and help relieve physical restlessness with meaningful activity.

CONCLUSION

When I think about the significance of teaching children, I cannot help but think of my own personal experience. Had it not been for the love and teaching of my childhood Sunday school teachers, I would not have known about God. Those teachers showed God's love to me, and they explained spiritual truths in such a way that I came to know and understand and accept them. Every time I reflect on that experience, I am thankful for those teachers.

Today's boys and girls still need Jesus. They still need teachers who will love them and teach them about God. Although God's instruction for parents to teach their children remains as the first curriculum for teaching spiritual truths, the church has its place as the "family of God," tied together by faith rather than blood. Jesus suggested this idea when he posed the question of the identity of his "mother" and his "brothers" (Matt. 12:48–50). Supporting and discipling parents is a priority but teaching children whose parents do not want to be discipled is also a priority. We must seek ways to teach and nurture children in their knowledge and understanding so that when the time is right, they will respond to God's call in their lives. We cannot neglect that responsibility.

FOR FURTHER STUDY

1. What parental needs do you see emerging as children move into elementary school? To what extent do you believe parents are seeking help from the church in addressing these needs?

2. How would you compare the world of children today with the world in which you grew up? What unique concerns do parents have today that your parents did not have to consider? How might the church be contributing to these concerns?

3. Compare the cognitive development of a first grade child and a sixth grade child. How might they differ in their views of God, the church, Jesus, and the Bible?

4. Observe a children's class in your church. Describe the activities used to teach. What evidences do you see of learning: doing, example, repetition, and concrete "hands on" learning. What content area was being taught during the session?

5. Using the lesson plan sheet provided in figure 13.1, select a curriculum resource for children and plan a lesson.

SUGGESTED READING

Allstrom, Elizabeth. *You Can Teach Creatively*. Nashville: Abingdon, 1970.

Almly, Millie C. *Young Children's Thinking: Studies of Some Aspects of Piaget Theory*. New York: Columbia U., Teachers College Press, 1966.

Bolton, B. J., C. T. Smith, and Wes Haystead. *Everything You Want to Know About Teaching Children, Grades 1–6*. Ventura, Calif.: Regal Books, 1987.

Chamberlain, Eugene. *Today's Children: A Profile for Teachers Leaders and Parents*. Nashville: Convention Press, 1993.

Clark, R. E., J. Brubaker, and R. B. Zuck. *Childhood Education in the Church*. Chicago: Moody Press, 1986.

Goldman, Ronald. *Religious Thinking from Childhood to Adolescence*. New York: Seabury, 1964.

Griggs, Patricia. *Using Storytelling in Christian Education*. Nashville: Abingdon, 1981.

Halverson, Delia. *Helping Your Child Discover Faith*. Valley Forge, Pa.: Judson, 1982.

Haystead, West. *Teaching Your Child About God*. Ventura, Calif.: Gospel Light, Regal Books, 1981.

Hendricks, William L. *A Theology for Children*. Nashville: Broadman, 1980.

Judith Allen Shelly, *The Spiritual Needs of Children*, Colorado Springs: InterVarsity Press, 1982.

Waldrop, C. Sybil. *Guiding Your Child Toward God*. Nashville: Convention Press, 1985.

CHAPTER 14

TEACHING YOUTH

—DARYL ELDRIDGE

All the other young men had gone to their tents, leaving fifteen-year-old Aaron alone with me at the campfire. As I looked into Aaron's eyes, I noticed he was crying. Aaron was a tough, street-wise kid who never cried, but now tears were streaming down his face. I asked, "What's wrong, Aaron?" For several minutes, he didn't say a word. As I waited, he took a stick, thrust it into the flames, and dragged a small piece of burning wood away from the fire. For several minutes we watched as the ember slowly turned from glowing orange to white ash. He finally broke the silence with this explanation: "I'm like this coal. Whenever I'm with the youth at our church, I burn brightly for Jesus. But, when I'm away from them, I turn cold, and my witness for Jesus dies."

What insight into our relationship with the Lord and his church! This young person could not spell theology, but he understood better than many adults the importance of relationships with fellow believers. Youth need the church. It is during adolescence that many youth make important spiritual decisions. In my seminary classes, I ask students how many were called into ministry as teenagers. Consistently, fifty to sixty percent of the seminary students accepted God's call into vocational ministry during these important years. Like Aaron, they examined their personal relationships with Jesus Christ and his church and made commitments to follow him.

Not only do youth need the church, the church needs them. Our churches benefit from their life, enthusiasm, and commitment to do God's will. Youth are seeking to discover who they are and why they are here. It is through Bible study that these and many other questions can be answered. If we are to reach a new generation of Aarons, we must understand who they are, how they learn, and how to teach them effectively.

CHARACTERISTICS AND NEEDS OF YOUTH

Effective lessons begin with knowing the needs and abilities of the students we teach. The terms *adolescence, youth,* and *teenagers* describe the period between child-hood and adulthood.

Adolescence ". . . begins with the emergence of the physiological characteristics that result in puberty. It is accompanied by the social attitudes and expectations that an individual is something other than a child. Adolescence draws to a close as persons begin to assume adult tasks such as work, self-support, marriage, or emotional independence from parents."[1]

Adolescence is a broader term than *youth.* For this chapter, *younger youth* are ages twelve to fourteen or grades seven to nine. *Older youth* are ages fifteen to seventeen or grades ten to twelve. Often called the "turbulent teens," these years involve rapid physical changes, caused by the onset of puberty. These physical changes affect the mental, emotional, social, and spiritual dimensions of young people. Following is a description of the characteristics of these two age groups:

CHARACTERISTICS OF YOUNGER YOUTH (GRADES 7–9)

Physical

1. Their bodies are rapidly changing.

2. Girls reach puberty earlier than boys.

3. Their changing bodies (or sometimes the slowness in comparison with others) can be a source of emotional concern with some youth.

4. They are sometimes awkward.

5. They are ready to perform tasks at a high level of physical stamina and strength, but they also will require periods of rest for their changing bodies.

Mental

1. They are creative and inventive.

2. They are beginning to think abstractly and learn difficult concepts.

3. They understand the consequences of actions.

---

1. Daniel O. Aleshire, *Understanding Today's Youth* (Nashville: Convention Press, 1982), 28–29.

4. They can think independently and may rebel against authority.

5. They can conceptualize time and space.

6. They can use their reading skills effectively.

7. They enjoy adventure and discovery.

Social

1. They want to belong to a group of their peers.

2. They seek adult status.

3. They desire the understanding and acceptance of adults, including parents.

4. They want to dress like their friends and those they admire.

5. They enjoy competition.

6. They are usually self-conscious.

Emotional

1. Their emotions are like a roller coaster.

2. They may feel misunderstood.

3. They have difficulty expressing their feelings.

4. They tend to rebel against authority.

5. They will commit to worthy causes or persons.

6. They are developing emotional independence.

7. Sometimes they have difficulty controlling their emotions.

Spiritual

1. They are idealistic in their expectations of the faith practices of others.

2. They have doubts about Christianity.

3. They are ready for personal encounters with God.

4. They think about death.

5. They recognize and appreciate honesty from peers and adults.

6. They want Bible study to be practical.

7. They are capable of serving the needs of others in ministry and mission activities.

CHARACTERISTICS OF OLDER YOUTH (GRADES 10–12)

Physical

1. They look like adults.

2. They are capable of adult physical activities.

3. They are capable of full sexual and reproductive activity, though they are not ready for it emotionally or economically.

4. They are outgrowing their clumsiness.

5. They consume large amounts of food (another way of saying their appetites increase).

Mental

1. They are capable of critical thinking.

2. They enjoy arguing for the sake of arguing.

3. They are creative and enjoy solving problems.

4. They can make and carry out plans of action.

5. They are ready to work hard for a sense of achievement and to reach immediate and distant goals.

6. Their decision-making skills are improving.

Social

1. They can take deliberate steps in improving their interpersonal skills.

2. They are concerned about relationships with the opposite sex.

3. They seek adult status.

4. They belong to a social group based on their interests and needs.

5. They want social approval.

6. They want a full social calendar.

Emotional

1. They have more ability to control their emotions.

2. They still have periods of moodiness.

3. They can still feel intense emotions.

4. Males are more aggressive to assume their sexual roles and females are generally less aggressive.

5. They react with great sensitivity to the arts, film, and media.

6. They need emotional security.

7. They are ready to accept their sexuality.

Spiritual

1. They question adult value systems.

2. They are developing a mature philosophy of life.

3. Their faith is emotional and personal.

4. They can express faith in their own terms.

5. They are capable of making lifelong commitments of their faith.

6. They want to relate spiritual truth to everyday life.

7. They are capable of meaningful worship experiences.[2]

Youth teachers should guide teenagers to become responsible adults. During these turbulent years, teenagers need lots of affirmation. Based on the developmental characteristics of youth, Wesley Black outlines the seven goals for youth ministry. They form the acrostic AFFIRMS.

A   Achievement realized

F   Friends gained

F   Feelings understood

I   Identity established

R   Responsibility accepted

M   Maturity gained

S   Sexuality understood[3]

HOW DO YOUTH LEARN?

1. Youth learn when they have adult models to follow.[4] No teaching method, despite its effectiveness, can replace the impact of a caring teacher. The most important element in the educational programs of our churches is not the facilities or the curriculum materials, but teachers. A teacher might be

2. These characteristics are outlined in the Church Curriculum Based Design of the Sunday School Board of the Southern Baptist Convention, Nashville, Tennessee, 1984. A fuller explanation of these characteristics can be found in G. Wade Rowatt, *Today's Youth: A Profile for Teachers, Leaders and Parents* (Nashville: Convention Press, 1993).

3. Wesley Black, *An Introduction to Youth Ministry* (Nashville: Broadman, 1991), 87.

4. The idea for these principles comes from LeRoy Ford, *Design for Teaching and Training* (Nashville: Broadman, 1978).

a great scholar of the Bible and possess understanding of teaching methodologies, and yet be ineffective because his walk doesn't match his talk. This
is because Christianity is caught more than taught.

When asked to describe their favorite teachers, teenagers use such phrases
as these: he is patient; she is interested in what I do; I feel I can be honest
with him; she listens; she shows us how to live a Christian life. Teenagers
recognize and appreciate honesty from adults. They are also aware when
adults do not practice what they preach.

Youth are growing in their cognitive ability to deal with abstract thoughts
and ideas. They are developing a philosophy of life. This is why adolescence is seen as a time of ideals.

Youth want to have relationships with adults they can model their lives after. This same idealism, however, leads youth to criticize adults when they
view them as being hypocritical. More than any other age group, youth
need workers whose lifestyles reflect a consistent walk with the Lord.

2. Youth learn when there is an atmosphere of love, trust, and acceptance.
    They want the understanding and acceptance of parents and other adults.
    At the same time they are questioning adult value systems. They need to
    determine if their faith is simply a product of their parents' wishes or a
    product of their own convictions. To develop a mature faith, youth must
    be allowed to raise difficult questions. Rather than putting youth down for
    suggesting answers different from theirs, teachers must lead youth to ex-
    plore scriptural evidence that supports or refutes their hypotheses. Youth
    must be helped to establish a scriptural basis for their faith. They need the
    freedom to be wrong. Adolescence is a time for testing ideas and weighing
    values. Teachers demonstrate their love by listening and not judging youth.
    Teenagers do not change their attitudes overnight, but they are more in-
    clined to make positive changes when they have the love and acceptance of
    adults.

3. Youth learn when they make discoveries for themselves. An old proverb says,
    "Never tell a student anything he can discover for himself." Youth recognize
    a teacher who loves to hear himself speak and will quickly tune him out. The
    teacher who can excite a class is one who enables class member to make dis-
    coveries. Researching Bible facts is important. However, the ultimate goal of
    teaching is to enable youth to apply the facts to their lives.

4. Youth learn when they are actively involved in the learning process. Rich-
    ard Ross discovered that active learning is more effective in changing the
    attitudes of youth.[5] Young people respond when given leadership respon-

5. Richard Ross, "The Effect of Teaching Methodology as Presented in the Southern Baptist
Curriculum Based Design on Selected Attitudes Related to Mate Selection Among High School
Students" (Ed.D. diss., Southwestern Baptist Theological Seminary, 1981), 87.

sibilities. A skilled teacher of youth is one who employs them as study leaders and who designs learning activities that involve the students in the learning process. Teachers can give youth outside assignments and arrange for them to present parts of the lesson.

5. Youth learn when they explore biblical truth with their peers. Young people play to an imaginary audience. A teenager often believes he is the only person in the world who feels the way he does. During adolescence, youth move from concrete to abstract thinking. They can evaluate the ideas of others. In a strange way this leads to a form of self-centered thinking. Because they can examine others' thoughts, they believe everyone is critically examining their thoughts, behavior, and dress. This is where peer pressure emerges. Youth will go to extremes to gain the approval and companionship of their peers. Peer pressure, however, is not always negative. The testimony of a peer often speaks louder than the experience of an adult. Upon hearing another teenager express his faith, a youth will remark, "I feel that way, too." Teenagers can learn some positive and powerful lessons from their peers. This is why youth-led revivals and youth versions of lay renewals have been successful. Teachers can ask youth to give their testimonies (especially as they relate to the lesson), invite popular youth known for their Christian convictions to speak, and arrange for youth to share their convictions in small groups led by one of their peers.

6. Youth learn when the lesson relates to their needs and interests. The writers of curriculum materials keep the needs of learners in mind when they design teaching materials. No writer, however, can write so that the lesson pinpoints the needs of every youth in every youth group. This is the job of the teacher. An effective teacher is one who can relate the lesson to the needs of the learners in his class. How can a teacher know the needs and interests of the class? Teachers can spend time with youth, see them in their environment, go to school functions, and attend youth fellowships. They also can plan one-on-one times with youth and use questionnaires on a variety of issues to discover their feelings and convictions.

7. Youth learn when the activities reflect their abilities. While some may have grown-up bodies and thought patterns, teenagers do not possess adult abilities. Adolescents, especially younger youth, do not possess the verbal skills of adults. Younger teenagers have difficulty expressing their feelings. They may have strong emotions concerning a particular discussion but they cannot express these feelings. Part of the spiritual development of youth involves learning how to verbalize one's faith. One characteristic of adolescence is low self-esteem, especially in grades seven through nine. When they need to put their faith into words, teenagers' concern for identity works against them. Youth often can't verbalize their faith. An effective teacher helps youth communicate nonverbally. Youth can express their faith through skits, role-playing, poetry, art, and music. Activities per-

ceived as fun-and-games by adults can be effective learning agents if conducted properly.

8. Youth learn when the learning goal has been identified. A wise teacher is
one who establishes the teaching aim. The learning objective helps the
teacher select the appropriate teaching methods for that lesson. Teaching
without an aim is simply talking. Youth learn more effectively when they
know the direction of the lesson. The teacher should share the learning
goal with the class members and tell them what they will be able to do as a
result of the study. Explaining the teaching aim can motivate youth to study
the lesson.

9. Youth learn when a variety of learning methods are employed. There is
an old teaching adage that says, "The worst teaching method is the one
that is used all the time." No matter how good an activity is, it loses its
effectiveness when used regularly. When it comes to teaching youth, variety is the spice of life. One way to avoid the methodology rut is for
teachers to keep a log of the activities they use. What works with one class
of youth may not work with another. A method should not be abandoned
just because it didn't work the first time. Often the methods selected by
the teacher reveal the interests of the teacher more than those of the
learner. If a teacher feels uncomfortable using a skit or role play, then it
is unlikely the teacher will employ this activity even though the curriculum materials suggest it.

10. Youth learn when they are provided with opportunities to take positive action regarding the lesson. The idea behind this principle is that you learn
by doing. The lesson should not end at the close of the hour. Often the best
learning takes place outside the classroom. Teenagers learn more about
missions by participating in a mission activity than by only hearing about a
mission endeavor. Youth should be encouraged to brainstorm ways they
can carry out the lesson. An effective teacher will guide them in ways to
practice their faith.

Teaching youth is more than a one-hour-a-week proposition. Teachers can take
youth to visit an inactive class member or arrange for teenagers to do volunteer
work at a school for the handicapped. Field trips, letters of gratitude to special persons in their lives, or projects to collect money for world hunger help the youth apply their faith. These meaningful emotional experiences will make the most impact
on the lives of youth.

Youth learn when they are taught as youth, not adults. When teachers consider
the unique tasks of adolescence, use methods that are appropriate for youth, and
display lifestyles consistent with the teachings of Jesus Christ, then teenagers learn.

USING YOUTH CURRICULUM

To get the most out of your curriculum there are several terms and ideas you will need to understand. Different terms may be used, but these concepts are common among the major publishers of youth material.

Total period teaching is the idea that the entire lesson relates to the "Central Bible Truth" and moves toward the accomplishment of the "Teaching Aim."[6] From the time youth walk into the department/class until they leave, every activity relates to the lesson.

The *background passage* is the larger Bible passage out of which the Bible study is developed. Usually, this is more content than can be examined during the lesson. It provides the setting and tone for understanding the central truth. The background passage used as an example for the following lesson elements is Luke 1:5–25, 57–80.[7]

The *central Bible truth* is a statement of the biblical principle contained in the passage of Scripture. The central Bible truth is stated in present tense, active voice, and in contemporary terms that apply to today's youth. For example, the central Bible truth for Luke 1:5–25, 57–80 might be, "God blesses and works through us when we are faithful to him."[8]

The *teaching aim* is the learning objective for the lesson. It is based on the central Bible truth. The teaching aim may be expressed as a cognitive goal (knowledge or understanding) or as an affective (attitude) goal. Or, the lesson may contain both cognitive and affective outcomes. An example of a teaching aim for Luke 1:5–25, 57–80 might be, Lead youth to: (Cognitive) explain how God used Zechariah and Elizabeth through the birth of John the Baptist; and (Affective) determine ways God can use youth's lives when they are faithful to him.

Focal passages are the heart of the Bible study. These Bible passages point toward the central truth of the lesson. They are usually contained within the larger background passage. The focal passage for the lesson on Luke 15:5–25, 57–80 is Luke 1:11–17, 23–25, and 76–80.[9]

The *memory verse* is a Scripture verse selected to help youth apply the central truth through memorization. The memory verse selected for the above lesson is, "Praise be to the Lord, the God of Israel, because he has come and has redeemed his people" (Luke 1:68).[10]

---

6. *Youth Sunday School Worker's Notebook* (Nashville: Convention Press, 1993), 132.

7. "People God Can Use," in *Youth in Action: Teacher* (Nashville: The Baptist Sunday School Board, December 4, 1994), 82.

8. Ibid.

9. Ibid.

10. Ibid.

LESSON PLANNING

There are three steps to an effective lesson plan for youth. They are: motivation, examination, and application. (The chapter "Preparing to Teach" explains these in more detail.) A variety of methods can be used successfully in each of these steps, if the method relates to that step. In the motivation step, use activities that stimulate youth to be involved in the lesson. In the examination step, use methods that help students understand the meaning of the passage. In the application step, use activities that help youth use what they have learned. The method should help reach the teaching aim and relate to the central truth.

Keep in mind that curriculum materials must be adapted to meet the needs of the youth in your church. Personalize the curriculum. What are the needs of those in your class or Bible study group? How does the lesson proposed in the literature relate to the needs of your youth? Rewrite the teaching aim and central truth to express the needs of your youth. If the curriculum materials involve more biblical content than can be covered in the time available, select one or maybe two focal passages that fit your teenagers' needs. Personalize your learning activities. Teachers should use methods that appeal to their youth.

METHODS

Youth are not adults, nor are they children. Teachers should use learning activities that fit the abilities and interests of youth. All teenagers do not learn the same way. They have different learning styles. Some learn by seeing (visual learners). Some learn by listening (auditory learners). Others learn by touching (tactile learners), and yet others by movement (kinesthetic learners). Some youth are social learners. They enjoy learning in small groups. Others prefer to work alone. Teachers will need to incorporate a variety of activities in their lesson plans. Remember, telling is not teaching. Listening is not learning. A variety of methods will help more youth to become involved.

Boredom is the death knell when teaching youth. If we are to reach this generation for our Lord, we must make the gospel relevant and exciting. We cannot be content to use yesterday's methods. The following is an overview of appropriate methods for teaching youth.

Art. Youth appreciate the aesthetic. Many youth are visual learners. Some youth have difficulty expressing themselves verbally but they can express their faith through drawings, cartoons, collages, bumper stickers, T-shirt logos, murals, photography, posters, and sculptures.

Drama. Drama doesn't have to be professional or scripted. It may be done live or shown on video. Drama can make the biblical story come alive. Some forms of drama include acting out a Bible event, contemporary skits, choral speaking, and dia-

YOUTH

SUNDAY

SCHOOL

PLAN SHEET

YOUTH NEEDS AND PRAYER CONCERNS

TEACHING-LEARNING

Date:

Focal Passage(s):

Central Bible Truth:

Teaching Aim:
   Knowledge:
   Application:

MY PLANS, STEPS, RESOURCES, TIME, ETC.

• Motivate Youth to Study the Bible

• Examine the Bible Passage

• Apply the Bible to Life

EVALUATING LAST SUNDAY

• Administering

• Reaching/Witnessing

• Caring/Fellowship

Figure 14.1

logues. Teachers can use drama as a discussion starter to create interest in the lesson. Youth enjoy playing a role and acting out a solution to a contemporary problem. Drama also can be used to interview a biblical personality. Other forms of drama might include monologues, pantomimes, puppet shows, and radio or television formats.[11]

Music. Teenagers fill their world with music. When they get into the car, youth turn on the radio and listen to their favorite music. Find out what music your youth like. Use their music to illustrate biblical principles. Junior high youth like to sing choruses with hand movements. Older youth, on the other hand, may be put off by perky music used first thing in the morning. Teachers can encourage youth to read and study the lyrics of the great hymns. Some youth can write lyrics. Use contemporary Christian music to illustrate biblical truth. Analyze secular music and help them see the values and messages contained in some music.[12]

Pencil and paper. Paper and pencils provide an economical way to get youth involved in studying God's Word. Use a variety of approaches to prevent youth from perceiving it as school work. Teachers can design activities requiring youth to research the Bible. Letter writing is another excellent method. Teachers can ask youth to write a letter to God, friends, or significant persons in their lives. Youth can write simulated newspaper articles, poetry, lyrics, stories, and skits. Don't forget acrostics, puzzles, coded messages, crossword puzzles, maps, and graphs. Keeping spiritual journals or constructing notebooks are effective means of keeping records of lengthy studies. Quizzes, fill-in-the blank items, pretests, posttests, multiple choice items, matching items, true-false statements, and worksheets are excellent ways of evaluating student learning. As you can see, there are many creative ways to use this old method.

Verbal techniques. Verbal methods are probably the most commonly used activities in Youth Bible study. Teachers must be taught how to use them effectively. Remember that all youth are not verbal learners. Use a variety of verbal methods and your youth will rise up and call you blessed. Youth enjoy brainstorming, discussing case studies, debating, and solving problems.

Youth will respond to lecturing if you use visuals, listening teams, and jot sheets, and tell stories or personal experiences. Some topics lend themselves to group lectures, interviews, or panel discussions. Teachers can also show a video clip and discuss it. Some youth can be challenged to research a topic and bring a report to the class. Teachers can challenge youth to discuss a problem or issue in small groups and report to the entire class. Youth also need opportunities to share testimonies with their peers.

---

11.   For further explanation of these methods consult Ann Cannon, *Bible Teaching for Youth Through the Sunday School* (Nashville: Broadman, 1984) or the *Youth Sunday School Workers Notebook*, 146–7.
12.   Ibid.

Visual techniques. Our challenge is to teach a timeless Book to a generation living in a multimedia world. Youth are accustomed to a collage of images interrupted every twelve minutes by a commercial. They are not linear and sequential thinkers. They watch several scenarios at once. Life is not in black and white, it's digital cinematography. So how do we compete? We don't. We can't. Most churches don't have the resources to produce multi-media that can compete with the world. But we can use the visual techniques available to us. The problem is often that we are using 1950's technology poorly. Visually enhance learning by incorporating objects, video clips, slides, overhead projectors, and computers. Teachers of youth can use music videos of contemporary Christian artists.

Personal experience. Youth learn best by doing. Find ways for them to apply what they have learned. Youth need avenues to share their faith and to serve others. Teachers can involve youth in mission action projects, outreach visitation, ministering to the homebound, and personal witnessing. The idealism of youth can be channeled to do great things for God.

Games. Youth enjoy competitive activities. These activities include relays and competition, Bible bowl, variations on TV game shows and table games, independent study work sheets, programmed instruction, assigned readings, research and report projects, and interviews.[13]

Match the method with the age of the youth. You also will want to consider the ages of the youth in your group. Younger youth learn differently than older youth. The following helps to delineate these differences. Younger youth prefer these methods:

- word games like mazes, acrostics, scrambled letters or words

- puzzles, including crosswords, fitting pieces together, and match-ups

- puppets or masks to hide behind rather than risk being in front of everyone

- art that completes a cartoon, makes a mobile, or draws something simple

- team games—since no one person has to appear to be ignorant

- action-oriented activities like moving around the room to agree or disagree or looking for clues to a Bible study

- writing down ideas before having to share them verbally

- expressing personal feelings rather than guessing about someone else's feelings

- any activity that asks for facts.[14]

Older youth prefer these methods:

- discussions that challenge them to think instead of just repeating facts

---

13. Black, 200.
14. *Youth Sunday School Worker's Notebook*, 137.

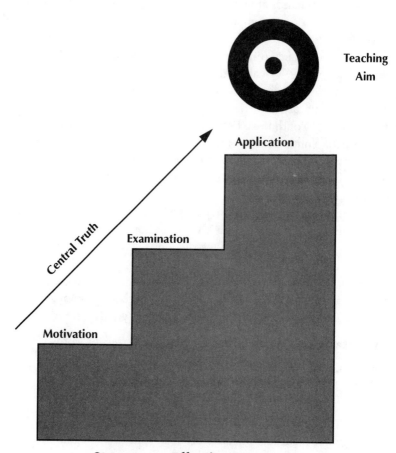

Steps to an Effective Lesson

Figure 14.2

- analyzing music and writing new lyrics
- case studies that relate to personal experiences
- learning games that teach, in addition to testing their own skills
- debating one or both points of view
- role plays that allow them to try on different personalities
- symbolic or abstract art[15]

Guidelines. If you or your youth are unaccustomed to active learning in Bible study, you will want to observe the following guidelines.

1. Start gradually.

2. Give clear instructions.

3. Choose a leader and recorder for each group.

4. Give realistic time limits.

5. Encourage students.

6. Let them do it alone.

7. Provide the resources.

8. Allow time for students to share their results.

9. Be affirming.[16]

Should sixth-graders be included in the youth ministry? In many communities, public schools organize sixth graders as part of a middle school program: grades six to eight or grades six to nine. This has caused youth programs to question if sixth-graders should be included in their youth Bible study programs. In addition, some parents apply pressure on youth ministers to allow their "mature" sixth-graders to move up to the youth program. What should churches do?

While this is a complex issue, there are several developmental issues that should be considered. Even where sixth-graders are in the middle school program, most public schools go to great efforts to keep them from mixing with older youth. Sixth-graders are often in separate buildings, on different schedules, with different lunch periods. They rarely, if ever, socialize with the older grades.

Sixth-graders promoted to the youth ministry immediately socialize with older youth. For many churches this means sixth-graders would be in the same social and study groups with seniors in high school. Many of these children are not ready for

---

15. Ibid.
16. Robert Joseph Choun, Jr., "Teaching Youth," in Kenneth O. Gangel and Howard G. Hendricks, *The Christian Educator's Handbook on Teaching* (Wheaton, Ill.: Victor, 1988). 144–45.

the social dynamics and expectations of adolescence. Early contact with older youth results in sixth-graders dating earlier.

Many sixth-graders are still concrete thinkers. They are not capable of discussing abstract ideas with older youth. Seniors intimidate sixth-graders and sixth-graders frustrate seniors. This results in juniors and seniors dropping out of the youth program. Furthermore, many teens who have been in the youth ministry since sixth grade drop out of the church program when they get their driver's license. They have been in the youth program for five years and feel they have outgrown it.

Considering the differences in developmental abilities between sixth-graders and older youth, sixth-graders should remain part of the children's ministry. You might consider developing special programs for fifth- and sixth- graders. Separate them from the younger grades and give them special attention. Youth ministers will want to begin developing relationships with them by planning functions for just sixth-graders. Our children grow up too fast the way it is. Let's allow sixth-graders to be children and not expect them to accept the roles and responsibilities required of youth.

CONCLUSION

Today's youth face a world much different than the one in which I grew up. Teenagers must contend with the fear of AIDS. They are concerned about personal security. Many of them come from diverse and complex families. The one constant in each generation of youth is their need for relationships with compassionate, encouraging teachers who walk alongside them through adolescence. They may forget the creative methods we used in Bible study. They will probably forget most of our words of wisdom. But if we have been good teachers, they won't forget us.

FOR FURTHER STUDY

1. Observe a youth class in your church. Evaluate the lesson. What were the strengths and weaknesses? What methods worked well, what didn't? How did the teacher achieve motivation, examination, and application?

2. Select youth curriculum from several different publishers and evaluate them.

3. Using the literature for youth teachers, develop a lesson plan for youth.

4. Interview four youth. Ask them what qualities they appreciate in their teachers. Ask them what they expect from Bible study and how teachers could improve Bible study.

SUGGESTED READING

Aleshire, Daniel O. *Understanding Today's Youth*. Nashville: Convention Press, 1982.

Anthony, Michael J. *Foundations of Ministry: An Introduction to Christian Education for a New Generation.* Wheaton, Ill.: Bridgepoint Books, 1992.

Benson, W. S. and M. H. Senter. *The Complete Book of Youth Ministry*. Chicago: Moody Press, 1987.

Black, Wesley. *Introduction to Youth Ministry*. Nashville: Broadman, 1991.

Burton, Janet. *Guiding Youth*. Nashville: Convention Press, 1969.

Cannon, Ann. *Bible Teaching for Youth Through the Sunday School*. Nashville: Convention Press, 1984.

Dean, B. J. *Teaching Youth in Sunday School*. Nashville: Convention Press, 1976.

Gangel, Kenneth O. and Howard G. Hendricks. *The Christian Educator's Handbook on Teaching.* Wheaton, Ill.: Victor, 1988.

Griffin, Kathryn. *Teaching Teens the Truth*. Nashville: Broadman Press, 1978.

Rowatt, G. Wade. *Today's Youth*. Nashville: Convention Press, 1993.

Sullivan, Ann. *How to Guide Youth*. Nashville: Convention Press, 1982.

Veach, Myrte. *Basic Youth Sunday School Work*. Nashville: Convention Press, 1981.

———. *Break Through: Youth Sunday School Work*. Nashville: Convention Press, 1982.

Youth Sunday School Worker's Notebook. Nashville: Convention Press, 1993.

CHAPTER 15

TEACHING ADULTS

—WILLIAM A. "BUDD" SMITH

> Consider it pure joy, my brothers, whenever you face trials of many kinds, because you know that the testing of your faith develops perseverance. Perseverance must finish its work so that you may be mature and complete, not lacking anything (James 1:2–4).

> When I was a child, I talked like a child, I thought like a child, I reasoned like a child. When I became a man, I put childish ways behind me (1 Cor. 13:11).

> But grow in the grace and knowledge of our Lord and Savior Jesus Christ (2 Pet. 3:18).

Developmental psychologists describe the development of the person as a linear process involving a progression through certain stages. Educators have linked certain forms of learning or methods of teaching with these developmental stages. Recently, theorists with a holistic approach to learning have challenged this paradigm. Still, they have not produced popular theories to replace the linear models.

The Continuum Model of Lifelong Learning, which follows, considers the complex nature of humans. It embraces the idea that people progress through stages in their development, but also stresses the holistic nature of learning and education. The model suggests that learning is a functional unit where all the processes operate or move in unison with one another to form an integral whole. The term "continuum" speaks of wholeness and continuity. The model provides a simple graphic form to express the complex nature of adults and how they learn through life experiences.

Much of the writing in the field of adult education, especially within the American scene, has been dominated by a psychological perspective. The main body of research focuses on the individual adult. However, studies in other parts of the world, particularly in Britain and Europe, view adulthood from a larger sociocultural perspective. Peter Jarvis suggests, "Learning is not just a psychological process that happens in splendid isolation from the world in which the learner lives, but is intimately related to that world and affected by it."[1] Jarvis argues that while the relationships between learners and their cultures impact learning, learning as a process largely occurs within the individual. He suggests that learning "commences and concludes with the person of the learner."[2] Though the Continuum Model of Lifelong Learning explains primarily the perspective of the individual learner, the model never ignores the social context within which the learner is acting and being acted upon. As we discussed in chapter 6, "The Church's Role in Teaching," one's Christian identity is not developed in a vacuum. It is cultivated within the context of a vital, living, cooperative body of believers, all growing toward the goal of Christian education—growing in the image of Christ. Individual growth and the context in which it takes place involves complicated processes. The Continuum Model provides a simple structure that sheds light on how this interchange may be organized and understood.

CONTINUUM MODEL OF LIFELONG LEARNING DEFINED

The model is built around three basic modes of learning: objective, subjective, and relational. The modes should be seen as innate, active processes used continuously by learners. The child approaches life experiences with these innate processes already intact and uses them until the point of death. They are always at work and they are at work simultaneously. The best way to describe how these modes operate is to liken them to "learning muscles." Just as children are born with all their physical muscles intact, so they also come with all their learning muscles. Naturally, they will use their learning muscles differently as they proceed through the developmental process, just as they will use their physical muscles differently in maturation. This process is not easy to illustrate. First, it must be dynamic, allowing the lines on the page to move at any given time. The only way to view this process from a somewhat static position is to see it as a generalization based upon multitudes of people of various ages over their complete life spans. The Continuum Model of Lifelong Learning is illustrated in figure 15.1:

---

1.   Peter Jarvis, *Adult Learning in the Social Context* (London: Croom-Helm, 1987), 11.
2.   Ibid., 37.

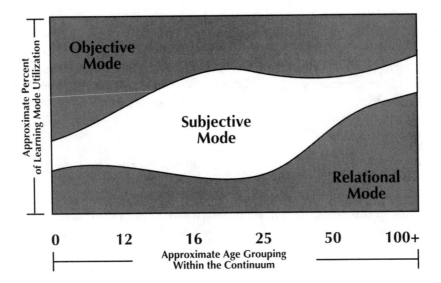

Figure 15.1

THE OBJECTIVE MODE

The objective mode or "learning muscle" is defined as the dynamic process of the learner accumulating raw data. In this mode, incoming data chunks are merely stored in some recognizable form. This accumulation of data takes place in both concrete and abstract form. In other words, learners are not only acquiring data from conscious, concrete experiences but are also collecting abstract data from the context or culture in which they learn. They may or (more likely) may not be aware that they are accumulating abstract data. The early stages of language development are an example of data acquisition.

In the early years of my ministry, I served as a minister to the deaf. I became aware that children who had the opportunity to hear for a short period before becoming deaf had much less trouble acquiring language later than those who had never heard anything from birth. Abstract language data stored in those first months of life became the basis for concrete formulation of language. This is also true for data involving values, attitudes, or ideologies.

SUBJECTIVE MODE

In the subjective mode, the learner can internalize, personalize, or own the meanings and experiences encountered in the objective mode. No longer is it a matter of knowing "Thou shalt not lie," but it becomes a matter of "I should not lie." No longer is it a matter of knowing the definition of "faith," but now it becomes a matter of understanding and expressing "my faith." This process sometimes occurs easily and quickly but it is more often long and arduous. It is filled with many question marks followed by exclamation points. It is a process that often requires return-ing to questions repeatedly. A person cannot make the internalized exclamation points until first he has faced the question marks. Every encounter that requires a personal response stretches this "learning muscle." A crisis creates a disequilibrium in the individual's usual system of thinking or operating. This disequilibrium causes the learner to personalize or internalize the meaning of the crisis.

RELATIONAL MODE

The learner uses the relational "learning muscle" to integrate and organize in-formation and experience into an interrelated, holistic pattern. In this mode, the learner relates socially to a community as both a receiving and contributing mem-ber. This process manifests both an individual and social nature. The learner is in-tegrating all his experiences (both internalized and non-internalized) to bring interpretation and meaning to the operations and problems of daily life. Compre-hending one's self as an integral part of the larger whole is paramount to this pro-cess.

The operations of the relational mode move the learner closer to a state of ma-turity or "wisdom." Maturity is more than recalling (objective) stored data, or find-ing personal meaning (subjective) in the data. Wisdom is using what we have learned in ways that positively impact both ourselves and our social environment. Wisdom is relational. Frederick Mayer writes: "Ultimately, we can be really creative only if we learn how to live. This is the final goal of education. Not mere knowl-edge, not theory, but wisdom applied to our lives."[3]

It follows that learners continuously use all three modes of learning, but well-bal-anced, growing persons use a higher proportion of the relational mode as they ma-ture.

THE KEY

The key to understanding the Continuum Model of Lifelong Learning is realiz-ing that all three modes operate continuously and simultaneously within the learn-er. The proportion of each mode in operation may vary, but learners use all three modes at any given moment. The earlier diagram (See fig. 15.1) suggests that even though children use all three modes of learning simultaneously, they predominantly use the objective mode. The child's principal task is to discover and define data and experience. While the adolescent uses all three modes of learning simultaneously, the subjective mode is the predominate learning muscle. Youth question all of life and personalize the meaning of learning experiences.

Finally, the diagram suggests that the adult learner, while using all three modes of learning simultaneously, predominantly uses the relational mode. It is the work

---

3.   Frederick Mayer, *The Goals of Education* (Washington, D.C.: Public Affairs Press, 1960), 97.

of the adult not only to come to a personal commitment to some integrated and balanced understanding of principles and relationships in life, but also to come to an ever-widening discovery of his involvement within the larger community of learners and the whole context of lifelong learning.

The following diagram shows the predominant modes for major developmental stages:

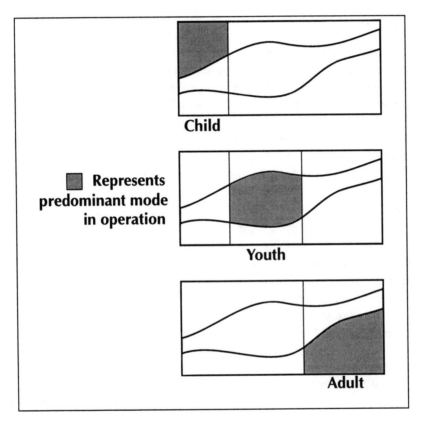

Figure 15.2

Remember the lines are fluid on the model and can move at any given time. When learners encounter new data or experience, they are using all three modes simultaneously. However, in those initial encounters with new material, they will all tend to use the objective mode predominantly. Therefore children, youth, and adults use the same learning "muscles."

If the adult learner is encountering new material, his diagram might look like that of the child. He will encounter new material primarily from his objective mode processes. Or if he is attempting to internalize new material into his systems of life operations, his diagram is similar to that of the adolescent. He will encounter accumulated material primarily from processes in the subjective mode. However, unlike the child or the youth, the adult learner usually does not see the objective mode or subjective mode as the main task. Adults tend to focus more on problem-centered tasks that correspond to the relational mode. Therefore, moment by moment, diagrams on the Continuum Model will not appear as they would when seen from the larger point of view of the developmental stages shown in figure 15.2, but over the extended period of a lifespan they will.

CHANGE EVENTS

Alan Knox writes about "change events" in adulthood that periodically punctuate the relative stability of adult life. He writes: "There are various ways in which adults try to adapt to change events. They include frantic activity, action, educative activity, seeking assistance, contemplation, and withdrawal. . . . Adults can be helped to broaden their perspective on alternatives and the process of change. As adults match needs and opportunities, they tend also to expand their ability to relate knowledge resources to action problems."[4]

Adults go through a series of passages. Each of these passages contains a set of challenges for the adult learner. (These passages are listed in figure15.3) There are some life events that profoundly affect the adult learner despite their chronological place in the life span. For example, the loss of a child, the death of a spouse, the loss of a job, or an accident resulting in serious emotional and physical injury will force the adult of any age to reassess his life and faith. (See figure 15.4).

Any time the adult learner experiences a crisis or change event, the individual will lean heavily on the subjective mode. The diagram will look similar to the expanded bubble of the subjective mode during adolescence. This may last for some time. The phenomenon termed "mid-life crisis" may exercise the expanded subjective mode bubble for an extended period. The duration and intensity of this bubble will be contingent upon the amount and severity of new information or experiences the individual must assimilate. In the midst of the change event there will be sudden rushes of the use of both the objective and the relational modes while the learner restores and rebuilds his network with his environment and normalizes the relationships that have suffered because of the crisis. (See figure 15.3)

An example of this kind of event is seen in the life of C. S. Lewis, when his wife, Joy, died.[5] This sudden crisis caused Lewis to question everything he had personally internalized into his belief system. Very few exclamation points could be observed at that point in Lewis' life, only great question marks. It was only after he had probed those deep, dark question marks that he came to conclude with the psalmist David that God could be found even at the bottom of Sheol (Ps. 139:8). Then came

---

4.   Alan B. Knox, *Helping Adults Learn* (San Francisco: Jossey-Bass Publishers, 1991), 550.
5.   C. S. Lewis was a Christian apologist. His experience is recorded in *A Grief Observed* (New York: Seabury Press, 1961).

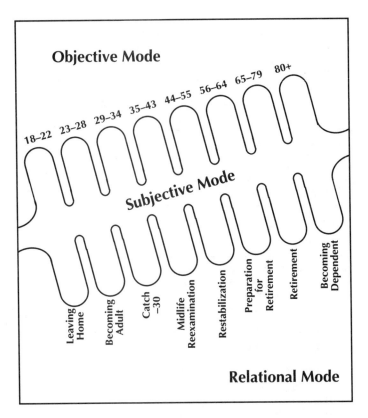

Figure 15.3

the normalizing of the relationships within his faith system, relationships that became even stronger than they were before the tragedy. Lewis and others who experience crises learn that a tested faith is a stronger faith.

Again, the processes of the modes within the Continuum Model should never be viewed as independent from one another. Some educators picture learning as putting sand into a bucket. When the bucket is full, learning has occurred. The Continuum Model does not view learning in this way. Learning is like pouring cream into coffee. It is a blending process. All modes work simultaneously. One may be the predominant mode, but it never operates independently from the others.

ADULT LEARNING: WHERE ARE WE?

In recent years, adult education has become a clearly-defined field of study. The question of whether learning for adults is entirely different from that for children has stimulated interest and investigation in this field. I will not attempt to cover the extent of this research in so small a space. I will only give a brief overview of the

Life Events or Experiences that Affect Stress Level[*]		
	Life Event	Value
1.	Death of spouse	100
2.	Divorce	73
3.	Marital separation	65
4.	Jail term	63
5.	Death of close family member	63
6.	Personal injury or illness	53
7.	Marriage	50
8.	Fired at work	47
9.	Marital reconciliation	45
10.	Retirement	45
11.	Change in health of family members	44
12.	Pregnancy	40
13.	Sex difficulties	39
14.	Gain of new family member	39
15.	Business readjustment	39
16.	Change in financial state	38
17.	Death of close friend	37
18.	Change to a different line of work	36
19.	Change in the number of arguments with spouse	35
20.	Mortgage over $40,000	31
21.	Foreclosure of mortgage or loan	30
22.	Change in responsibilities at work	29
23.	Son or daughter leaving home	29
24.	Trouble with in-laws	29
25.	Outstanding personal achievement	28
26.	Spouse begins or stops work	26

Life Events or Experiences that Affect Stress Level[*] (Continued)		
27.	Begin or end school	26
28.	Change in living conditions	25
29.	Revision of personal habits	24
30.	Trouble with the boss	23
31.	Change in work hours or conditions	20
32.	Change in residence	20
33.	Change in schools	20
34.	Change in recreation	19
35.	Change in church activities	19
36.	Change in social activities	18
37.	Mortgage or loan of less than $40,000	17
38.	Change in the number of family get-togethers	15
39.	Change in sleeping habits	15
40.	Change in eating habits	15

Figure 15.4

[*]   Keith W. Sehnert, *Stress/Unstress: How You Can Control Stress at Home and on the Job* (Minneapolis: Augsburg Publishing House, 1981), 68–69.

three major efforts at distinguishing adult education from childhood education: andragogy, self-directed learning, and perspective transformation.

ANDRAGOGY

Malcolm Knowles introduced the concept of andragogy as "the art and science of helping adults learn."[6] He contrasted andragogy with what educators had for years called pedagogy, the art and science of helping children learn. Knowles builds his model around five assumptions about the characteristics of adult learners: (1) self-concept, (2) prior experience, (3) readiness to learn, (4) orientation, and (5) motivation to learn. Daniel Pratt paints the following portrait of Knowles' process model:

6.   Malcolm Knowles, *The Modern Practice of Adult Education: From Pedagogy to Andragogy*, 2d ed. (New York: Cambridge Books, 1980), 43.

> First there is an emphasis on the psychological and individualistic nature of the learner with the person's self-concept, prior experience, and perceived needs as antecedents to learning. Second, each individual is assumed to be, by nature, autonomous and desiring of self-improvement, and to have the capacity to be self-directed in learning quite apart from the social structures. . . . Third, each person is believed to be unique, and individual differences, whether arising from experience, felt needs, or genetic nature, are to be respected and nurtured as individuals move toward self-fulfillment.[7]

Knowles' process model contrasts to the content models of the developmental and educational psychologists writing in the first half of this century. His work focuses more on the methods of adult education than it does on any unique differences between adult learning and other age-group learning. Knowles's earlier writings seem to suggest that the methods of andragogy were unique and exclusive to the adult learner. Sharan Merriam suggests that a shift in Knowles's thinking occurred:

> However, close scrutiny of the five assumptions and their implications for practice by educators in and out of adult education led Knowles to back off his original stance that andragogy characterized only adult learning. The clearest indication of this rethinking is the change in the subtitles of the 1970 and 1980 editions of *The Modern Practice of Adult Education*. The 1970 subtitle is *Andragogy Versus Pedagogy*, whereas the 1980 subtitle is *From Pedagogy to Andragogy*. Knowles's later position, as reflected in the 1980 subtitle, is that pedagogy-andragogy represents a continuum ranging from teacher-directed to student-directed learning and that both approaches are appropriate with children and adults depending on the situation.[8]

Again, when Knowles speaks of teacher-directed or student-directed learning, he is dealing with methodology, not the concept of learning itself. The methods attached to any of the three modes of learning in the Continuum Model could be either teacher- or self-directed. Certain methods might lend themselves more to one mode than to others in the Continuum Model. Whether they are teacher-directed or student-directed is of little consequence. Even in his later writing, Knowles still seems to relegate the child to teacher-directed learning.

SELF-DIRECTED LEARNING

The second major attempt at distinguishing adult learning from childhood learning is known as self-directed learning. Rosemary Caffarella enumerates the basic ideas of this approach as follows: "Currently three principal, but distinct, ideas are incorporated into the concept of self-directed learning: a self-initiated process of learning that stresses the ability of individuals to plan and manage their own learning, an attribute or characteristic or learners with personal autonomy as its hall-

7.   Daniel D. Pratt, "Andragogy After Twenty-Five Years," in *An Update on Adult Learning Theory*, Sharan B. Merriam (San Francisco: Jossey-Bass Publishers, 1993), 17.

8.   Sharan B. Merriam, "Adult Learning: Where Have We Come From? Where Are We Headed?" in *An Update on Adult Learning Theory*, Sharan B. Merriam (San Francisco: Jossey-Bass, 1993), 8.

mark, and a way of organizing instruction in formal settings that allow for greater learner control."[9]

The philosophy of self-directed learning is humanism, which centers on the individual and self-development. Steven Brookfield provides a critical perspective:

> The most fully adult form of self-directed learning, however, is one in which critical reflection on the contingent aspects of reality, the exploration of alternative perspectives and meaning systems, and the alteration of personal and social circumstances are all present. The external technical and the internal reflective dimensions of self-directed learning are fused when adults come to appreciate the culturally constructed nature of knowledge and values and when they act on the basis of that appreciation to reinterpret and recreate their personal and social worlds. In such a praxis of thought and action is manifested a fully adult form of self-directed learning.[10]

Brookfield is saying that the truly self-directed learner will be concerned with the integration of the grand scheme of things from both an individual and social perspective. However, he later belittles the importance of social order among humans and raises individual independence to the highest plane of importance.[11] His concept of "empirical rarity" is interesting. He notes that the majority of the members of a society enjoy the security that a social system provides although certain individual freedoms must be sacrificed in order for the society to exist. He further insists that the "enhancement of self-directedness is the proper purpose of education" and that "educators should pursue this end with unflagging zeal."[12] This seeming contradiction of purpose leaves one with an uncomfortable feeling that perhaps the self-directedness Brookfield would have us strive for is less than fully mature.

Probably the worst temptation is to relegate self-directed learning to one mode of learning. Still, it does seem reasonable that Brookfield's definition of self-directedness applies to the subjective mode with a flavoring of the relational mode.

Brookfield might argue that a fully self-directed learner would be more completely developed than one who is not. I would argue that his self-directed individual still has a way to go to be fully mature. That is, he still needs to arrive at the point of realizing that his personal autonomy may need to be subjugated to the needs of others within his community. This argument is not without support of other adult educators. Sharan Merriam and Rosemary Caffarella report that Boucouvalas with Tough and Knowles has "challenged the exclusive emphasis on autonomous self as only a partial explanation of what selfhood is all about."[13] Indeed the message of

---

9.   Rosemary Caffarella, "Self-Directed Learning," in *An Update on Adult Learning Theory*, Sharan B. Merriam (San Francisco: Jossey-Bass, 1993), 25–26.

10.   Steven D. Brookfield, *Understanding and Facilitating Adult Learning* (San Francisco: Jossey-Bass Publishers, 1986), 59.

11.   Brookfield, 94–95.

12.   Ibid., 95.

13.   Sharan B. Merriam and Rosemary S. Caffarella, *Learning in Adulthood* (San Francisco: Jossey-Bass Publishers, 1991), 218.

Christianity is to "deny self." Our Lord modeled self-denial when he said, "Not my will, but yours be done" (Luke 22:42).

At its best, the idea of self-directed learning is, as Merriam put it, "this complex web of concepts and practices."[14] While few adult educators question whether adults are self-directed in their learning habits, there are few who agree on just what that means.

PERSPECTIVE TRANSFORMATION

A third major effort at distinguishing adult education from childhood education is Jack Mezirow's theory of perspective transformation. He suggests that critical reflection and awareness of "why we attach the meanings we do to reality may be the most significant distinguishing characteristics of adult learning."[15] Mezirow states that the hallmark of adult learning is:

> Becoming critically aware of how and why our presuppositions have come to constrain the way we perceive, understand, and feel about our world; of reformulating these assumptions to permit a more inclusive, discriminating, permeable, and integrative perspective, and of making decisions or otherwise acting upon these new understandings. More inclusive, discriminating, permeable, and integrative perspectives are superior perspectives that adults choose if they can because they are motivated to better understand the meaning of their existence.[16]

This perspective comes closer to the relational mode of the Continuum Model of Lifelong Learning. However, I believe this activity is not limited to adults. Although the child would be greatly limited in his capacity to use the dynamic processes of the relational mode, the young person has the innate capacity for these activities.

CONTINUUM MODEL AS A CURRICULUM ORGANIZER

There are many ways to classify the learning process from the linear perspective of learning levels. Benjamin Bloom and associates developed the most precise system of classification. They divided learning into three domains: cognitive, affective, and psychomotor.[17]

The cognitive domain includes learning processes that "deal with the recall or recognition of knowledge and the development of intellectual abilities and skills."[18]

---

14.   Merriam and Caffarella, *Learning in Adulthood*, 224.
15.   Jack D. Mezirow, "A Critical Theory of Adult Learning and Education," *Adult Education Quarterly* 32 (1981): 11.
16.   Jack D. Mezirow, *Fostering Critical Reflection in Adulthood: A Guide to Transformation and Emancipatory Learning* (San Francisco: Jossey-Bass Publishers, 1990), 14.
17.   Benjamin S. Bloom, ed., *Taxonomy of Educational Objectives: Handbook I* (New York: David McKay Company, 1956), 7.
18.   Bloom, 7.

The six major classes for this domain are: knowledge, comprehension, application, analysis, synthesis, and evaluation.[19] In his *Design for Teaching and Training*, LeRoy Ford provides the following definitions for Bloom's six cognitive classes:

1. *Knowledge* involves the ability to recall facts and information. "Recall" suggests the lowest—but a worthy—level of learning.

2. *Comprehension*. This second level of learning suggests ability to express ideas in new ways. One who comprehends can explain how one idea relates to another.

3. *Application*. This third level of learning suggests the ability to use in a new situation something one has learned before. It suggests a transfer of learning.

4. *Analysis*. The level of learning at which the pupil breaks material down into its parts or solves problems in a systematic way. For example, a pupil outlines a book or predicts what effects a new law may have on gambling.

5. *Synthesis*. The level of learning at which the pupil puts parts together to form something new. He may write a newspaper article or a new lesson plan.

6. *Evaluation*. The level of learning at which the pupil judges the value of something based on certain standards. For example, a pupil may decide which of three Sunday school lesson plans would best meet the needs of senior adults.[20]

Bloom's second domain is the *affective* domain. It is defined as "objectives which describe changes in interest, attitudes, and values, and the development of appreciations and adequate adjustment."[21] David Krathwohl, Benjamin Bloom, and Bertram Masia developed the five following classes for this domain: receiving, responding, valuing, organization, and characterization.[22] They suggest that a key to the activity of the learner in this domain is "in the 'willingness,' with its implication of capacity for voluntary activity. There is the implication that the learner is sufficiently committed to exhibiting the behavior that he does . . .'on his own' or voluntarily."[23] They finally get to the essence when they describe the process of valuing as "the ascribing of worth to a phenomenon, behavior, object, etc. The term 'belief' describes what may be thought of as the dominant characteristic here."[24]

19. Bloom, 18.
20. LeRoy Ford, *Design for Teaching and Training* (Nashville: Broadman Press, 1978), 81, 100.
21. Bloom, 7.
22. David Krathwohl, Benjamin Bloom, and Bertram Masia, *Taxonomy of Educational Objectives: Handbook 2* (New York: David McKay Company, 1964), 35.
23. Krathwohl, 181.
24. Ibid.

Again Ford provides the following definitions for the five levels of the affective domain:

1. *Receiving*. The level of attitude learning at which the learner simply becomes aware that a thing exists.

2. *Responding*. The level of attitude at which the learner to some small degree commits himself to something. He has not acted on his feelings as yet.

3. *Valuing*. The level of attitude learning at which the learner attaches worth to something. He commits himself to the extent that he pursues what he values.

4. *Organization*. The level of attitude learning at which the learner brings several values to bear on a situation. He must decide which of several good things has priority.

5. *Characterization*. The level of attitude learning at which the learner has a lifestyle that reflects day-by-day his attitude and values.[25]

The implications of the affective domain for Christian education are more far-reaching than we are usually willing to explore. It is this domain that deals with the volition of the learner. The affective domain focuses on the will of the learner in a commitment to something of value. Most Christians would agree that the supreme value in life is a personal commitment to Jesus Christ. It involves the volition of the learner.

A beautiful picture of the commitment process can be seen in the story of the woman of Samaria (John 4:7–42). Here, Jesus encounters a woman in such a way as to obligate himself to her by asking for a drink of water. Not only does this Jewish man speak to a woman, but he breaks all cultural barriers by suggesting that he will put his lips on the rim of a jug from which she recently drank. They discuss "living water" and the cultural differences and attitudes about the place of worship. They discuss her personal life and the number of husbands she has had and the man with whom she is presently living. This discussion does not offend her. Rather, it causes her to become more open. Here we see the receiving stage of the affective domain.

The next scene in this story depicts the woman returning to her village to tell the others of her encounter with Jesus. Then she asks a most important question, "Can this be the Christ?" (John 4:29). I see this as a poignant example of the responding stage of the affective domain. For me, this stage is filled with questions. How can one make a commitment until one has first asked questions? Each person will ask questions in his or her own way. Some will ask forcefully and some gently. Regardless, each will ask the questions.

---

25. Ford, 271.

Later in the story, we read that many "believed" with the woman (John 4:41–42). This belief process is the valuing stage of the affective domain where the learner, through the action of the will, makes a definite commitment.

The new convert will often find he is committed to values that now have to be reorganized in light of what it means to follow Christ. For example, the value of success must be reorganized in light of Christlike integrity. In the organization stage of the affective domain, the learner stops and asks, "What would a good Christian do in a similar situation?"

After the believer has walked with Christ for a while, his lifestyle becomes Christlike because he is being transformed by the person of Christ. This is what the apostle Paul meant when he said, "in all things grow up into him who is the Head, that is, Christ" (Eph. 4:15). It is an example of the characterization stage of the affective domain.

Students of the learning process do not correlate the cognitive and affective domains for teaching purposes, but view them as separate actions. The following graphic shows how these domains relate to the three modes of the Continuum Model.

In the Continuum Model, all learners work in all the modes of learning simultaneously and everyone is capable of working, to some extent, with all levels of learning. Yet, a close observation of this correlation would suggest that adult education should concentrate, more than it often does, on learning activities associated with the higher levels of learning. These higher levels correlate with the dynamic processes of the relational mode. Adult learners, by virtue of where they are in the developmental processes, tend to focus more on the activities of the relational mode. Facilitators of adult education should, therefore, spend more of their time using learning activities that reflect the levels of learning related to the relational mode as seen in figure 15.5.

GUIDELINES FOR TEACHING ADULTS

If adult learning focuses on the dynamic processes of the relational mode, then lesson plans need to consider those methods and learning activities that elicit personal responsibility for the meanings that have been discovered in the Bible passage. Methods that call for problem solving, particularly those that allow for more than one possible solution, move learners into the processes of the relational mode. Methods that introduce controversy are a part of the methodological fabric of the relational mode. Remember, it is difficult for persons to make commitments until they have wrestled with faith questions. Any method that requires the integration of thinking and organization of thought patterns will be effective with adults. Adult education facilitators who fear controversy will have difficulty moving lessons to the higher levels of learning and using the processes in the subjective and relational

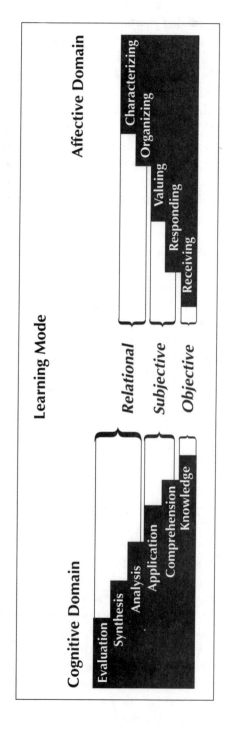

Figure 15.5

modes. It will help if facilitators of adult learning recognize that all of life is a classroom. When we come to the formal classroom, it should look more like a microcosm of the larger classroom of life. Because we often do not view the formal classroom in this way, we sometimes make artificial prescriptions that will not integrate into the reality of life. Adult learning is more effective when:

1. new learning builds upon the learner's background of experience.

2. learning activities are in keeping with the maturity level of the learner.

3. learning activities involve more than one of the senses.

4. the learner takes part in a variety of activities.

5. learning is reinforced shortly after the initial learning experience.

6. learning is accompanied by a satisfying state of affairs.

7. the learner responds in an active way.

8. the learner helps determine the purpose.

9. the learner repeats in some way what is learned.

10. the learner relates to life situations what has been learned.

11. the learner is allowed to progress at a personal rate.

12. the learner begins with the simple aspect of a problem and progresses gradually toward aspects or problems that are more complex.

13. the learner receives immediate knowledge of results.

14. the learner shares in the leadership of the group.

15. the learner feels accepted and free to take part in an atmosphere of security and belonging.

16. the issue at hand is urgent.

17. the learner's readiness to learn is met by the teacher's readiness to teach.

18. both teacher and learner recognize the need for divine assistance in learning.

19. the learning materials are characterized by good arrangement.

20. the learner feels that what is learned is worthwhile.

21. the learning task and activities fall within the learner's "range of challenge."

22. concepts are presented in numerous and varied specific situations.

23. tests and the goals and objectives are compatible.

24. the group is of the right size.

25. group members work toward a common goal.

26. the learner sees an advance organizer.

27. the learner has pleasant emotional experiences in the learning experience.

28. the learner participates in group experiences.

29. the learner gains information about a subject.

30. the learner uses his or her own approach to problem solving.

31. the teacher uses novel approaches.[26]

SUMMARY

Learners and learning processes are very complex. Educational theorists have often presented a fractured picture of the processes of learning by placing portions of these processes into little boxes. The Continuum Model of Lifelong Learning attempts to approach the concept of learning in a way that considers the complex nature of individuals and the context within which they learn, and also fulfills a need for a simple graphic form to communicate ideas about the way complex individuals develop and learn.

The Continuum Model of Lifelong Learning embraces the idea that people progress through stages in their development while stressing the systemic nature of learning and education. Learning is a functional unit where all the processes (explained by objective, subjective, and relational modes) operate or move in unison with one another to form an integral whole. The Continuum Model provides a simple structure to shed some light on how this interchange may be organized to explain the concept of learning and to develop curriculum structures that will better use the learning processes that are predominant in the developmental stages of life.

This chapter has explained how the Continuum Model can be used in the planning of adult learning experiences. I hope this study will stimulate further thinking on the nature of learning. The Continuum Model recognizes that many schools of educational thought have validity, and it seeks to integrate them. These educational philosophies and psychologies can be affiliated with one or more of the learning modes or learning muscles delineated in the model. The Continuum Model suggests that learners use one predominant mode during each developmental stage. Therefore, some methodologies are more appropriate for certain developmental stages. Curriculum planners and age-group specialists should consider these modes of learning when designing learning experiences.

26. Richard E. Dodge, comp., *Adult Sunday School Worker's Notebook* (Nashville: Convention Press, 1993), 5:10.

FOR FURTHER STUDY

1. Diagram your personal continuum of lifelong learning. Explain the experiences that created bubbles in your continuum.

2. Observe an adult class. Evaluate the lesson. What were the strengths and weaknesses? What mode was predominantly used in the lesson? Objective? Subjective? Relational?

3. Discuss the methods that would help adults operate in the relational mode.

4. Design ministry strategies for each passage of adulthood.

5. Using the literature for adult teachers, develop a lesson plan for young adults, median adults, and senior adults.

6. Based on a passage of Scripture of your choosing, write appropriate questions for adults at the higher levels of the cognitive and affective domains.

7. Interview adults from each phase of adulthood. Ask them what they expect from Bible study and how teachers could improve Bible study.

SUGGESTED READING

Bradshaw, C. O. *Faith Development: The Lifelong Process*. Elgin, Ill.: David C. Cook Publishing, 1983.

Crawford, Dan R. *Single Adults: Resource and Recipients for Revival*. Nashville: Broadman Press, 1985.

DeBoy, J. J., Jr. *Getting Started in Adult Religious Education*. New York: Paulist Press, 1970.

Dodge, Richard E., comp. *Adult Sunday School Worker's Notebook*. Nashville: Convention Press, 1993.

Elias, J. L. *The Foundations and Practice of Adult Religious Education*. Malabar, Fla.: Kriegen Publishing Co., 1982.

Foltz, N. T. *Handbook of Adult Religious Education*. Birmingham, Ala.: Religious Education Press, 1986.

Fowler, J. W. *Becoming Adult, Becoming Christian: Adult Development and Christian Faith*. San Francisco: Harper and Row, Publishers, 1984.

Knowles, M. *The Adult Learner: A Neglected Species*. 4th ed. Houston: Gulf Publications, 1990.

———. *The Modern Practice of Adult Education*. rev. ed. Englewood Cliffs, N.J.: Cambridge, 1988.

Knox, A. B. *Helping Adults Learn*. San Francisco: Jossey-Bass Publishers, 1985.

Levinson, Daniel. *The Seasons of a Man's Life*. New York: Knopf, 1978.

McKenzie, L. *The Religious Education of Adults*. Birmingham, Ala.: Religious Education Press, 1982.

Peterson, G. A., ed. *The Christian Education of Adults*. Chicago: Moody Press, 1985.

Sell, C. M. *Transitions Through Adult Life*. Grand Rapids: Zondervan Publishing House, 1991.

Stokes, K., ed. *Faith Development in the Adult Life Cycle*. New York: Sadlier, 1983.

Vogel, Linda Jane. *The Religious Education of Older Adults*. Birmingham, Ala: Religious Education Press, 1984.

Wilbert, W. N. *Strategies for Teaching Christian Adults*. Grand Rapids: Baker Book House, 1984.

CHAPTER 16

HOW TO SELECT AND EVALUATE CURRICULUM MATERIALS

—NORMA S. HEDIN

Consider the following case studies:

Case Study #1

> An adult men's teacher comes to see you concerning the Sunday school litera-
> ture. He feels that the material currently used is not challenging enough for his
> class. He has a book on biblical prophecy that he wants to use in his class for the
> next three months. How would you respond to his idea?

Case Study #2

> A woman makes an appointment with you to discuss the possibility of writing
> Sunday school curriculum for your church to use. She is a public school teacher and
> feels that she can write better lessons that the ones currently used. How would you
> respond?

How do you respond to well-meaning people who want to change curriculum materials? What's wrong with letting teachers decide what they want to teach? How do you encourage enthusiasm without compromising curriculum decisions? How can you communicate the importance of curriculum evaluation and selection?

The choice of curriculum is central to educational programming in most church-es. The materials selected guide both the content used in the classroom and the process used to teach and learn that content. Although church curriculum includes all materials used for educational purposes, this chapter focuses specifically on Sunday school curriculum, since Sunday school is generally the largest teaching organization.

WHO IS MAKING THE DECISION?

Search Institute's study of youth and adults in six denominations in the United States found that the responsibility for choosing curriculum varies among congregations. Most commonly, a Christian education committee, the teachers, either individually or collectively, or the staff member responsible for Christian education decides which curriculum to use.[1] According to Search Institute's findings, most churches are satisfied with curriculum choices, although more so for children than for youth and adults. Southern Baptist congregations were almost twice as likely as any of the other denominations in the study to use exclusively denominational material for their adult Bible study. However, researchers found a trend toward diverse curriculum use in all denominations studied. Churches are turning to special interest organizations for resources more frequently than in the past.[2]

WHO SHOULD BE DECIDING?

The process of evaluating and choosing curriculum[3] should be approved and supervised by the church and should be part of the overall planning process in a church. Effective churches determine the best direction for their members and make plans to move in that direction. Curriculum decisions should grow out of the church's direction, which is driven by its purpose or vision. Purpose or vision, according to leadership resources,[4] is based on scriptural norms, the evaluation of the needs of the church and its people, and the goals of the church based on those needs. Once the direction has been established, then educational goals are outlined and curriculum is examined to determine how it addresses the goals.

---

1. Eugene C. Roehlkepartain, *The Teaching Church: Moving Christian Education to Center Stage* (Nashville: Abingdon Press, 1993), 80.
2. Ibid., 81.
3. Although we have defined curriculum earlier as "student activities related to scriptural content that are implemented by Christian leadership to bring students closer to maturity in Christ," in this chapter, the term *curriculum* will be used interchangeably with *literature*.
4. There are several helpful resources regarding creating vision, purpose, and mission statements and how to set church goals based on these. Effective curriculum for Christian education must lead members to accomplish the goals set for the church. See Leith Anderson, *Dying for Change* (Minneapolis: Bethany House Publishers, 1990); George Barna, *The Power of Vision* (Ventura, Calif.: Regal Books, 1992); J. Truman Brown, compiler, *Visionary Leadership for Church Growth* (Nashville: Convention Press, 1991); Leighton Ford, *Transforming Leadership* (Downers Grove, Ill.: InterVarsity Press, 1991).

Unfortunately, curriculum decisions are often based on how easy the lessons are to prepare or how colorful the materials are. Or they may be based on someone's experience with particular curriculum materials. The Bible is our textbook and it provides the content for Christian teaching. But curriculum materials provide instruction as well. In fact, we know that some students read or hear lessons prepared with the curriculum materials without picking up a Bible. What do the materials say about the Bible?

How does a church go about determining its instructional needs and then match a curriculum to those needs? If you feel you have a clear picture of your congregation's educational needs and want to move on to the process of curriculum evaluation, you may want to skip the following section. However, if you have not gone through the process of looking at church needs as they relate to curriculum, the following is a plan for moving from the needs of individuals and the church to curriculum decisions.

DETERMINING YOUR CHURCH'S EDUCATIONAL NEEDS

Various writings address the task of determining a church's needs. Current emphasis on "marketing" your church deals with surveying the community and market of your church. Curriculum should assist in meeting the needs discovered through surveys or studies. "Assessing needs is important for Christian education for several reasons. First, if the gospel is indeed to touch people's lives, we must identify places where they need to hear the gospel. Second, assessing needs helps planners step back and refocus programs. This process gives clues to the time when particular emphases or programs may no longer be needed. Finally, assessing needs opens doors for unique ministries that can impact people's lives in significant ways."[5] Once needs have been discovered and a clear picture of your church and educational goal has been established, you can move on to evaluating curriculum as it addresses the discovered needs.

One of the most efficient ways to determine a church's needs is to simply ask church members what they think their learning needs are. There are various ways to elicit responses from individuals.

PERSONALLY ASK CHURCH MEMBERS

Gather groups together and ask them such questions as: "What issues do you struggle with the most in your workplace? What are your greatest family concerns? What are the greatest needs in your church family? How could the church help you in addressing these issues? If you could study any book of the Bible, what would it be? What kind of learning experiences do you enjoy most?"

---

5.   Roehlkepartain, 96.

This approach is appropriate for Bible study classes, weekly workers' meetings, deacons' meetings, Wednesday evening prayer meetings, or other naturally occurring groups. Meeting in groups allows for "bouncing around" ideas and stimulating thinking. Questions should focus on the concerns of members and their learning needs related to those concerns.

SURVEY THE CONGREGATION

Using a printed questionnaire, employ open-ended questions, like the ones listed above or closed questions, such as "Rank the following in order of importance to your family: quality Bible study, fellowship, discipline in the home, family relationships, effects of peer pressure . . ." or "What type of learning situation do you benefit from most? Small group discussion, lecture, individualized instruction, or watching videos?"

You may also include demographic information about church members which will be helpful in describing your church. Local associations and state and national organizations exist to help in gathering data and designing questionnaires to gather information.[6]

Printed questionnaires are helpful in gathering information because: 1) respondents often write anonymously what they will not say out loud; 2) responses can be categorized and compared more readily, particularly when using closed questions.

However, printed questionnaires have their disadvantages. First, the responses may not represent the needs of the church as a whole. Without a "significant number" of questionnaires returned, one cannot claim that the responses represent the majority. Appropriate publicity and emphasis on the survey's importance will yield a more enthusiastic response. Second, the amount of time involved in filling out a questionnaire can be a problem. Thoughtful respondents require time to think seriously about their responses. Mailing questionnaires to homes with a return envelope provides better responses, but cost may be prohibitive. Personally going to Bible study classes and handing out the questionnaire, going over each question, and giving members time to answer secures improved responses.

VISIT FAMILIES

Carefully prepare questions based on the information you want to seek before visiting. Use deacons, teachers, church council members, or staff members for these visits.

---

6.   Southern Baptist churches receive materials for conducting surveys through the association or state offices. Search Institute's *Profile of Congregational Life* is an extensive survey to help congregations to assess attitudes, beliefs, perceptions, and religious experiences of their members. Congregations administer the survey, then Search Institute analyzes the results and sends a custom report to the congregation. A self-administered survey of youth developed by Search Institute is available in Peter L. Benson and Dorothy L. Williams, *Determining Needs in Your Youth Ministry* (Loveland, Colo.: Group Books, 1987).

SURVEY TEACHERS

Ask teachers about the needs of students, learning activity preferences, and teaching style preferences. What are your teachers like? What teaching methods do they use in teaching? In what areas do they need help to improve their teaching? What must the literature include to assist them week by week? This information will be most helpful as you evaluate the actual literature pieces. Teachers have on-going contact with their class members and provide insight into specific needs.

Regardless of the method of gathering information, come to an agreement on the kind of information needed and how it is to be used. Focus on general needs as well as specific needs of individuals. Reading about developmental needs of age groups will add to your understanding of general needs. The information you gather from individuals or groups will address the specific perceived needs of the congregation. Once you gather the information, write a description of educational needs or compile a list in rank order. Then you are ready to write a church description.

WRITE A CHURCH DESCRIPTION

Using the data gathered, write a description of your church. This can be an overall description of your church or it can be broken down into age group or department descriptions. It is helpful for workers to be involved in this process of describing their educational needs based on who their learners are.

DESCRIBE YOUR CHURCH MEMBERS

What are the attitudes of your members toward church and religion? Describe the professional and economic status of members. What is the average educational level? What unique needs do members in your church have that affect their time, values, and commitment to church activities?

Case Study #3

> Our church is located in the northern part of a busy metropolitan area. The most active members are high-level professionals who spend long hours at their jobs. They commute to work, so their weekday time is limited. They are basically Baptist in orientation, but not as loyal to the Baptist denomination as their parents. The average educational level is college, with several holding advanced degrees. They are white, upper-middle to upper class. The average age is 40–45, with very few older adults. They are generally committed to the church, but their time is limited, particularly during weekdays. Since they are successful professionally, they want to be challenged in thinking and learning. They prefer discussion-type methods, with the exception of the oldest group of adults. Everyone is concerned about family relationships, particularly teenage issues regarding drugs, sex, and peer pressure.

Case Study #4

> Our church is a rural church. Most members are employed by local textile mills or on farms. Economically, they are comfortable for this part of the country, but overall considered lower-middle class. They work various shifts and thus their schedules change from time to time. The average educational level is high school, with a few educators holding college degrees. The average age is 50–60 with very few children or teenagers. They are committed to church attendance and to church programs. They prefer lecture methodology and Bible study that focuses on in-depth examination of the passage of Scripture. They are concerned about community issues, such as rising crime rates, lack of religious influence in children's lives, and personal issues such as aging parents and finances.

DESCRIBE YOUR CHURCH PROGRAM.

What do the records say about trends in enrollment, attendance, and growth? Look at the times when your church was growing and determine the factors that made such growth possible. What are the prospects for growth? What are the educational needs of the potential prospects? What facilities does the church have? What programs are in place that could be used to address the needs of your members? What areas are addressed by other church programs that do not necessarily need to be addressed by Bible study curriculum? For example:

Case Study #5

> Our church went through a period of rapid growth in the early 1980s when the pastor placed an emphasis on evangelism training. Since that time, we have declined, possibly due to building emphases and changes in Sunday school organization. We lost a large group of families due to a disagreement among staff members. We have been rebuilding in attendance since that point. We have the traditional Southern Baptist Convention organizations in place: Sunday school, discipleship training, Baptist women, mission organizations for children, music ministry, Baptist men, a beginning singles' ministry, an active senior adult ministry, a limited recreation ministry, and a beginning womens' ministry which includes ladies' retreats, and a craft emphasis. We have a pastor, minister of education, minister of music, part-time youth minister, and part-time preschool/children's minister. Our prospects for growth include in all age groups, but particularly singles and senior adults.

DESCRIBE YOUR CONTEXT

Include facts about the location of the church that affect its ministry, such as visibility, accessibility, surrounding neighborhood, and proximity to ministry areas such as apartments, nursing homes, and universities. Use a map to plot the distance members travel to church and pinpoint the areas from which members and visitors are drawn.

Case study #6

> Our church is located in the middle of a suburban neighborhood. The immediate neighborhood is declining and most of our members come from neighborhoods two to three miles away from the church. We are on a busy major road that

connects one end of town to another. We often get visitors who just drive by because of our location. We are next door to an elementary school which has potential for space if needed. We own an additional piece of land across the street that can be used for expansion. We are two blocks from a large apartment complex and about one to two miles from the site of a proposed nursing home complex. We draw many children from the apartment complex for Vacation Bible School. We have begun to draw singles from an apartment located several miles away.

WRITE EDUCATIONAL GOALS

Once the needs of the church are identified and the church description is completed, write specific educational goals based on the unique needs of your church. Pay particular attention to specific problem areas faced by your particular church in its own setting. A few significant goals are better than a long list of less significant ones. These goals give direction in selecting curriculum for your church. For example:

1. The goal of our church is to increase Bible study attendance by 10 percent in eight months.

2. The goal of our church is to reach twenty-five new singles through small group Bible studies in six months.

3. The goal of our church is to provide spiritual training for one hundred families in a year.

Once your goals have been set, you will want to evaluate prospective curriculum in light of its effectiveness in helping you reach those goals. For example, goal #1 would call for curriculum that draws members into Bible study. For some age groups that would mean a focus on the needs of that group. For others, it may be an in-depth approach to Bible study with emphasis on increasing Bible knowledge. If your goal is to reach families, you will need curriculum that focuses on family themes, studies the same Scripture passages, or provides suggestions for strengthening family relationships. If your goal is to train people in evangelism, look for curriculum that focuses on evangelistic themes, witnessing, sharing your faith with coworkers, and Bible studies that give learners a chance to respond to the gospel. Curriculum for singles would need to focus on evangelism and discipleship based on the unique needs of singles. As you examine curriculum pieces, look for these emphases and how units or lessons could assist the church in reaching those goals. If you are committed to the goals, then you must find resources that are supportive of the goals. As you evaluate Sunday school, discipleship training, or mission materials, you will want to identify which curriculum materials will help you meet your goals. As you look at each goal, identify the parts of the curriculum materials that will help move the church toward the designated goal.

SELECT YOUR RESOURCES

Many denominations provide curriculum materials for their congregations. Some make available several lines from which to choose. It is almost always best for churches to consider materials from their own denomination. However, at times you may want to consider other publishers. Choose the materials that best meet the needs of those who will use the materials and those who will help reach the set goals.

Evaluation of curriculum plans is not a short-term project. It takes time to seriously consider the needs of your church and to evaluate the curriculum's potential to meet those needs. Consider such issues as cost, use of content, use of experience, educational approach, relationship to church goals, and how well a curriculum meets the needs of teachers and students. Careful evaluation is particularly important when using materials from a publisher with whom you are not familiar. The following questions will aide in evaluating literature for comparison purposes.

USE OF CONTENT

Theological considerations head the list of concerns for the Christian educator. Since evangelicals consider the Scriptures the primary sourcebook in Christian education, other books, however relevant, rank as secondary sources. We reject any curriculum that treats the Scriptures negatively, views God's power as limited, or views miracles as myths. The following are some questions that should be asked concerning content:

1. Is the Bible regarded as authoritative, the guide to faith and practice?

2. Is the curriculum centered in the Word of God?

3. Does the content emphasize biblical essentials—salvation, discipleship, service?

4. Is the extra-biblical content true to scriptural principles and introduced for the purpose of making the Bible relevant to daily life?

5. Does the content emphasize the doctrinal distinctives of your particular denomination?

6. Do the materials encourage learners to commit themselves to Jesus Christ as personal Savior?

USE OF EXPERIENCE

Although the Scripture is the foundational textbook for religious education, a person's experience plays a secondary, although important, part in growth and development as a Christian. Content should emphasize the importance of the application of Bible content to personal experience so that the Bible is not merely viewed as relevant to the past. You may want to ask:

1. Is the individual helped to grow continually and to take definite steps toward maturity in Christ?

2. Is provision made for making decisions and solving problems so that the pupils develop their own personal convictions?

3. Are pupils encouraged to apply faith to moral decision-making about life issues?

4. Are the pupils' personal life experiences used as occasions for spiritual insight?

5. Does the material encourage independent thinking and questioning?[7]

EDUCATIONAL APPROACH AND ORGANIZATION

Most publishers provide promotional material that describes the educational approach of the curriculum. Some periodicals focus more on learning Bible content or securing Bible knowledge. Other sources focus more on exploring and assimilating truth and dealing with biblical concepts and ideas. Other materials focus more on applying Bible truths, with a concern for needs of students. Depending on the maturity level of the people in your church, you may consider any of these approaches. Some curriculum publishers offer a series that focuses on studying a Bible book, with greater emphasis on the Bible as it speaks to needs. Another series may focus more on needs and how Scripture can speak to those needs. The insight of teachers is particularly helpful in choosing material that is most appropriate for a particular class. All curriculum, however, should attempt to intersect the Bible content with the needs of learners. Age-graded materials seem to do this best since they are able to focus more on developmental needs. For example, studies written for senior adults address the unique needs of senior adults as they mature. Single adult materials focus more on the unique needs of singles. Read through the introduction to units and lessons. Look through the introductory material to determine the focus of a particular periodical. Look for themes and main ideas and how they are related to the needs of learners. Of particular importance will be the stated objectives. Clearly stated objectives should provide direction for the content and the teaching of materials. Quality materials provide instruction in all essential biblical teachings. Study materials should increase in difficulty as students mature.

If you have difficulty in determining the answers to the following questions, contact a representative from the publisher and ask for assistance. Most publishers have editors or consultants who can answer all of these questions. You should ask:

---

7. The questions listed are adapted from suggestions from the following sources: Lois LeBar, *Education That Is Christian* (Wheaton, Ill.: Victor Books, 1989), 270–72; Ronald C. Doll, "Twenty Questions to Ask About Sunday-School Materials," *Christianity Today*, Reprint, 1972; and "Choosing Sunday School Materials," pamphlet produced by the Sunday School Board of the Southern Baptist Convention, Nashville, Tenn.

1. Do the materials state understandable and acceptable objectives that speak to the needs of the targeted age group (what the learner will know, feel, or do as a result of study)?

2. Do lessons offer a balance of biblical exposition and application to life?

3. Are the materials appropriate to learners' abilities, needs and interests? (See chapters 12, 13, 14, and 15 on age group learning.)

4. Do the materials increase in difficulty throughout the span of years they cover?

5. Do the materials offer a systematic plan of study of the entire Bible? (Look in catalogs or promotional material for overall view of study.)

NEEDS OF CHURCH

Although meeting the needs of the individual is basic to the purpose of a curriculum, the needs of the church or congregation must also be considered. Since Christian literature is used in all ministries of the church, coordination and correlation of topics for various age groups is helpful. Although it is not necessary to use just one curriculum line, it is helpful if a publisher can provide materials that are distinctly related to the needs of all ministries and age groups in the church. You may ask:

1. Does the curriculum provide a broadly based plan for the entire church?

2. Does the curriculum take advantage of the distinctive needs and possibilities of the ministry for which it is prepared (Sunday school, discipleship training, missions, etc.)?

3. Does the curriculum correlate with or complement other materials being used in the church?

4. Is the material reasonably priced, both for the church and for pupils who may be asked to purchase materials?

NEEDS OF TEACHERS

Most teachers need help in planning their teaching and selecting appropriate teaching methods and materials for various age groups. Materials should distinguish between basic and essential methods and teaching aids, and more elaborate and optional methods and aids. Practical suggestions for teaching content are needed as well as explanations for suggested procedures such as case studies and role playing. At least one detailed lesson plan should be provided for the teacher. Good teachers also want their materials and teaching aids to be evaluated. Evaluators should ask:

1. Is the material self-explanatory and practical?

2. Is the material flexible enough to meet the needs of large and small churches, trained and untrained teachers, pupils with diverse backgrounds, living in diverse geographical areas?

3. Does the curriculum provide biblical background, illustrations, and teaching principles in addition to definite suggestions for lessons?

4. Does it guide the teacher to use life situations of his or her pupils to make the Bible real to them?

5. Do the periodicals suggest a variety of learning activities based on sound educational principles?

6. Do the teacher helps give guidance and insight into educational theory and methods?

7. Do teacher helps provide at least one detailed lesson plan and additional teacher helps and resources?

8. Does the publisher provide training materials that facilitate training in the use of materials?

9. Are additional helps available: resource kits, visuals, commentaries, tapes, etc.?

NEEDS OF PUPILS

We know that attractive, stimulating materials prod people to learn. Materials, regardless of design, should emphasize learners' interests and should take into account the normal developmental tasks of the age they are intended for. Materials should also emphasize problem solving and involve all the senses through the use of a variety of learning activities. Ask:

1. Does the material appeal to and challenge the individual?

2. In the activities suggested for pupils, is provision made for individual differences—between pupils, classes, geographical areas, and so forth?

3. Are illustrations and application suggestions appropriate for the age group for which they are written?

4. Do educational processes or teaching methods create a sense of community among adults?

MECHANICAL FEATURES

The way a periodical is put together reveals the concern of the publisher for quality. Its visual appeal—use of color, type style, illustrations—and writing style help to determine how effective the publication will be for teaching and learning. We know that short paragraphs and sentences are easier to read, and that attractive graphics and use of white space give psychological appeal. We also know that photos from twenty years ago make periodicals appear outdated, and that abstract illustrations and surrealistic art are not appropriate for young children. Although perhaps the least important of the areas considered, the mechanical features should be evaluated as well:

1. Do the high quality and standards of the material reflect its eternal values?

2. Is it well-written and readable? Does it include short paragraphs and sentences?

3. Is the material printed in a manner that facilitates teaching and learning: layout, type, binding, vocabulary, illustrations?

4. Are graphics and layout attractive, contemporary, and interesting?

5. Are illustrations and art appropriate for the age group targeted?

USING THE QUESTIONS

You may want to use a form like the one in figure 16.1 to list the questions of greatest concern to your church. Using the list to compare curriculum lines will give an overview of the strengths and weaknesses of each one. Another approach is the one in figure 16.2 that gives you more than just a yes or no response. You could add the numbers and come up with a numerical score for comparison. This is a 5-point Likert scale where questions are rated on a scale of 1 to 5 with 1 being low and 5 being high.

Another approach is to use the questions to facilitate discussion of potential materials or to initiate discussion among committee members concerning the importance of these items. When approached by an enthusiastic teacher who wants to change or write a curriculum, these questions can be used to communicate the critical task of selecting curriculum. It is the church's responsibility to choose appropriate curriculum materials for religious education. Asking these questions will help the evaluator to be more objective in a seemingly subjective task.

Again, the Bible is our textbook, but the materials we use to teach the Bible—whether study outlines, commentaries, teachers' books, or pupil books—communicate Bible truths and should be of the highest quality. Our choice of literature is a reflection of the importance that we place on the Bible teaching ministry of the church. And considering the high objectives and eternal subject matter of Christian education, choosing the right curriculum materials is serious business.

Curriculum Evaluation Checklist		
Curriculum		
Age		
Group		
Educational Goals		
Use of Content		
Regards the Bible as the authoritative guide.	Yes	No
Emphasizes biblical essentials—salvation, discipleship, service.	Yes	No
Emphasizes the doctrinal distinctives of your particular denomination.	Yes	No
Encourages commitment to Jesus Christ as personal Savior and Lord.	Yes	No
Encourages independent thinking and questioning.	Yes	No
Uses personal life experiences of members as occasions for spiritual insight.	Yes	No
Recognizes and affirms the uniqueness of each person's spiritual journey.	Yes	No
Regards the Bible as the authoritative guide to faith and practice.	Yes	No
Emphasizes applying faith to moral decision-making and life issues.	Yes	No
Relationship to Goals		
Focuses on outreach and ministry to others.	Yes	No
Provides resources related to the needs of singles.	Yes	No
Provides resources for all age groups for family Bible study.	Yes	No
Focuses on spiritual disciplines, with practical suggestions for family relationships and growth.	Yes	No
Educational Approach and Organization		
Gives clear and understandable objectives for teaching and learning.	Yes	No
Offers a balance of biblical exposition and application to life.	Yes	No

Curriculum Evaluation Checklist (Continued)		
Materials are appropriate to learners' needs, abilities, and interests.	Yes	No
Needs of Church and Teachers		
Allows for flexibility to meet the needs of various-size churches and diversity of teachers and pupils.	Yes	No
Gives teachers guidance and insight into educational theory and methods for adults.	Yes	No
Provides inspiration, biblical background, and teaching principles for teachers.	Yes	No
Provides at least one detailed lesson plan with additional teacher helps and resources.	Yes	No
Provides illustrations and application suggestions appropriate for the age group for which it is written.	Yes	No
Suggests a variety of learning activities based on sound educational principles.	Yes	No
Mechanical Features		
Material is well-written and readable, using short paragraphs and sentences.	Yes	No
Graphics and layout are attractive, contemporary, and interesting.	Yes	No
Designed for ease of use for teacher and student.	Yes	No
Comments and Overall Assessment		

Figure 16.1

Curriculum Evaluation Worksheet[*]	
Curriculum	
As you evaluate each curriculum piece, answer the question: To what extent does this curriculum reveal this characteristic. A score of 1 = very poor; 2 = poor; 3 = average; 4 = good; 5 = excellent.	
Curriculum is centered in the Word of God.	1 2 3 4 5

Curriculum Evaluation Worksheet*					
Emphasizes salvation, discipleship, service.	1	2	3	4	5
Emphasizes the doctrinal distinctives of our denomination.	1	2	3	4	5
Encourages commitment to Jesus Christ as personal Saviour and Lord.	1	2	3	4	5
Emphasizes biblical knowledge and understanding, and application of Bible truths.	1	2	3	4	5
Encourages independent thinking and questioning.	1	2	3	4	5
Uses educational processes that actively involve learners.	1	2	3	4	5
Gives teachers guidance and insight into educational theory and methods.	1	2	3	4	5
Gives clear and understandable objectives for teaching and learning.	1	2	3	4	5
Flexible enough to meet the needs of various teachers and pupils in our church.	1	2	3	4	5
Provides biblical background, illustrations, and teaching helps for teachers.	1	2	3	4	5
Provides at least one detailed lesson plan with additional teacher helps and resources.	1	2	3	4	5
Provides illustrations and application suggestions appropriate for the age group for which it is written.	1	2	3	4	5
Material is well-written and readable, using short paragraphs and sentences.	1	2	3	4	5
Graphics and layout are attractive, contemporary, and interesting.	1	2	3	4	5
Easy for teachers and students to use.	1	2	3	4	5

Figure 16.2

*When using to compare several curriculum lines, simply add all the circle numbers for a total score, or compare individual characteristics and their importance to your church. It may be that you can overcome the lack of ease of use, for example by proper training. Or someone may be able to provide additional teaching helps if these are not provided. However, issues such as biblical foundation and emphasis on biblical essentials cannot be compromised.

FOR FURTHER STUDY

1. Discuss case studies 1 and 2 with another person. How should a church educator respond to these situations?

2. How would you describe your church? List several specific needs that you want the curriculum to address.

3. Who makes the curriculum decisions in your church? What steps could be added to improve the selection/evaluation process?

4. Read case studies 3 and 4. Discuss how the curriculum would differ according to the membership of the church.

5. Read case study 5. What dynamics of this church would affect the selection of curriculum? What type of curriculum would you recommend?

6. Read case study 6. How would the context of this church affect the selection of curriculum? What is the context of your church? How would the curriculum plan for your church be different or similar to the one in the case study?

7. Based on your church's needs and context, what would you see as the educational goals for your church?

8. Select the literature from a specific series and age group. Use one of the evaluation forms at the end of the chapter and evaluate the literature.

SUGGESTED READING

Braunius, Burt D. "Orientations to Curriculum Development for Church Education." *Christian Education Journal*. 6(1): 52–61.

Colson, Howard, and Raymond M. Rigdon. *Understanding Your Church's Curriculum*. Nashville: Broadman Press, 1981.

Cully, Iris V. *Planning and Selecting Curriculum for Christian Education*. Valley Forge, Pa.: Judson Press, 1983.

Harris, Maria. *Fashion Me a People: Curriculum in the Church*. Louisville: Westminster/John Knox, 1989.

Joy, D. J. "Introduction." *Christian Education Journal*. 10(1): 9–11.

Leigh, R. W. "Evaluating Your Curriculum." *Christian Education Journal*. 3(1): 41–46.

Lewis, K. "The State of the Art in Evangelical Curriculum Publishing." *Christian Education Journal*. 8(1): 9–24.

Marlow, Joe D. "Analyzing the Curriculum Debate," *Christian Education Journal*. 13(3): 95–101.

Plueddemann, J. E. "Curriculum Improvement Through Evaluation," *Christian Education Journal*. 8(1): 55–60.

Tyler, R. W. *Basic Principles of Curriculum and Instruction*. Chicago: University of Chicago Press, 1949.

Wilhoit, J. *Christian Education and the Search for Meaning*. Grand Rapids: Baker, 1986.

Wyckoff, D. Campbell. *Theory and Design of Christian Education Curriculum*. Philadelphia: Westminster Press, 1961.

Part Four:
Training Others to Teach

CHAPTER 17

TEACHER TRAINING

—TERRELL PEACE

Much of the content of this book serves as a testimony for well-trained teachers. Jesus modeled a thoroughly prepared teacher. The Scripture is worthy of our best preparation and the church is responsible for teaching it. It is obvious that teaching is an awesome responsibility and requires persons who are not only committed, but also equipped. Dozens of scriptural admonitions could be cited, but two are of primary importance. "Do your best to present yourself to God as one approved, a workman who does not need to be ashamed and who correctly handles the word of truth" (2 Tim. 2:15).

Teachers are some of those who "handle" God's Word. Neither "giftedness" nor natural ability alone will qualify us as God-approved teachers. We have to develop our skills. Development of those skills comes most easily through effective training.

"It was he who gave some to be apostles, some to be prophets, some to be evangelists, and some to be pastors and teachers, to prepare God's people for works of service, so that the body of Christ may be built up" (Eph. 4:11–12). Those who function in leadership positions in the church have a primary responsibility for training and equipping those who teach the body of Christ.

CONTENT OF TRAINING

When discussing teacher training, we must not make the mistake of thinking only in terms of helping teachers to "teach the lesson." The teaching/learning experience and the teacher-student relationship are complex. Therefore, we need to look at the content of training in terms of what the teacher should be, what the teacher should know, and what the teacher should do.

WHAT A TEACHER SHOULD BE

A teacher should be a "pressing" example. I hesitate to say that teachers should be role models because we sometimes think of role models as perfect people. Teachers have enough pressure without those kinds of expectations! What I have in mind is Paul's description of himself in Philippians 3:12; "Not that I have already obtained all this, or have already been made perfect, but I press on to take hold of that for which Christ Jesus took hold of me." Teachers should be examples of those who are pressing on, those who are growing and maturing in their faith.

A teacher should be faithful. God does not expect teachers to be perfect, talented, or successful. Paul writes, "Now it is required that those who have been given a trust must prove faithful" (1 Cor. 4:2). God does require teachers to be faithful. God desires our devotion, steadfast loyalty, unswerving commitment, and dedication. Teachers must be faithful to the Bible. Loyalty to God's Word must never be compromised. Teachers must also be faithful to the church. We should take every opportunity to be supportive of church leadership and ministries. Teachers must be faithful to class members. Those in a Bible study class need to know that a teacher will be consistently present, adequately prepared, and personally interested in their lives.

A teacher should be loving. If you ask people to name the characteristics of a good teacher, what would they identify? You probably would hear such things as a dynamic personality, a good speaking voice, and a thorough knowledge of Scripture. Although these are all commendable qualities, Paul identifies the most important characteristic of a good teacher. "If I have the gift of prophecy and can fathom all mysteries and all knowledge, and if I have a faith that can move mountains, but have not love, I am nothing" (1 Cor. 13:2).

Superior Bible knowledge and personal giftedness cannot replace a heart filled with love for God and for other people. We are not talking about mushy sentimentality, but a genuine committed concern for the well-being of others. Jesus went so far as to call love a new commandment, and said it was the means by which people would recognize Christians as his followers. "A new command I give you: Love one another. As I have loved you, so you must love one another. By this all men will know that you are my disciples, if you love one another" (John 13:34–35).

A teacher should be trained. A common and faulty notion exists that good teachers are born, not made. Teaching involves many skills that have little or nothing to do with natural endowments. Furthermore, those who are gifted benefit from training and preparation. We would never consider going to an untrained person for medical attention. The teaching of God's Word is important, and those who are responsible for its communication should be trained to be more effective.

WHAT A TEACHER SHOULD KNOW

A teacher should know how to study the Bible. Though most Bible study teachers use a curriculum guide in their preparation, the fact remains that the Bible is the content that is taught. If the teacher is to do an adequate job of teaching God's Word, then he or she should be equipped to be an effective Bible student. It is difficult to communicate the truths of Scripture by relying on second hand experiences. The encounter with God occurring during the personal study of God's Word will enhance any teacher's ability, despite how good their Bible study curriculum might be. You should find chapter 10, "How to Study the Bible" helpful in accomplishing this training need.

A teacher should know how to teach effectively. College students frequently complain that professors do not communicate their knowledge on a level students can understand. The same thing can take place in a Bible study class. In-depth knowledge of a passage of Scripture does not necessarily translate into effective Bible teaching. Besides a good working knowledge of Scripture, teachers need some understanding of the learning process.

A teacher should know how to minister in Christ's name. Because we are not only mental and spiritual beings, but also physical and emotional beings, our needs go beyond the mere transmission of biblical knowledge. The Bible teacher has opportunity to express care for the whole person. This type of ministry may not be available to the vocational minister. The intimacy of a Bible study class lends itself to the development of strong personal relationships that are beneficial in many ministry situations. A pastor or other church staff member may not have this kind of relationship with a class member and therefore cannot minister in the same way that the teacher can. Relationships build bridges for ministry.

WHAT A TEACHER SHOULD DO—PREPARE, PREPARE, PREPARE

A teacher should prepare his or her heart in prayer. In emphasizing the technical aspects of Bible study and lesson preparation, we in no way want to lessen the part spiritual preparation plays in effective teaching. We have spiritual knowledge only as the Holy Spirit imparts that knowledge to us (See chapter 3, "The Role of the Holy Spirit in Teaching"). Therefore, an intimate, personal, ongoing prayer life is essential if we are to be the teachers that God wants us to be. Remember to pray for the people in your Bible study class. Pray that their hearts would be fertile ground in which the seed of God's Word can be cultivated by the Holy Spirit.

A teacher should prepare the lesson. Refer to chapter 11, "Planning to Teach" for general knowledge in the area of lesson planning. In addition, commit yourself to using whatever resources you have available to prepare for each specific Bible study. Curriculum teaching plans, commentaries, Bible handbooks, and other reference materials provide needed insight into many aspects of the text under consideration. Still, don't allow these to replace your personal study of the Scripture. The purpose of your study and planning is not to see how much you can learn. The purpose of lesson preparation is to help students learn and apply the Scripture. Prepare with your students in mind.

A teacher should prepare to let the Holy Spirit work. I am a firm believer that a teacher ought to have everything well-planned before going to teach a class. Every activity, every question, every visual ought to be thoughtfully and prayerfully planned and arranged. The Holy Spirit can be just as influential in "preparation" as in "presentation." The other side of this argument is that we can become so locked into our plan that we do not allow the Spirit to work. Plan diligently and faithfully, but do not be so rigid that you are not willing to deviate from your plan when the Holy Spirit is leading in a different direction.

It is essential that we let the Holy Spirit do his work in our students. Ultimately, we are not responsible for changing the lives of the people in our Bible study class. This is not an excuse for doing shoddy preparation or sloppy teaching. We should earnestly pray, diligently study, and deliberately plan. We can and should do all those things; but we cannot change peoples' lives—only God can do that.

APPROACHES TO TRAINING

People would probably agree that teachers need to be trained. There is, however, a diversity of opinions concerning how that training should be accomplished. Generally, we can group the various views toward teacher training into three approaches: the pre-service approach, the on-the-job approach, and the periodic enrichment approach. These approaches are not mutually exclusive, but there are specific kinds of training that lend themselves more readily to each approach.

THE PRE-SERVICE APPROACH TO TEACHER TRAINING

The pre-service teacher training course. This training approach is an excellent way to help establish and maintain training as a priority in your church. It typically involves six-to-eighteen hours of training over a six-to-twelve week period. The training can be as general or as age-specific and curriculum-specific as your particular situation demands. Establishing such a course as a minimum level of training expected of teachers has several advantages. First, a "trial by fire" can be avoided for inexperienced teachers by providing them opportunities to develop their skills before taking on a class full-time. Second, the course will provide a pool of potential workers, already trained, who can be recruited for specific teaching needs. Having a reservoir of willing, trained persons should help leaders avoid desperate enlistment tactics when an unexpected vacancy occurs. Another benefit of the pre-service training course is that it elevates the church's view of the teaching ministry. If we care enough to expect our teachers to be trained, people will have a greater respect for Bible study. Churches that provide pre-service training may find it helpful to enlist those who are already teaching to take the course as a refresher. This will reinforce the idea of minimum training expectations for all teachers.

Apprenticeship. The idea of apprenticeship, as it applies to teacher training, is to place a novice teacher under the tutelage of a skilled, experienced teacher. The apprentice can observe, question, experiment, and gain experience under the watchful eye of the mentor. There are at least three key ingredients to a successful apprenticeship program. First, you must choose your mentor teachers carefully. Since the apprentice is likely to adopt many of his mentor's teaching traits, use only your best teachers in this role. Secondly, outline for both the mentor and the apprentice the specific activities and responsibilities this relationship requires. New teachers need to experience all aspects of teaching, including research, preparation, presentation, and visitation. The apprentice who is encouraged to participate in a broad range of responsibilities will be better prepared to assume responsibility for a class. The third necessary ingredient for a successful apprenticeship program is to specify the time period during which the training will take place. This gives the apprentice and the mentor extra incentive to be diligent in their responsibilities.

The apprentice approach is especially helpful for smaller churches that might have a difficult time fielding enough prospective teachers to have a pre-service training course. If you fear some adults may react negatively to the term "apprentice" call them "associates" or "associate teachers."

On-the-job training. Pre-service training is essential. You expect only trained personnel to prepare and interpret your x-ray or dental records. People who come to Bible study also expect trained teachers to communicate the life-changing truths of God's Word. Therefore, on-the-job training does not preclude pre-service training; it is a necessary supplement to it. One training course is not sufficient for a lifetime of work. Those who supervise any kind of workers continue to give them assistance regularly, enabling them to meet the changing demands of their particular work situations. Likewise, those who are responsible for the educational ministries of the church need to help teachers be fresh and effective in the study and teaching of the Bible.

Weekly teachers' meetings. The purpose of the weekly meeting is to provide teachers with very specific help in preparing for the upcoming lesson. The weekly meeting typically includes discussion of the biblical text, teaching procedures and activities, and ideas for application. The specific format may change depending on need. Teachers may want help interpreting Scripture passages that are difficult to understand. On the other hand, studying a familiar passage will allow time to help teachers apply the lesson to their students. Obviously this approach presupposes that teachers are using a common curriculum. Weekly meetings with teachers also provide an excellent opportunity for the educational leadership to model effective teaching techniques and introduce new ideas and methodologies.

Quarterly planning meetings. These should be supplements and not substitutes for weekly meetings. This meeting can be used to preview an upcoming unit of study in order for teachers to have an overview of where they are going as they begin a new series of preparations. Quarterly meetings are also helpful in conducting business such as visitation, absenteeism, behavior problems, space needs, or starting new classes.

Individual study. Even experienced teachers need to be challenged to grow in their classroom skills. Complacency in any field is the breeding ground for mediocrity, and there is no room for mediocrity in the teaching of God's Word. Encourage teachers to read books and articles, watch video tapes, and participate in other kinds of personal study to enhance their teaching.

Individual study can also help reach those whose work schedules prohibit attendance at regular teachers' meetings. The Church Study Course Program is an excellent system for training potential and experienced church leaders. The system provides course recognition, record keeping, and regular reports for participants and church. The courses range from two-and-a-half to ten hours in length. They can be studied individually or in groups. Most diplomas require a study of six books. All types of educational program ministries are included in this system. (See address in "Suggested Resources.")

Church media library. The quality of a school can be judged by the quality of its library. This important part of the educational program of a church is often neglected by church leaders. The church media library is more than a storehouse for books. It can be the teaching training center of the church. It provides videos, audio-visual equipment and resources, and teaching materials. The media library director can recommend books and resources that improve the quality of teaching. Your church also may want to develop a curriculum center in the library. A curriculum center contains a selection of present and old curriculum. This can be helpful in making curriculum decisions and training teachers in the use of curriculum.

PERIODIC TEACHER ENRICHMENT

Besides pre-service and ongoing kinds of training, it is beneficial to provide opportunities for teachers to deepen their understanding of the Bible and the teaching/learning process.

Age-specific conferences. Training geared toward helping teachers focus on the specific learning characteristics and needs of the age group they are working with is a vital link in teacher preparation. A typical conference has qualified leaders in preschool, childhood, youth, and adult education simultaneously leading in six to eight hours of intense instruction. A common practice is to schedule such a conference on Friday evening and Saturday morning. But, do not hesitate to use another schedule if it better fits the needs of your teachers and conference leaders. Depending on the needs of your particular congregation, you may need to enlist leaders for sessions on teaching college students, single adults, senior adults, special ministries, or another group. Including one or two brief general sessions in the schedule for all teachers can help to build bonds of unity, loyalty, and mutual encouragement among your teaching corps.

Skill development training. In today's busy world, many people will not or cannot take out large blocks of time for teacher training, especially if they are not sure exactly what they are going to get out of it. One approach that takes both of those problems into consideration is to use short, one hour clinics, and to focus on developing expertise in one specific teaching method or skill. For example, you might have a session dealing with how to formulate and ask good discussion questions, or a clinic to help preschool teachers know how to minister to new parents, or a session for children's teachers on developing skills for dealing with behavior problems. Teaching is such a complex activity that the list of possible topics is almost endless. This format has much potential because of the ease of scheduling and because you can tell persons ahead of time exactly how this training is going to help them become better teachers.

Independent and denominational conferences. Many denominations and independent groups sponsor state or regional workshops for Bible study teachers. Such conferences expose your teachers to persons sometimes unattainable by your church. Church leaders also are spared the tedious duties of planning and scheduling such an event. The disadvantage is that you have little or no control over the types of sessions offered. Normally though, a conference like this has plenty of topics to choose from and serves as a good source of motivation and inspiration for teachers.

Curriculum preview and curriculum resource clinics. Teachers need help in the use of curriculum. In a curriculum resource clinic, leaders interpret the curriculum used by the church. They also display pupil literature, resources kits, leadership guides, and other helpful materials. Teachers also appreciate a preview of the upcoming study or curriculum. The clinician suggests books, methods, and ways of making the study more effective. A preview of the curriculum provides teachers an opportunity to plan and prepare for an effective study of God's Word.

Advanced training. Some churches are blessed with persons who have extensive academic preparation or experience in teaching. Challenge veteran teachers with specialized training experiences. Provide books in your media library on recent research in teaching. Encourage experienced teachers to read. Form book clubs that meet regularly to discuss contemporary Christian works.

Seminaries and colleges often provide lay institutes for those interested in theological studies. Some church leaders find university and seminary correspondence courses helpful. (For more information, consult the resources at the end of this chapter.)

One of the highest forms of compliments is an invitation to address your peers. Send experienced teachers to training conferences so that they can develop a training course for other teachers in the church. Veteran teachers can also assist your church's educational staff when they conduct denominational training conferences or teacher training conferences for other churches. Experienced teachers are often an untapped resource for training other teachers. Support and encourage them to maximize their contribution to the teaching ministry of the church.

RESULTS OF TRAINING

Most training in a church is directed toward Sunday school workers. Don't forget the cadre of teachers in other educational ministries such as mission education, Vacation Bible School, discipleship groups, women's and men's ministries, small group ministries, and self-help groups. All who are involved in the teaching ministry of the church should expect training.

The purpose of this chapter has been to present a representative list of ways church leaders can train teachers. You will think of more innovative and timely ways to train your teachers. My concern is not so much for how you do it, but that you do it, "so that the body of Christ may be built up until we all reach unity in the faith and in the knowledge of the Son of God and become mature, attaining to the whole measure of the fullness of Christ" (Eph. 4:12b–13).

FOR FURTHER STUDY

1. Design a six-to-eight week teacher training course for your church. Briefly describe each session and state the learning goal for the course and session.

2. Develop a yearly calendar of training for your church. Include training for not only Sunday school teachers, but also for mission education, discipleship training, and other Bible study leaders.

3. Preview a recent teacher training book or video series. Evaluate its strengths and weaknesses. How could you use it in your church?

4. Attend a teacher training workshop or conference. Observe how the conference was conducted. What did you learn about planning and conducting such an event in your church?

5. Survey several churches in your area to determine what they are doing in the way of pre-service teacher training. Collect samples of various pre-service training programs.

TEACHER TRAINING RESOURCES

CONFERENCE CENTERS & ASSOCIATIONS:

Christian Ministries Conference Network. This is a network for state and regional non-denominational Sunday School Conferences in the U.S. Contact your Christian bookstore or curriculum publisher for more information.

Church Study Course Resources Section. The Baptist Sunday School Board of the Southern Baptist Convention, 127 Ninth Avenue North, MSN 117 Nashville, TN 37234.

Evangelical Training Association. 110 Bridge Street, Box 327, Wheaton, IL 60189, (800) 369–8291.

Glorieta Conference Center. P.O. Box 8, Glorieta, NM 87535, (505) 757–6161.

Ridgecrest Conference Center. P.O. Box 128, Ridgecrest, NC 28770, (704) 669–8022.

Seminary Extension Department, Seminary External Education Division, 901 Commerce Street, Suite 500, Nashville, TN 36203–3697, (615) 242–2453.

VIDEO TRAINING SERIES:

Adult Sunday School Teacher of the Year. Nashville: Convention Press, 1994.

Design for Teaching Videos. Standard Publishing, 8121 Hamilton Avenue, Cincinnati, OH 45231. (800) 543–1353.

Improving Bible Teaching. A video analysis of seven administrative steps general officers can use to conduct a teaching improvement program. Baptist Sunday School Board, 127 Ninth Ave. North, Nashville, TN 37234.

The Leading Edge Video Series. Dallas: The Sampson Company, 1993. 5050 Quorum Drive, Suite 245, Dallas, TX 75240, (214) 387–2806.

Seven Laws of the Learner. Walk Thru The Bible Ministries. P.O. Box 80587, Atlanta, GA 30366–9978. (800) 763–LIFE.

Taylor, Bill. *Teaching to Make a Difference*. Dallas: The Sampson Company, 1993. 5050 Quorum Drive, Suite 245, Dallas, TX 75240, (214) 387–2806.

Yount, William R. *The Discipler's Model Video Series*. Box 22000, Fort Worth, Tex. 76122. (817) 923–1921.

Youth Sunday School—A Live Demonstration Video. Baptist Sunday School Board, 127 Ninth Ave. North, Nashville, TN 37234.

BOOKS

Burcham, Arthur D. *Teaching People the Bible*. Nashville: Convention Press, 1991. This also has an accompanying teaching resource kit.

Caldwell, Louise. *How to Guide Children*. Nashville: Convention Press, 1981. This also has an accompanying video tape.

Ford, LeRoy. *Design for Teaching and Training*. Nashville: Broadman Press, 1978.

Gartman, Chuck. *Potential Youth Sunday School Worker Manual*. Nashville: Convention Press, 1993.

Hobbs, Herschel H. *Getting Acquainted with the Bible*. Nashville: Convention Press, 1991. This also has an accompanying teaching resource kit.

Poling, Wayne, compiler. *Conducting Potential Sunday School Worker Training*. Nashville: Convention Press, 1992. This also has an accompanying teaching resource kit.

Strickland, Jennel. *How to Guide Preschoolers*. Nashville: Convention Press, 1982. This also has an accompanying video tape.

Figure 17.1

SAMPLE POTENTIAL TEACHER TRAINING PROGRAM

SESSION 1: WHY TEACH?

Goal : The student will demonstrate an understanding of the purpose of the educational ministry of our church by:
1. listing the seven objectives of our teaching ministry.
2. listing and explaining the tasks of the Bible teaching program.
3. identifying proper motivations for teaching the Word of God.

SESSION 2: WHAT MAKES A GOOD TEACHER?

Goal: The student will understand the qualities of an effective teacher by:
1. naming the qualities of a good teacher.
2. identifying what the church expects of every teacher.
3. identifying the characteristics that made Jesus a Master Teacher.

SESSION 3: WHAT DO WE BELIEVE?

Goal: The learner will demonstrate an understanding of the major doctrinal beliefs of our church by:
1. naming the number one belief of our church.
2. identifying statements that describe our doctrinal position.

SESSION 4: HOW DO YOU PREPARE FOR BIBLE STUDY?

Goal: The learner will demonstrate an understanding of the steps in preparing to teach a Bible study by:
1. listing the steps in lesson preparation.
2. rewriting a central truth and teaching aim from a given lesson.
3. identifying needs of class members as they relate to a given lesson.
4. developing a notebook containing profiles of class members.

SESSION 5: WHAT ARE SOME GOOD TEACHING RESOURCES?

Goal: The learner will demonstrate an understanding of Bible study resources by:
1. naming at least five Bible study resources.
2. writing a background study for a given passage of Scripture using principles of biblical interpretation outlined in class.

SESSION 6: HOW DO YOU TEACH PRESCHOOLERS, CHILDREN, YOUTH, AND ADULTS?

Goal: The learner will demonstrate an understanding of the differences in teaching in the various age-groups by:

1. charting the differences in educational approaches among the various age-groups.
2. analyzing the differences in curriculum pieces among the age-groups.

SESSIONS FOR THE ADULT DIVISION
SESSION 7: WHAT MAKES A GOOD LESSON?

Goal: The learner will demonstrate an understanding of the parts of a lesson plan by:

1. listing and explaining the importance of each part of a lesson.
2. identifying methods that are appropriate for each step.

SESSION 8: HOW DO YOU BEGIN A LESSON?

Goal: The learner will demonstrate an understanding of how to create learning readiness by:

1. naming four ways to create learning readiness.
2. identifying the parts of an effective learning readiness activity.
3. writing a learning readiness activity for a given passage of Scripture.

SESSION 9: WHY DON'T THEY RESPOND TO MY QUESTIONS?

Goal: The learner will demonstrate an understanding of the use of effective questions to stimulate discussion by:

1. writing effective questions for a given passage of Scripture.
2. categorizing questions as to the stage of the lesson they should be employed.

SESSION 10: HOW CAN I MOTIVATE MY CLASS TO STUDY THE BIBLE?

Goal: The learner will demonstrate an understanding of creative teaching methods by:

1. designing a creative teaching method for a given passage of Scripture.
2. naming methods that involve members in Bible research.
3. identifying methods appropriate to secure application.

SESSION 11:
HOW CAN I DEVELOP A CARING MINISTRY IN MY CLASS?

Goal: The learner will demonstrate an understanding of the task of ministry in the Adult bible study class by:

1. explaining the adult class ministry organization.
2. describing the responsibilities of the adult class officers.
3. identifying the characteristics and needs of various age-groups within the adult division.
4. identifying ways to develop a caring class.

CHAPTER 18

EVALUATING THE TEACHING MINISTRY OF A CHURCH

—DARYL ELDRIDGE

I was the minister of education at a rapidly growing church that nearly tripled in attendance in five years in addition to starting three mission churches. We were in the top one percent of the denomination in baptisms. Giving was up. Worship attendance was up. Denominational officials came to our church to see how we were doing it. We were a growing church. Or were we? What are the criteria for effective ministry and church growth? Are attendance, baptisms, or church budget reliable measurements of the effectiveness of the church's ministry? Do those numbers reflect a measure of spiritual growth as well?

I became increasingly aware that even our veteran Christians were ignorant of basic biblical knowledge and Christian doctrine. While a number of our members had been through discipleship courses, they were not actively involved in winning others to Christ or producing believers. Was there evidence of the fruit of the Spirit in our congregation? Were we becoming a more patient, long-suffering congregation? Was there evidence of spiritual growth in our members?

Then it dawned on me that I had the responsibility for an educational enterprise that never gave tests, never gave grade reports, never marked student progress, never graduated students, and rarely evaluated its program. Through a long-range planning process, the church evaluated every statistic of our church, and being a Baptist church we kept lots of statistics. We knew the enrollment and average attendance of every program. We knew the percentage of giving in our congregation, the number of tithers, the number of baptisms. We probably knew the number of red-headed preschoolers who liked applesauce. But did we know the spirituality of our members? Did we know the maturity of their faith? Had we evaluated the important things or had we merely measured the things that are easily reported? We were growing, but were we being effective? Growth can occur because you are doing things right. The more important question is, "Are we doing the right things?"

When asked whether or not their church is spiritually growing, church leaders often reply, "I hope so. After all, spiritual growth is subjective, difficult to measure. The only one who really knows whether or not people are growing in their faith is God."

So, is that it? Do we continue to count noses and spend thousands of dollars in curriculum, facilities, and training of workers hoping that what we are doing is effective? As Coleman states, "Can we afford to just leave it to chance that we are being good stewards of all these resources?"[1] The answer to these questions may be found in applying the concept called "Educational Evaluation" to the teaching ministry of the church.

DEFINITION OF EDUCATIONAL EVALUATION

What is educational evaluation? Ralph Tyler (1949) defines it as documenting the congruence of learner outcomes and program objectives. Popham (1971) says it is a comparison of performance data with a commonly accepted standard. It is also viewed as specifying, obtaining, and providing relevant information for judging decision alternatives (Stufflebeam, 1971). D. Campbell Wyckoff defines evaluation as "a process of comparing what is with what ought to be, in order to determine areas and directions for improvement."[2]

Evaluation is more than gathering data, it is determining worth or merit. Assessment is often used synonymously with evaluation. However, assessment is a value-less measurement. The purpose of evaluation is not to measure or acquire facts, but to make decisions.[3] In addition to counting noses or offerings, we need to measure the biblical knowledge and Christian behavior of our congregation. This information should be acquired for the purpose of making decisions on how to increase the impact of educational experiences in the church. The basic purpose of educational evaluation is to determine the effectiveness of the educational program in order to improve the quality of teaching and learning. In other words, "Are we doing what we should be doing?" and "How can we strengthen the educational ministry of the church?"

---

1.   Lucien Coleman, "The Need for Evaluation," section 2 in *How to Improve Bible Teaching and Learning in Sunday School* (Nashville: Convention Press, 1976), 40.

2.   D. Campbell Wyckoff, *How to Evaluate Your Christian Education Program* (Philadelphia: Westminster Press, 1962), 9.

3.   W. James Popham, *Educational Evaluation* (Englewood Cliffs, N.J.: Prentice-Hall, 1975), 11.

HISTORICAL PERSPECTIVE OF EDUCATIONAL EVALUATION

Educational evaluation is not new. In fact, the emperor of China instituted educational proficiency requirements for his public officials as early as 2200 B.C.[4] While the first formal educational evaluation in America is recognized to have taken place as early as 1845, it became a significant force in the 1950s when critics contended that public schools were ineffectual. When the Soviets put a satellite into space before the United States did, it sent shock waves that continue to ripple throughout our educational system.[5]

In the 1980s, the public began to expect greater accountability from our schools. In 1987, Allan Bloom, a professor of social thought at the University of Chicago, wrote a powerful critique of the intellectual and moral confusion of our age.[6] According to Bloom, our universities no longer provide knowledge of the great tradition of philosophy and literature that made students aware of the world and man's place within it. In the same year, E. D. Hirsch, Jr. wrote *Cultural Literacy: What Every American Needs to Know*. Cultural literacy is the knowledge of the common information needed by people to make sense of what they read. Hirsch calls for a new emphasis on information in education. He advocates a straightforward plan for making cultural literacy our educational priority by defining core knowledge, putting more of that information into school textbooks, and developing tests of core learning to help students measure their progress. One of the outgrowths of his work was the development of *The Dictionary of Cultural Literacy* (which contains many names and concepts from the Bible) and "The Core Knowledge Series," a collection of books for each grade, such as *What Your 4th Grader Needs to Know*. Numerous institutions of higher learning began developing a core curriculum composed of a set of courses defining the basic knowledge students should acquire in their degree programs.

In an effort to raise standards and increase student performance, local and state education boards have begun to identify student competencies, using standardized tests, more stringent teacher evaluations, and competency tests such as the Texas Assessment of Academic Skills (TAAS). Guidelines such as the "No Pass, No Play" rule were developed to emphasize academics over athletics and other extracurricular activities.

The idea of assuring the public of the quality of its institutions of higher learning led to the practice of accreditation. When you hear that a college or university is an "accredited institution," it is referring to the school passing certain performance standards set by a certification board. Each school goes through an elaborate self-evaluation process. This process identifies the school's strengths and weaknesses in

---

4.   Egon G. Guba and Yvonna S. Lincoln, *Effective Evaluation* (San Francisco: Jossey-Bass Publishers, 1981), 1.

5.   Popham, 2.

6.   Allan Bloom, *The Closing of the American Mind* (New York: Simon and Schuster, 1987).

several categories, such as administration, faculty, facilities, finances, educational program, and student body. Part of the self-evaluation process includes teacher evaluations and curriculum reviews.

After the college or university completes its report, a team of experts visits the campus to determine if the self-assessment is accurate. The team reports its findings and recommends to its board whether or not the school is to receive accreditation. The school may be granted accreditation with notations of changes that must be made within a given time period. Or, the school may be given pre-accreditation status, which means that several items must be improved before the council grants accreditation. The accreditation process is repeated every five to ten years.

Mediocrity can easily slip into any organization. The purpose of an accrediting agency is to help schools achieve standards they would not otherwise achieve. Accrediting agencies challenge schools to continually improve the quality of education.

The idea of evaluating the quality of the teaching ministry of the church is also not a new idea. In the 1920s, Arthur Flake led Southern Baptists in the development of a Standard of Excellence for the Bible Teaching Program. The aims of the Standard were twofold:

1.   To Set Out the Essentials of a Good Sunday school

   The leaders should be informed as to the things which go to make up an efficient Sunday school. The qualities which make for efficiency should be kept before the school to guide the officers and teachers in building the school.

   The Standard of Excellence presents these. It emphasizes certain fundamental things that should characterize a good Sunday school, such as the school's relation to the church, its enrollment, its literature, its Bible study, its work in winning souls, its denominational affiliation, and other worthwhile things.

2.   To Present Plans for Building a Good Sunday school

   Knowing the essentials of a good Sunday school is not enough; the plans for building such a school must be understood. Vagueness, indefiniteness, and aimlessness always hinder progress. A good Sunday school can no more be built without the builder having well-defined plans to work by than a watch that will keep correct time can be made by throwing the material together without a plan and a working knowledge of that plan.[7]

The purpose of creating a Sunday school standard was "in order that the school may do first-class work."[8] Another contribution of Flake was the "Six-Point Record System" which helped the church identify how many persons were present, brought

---

7.   Arthur Flake, *Building a Standard Sunday School* (Nashville: Sunday School Board, 1922), 4-5.
8.   Ibid., 6.

their Bibles, read their Bibles daily, studied their lessons, gave an offering, and attended worship. These six points were printed on the offering envelopes, normally collected in Sunday school.

In 1962, D. Campbell Wyckoff made a significant contribution to religious education through his work, *How to Evaluate Your Christian Education Program*. In this book, Wyckoff gives a step-by-step approach for conducting an evaluation of the entire Christian education ministry of a church and includes several assessment instruments.

Gaines S. Dobbins, one of the outstanding leaders in Christian education in the twentieth century, wrote *The Improvement of Teaching in the Sunday School* (1973). While this book does not address a systematic formal evaluation of the Sunday school, it does point to the need for continual improvement of teaching in the church.

In a manual for Sunday school directors and pastors entitled, *How to Improve Bible Teaching and Learning in Sunday School* (1976), Lucien Coleman contributed a chapter on "The Need for Evaluation." In it he discusses not only the need for evaluating the work of the Sunday school, but he gives specific ways in which the evaluation process might be accomplished.

Since the 1950s, Search Institute has conducted research and developed resources and services to help educators, leaders, practitioners, and organizations understand how to address young people's needs in constructive, effective ways. In 1990, Search Institute released the results of its study, "Effective Christian Education: A National Study of Protestant Congregations," which surveyed more than eleven thousand people in six major Protestant denominations: Christian Church (Disciples of Christ), Evangelical Lutheran Church in America, Presbyterian Church (USA), Southern Baptist Convention, United Church of Christ, and United Methodist Church. The study examined such facets of religious expression as faith maturity, beliefs, practices, and congregational life. The outgrowth of this study was the development of an instrument for measuring the faith maturity of an individual and a congregation.

In recent years churches have abandoned the idea of the Sunday school standard, and few churches today bother keeping the "Six-Point Record System." The validity of these instruments may be debated, but if the church is to provide quality education in its teaching ministry, there must be some organized effort to evaluate its effectiveness. While any measurement or evaluation of the teaching ministry of the church may be incomplete, we should not refrain from whatever means are at our disposal to evaluate its effectiveness.

HOW TO CONDUCT A FORMAL EVALUATION

Wyckoff's plan for evaluating the educational ministry of a church involves an institutional self-study (similar to self-studies done by universities), studying the program and curriculum, evaluating the teaching/learning process, and remaining "in character" throughout the experience.[9] By "in character" Wyckoff means that throughout the evaluation the church should use methods and processes that honor the nature and purpose of the church.[10]

There are several approaches the church might take in conducting the evaluation. If the church has a Christian Education Committee, it might be charged with conducting the evaluation. In other churches, the long-range planning committee or the church council might assume this responsibility. Wyckoff suggests that a church work through five subcommittees:

1. Christian education in the congregation at large

2. Christian education in the family

3. Christian education of children

4. Christian education of youth

5. Christian education of adults[11]

Regardless of how the church goes about the evaluation, the following guidelines should be observed. The evaluation must:

1. Grow out of the church's objectives

2. Be based on standards understood by all

3. Be done by all

4. Cover all aspects of the program[12]

The evaluation of the educational ministry should be a thorough process, involving the entire membership of the church. It is important for all programs, organizations, and age groups to have a part in the process. Since the evaluation by definition will require change, the more people who buy into the evaluation the more likely it is that new strategies can be implemented. The evaluation should not focus on personalities, but on principles, processes, and procedures. The evaluation should seek to answer four questions:

---

9.   Wyckoff, 26.
10. Ibid., 27.
11. Ibid., 35.
12. Coleman, "The Need for Evaluation," 42–3.

1. What are the facts about the situation?

2. What are our objectives?

3. What are we accomplishing?

4. What, then, do we need?

5. What next steps shall we take?[13]

What are the facts about the situation? In order for the church to better meet the needs of its members and prospects in the community, the evaluation should begin with community and church case studies. Materials such as the *Church and Community Diagnosis Workbook*[14] and *Planning for the Next Five Years in a Southern Baptist Church*[15] provide several helpful questionnaires and surveys for studying the effectiveness of the church's internal operation, programming, and environment. In this step the church should gain an understanding of the demographics of its community. The data-gathering stage should study the following:

Location of the church—What is there about the location of the church that provides data pertinent to the teaching ministry of the church? Describe the community or neighborhood.

Membership of the church—Who are the members with respect to attitudes, professional status, economic factors, divisive issues, educational levels, etc.? What needs do church members have?

Church program—What do the records say about trends in enrollment, attendance, growth, etc.? What are the prospects for growth? What are the needs of the prospects? What are the bounds within which the church council must operate? How do policies and procedures of the church limit what can be done? What facilities does the church have?[16]

In addition, Wyckoff suggests that the following facts should be collected:

1. Basic historical, sociological, and operational data are gathered on the community and the congregation.

2. Each group and its activities are canvassed.

3. Data on each teacher, leader, and administrator are secured.

4. Classes, groups, and committees are visited and observed in operation.

5. Participants are questioned about their activities and reactions.

---

13. Wyckoff, 35.
14. J. Truman Brown, Jr. and Jere Allen, *Church and Community Diagnosis Workbook* (Nashville: Convention Press, 1990).
15. J. Truman Brown, Compiler, *Planning for the Next Five Years in a Southern Baptist Church* (Nashville: Convention Press, 1989).
16. LeRoy Ford, Notes from his course, "Building a Church Curriculum Plan," Southwestern Baptist Theological Seminary.

6. Parents are asked to give their impressions and reactions.

7. Basic information is gathered on the church's work with and programs for families.[17]

What are our objectives? In this stage the church determines "what ought to be" in order to make value judgments as to what the church is doing. What is the purpose of the educational ministry of the church? Ralph W. Tyler writes:

> If an educational program is to be planned and if efforts for continued improvement are to be made, it is very necessary to have some conception of the goals that are being aimed at. These educational objectives become the criteria by which materials are selected, content is outlined, instructional procedures are developed and tests and examinations are prepared. All aspects of the educational program are really means to accomplish basic educational purposes. Hence, if we are to study an educational program systematically and intelligently we must first be sure as to the educational objectives aimed at.[18]

The educational objective is a statement of the ultimate end or intention of a church's total curriculum. It is a summary of the church's goals for its nurturing and teaching functions. This objective is stated broadly enough to apply to persons at every level of maturity. It serves as the purpose for the church's total curriculum and for each segment thereof. Individuals' relationships with God and their growth toward Christlikeness are central concerns expressed in an educational objective. Therefore, an educational objective is Christian in nature and application. The following is an example of an educational objective for a church: "To help persons become aware of God as revealed in Scripture and most fully in Jesus Christ, respond to him in a personal commitment of faith, strive to follow him in the full meaning of discipleship, relate effectively to his church and its mission in the world, live in conscious recognition of the guidance and power of the Holy Spirit, and grow toward Christian maturity."[19]

The educational objective, while helpful, is rather broad. What kinds of changes is your church wanting to see as a result of the teaching and training in the educational ministry? In other words, what are the objectives of teaching and training, regardless of the program organization or the content area? What do you want to see take place in the lives of your learners? Each age group should adapt and write its own teaching objectives, based on its developmental readiness. The following are examples of objectives for adults:

---

17. Wyckoff, 22–23.
18. Ralph W. Tyler, *Basic Principles of Curriculum and Instruction* (Chicago: University of Chicago Press, 1949), 3.
19. Howard P. Colson and Raymond M. Rigdon, *Understanding Your Church's Curriculum* (Nashville: Broadman Press, 1981), 143-44.

1. *Christian conversion.* To help each unsaved adult to have a genuine experience of the forgiving and saving grace of God through Jesus Christ, and to make a conscious commitment of his life to Christ's lordship.

2. *Church membership.* To help each Christian adult to become an intelligent, active, and devoted part of the family and fellowship of a New Testament church.

3. *Christian worship.* To help each adult develop the understanding and skills to make Christian worship a vital and constant part of his expanding experience.

4. *Christian knowledge and understanding.* To help each adult to grow toward mature Christian knowledge and understanding.

5. *Christian attitudes and convictions.* To assist each adult in developing such Christian attitudes and convictions that he will have a Christian approach to all of life.

6. *Christian living.* To help each adult develop habits and skills that promote Christian growth and live the Christian style of life he has committed himself to.

7. *Christian service.* To help each adult to invest his talents and skills in Christian service.[20]

In addition to these objectives for individuals, each educational program and ministry should have a set of objectives (and tasks). They should be stated in such a way that the church can determine if it is making progress toward these objectives. The Sunday school standard is one example of criteria for judging the effectiveness of that organization.

What are we accomplishing? Once again, "evaluation is the comparison of what is with what ought to be." Using the objectives as criteria, each area of the Christian education program may be evaluated and judgments made concerning necessary improvements to the program. The following are some areas you will want to assess, and some questions for accomplishing your analysis. These questions are simply given as a starter set. Each church will want to expand and adapt these questions to meet its own evaluation needs.

ADMINISTRATION

1. How is the educational ministry organized? Diagram the organizational structure of the teaching ministry of the church.

2. How is the church staff involved in the teaching ministry?

---

20. These objectives of teaching and training were developed in the Church Curriculum Based Design of the Sunday School Board of the Southern Baptist Convention, Nashville, Tennessee, 1984. Similar objectives are developed for each age division.

3. Does the church have a set of written policies relevant to the teaching ministry?

4. How much of the church budget relates to the educational ministry? How is the budget itemized? Are the funds adequate? What areas need more funding?

5. How stable are the educational programs?

6. What kind of records (enrollment, attendance, activities) are kept?

TEACHERS

7. What is the number of teachers? What is the ratio of students to teachers?

8. How are teachers enlisted?

9. Is there a pre-service training program for new teachers?

10. Does the church provide weekly planning and preparation for teachers?

11. What is the commitment level of teachers?

12. Does the church provide a set of written job descriptions and qualifications for teachers?

FACILITIES

13. Draw a floor plan of the space used for Christian education. Utilize standards set in *Designing Educational Buildings*,[21] and evaluate the space allotted, lighting, equipment, and furnishings.

14. Describe the classroom environment. Is it conducive to learning? Does it invite discussion and participation? Imagine you are a first-time visitor. What would be your impressions?[22]

15. Does the church have a media library? What resources are available? How many holdings does the library have? How often do members use the facilities? How is it funded? Is the funding adequate?

16. Are there plans for future development or remodeling of the facilities?

PROGRAM

17. Describe the various educational programs of the church.

18. Are the programs relevant to the needs of the church and community?

21. Robert N. Lowry, *Designing Educational Buildings* (Nashville: Broadman, 1994).
22. For ideas on evaluating the environment, refer to Lucien Coleman, *How to Teach the Bible* (Nashville: Broadman, 1979).

19. Does the curriculum cover all subject areas of Christian education? Which content areas are strong? Which are weak?

20. Do teachers use learning objectives in the classroom?

21. What programs are designed to equip members in discipleship?

22. How are members educated in missions, church polity and organization, church doctrine, Christian ethics, and Christian history?

23. What is the ratio of enrollment to church membership for each program organization?

24. What evaluation processes are in place to determine the effectiveness of programs?

25. How are the programs interpreted to members, the church, and the community?

26. In what ways are members trained to share their faith with others?

27. How effective is the outreach program of the church?

28. Describe the strengths and weaknesses of programs designed for each age-group (examples: preschool, children, youth, single adults, young adults, median adults, and senior adults).

STUDENTS

29. Do teachers show an understanding of the developmental stages of their students?

30. Do students have opportunities to assess/measure their spiritual growth? Through what means?

31. Does the church inventory its membership using spiritual gifts profiles and interest/service surveys?

32. Describe the quality of fellowship among the membership. How is this fellowship evidenced?

33. How well are new members integrated into the life of the church?

34. What is the level of biblical knowledge and understanding of Christian doctrine among members? How is their biblical knowledge evaluated?

35. What kinds of problems do families face in your church? How is the church addressing these problems?

36. What kinds of counseling are available to the membership?

37. What objectives, plans, and programs does the church have for strengthening families?

38. Describe ways in which the church equips adults in their roles as Christian parents?

39. What evidence of Christian growth is observed among families?

What, then, do we need? With each aspect evaluated, a set of needs is developed. The evaluation should pinpoint specific areas needing improvement. In each of these stages, as many people as possible need to be involved. Do these needs reflect significant concerns? Where possible, prioritize these needs for each area of concern and report the findings to the church.

What next steps shall we take? At this stage, a strategy and set of actions are proposed to meet those needs. Specific recommendations should be formulated for individuals, organizations, and groups. The recommendations should include a timetable for completing the actions, and how each action will be evaluated. The recommendations should then be approved by the church.

OTHER EVALUATION STRATEGIES

1. Visit classes and take mental notes on the strengths and weaknesses of the teaching/learning process. Then meet with the teacher and discuss how he or she felt about the learning process and how it can be improved. Major on strengths rather than weaknesses.

2. Spiritual gift inventories. There are a number of excellent spiritual gift inventories available on the market. Set a goal of inventorying all of your youth and adult members in the coming year. There are several inventories listed at the end of this chapter.

3. Conduct age-group tours. Ask age-group specialists to visit your church and evaluate the strengths and weaknesses of the educational ministry.

4. Use surveys to discover the interests and needs of church members.

5. Develop a Bible knowledge inventory and regularly check on the progress of church members.

6. Keep training records on all church members to track their involvement in the educational ministry of the church.

7. Periodically review the church roll and assess the growth of your church members.

8. Conduct student evaluations of teachers.

9. Conduct peer evaluations of teachers.

10. Use the "Sunday school standards" to evaluate the strengths and weaknesses of the Bible teaching program.

11. Review job descriptions with every worker.

12. Review church rolls and Sunday school rolls for prospects.

13. Conduct "town hall meetings."

14. Videotape lessons and critique them with teachers.

15. Send grade cards to members each quarter that would indicate their level of involvement and growth.

16. Write objectives for the educational ministry and periodically review them.

17. Send teams to evaluate other churches and gain new ideas on how to improve the teaching ministry.

18. Give "teacher of the year" awards in each age division.

19. Ask teachers to write learning goals for themselves each year and periodically review their progress.

20. Publish vital statistics each month on the growth of the educational ministry, including growth ratios, baptisms per church member, teacher-student ratios, new members, etc.

21. Develop your own "standard of excellence."

22. Use pre-tests and post-tests in lessons to determine the knowledge of class members.

23. Survey drop-outs and prospects who join other churches to gain clues on how to improve the teaching ministry.

24. Establish a "school board" that evaluates and coordinates the educational ministry.

25. In teacher planning meetings, evaluate the previous lesson. Develop a post-mortem sheet for this purpose.

TEN THINGS TO DISCOVER IN AN AGE-GROUP TOUR[23]

Great insight into the quality of the teaching ministry can be gained by conducting a tour through the building. As you walk through the facilities, try to view the educational space from the perspective of a first time visitor. You might want to consider asking an educational consultant to evaluate your facilities. Here are some questions you will want to consider as you conduct a walk-through.

23. "Ten Things to Discover in Age-Group Tour," *Helping Teachers Teach: Resource Kit*, item 9 (Nashville: Convention Press, 1976).

1. What age group meets here? What is the department enrollment? Average attendance?

2. Is this department easy or hard to find?

3. Is the supply of tables and chairs adequate?

4. Describe the first things you were aware of when you entered the room.

5. Identify five pieces of equipment for teaching/learning that seemed to be missing from the room. Did you see equipment that did not belong there or was not worth the space it required?

6. Search for resources. Identify five teaching resources (maps, books, kits, etc.)

7. What extraneous matter was there? Was the room clean?

8. How effectively is available space being used?

9. What evidence do you see of adaptation in the absence of needed equipment?

10. What kind of teaching/learning seems to be going on in the room?

11. Make a proposal for immediate improvement of the learning environment. List five things that could be done at once with a minimum of expenditure.

STUDENT EVALUATION OF TEACHING

Some educators may argue that students are not qualified to evaluate teacher effectiveness. While students may not be experts in course design, their input can provide a valuable source of information for improving the classroom experience. Most colleges and seminaries regularly use student evaluations of teaching to help professors improve their teaching skills. The following are sample questions for constructing a form (teacher's report card) to be used in evaluating the classroom experience in the church. In completing an evaluation of teaching, class members should not be expected to give their name. Since the instrument is designed to help teachers improve their skills, class members should be encouraged to comment freely.

1. Does your teacher start the class period in a timely manner?

2. How long do you usually spend taking prayer requests in the class?

3. Does your teacher normally prepare the room for teaching before you arrive?

4. How would you characterize your teacher's style: brainstorming, open discussion, lecture, or question-and-answer?

5. Does your teacher use audiovisual aids? Check all that apply: chalkboard, maps, overhead projector, video, pictures.

6. Is your teacher generally well-prepared and able to keep the class's attention?

7. Does your teacher use the curriculum the church provides?

8. Does your teacher attempt to make sure you have a book so at you can study and be prepared each Sunday?

9. Does your teacher use outside resources, such as commentaries, dictionaries, etc.?

10. Does your teacher use illustrations to make points?

11. Does your teacher make sure that the points of the lesson are clear?

12. Does your teacher encourage you to ask questions?

13. Does your teacher introduce visitors when they are present?

14. Does your teacher use every opportunity to present the plan of salvation in the lesson?

15. Does your teacher complete the lesson before the time runs out?

16. Does your teacher ever contact you during the week?

17. If you had a crisis in your life that required advice, who would you contact? (pastor, teacher, class member, friend)

18. What would you suggest for improving the teaching ministry of our church?

CONCLUSION

In the secular world, the philosophy of total quality management, attributed to Ed Deming, has influenced every segment of our society, including government, business, and education. His fourteen-point treatise is based on the premise that everything must be continually improved if organizations are to survive in the marketplace. Improvement is not a one-time effort. Organizations should seek to look for ways to reduce waste and improve quality.[24]

I believe this premise of continual improvement also applies to the church. Our congregations and community should not tolerate shoddy teaching from the pulpit or in the classroom. We should not stand for mediocrity in any area of the educational ministry of the church. God deserves our best. His Word deserves our best and his people deserve our best. Providing the best possible learning experiences in

---

24. Mary Walton, *The Deming Management Method* (New York: Dodd, Mead, & Company, 1986), 35.

our churches will mean that we continually evaluate the teaching ministry of the church.

Hopefully, this chapter has challenged you to think seriously about the evaluation process of your Christian education program. Let's capture a vision of what Christian education ought to be, evaluate where we are, and then implement a strategy for improving the quality of the teaching ministry. May it be said of our generation, "It left a legacy of commitment to teaching God's Word with excellence and power!"

FOR FURTHER STUDY

1. Pretend you are a member of a committee selected by your church to develop a process and instruments for evaluating the quality of the teaching ministry of the church. Use the following areas to draw up a set of standards for the teaching ministry of your church: administration, teachers, facilities, educational program, and students.

2. If your church were to take a basic Bible knowledge test, how do you think it would measure up?

3. If the church were to develop a core curriculum, what do you think it should include for preschoolers, children, youth, and adults?

4. Do you think it is possible to measure the faith maturity of believers? Explain your answer.

5. Does your church have a set of clearly defined objectives for its teaching ministry? If not, describe what the objectives should include.

6. Should Sunday school teachers be regularly evaluated? Is so, how would you suggest the evaluation be conducted?

EVALUATION INSTRUMENTS, SURVEYS, AND ASSESSMENT GUIDES

Exploring Christian Education Effectiveness: An Inventory for Congregational Leaders. Eugene C. Roehlkepartain. Search Institute, 700 South Third St., Suite 210. Minneapolis, MN 55415, (800) 888-7828.

Exploring Faith Maturity. Dorothy L. Williams and Eugene C. Roehlkepartain. Search Institute, 700 South Third St., Suite 210. Minneapolis, MN 55415, (800) 888-7828.

An Adult's Guide to Style. Gregorc Style Delineator and Anthony F. Gregorc, Gabriel Systems, Inc., P.O. Box 357, Maynard, MA 01754.

Learning Style Inventory (LSI). Rita and Kenneth Dunn. Obtainable from Price Systems, Box 3067, Lawrence, KS 66044. Specimen Set: $12.00.

Partial Index of Modernization: Measurement of Attitudes Toward Morality. Panos D. Bardis. University of Toledo. 2801 W. Bancroft Street, Toledo, OH 43606, (419) 537-4242.

Profile of Adaptation to Life—Holistic (PAL-H). Publisher: Consulting Psychologists Press, Inc. 577 College Ave., P.O. Box 60070, Palo Alto, CA 94306. (415) 857-1444.

Religion Scale. Panos D. Bardis. University of Toledo. 2801 W. Bancroft Street, Toledo, OH 43606, (419) 537-4242.

Religious Attitudes Inventory. W.E. Crane and J. Henry Coffer. Family Life Publications, Inc. P.O. Box 427, Saluda, NC 28773.

Standardized Bible Content Tests, Form SP. American Association Bible Colleges. P.O. Box 1523, Fayetteville, AR 72702, (501) 521-8164.

SPIRITUAL GIFTS AND PERSONALITY INVENTORIES

Mels Carbonell, *Uniquely You*. P.O. Box 1826, Fayetteville, GA 30214. (404) 461-4243. Combination Personality and Spiritual Gifts Profile, as well as an interest survey. Features 36 blends of spiritual gifts, personality types, how to handle conflicts, and opportunities for ministry. Capabilities of producing computer-generated reports.

The Keirsey Temperament Sorter. Companion Book: *Please Understand Me: Character & Temperament Types*, David Keirsey and Marilyn Bates, Prometheus Nemesis, Box 2748, Del Mar, CA 92014, (619) 632-1575, Fax: (619) 481-0535.

Lay Ministry Involvement Program, Bellevue Baptist Church, 2000 Appling Road, Cordova, Tenn. 38018, (901) 385-2000.

Ken Voges and Ron Braund. *Understanding How Others Misunderstand You*. Chicago: Moody Press, 1990.

Willow Creek Resource, 5300 Patterson Ave. D.E., Grand Rapids, MI 49530, (800) 876-SEEK or (616) 698-6900. System, called "Network," helps believers identify their unique passion, spiritual gifts, and personal style, and integrate them into a fulfilling place of service in the church.

SUGGESTED RESOURCES

BREAKTHROUGH: Sunday School Work Series, (Nashville: Convention Press).

Designing Educational Buildings. Compiled by Robert N. Lowry. (Nashville: Convention Press, 1994).

Sunday School Handbook (For each age group). The Sunday School Board of the Southern Baptist Convention. 127 Ninth Avenue, North, Nashville, TN 37234.

"The Sunday School Standard," for all age groups. This can be ordered from any State Convention of the Southern Baptist Convention.

Teaching the Bible Series, Nashville: Convention Press.

SUGGESTED READING

Bloom, Allan. *The Closing of the American Mind*. New York: Simon and Schuster, 1987.

Coleman, Lucien. "The Need for Evaluation," Section 2 in *How to Improve Bible Teaching and Learning in Sunday School*. Nashville: Convention Press, 1976.

Colson, Howard P., and Raymond M. Rigdon. *Understanding Your Church's Curriculum*. Nashville: Broadman Press, 1981.

Dobbins, Gaines S. *The Improvement of Teaching in the Sunday School*. Nashville: Convention Press, 1973.

Flake, Arthur. *Building a Standard Sunday School*. Nashville: Sunday School Board, 1922.

Guba, Egon G., and Yvonna S. Lincoln. *Effective Evaluation*. San Francisco: Jossey-Bass Publishers, 1981.

Hirsch, E. D., Jr., Joseph F. Kett and James Trefil. *Dictionary of Cultural Literacy: What Every American Needs to Know*. Boston: Houghton Mifflin Company, 1988.

Hirsch, E. D., Jr., ed. *What Your 4th Grader Needs to Know*. New York: Doubleday, 1992.

Popham, James W. *Criterion-referenced Measurement*. Englewood Cliffs, N.J.: Educational Technology Publications, 1971.

———. *Educational Evaluation*. Englewood Cliffs, N. J.: Prentice-Hall, 1975.

Stufflebeam, D. L. et al. *Educational Evaluation and Decision-Making*. Ithaca, Ill.: Peacock Publishers, 1971.

Tyler, Ralph W. *Basic Principles of Curriculum and Instruction*. Chicago: University of Chicago Press, 1949.

Walton, Mary. *The Deming Management Method*. New York: Dodd, Mead, & Company, 1986.

Wyckoff, D. Campbell. *How to Evaluate Your Christian Education Program*. Philadelphia: Westminster Press, 1962.